D1095182

UNRULY
GIRLS,
UNREPENTANT
MOTHERS

UNRULY GIRLS,
UNREPENTANT
MOTHERS

Redefining Feminism on Screen

BY KATHLEEN ROWE KARLYN

UNIVERSITY OF TEXAS PRESS ⌄ AUSTIN

Copyright © 2011 by the University of Texas Press
All rights reserved
Printed in the United States of America
First edition, 2011

Requests for permission to reproduce material
from this work should be sent to:
 Permissions
 University of Texas Press
 P.O. Box 7819
 Austin, TX 78713-7819
 www.utexas.edu/utpress/about/bpermission.html

The paper used in this book meets the minimum requirements
of ANSI/NISO Z39.48-1992 (R1997) (Permanence of Paper). ∞

Library of Congress Cataloging-in-Publication Data

Karlyn, Kathleen Rowe
 Unruly girls, unrepentant mothers : redefining feminism
on screen / by Kathleen Rowe Karlyn. — 1st ed.
  p.   cm.
 Includes bibliographical references and index.
 ISBN 978-0-292-71833-3 (cl. : alk. paper)
 1. Women in motion pictures. 2. Feminism and motion
pictures. 3. Motion pictures for women. I. Title.
 PN1995.9.W6K37 2010
 791.43'6522—dc22   2010012585

FOR MY DAUGHTERS

Elizabeth Rowe,
Miranda Rowe Harper, and
Helen Rowe

CONTENTS

ACKNOWLEDGMENTS

RANTS FROM THE University of Oregon Humanities Center and the Center for the Study of Women in Society funded preliminary research for this book. Part of that research appeared in the following essays: "*Scream*, Popular Culture, and Feminism's Third Wave," *Genders* OnLine Journal, issue 38, 2003; "'Too Close for Comfort': *American Beauty* and the Incest Motif," *Cinema Journal* 44.1 (2004): 69–93; and "Film as Cultural Antidote: *Thirteen* and the Maternal Melodrama," *Feminist Media Studies* 6.4 (2006): 453–468. I am grateful to the external reviewers and editors of these journals for their helpful advice.

I am also grateful for abundant support of all kinds from my family, friends, colleagues, and students. Members of my original women's group—the Ladies from Kansas—have been faithful cheerleaders, as has my walking and shopping pal Joanne Kent. Donna Laue, my department's computer guru, set me up with the perfect machine when I began this book in earnest, and gave expert technical help along the way.

My students and former students have been my teachers on much of the subject matter of this book. I learned from the young women in my classes about their hunger to study the popular texts that matter most to them. I have benefited from Elaine Roth's work on melodrama and Kate Sullivan's on horror. My conversations with Carter Soles about slacker cinema while he was writing his dissertation provided a stimulating counterpoint to my interests in Girl Culture. With assistance from Emily Afanador, Carter also gave invaluable help with the illustrations.

Chuck Kleinhans and Julia Lesage have been generous mentors and friends since I was a graduate student, and their imprint on my thinking is indelible. Diane Negra and Yvonne Tasker brought my voice into influential debates about postfeminism through their own scholarship and their invitation to speak at the Interrogating Postfeminism Conference in the UK in 2004. I am grateful to them and to my other colleagues across the Atlantic, including Jane Arthurs, Rosalind Gill, Julia Hallam, Joanne Hollows, Rachel Moseley, Janet Thumin, and Beverley Skeggs, for their interest in my work. Among my Oregon colleagues, Liz Bohls gave me a strong nudge at the right time to write this book. Jennifer Freyd, Michael Hames-Garcia, and Priscilla Peña Ovalle shared their expertise on key sections of the book. Priscilla also stepped in for a last-minute rescue with the illustrations, even though that last "minute" became hours. Michael Aronson cheerfully picked up the slack on departmental matters large and small, whenever I needed a helping hand.

Serendipitous conversations with Sarah Kozloff, Linda Mizejewski, and Carol Siegel at the 2006 Society for Cinema and Media Studies conference in Vancouver were pivotal in setting this book in motion. Sarah read every chapter as I wrote it, responding to each with criticism that was both sensitive and tough-minded. Carol and Linda gave superb editorial advice on the completed manuscript. I am grateful to all three for their enthusiasm for my earlier work, their rigorous attention to this project, and the gift of their friendship. I am also grateful to Laura Griffin for her sharp editing skills and formidable knowledge of popular culture. Jim Burr at the University of Texas Press has been the perfect editor, a dream to work with at every step of the way.

Cara DiMarco's wisdom and warmth have sustained me since long before I began this book. Louise Bishop and I have shared our lives and our work for more than twenty years, and I thank her for being more a sister to me than a colleague or friend. Maxine Scates and Bill Cadbury have been the dearest of friends and the most dedicated of readers. Their support in every aspect of my life has made all the difference.

I thank my father Al Karlyn for his generous heart and abundant good cheer. Glen Cherry and Jason Harper have been the sons I never had. Finally, this book is for Elizabeth Rowe, Miranda Rowe Harper, and Helen Rowe, my beloved and altogether fabulous girls.

Introduction

BAD MOTHERS, ANGRY GIRLS

Everything will be changed once woman
gives woman to the other woman. There
is hidden and always ready in woman the
source, the locus for the other. The mother,
too, is a metaphor. —HÉLÈNE CIXOUS

Oh, Mother, shut up. —ROSE TO HER
MOTHER RUTH, IN *TITANIC*

NE OF THE EMOTIONAL turning points of the 1997 block-
buster *Titanic* occurs soon after the ship's collision with
the iceberg that will sink it within hours. In a scene of
escalating panic and chaos, Ruth (Frances Fisher), the
mother of the film's headstrong protagonist Rose (Kate
Winslet), urges her daughter to join her in a lifeboat quickly filling with other
members of the upper class. Rose is revolted by her mother's snobbery and
yearns to remain with her newfound love Jack (Leonardo DiCaprio), a frisky
young fellow traveling in steerage. She pauses, fixes her gaze on her mother,
then refuses with a resolute, "No, Mother." In doing so, she turns her back not
only on her old life but also, in all likelihood, on life itself rather than follow
the path laid out for her by her mother.

The film has dramatized her choice with the laserlike clarity of melodrama:
Jack stands for innocence, art, freedom, and love, and Ruth stands for all that
the film vilifies—the weight of convention, especially on women, but more
important, the oppressiveness of the class structure symbolized by the opu-
lent excesses of the ship. The film validates Rose's moment of self-definition

by enabling her to survive the disaster and live a long life, rich in adventure. Jack becomes the sacrificial lamb who rescues her first by instilling in her his zest for life, then by giving up his own life for her.

Titanic's reviews were mixed, to say the least. Some praised it for its unabashed romanticism, extravagant special effects, and return to the lost grandeur of Hollywood's Golden Age. Others welcomed it as a respite from "shallow postmodern irony" (Lubin 1999, 10).[1] Still others slammed it for its anachronisms, dialogue clunkers, and melodramatic flourishes. (Billy Zane, for example, wearing eyeliner and costumed in black, plays Rose's upper-class fiancé Cal in a performance evoking the dark-cloaked, mustache-swirling villains of the earliest melodramas.) But there is no question that the film was an extraordinary phenomenon, both a prestige pic and super-expensive blockbuster with an array of statistics as impressive as the ship that was its subject. It was the most expensive movie ever made and won eleven Academy Awards, including best picture. It uniquely positioned itself for a global market by opening in Tokyo, then demonstrated record-breaking worldwide appeal.[2]

Clearly the film captured the historical moment of its release, and in several interesting ways. First, it spoke to the enduring power of melodrama to move audiences, especially during a period—four years before 9/11 shook the emotional core of the United States—when the tone of movies tended more toward postmodern irony. Titanic celebrated emotion, moral certainties, and spectacle in a nostalgic package recalling old Hollywood's epic romances, such as Gone with the Wind (1939) and Doctor Zhivago (1965).

Titanic also signaled something new: the rising power of teen girls as a demographic group to be reckoned with. This power, a likely legacy of feminism's Second Wave, was recognized by cultural critics and named variously "Girl Power" or "Girl Culture," after the terms used by riot grrrls and then the Spice Girls. The film's unexpected box office success was credited to its teen-girl fans, who came in groups to theaters for multiple viewings. Critics and the fans themselves attributed the film's teen-girl appeal to Leonardo DiCaprio's star power. However, the character of Rose, who dominates the narrative, offered an image of femininity particularly suited to the times. With her feisty rebelliousness, she evokes the tradition of female unruliness I mapped in my first book, The Unruly Woman. Yet with her faith in romantic love and individual freedom, she also embodies the contradictions of postfeminism, a phenomenon associated with young women who have benefited from the gains achieved by feminism's Second Wave, but often disavowed the movement itself, or redefined it in ways that are not always clear to their mothers.[3]

Titanic's Rose (Kate Winslet) rejects her mother's offer of safety to take her chances with Jack. A protagonist for the postfeminist era, Rose puts her faith in individual freedom and romantic love.

If *Titanic* pointed to something new, it also recalled something old, an enduring ambivalence about mothers, motherhood, and mother-daughter relations that dates from the earliest myths of Western culture and persists into media today. Since the late 1990s, motherhood has become an increasingly charged site on which unresolved conflicts about ideologies of gender, race, and class collide.

Consider the new "momism," a cultural trend that surfaced in the 1990s and purports to celebrate motherhood, but by making mothers subservient to their children rather than their husbands. Judith Warner describes this pursuit of perfect mothering as the road to "perfect madness," the title of her book on modern motherhood.[4] This new "mommy mystique," which is very much a white, middle-class phenomenon, ties good mothering to consumerism. It also recalls Betty Friedan's concept of the feminine mystique, or the bondage to which women unthinkingly submitted, especially during the 1950s, a time since associated with Stepford Wives. The very term "mom" infantilizes mothers by naming them with a term of address used by children. It also figures in the so-called "mommy wars," which have encouraged women to turn their frustrations toward each other rather than toward the social institutions that continue to fail mothers and families.

Titanic is a rare example of a major film focalized around a woman's point of view. Indeed, Rose's subjectivity, often conveyed through the powerful form of voice-over, anchors the film, conveying not only the story of her life but also that of the *Titanic*, one of the defining events of modernity. However, even though the film encompasses the span of her long life and includes her granddaughter in its frame story, Rose's voice is always that of the daughter, the girl who in taking Jack's name refuses to keep the name her mother took and who makes a life for herself as Jack's widow. Through narrative and visual means, Ruth is relentlessly aligned with Cal in opposition to her daughter's happiness, and we never hear her story.

Finally, *Titanic* is a story about a historical event, told with a certain awareness of the act of remembering and recording the past, thus telling us something about the pull of history even in an age noted for its historical amnesia. As such, it resonates with the struggles of a new generation of women to place their own lives and priorities in relation to those of the generations that preceded them. The girls who came of age during a decade of Girl Power generally considered feminism to be dated and irrelevant to them. And the feminism that emerged in the 1990s, generally called the Third Wave, occurred in the context of intense debates about the relation between the past—especially the Second Wave—and the present. As Astrid Henry has argued in *Not My Mother's Sister: Generational Conflict and Third-Wave Feminism*, feminism, for better or worse and perhaps inevitably, has understood itself and its history in generational terms through use of the metaphor of the mother-daughter relation, which she refers to as the "matrophor."[5] More often than not, the matrophor has created deep fissures within feminism as both an activist movement and as a now-institutionalized body of knowledge.

This book takes as its starting point the ambivalence around mothers that persists in widely consumed forms of popular culture today, not only in such award-winning films as *Titanic* and *American Beauty* (1999) that are aimed at mass audiences, but in films and television shows directly targeting young female audiences, from *Buffy the Vampire Slayer* (1997–2003) to *Clueless* (1995), *Scream* (1996), and *Mean Girls* (2004). My purpose is to consider the ways feminism has absorbed this ambivalence when, in renewing itself, it has distanced itself from the generations that preceded it, thereby replicating that very misogyny it wishes to eradicate. What does it mean that Rose's vibrant, unruly independence can come only by repudiating her mother? At the same time, to what extent do older feminists widen generational gaps through their own failures to understand new models of femininity and feminism that in fact may be expressions of unruliness for a new age?

The issue of motherhood has haunted Western feminism from its outset, in its struggle to free women from a biological determinism that links female bodies to reproduction. Indeed, ideologies of femininity are nowhere more intensely charged than around motherhood.[6] Concerns about the dangers of essentialized identity categories (such as "woman" or "mother") have caused feminists, especially after the Second Wave, to be wary of universalizing terms that can minimize or conceal the differences among us. This retreat, however, has coincided with a turn in the political sphere toward social conservatism that has increasingly challenged feminism to face and name the injustices suffered by poor women and working women of all classes and races. Many of these women are mothers and carry a disproportionate share of responsibility for the oldest and youngest among us. The feminist struggle for social transformation and justice can only benefit from our continued willingness to think about the institution of motherhood, and to reflect on and strengthen our generational connections.

Feminism's Mothers, Teen Girls, and Popular Culture

The 1990s might well be remembered as the decade of Girl Culture and Girl Power. New phrases began sounding in the air and new images surfacing in the media, changing the face of popular culture in a decidedly more youthful and female direction.[7] This change had already been anticipated by the rise of shopping malls in the 1980s as a place where young people congregated, and the related spread of multiplexes showing movies catering to young audiences.[8] In 1994, Mary Pipher's *Reviving Ophelia* helped put the issue of teen girls on the national cultural agenda. Indicting our "media-saturated culture" for "poisoning" our girls, the book sold 1.6 million copies.[9] In cinema, teen girls created surprise hits out of not only *Titanic* but also the low-budget romantic comedy *Clueless* and the slasher parody *Scream*. *Clueless's* success was followed by a television spin-off and a wave of romantic teen flicks, and the cult around *Scream* led to two sequels and the parody *Scary Movie* (2000), with its own sequels (2001, 2003, 2006).

On television, more programming than ever began featuring teen-girl protagonists in situations ranging from the everyday (*Felicity* and *Dawson's Creek*) to the fantastic (*Buffy the Vampire Slayer*, based on a 1992 movie of the same name). In music, phrases such as "Girl Power," first articulated by the underground riot grrrls, moved into the mainstream with the international if short-lived phenomenon of the Spice Girls, adored by very young girls, if reviled by al-most everyone else. "By sheer bulk," according to one studio executive, "young girls are driving cultural tastes now. They're amazing consumers."[10] Girls now control enough money to attract attention as a demographic group. This may or may not represent an advance in terms of girls' actual social power, but it does indicate that cultural producers are taking them seriously.

That hasn't necessarily been the case, however, for people with far more compelling personal and political stakes in understanding young women: their mothers, their teachers, and feminist thinkers in general. During the 1990s, academic feminists began to examine the relation between feminism and youth cultures, but these investigations focused more often on alterna-tive, independent, and subcultural venues, such as riot grrrls, than on main-stream popular culture.[11] Like Mary Pipher, educated and liberal-minded adults from widely differing backgrounds have more often felt a deep unease about the connections between girls and popular culture, especially youth-oriented genre films and TV.

Let me cite a few examples. During the emergence of Girl Culture in the 1990s, I spoke many times to academics and other professionals who work with girls about the ways such media icons as Buffy the Vampire Slayer, Xena the Warrior Princess, and the Spice Girls challenge familiar representations of femininity by affirming female friendship, agency, and physical power. While my audiences were usually entertained by my examples, many could not see past the violence, overt sexuality, and commercialism in the clips I showed and were troubled by my argument. Similarly, mothers in my classes ac-knowledged that they battled with their daughters over their tastes in popular culture. *Scream* was a particular flashpoint. Despite its influence among teen girls, these women discouraged or even forbade their daughters from watch-ing it, and they certainly avoided watching it with them.[12]

These responses speak to real fears about the effects of popular culture on young people, and to sincere desires to protect girls from those effects. More important, however, they stand as poignant examples of missed opportuni-ties for women of my generation—the "mothers" of contemporary feminism, or feminists of the Second Wave—to learn more about our daughters and to mend or at least better understand some of the rifts that divide us. For, despite the preferences of many educated adults for more refined examples of culture, choosing Jane Austen's *Emma* over Amy Heckerling's *Clueless*, or Mary Shel-ley's *Frankenstein* over Wes Craven's *Scream* trilogy, popular culture infuses the

Media icons such as Xena (Lucy Lawless) challenge normative femininity by affirming female friendship, agency, and physical prowess.

world in which today's young women live, and the face of feminism today, for better or worse, is being written across media culture. Over the years, *Time* magazine has heralded the end of feminism on numerous occasions, but the cover of its June 29, 1998, issue was especially suggestive. The image depicted succeeding generations of American feminism with the faces of Susan B. Anthony, Betty Friedan, and Gloria Steinem in black and white, followed by Ally McBeal, TV's most popular female character that year, in "living color." The headline "Is Feminism Dead?" suggested that if feminism lives, it does so in the fictionalized characters of popular culture.

The tension I've observed between mothers and daughters on the issue of popular culture resonates elsewhere in the U.S. feminist movement today. On the one hand, since the 1990s, "Girl Power" and "Girls Kick Butt" have become familiar phrases on magazine covers, bumper stickers, and T-shirts, one sign of the ways the Second Wave has changed the world our daughters are growing up in. On the other hand, feminism itself seems most evident as a structuring absence for middle-class young women attempting to define their identity. "I'm not a feminist, but . . ." has become the most ubiquitous reference to feminism today, heard in university classrooms, the popular press, and a wave of recent books on contemporary feminism.

Brought up during a period of social conservatism, young women are reluctant to identify themselves with any political movement and instead are more likely to place their faith in free-market individualism. This resistance to thinking collectively, however, has serious consequences at a time when collective action remains necessary not only to advance feminist goals in an age of globalization but to protect its still-vulnerable achievements in the areas of abortion rights, affirmative action, education, and healthcare, not to mention maintaining a social safety net for poor women and the families of illegal immigrants.

Thinking collectively requires both real and imaginative models of productive relationship, which have been hard to come by for girls and women in both high art and popular culture. Sisterhood was the rallying cry of the Second Wave, and while representations of sisterhood or female friendship have begun to appear with more frequency in popular culture, the mother-daughter bond, a key model of female connection, remains invisible and unexplored.[13] With a few important exceptions (including the *Alien* films, especially the second and fourth, *Species II*, and a handful of more recent examples), movies dispatch mothers with a vengeance, relegating them to sentimentality (*Stepmom*), hysteria (*American Beauty*), monstrosity (*Titanic*), or mere invisibility (*Rushmore*).[14] As a result, girls have been hard pressed to imagine what female collectivity might look like among women of their own generation or across time. Sentimentalizing sisterhood as an ideal is not the answer, especially when that ideal obscures real differences among women and the power differentials that accompany those differences. However, without models of common goals and action, the ideology of free-market individual power can and does thrive.

Women who care about the next generation of girls need to learn more about the popular texts they're drawn to, whether they are *Sex and the City* or *Buffy the Vampire Slayer*, the *Twilight* books or MTV. Productive conversations about the future of the feminist movement must take place on the terrain of popular culture, where young women are refashioning feminism toward their own ends.[15] As Australian feminist Catherine Lumby argues, "If feminism is to remain engaged with and relevant to the everyday lives of women, then feminists desperately need the tools to understand everyday culture. We need to engage with the debates in popular culture rather than taking an elitist and dismissive attitude toward the prime medium of communication today" (Lumby 1997, 174).[16]

Female Unruliness Redux

Unruly Girls, Unrepentant Mothers continues the work I began with *The Unruly Woman*, which was shaped by my own roots in the Second Wave. Highlighting the framework of generation and history, this book looks at unruly girls who rebel in ways suited to their own times, and at unrepentant mothers who refuse to be sentimentalized, demonized, or forced to disappear, the typical fate of mothers in popular culture. In contrast to *The Unruly Woman*, however, which emphasized the transhistorical figure of the unruly woman, *Unruly Girls, Unrepentant Mothers* emphasizes a single historical period, beginning in the early 1990s, a period that saw the emergence of Girl Culture and Third Wave feminism, but also a strong turn toward conservatism.

As with the earlier book, *Unruly Girls, Unrepentant Mothers* builds its argument from several sources. The first is popular culture, which I limit primarily to film and television. The second is the broad field of journalistic discourse, which creates and contests ideologies around the topics, such as romance, motherhood, and heroism, explored in popular culture. The third is feminist cultural theory, which applies to both a politicized analysis of gender, class, race, and other identity categories. Film and television are significantly different objects of study because of the industrial, technological, and economic factors that influence their production and reception. However, with increasing media convergence worldwide and the new delivery systems made possible by digital technologies, the boundaries between the two forms continue to soften. In looking at various film and television texts, I consider how the meaning of each is shaped by the aesthetic and narrative properties of its medium.

As I argued in *The Unruly Woman*, comedy as a narrative and performative mode is a key site for examining the transgressive power of female unruliness, which in *romantic* comedy confronts and challenges the ways the institution of (hetero)sexuality maintains unequal social power. In addition to its other social functions, melodrama has long been the primary popular narrative form available for examining mothers and mother-daughter relationships, and in this book I turn more fully to melodrama for its explorations of unruly women in relation not just to romantic partners but to each other, as mothers and daughters. In doing so, I take inspiration from a generation of feminist scholars who built the foundations of feminist film theory on melodrama: Julia Lesage, E. Ann Kaplan, Ellen Seiter, Christine Gledhill, Linda Williams, Mary Anne Doane, and others.

In returning to female unruliness, I also have the good fortune of following the lead of scholars who have extended my ideas beyond my initial focus on gender and class to differences of race and sexual orientation.[17] Like *The Unruly Woman*, *Unruly Girls, Unrepentant Mothers* draws primarily on mainstream popular culture, which continues to reflect the hegemony of whiteness in American culture. However, in bringing a heightened awareness of how the cultural texts I study help maintain that hegemony, I hope to help expand the concept of female unruliness in terms of not only generation and age but also racial and sexual identity.

I have also been inspired by independent filmmakers in the United States, such as Allison Anders and Julie Dash, and international ones such as Pedro Almodóvar and Marleen Gorris, who have turned to melodrama to reimagine women's connections across time. While all of these directors do not figure in this book, work by them and others begins to free motherhood and mother-daughter relations from the claustrophobia of the white, middle-class family, which limits the very idea of mothering to the mother-daughter dyad—a figuration rooted in the nineteenth-century middle-class European family. Similarly, scholarship associated with the Third Wave, transnational, U.S. Third World, and other forms of feminism offers powerful perspectives on the family that help "unthink" the Eurocentrism of academic white feminism while stimulating new ways of imagining generational relations among women.

In *The Unruly Woman*, I defined female unruliness as a cluster of attributes that challenge patriarchal power by defying norms of femininity intended to keep a woman in her place. The unruly woman creates disorder by dominating men and refusing to confine herself to her proper place. Her body is excessive, especially in terms of fatness, and her speech breaks conventions of female decorum. She may be androgynous, drawing attention to the social construction of gender by exaggerating or challenging its signifiers. She may be old, a masculinized crone who refuses to become invisible. Her behavior is defined by looseness, including sexually, and she may be pregnant. Associated with dirt, liminality, and taboo, she is above all a figure of the grotesque.

Within this conceptual framework, the term grotesque is not negative but rather ambivalent, deriving its representational and social power through its embrace of conflicting poles of meaning. By this definition, unruliness is implicitly feminist because it destabilizes patriarchal norms, although that connection may not be overtly acknowledged. This book seeks to understand the ways the Girl Culture of the 1990s and early 2000s takes up female unruliness while overtly distancing itself from feminism.

Unruly Girls, Unrepentant Mothers rests on the grotesqueness of the maternal body, the female body that is always defined by its relation to reproduction, coded as pregnant or potentially pregnant during its childbearing years and as nonsexual or masculine thereafter. The pregnant body epitomizes the grotesque by destabilizing the boundaries between inside and outside, self and other. The disruptive power of Roseanne Barr's persona in her standup comedy and sitcom (1988–1997) arose from her refusal to conceal the reproductive aspects of her fat, menstruating body and the consequences of her sexuality—in a word, her children, and the necessity of assuming primary responsibility for their day-to-day care. The pregnant body has returned to popular culture in a series of films and TV shows about unplanned pregnancies: *Waitress* (2007), *Knocked Up* (2007), *Juno* (2007), *Baby Mama* (2008), Fox's TV series *Glee* (2009–present), which also includes a faked (or "hysterical") pregnancy.

If Roseanne's fertile body bore the signs of one aspect of the grotesque, the enforced invisibility of old women suggests yet another, deriving from the potential power inherent in their aged bodies. The category of the mother, especially in her postmenopausal years, warrants more study from the perspective of female unruliness, and I will return to the old woman in chapter eight, the concluding chapter of this book. Sadly, even more than mothers of daughters, the old woman in popular culture, as in this book, is largely a structuring absence. Yet throughout, I seek to hear the suppressed voices of mothers I call "unrepentant," a term that suggests unruliness over time, the stubborn refusal of women later in life to apologize for who they are or have become.[18]

In an astute analysis of the ways the discourse of the bad mother is used against the mothers of celebrities, Shelley Cobb explains how the mothers of Britney Spears, Lindsay Lohan, and Paris Hilton have been harshly criticized for including their own desires in their ambitions for their daughters. "Worse, perhaps, is that they refuse to apologize for their unconventional behavior," Cobb writes.[19] By making spectacles of themselves (they have "gone wild") and not being "suitably, exclusively maternal," these mothers recall Stella Dallas, the iconic heroine of the maternal melodrama of that name, who was also punished for refusing to rein in her own desires to have a good time, to seek a better life for herself and her daughter, and finally to be "something else besides a mother."

I limited my earlier exploration of female unruliness primarily to comedy because of its affinities with the carnivalesque and the grotesque as well as its neglect by most feminist film scholars at that time, and comedy remains an important site for unruly teen girls, as I will show in chapter three. However, romantic comedy and melodrama are closely bound to each other.[20] Both turn on the ideological tensions that occur around female unruliness, or expressions of female desire that exceed cultural norms.

Melodrama, of course, deals with how men as well as women are victimized by patriarchy, but the form is particularly well suited to explore the pain of the banished mother, or the bride the morning after, or any woman who insists on leaving the pre-Oedipal mother-daughter bond intact, thereby violating culture's primary taboo.[21] As such, the form has been effective in dramatizing the costs to women of pursuing unruly desire, and it remains an uneasy reminder that the unruly woman's power is fragile and subject to social and generic forces that would shift her outrageousness from comedy to pathos. In poet Adrienne Rich's words, the rent between mother and daughter, ignored in our culture, is "the essential female tragedy."[22] Developing a better understanding of this tragedy is the project of this book.

Goddesses, Monsters, and Other Mythic Mothers

Some of the tension within contemporary feminism has arisen from a perceived failure by the Second Wave—the "mothers" of today's young feminists—to listen to their daughters, but meaningful cross-generational conversation among girls and women has also been stymied by a massive set of cinematic conventions establishing mothers as having nothing to say. In popular culture, especially in the more prestigious forms of film and primetime television, women have rarely existed as interesting characters once they are mothers, especially mothers of daughters. While occasionally sentimentalized and idealized, they are more often incompetent, monstrous, or just not there.

Cinema's visual vocabulary of motherhood, established in the earliest years of film history, reflects enduring moral polarities that structure Western thinking around motherhood.[23] This polarity begins with the severing of body from mind, which, as feminist thinkers such as Jane Gallop and Jane Flax have argued, has provided the foundation for associating the feminine with the body and the masculine with the mind. From there, it is a small step to "abjecting" motherhood (and procreation) in order to uphold the more esteemed categories of the mind and creation.[24] This mode of thinking helps explain why melodrama, driven by Manichean oppositions, has long been the generic home for stories about mothers. Bad Mothers loom large in the imagination of men, who fear their power to punish them.[25] The specter of the Good Mother, in contrast, highlights what is missing from popular representations of motherhood: good mothers who are also sexual; good mothers who enjoy affectionate exchanges with their daughters; and most tellingly, good mothers, period. Where in film history is Marmee, the strong and beloved mother of four daughters in Louisa May Alcott's *Little Women?* The 1868 novel has been made into movies numerous times, but failed to inspire other, similarly rich treatments of mothers and daughters.[26]

Since the 1990s, cinema has silenced mothers in new ways, revealing cultural anxiety about the empowerment of white middle-class women of the baby boom generation as a result of the Second Wave. As Elaine Roth notes, in popular films, advertisements, and television shows, mothers, especially older ones, may appear physically more present than ever, but they are also "cognitively and emotionally" more absent. Mute, abjected, and often institutionalized, these mothers are "portraits of utter passivity and incompetence" (2005).[27] For example, in ABC's drama *Grey's Anatomy* (2005–present), which is immensely popular among young women, the brilliant, once-accomplished mother of protagonist Meredith Grey suffers from Alzheimer's disease. But these mothers are also figures of ambivalence who often motivate their adult children to necessary action. And their painful visibility forces audiences to confront cultural anxieties around aging but still powerful women.

Consider also the wave of monstrous and otherwise compelling mothers who have appeared on HBO during this period. *The Sopranos* (1999–2007), one of TV's most acclaimed shows, includes interesting maternal figures such as Carmela, "capo" gangster Tony's wife, and Dr. Melfi, his shrink. However, Livia Soprano, his sour and overbearing mother, provides the driving narrative force behind the series. The key to her son's neurotic psyche and the author of a failed attempt on his life, she was dubbed by critics "the Medea of North Jersey," evoking her mythic stature. *Six Feet Under* (2001–2005), set in the grotesque space of a funeral home, dramatizes the saga of a family of undertakers headed by the widowed mother of two adult sons and a teenage daughter. At the beginning of the series, the mother (Frances Conroy) is infantilized and annoying, but soon begins to take lovers and otherwise violate her children's expectations of her. The female protagonists of both series are unrepentant mothers, mothers who make no apologies for who they are.

The more recent *Big Love* (2006–present), tells the story of a white suburban family that is utterly ordinary except that it is polygamous. As the series unfolds, the web of relations among the wives begins to eclipse the trials of the husband, who appears increasingly victimized despite his economic power and sexual privilege. The series slyly exposes the isolation and pain mothers have endured within the conventional nuclear family.

Yet another recent expression of ambivalence around motherhood is *The Da Vinci Code*, which was first a best-selling novel (2003) and then a film (2006). If momophobic movies express the urge to squelch maternal power, *The Da Vinci Code* shows the impulse to fetishize it, probing deep into the religious traditions of Western culture. A worldwide bestseller with more than sixty million copies in print and translated into forty-four languages, the book tells the story of a professor who tries to help a young woman decipher a cryptic message left by her grandfather before his violent and mysterious death. The answer involves legends of the Holy Grail, secret societies, initiates, codes, bloodlines, and esoterica covering two thousand years of Western art, philosophy, and religion. The book concerns what it considers the greatest erasure of maternal power in Western history: the Catholic Church's two-thousand-year cover-up of Jesus's marriage to Mary Magdalene and the bloodline descending from their union. This erasure has worked by substituting the virgin mother Mary in her place, a figure that became the Christian model of desexualized, disembodied, and passive femininity underlying Western ideologies of gender and whiteness.[28] According to this story, Magdalene is not only the mother and real heart of the church but she is also descended from archaic pagan roots in the Goddess.

The Da Vinci Code speaks to anxieties of the post-9/11 years, when news about conspiracies and domestic surveillance had become a part of everyday life. Like *Titanic*, it suggests a desire to uncover repressed historical truths and authenticity, a nostalgia for a lost innocence central to melodrama. Typical of popular culture, it mixes progressive messages with reactionary ones, here conveyed by the tired trope of a wise male professor who educates a wide-eyed young woman about the alluring mysteries of female wisdom and power.

As *The Da Vinci Code* shows, Western thinking about mothers and motherhood is rooted in ancient mythologies that have influenced canonical literature, philosophy, and other forms of art and popular culture for centuries. The myth of Oedipus is the most obvious example of how Greek sagas of conflicted families endure and lend themselves to contemporary interpretation.[29] According to Marianne Hirsch, patriarchal versions of the myth, from Sophocles to Freud, focus on Oedipus, the son, at the expense of the story's female figures—his wife/mother Jocasta and the mysterious Sphinx (1989).[30] Even feminist retellings of the plot, such as those of Teresa De Lauretis and Muriel Rukeyser, give precedence to the Sphinx over Jocasta.[31] Describing the Sphinx as "enigmatic, powerful, monstrous, terrifying," and Jocasta as "powerless, maternal, emotional, and virtually silent" (2–3), Hirsch asks, "What earns the Sphinx, the nonmaternal woman, privilege over Jocasta, the mother?"

The related story of Elektra is often offered as a competing model to Oedipus. Elektra inspired her brother Orestes to kill their mother Clytemnestra to avenge Clytemnestra's murder of their father Agamemnon.[32] Clytemnestra is typically seen as one of mythology's monstrous women, although her motive was avenging Agamemnon's earlier sacrifice of their daughter Iphigenia to ensure his success in war. As Hirsch notes, Elektra, serving as the passion behind her brother Orestes, is male-identified (31), and her story is generally told in terms of her relation to her father and desire to avenge his death, not her struggle with her mother. Antigone, Oedipus's daughter, offers yet another challenge to Oedipus, and her defiance of the state has fascinated philosophers from Hegel, Lacan, and Irigaray, to Judith Butler (2000). In burying her brother against state sanctions, Antigone demonstrated her allegiance to the claims of a more ancient system of law, and her story is often seen as mediating the transition from matriarchy to patriarchy. Yet she herself is not a mother and in fact derives her power from her liminal status in patriarchal law.

Shakespeare's treatment of mothers is notorious, with mothers conspicuously missing from his major romances, tragedies, and problem plays, as well as many of the comedies.[33] During the social and economic upheavals of the Renaissance, Protestantism ushered in a new emphasis on the individual that empowered women and mothers. Maternal power has generally originated in a woman's ability to assign paternity and thus control the transfer of property, but in Mary Beth Rose's account, as women began to assert more influence in choosing their own husbands or those of their children, their ability to effect cultural change became both widely recognized and feared (1991,

310). The resulting anxiety led to increasingly severe laws about infanticide and adultery, as well as endless jokes about cuckoldry. These seismic social clashes were played out in the great dramas of the era, in which, as Rose demonstrates, "the best mother is an absent or dead mother, and the ideal society is based upon the sacrifice of the mother's desire" (307)—a description that continues to ring true in much of today's popular culture.[34]

Narrative conventions for telling the stories of women's lives remain stubbornly fixated on fathers and sons, with no enduring recognition of mother-daughter "passion and rupture," in Adrienne Rich's words.[35] Similarly, Hirsch calls for a transformation of the narrative conventions that have shaped canonical Western literature to make space for the voices of mothers and daughters, speaking for themselves and for each other, but most importantly to each other (1989, 8). An obvious source of new models lies in traditions outside the Eurocentric framework that has so powerfully circumscribed Western thinking on mothers. Rich turns to texts by nonwhite women influenced by other traditions and collective experiences, as I will later in this book, for visions of motherhood and mother-daughter relations based on different traditions and social values.

Other answers lie in strains of Western mythology that have been repressed from patriarchal retellings, such as the story of Demeter, found in a Homeric hymn set in a period that preceded the arrival of the Olympian pantheon. Demeter, the goddess of Mother Earth, fertility, and grain, is best known for her fearless and protective love for her daughter Persephone. After Hades abducts Persephone to become queen of the underworld, Demeter, wild with grief, lets the earth begin to die. Zeus takes pity on her and allows Persephone to return for part of the year, instituting the cycle of the seasons. Demeter exists at the edge of representation and, like Clytemnestra, points to the deep anxieties around maternal agency and anger—Demeter, the mother who can destroy the earth, and Clytemnestra, the wife who can kill her husband and punish her children. Like Clytemnestra, Demeter stands as a figure of female rage and impassioned desire, validating a mother's grief at the loss of her daughter while also acknowledging the inevitability of that separation, as well as the daughter's own desire. In its cyclicality, with the annual return of Persephone from the underworld, the Demeter myth offers an alternative model to the linearity of Oedipal plots, and it resonates in *Antonia's Line*, the beautiful film that is the subject of this book's final chapter.

The traditions and conventions I have touched on above have had endur-ing traction not only in high culture and art films such as *Antonia's Line*, but in the more popular texts of Girl Culture. *Romeo + Juliet* (1996) and *10 Things I Hate About You* (1999), which is a remake of Shakespeare's *Taming of the Shrew*, as well as Jane Austen's *Emma*, remade as *Clueless* (see chapter three), are obvious examples of Generation X's taste for "classics lite."[36] Other allusions exist as well, including ones to Elektra, who figured not only in art films such as Ing-mar Bergman's angst-ridden, mother-obsessed *Persona* (1966) but in Wes Cra-ven's *Scream* trilogy (discussed in chapter four), which is also obsessed with a mother, but from the perspective of a daughter who comes to understand her and avenge her death. And in *Titanic*, the heroine Rose recalls the pagan and proto-Christian mythologies explored in *The Da Vinci Code*, both in the grail-like quest of the contemporary explorers for the Heart of the Ocean diamond and in her name, which according to *The Da Vinci Code* refers to Magdalene, who is still worshipped "to this day . . . as the Goddess, the Holy Grail, the Rose, and the Divine Mother."

What Is a Mother? Who Is a Mother?

Motherhood has been as contentious and difficult an issue as any that femi-nism has had to navigate. The struggle to understand and transform the insti-tution of the family, and women's place in it, was foundational to the First and Second Waves of feminism, yet many women with children did not identify with the Second Wave because they did not see what it offered them as moth-ers. Media depictions of the Second Wave's agenda included such issues as sexual and reproductive freedom, reallocations of household and childrearing labor, and matters of personal dress and grooming. But the push to pass the Equal Rights Amendment dominated the public face of the movement, and the benefits of transforming the workplace did not appear obvious to white middle-class mothers who did not work outside the home. Nor did the move-ment speak effectively to women of color who were alienated by its failure to integrate race and class into its analysis of gender.

In seeking to understand its relation to its past, today's young feminists have resisted identifying themselves as part of a new *generation* of feminism in part because the concept of generation brings to mind the mother-daughter relation, which many see as overly fraught with ambivalence. In this book, however, I choose to use the language of generations and mother-daughter relations with political intent. First, the idea of generations puts the erasure of mothers from representation within a broader political order that tends to erase all historical consciousness through the workings of capitalism, especially in postmodernity. Second, given the cultural tradition of mother-blaming as well as the expectations that older women "disappear," I believe feminist scholars should not shrink from using the matrophor, despite its inadequacies, to conceptualize women's relations across time. Not all of us are mothers, but we all have mothers. And we all have a stake in the future of girls and young women, whether we see them as our daughters or not.

Here I would like to return to Mary Russo's "Female Grotesques: Carnival and Theory," an article that was foundational to *The Unruly Woman*. Russo begins with an anecdote recalling a phrase she heard in her childhood, spoken by "the mother's voice—not my own mother's, perhaps, but the voice of an aunt, an older sister, or the mother of a friend. It is a harsh, matronizing phrase, and it is directed toward the behavior of other women: 'She [the other woman] is making a spectacle of herself'" (1986, 213). When thinking about comedy and the unruly woman, I was compelled by the idea of spectacle-making in the embedded quotation. Now the words framing that phrase leap out at me for the generational tension they convey. That framing voice is the daughter's, bristling at the censorious gaze of the mother. Russo identifies the maternal and aging body as quintessentially grotesque, but mothers themselves—colonized by patriarchy—occupy a more shadowy position in her analysis. This is the dynamic between Rose and Ruth in *Titanic*. One could imagine an empowered Rose replying to that matronizing voice as she does to her own mother in the film, with barely suppressed anger: "Oh, Mother, shut up."

This conflicted and often hostile attitude toward the mother characterized much academic feminism of the Second Wave and still haunts the Third.[37] In 1979, Audre Lorde exposed the entanglements of matrophobia, Eurocentrism, and race when she asked Mary Daly, in an open letter, why she omitted Afrekete and the other great goddesses of African tradition from *Gyn/Ecology*, Daly's influential 1978 work on religion, mythology, and radical feminism.[38] In 1981, not long after Rich's *Of Woman Born*, Marianne Hirsch charged much of the Second Wave with theorizing "at a distance from the maternal" (25) and exclusively from the position of daughters. She argued that there would be no systematic study of women's oppression that did not take into account women's roles as mothers and daughters and their relation to previous and

Bristling at the censorious gaze of her mother, Rose enacts the tradition of mother-blaming when she tells Ruth (Frances Fisher), "Oh, Mother, shut up."

subsequent generations of women in patriarchy.[39] In 1997, Ruthe Thompson wrote that feminists, academic and otherwise, were still failing to seriously engage with the issue of motherhood, despite a proliferation of articles, books, and conferences on the subject (199). And in 2004, Astrid Henry, writing from the Third Wave, argued that feminism has continued to undermine itself through inadequately understanding its own relation to previous generations.

To move beyond this impasse requires analytical steps that are basic but not always simple, such as defining terms: what, and who, is a mother? Motherhood, of course, has not meant the same thing at all times. In the United States today, the ideology of the (white, middle-class) family is in particular flux, challenged by the influence of the religious Right as well as the claims of single women and same-sex couples to the rights of parenting. And new reproductive technologies have provided dramatic opportunities, from in vitro fertilization to postmenopausal pregnancy, for people with the financial resources to afford them (Orenstein 2007). Like other liberation movements, feminism has long struggled with the consequences of trying to create political solidarity around an identity based on a universalized definition of "woman" rather than on the experiences of particular, historically situated women. These consequences weighed particularly heavily on women whose perspectives were marginalized by other women more privileged by race and class. Poststructuralist theory further challenged identity as a theoretical category and a basis for political action by striking a powerful blow against the belief in any transparent relation between the body and subjectivity, thereby helping to usher in the age of "postfeminism," "post-race" and "post-queerness" (Greene 2002).

Feminism needs to find a way to talk about motherhood and the lives of real women and children without undue fear of taking a position that is deemed essentialist or that can be co-opted by the religious Right. Similar issues have vexed feminism in the past, and notions of not only gender but also race and sexual orientation (not to mention national identity, at a time when the status of the nation-state is in flux) remain contested. However, as Biddy Martin and Chandra Talpade Mohanty remind us, "the claim to a lack of identity or positionality is itself based on privilege, on a refusal to accept responsibility for one's implication in actual historical or social relations, on a denial that positionalities exist or that they matter" (1986, 208).[40]

One route out of this impasse draws on Rich's distinction between motherhood as an institution, shaped by the interests of patriarchy, and motherhood as any woman's potential relation to her own reproductive powers and to children under her care. Both pave the way toward understanding that motherhood, like any other identity category, derives not from an "essential" biological condition or relationship but from a set of historically specific conditions. Women who identify unquestioningly with the *institution* of motherhood become patriarchy's cops, raising daughters who support the status quo not only by becoming "good girls" but also by internalizing patriarchy's matrophobia. In *Titanic*, Ruth can see no other way to ensure her own survival and that of her daughter than by following the rules. Rose chafes at those rules and contemplates jumping off the ship rather than marrying the fiancé Ruth has chosen for her. Her rebellion against patriarchy, then, necessitates her rejection of her mother.

Yet another suggestive perspective considers motherhood as the active labor involved in caring for children. For feminist philosopher Sara Ruddick, using the term "maternal" in place of "mother" shifts the emphasis from biology toward the work done by people who care for children as fully human beings demanding "protection, nurturance, and training" (1989, xi).[41] This concept nudges theories of motherhood beyond the mother-daughter dyad toward larger questions of community and ethics, governing how we care not only for children but for the aged, and not only for the people in our immediate circle but for the planet that sustains us all. This view transforms mothering into a broad-reaching and profound political practice.

Titanic was among the first films identified with Girl Culture, and it valorized a model of unruly femininity that spoke to teen girls. As I will show in the next chapter, it is also an exemplary postfeminist text. But it did not offer the only or the last word about unruly daughters and mothers. Despite its extravagance and breadth, its vision of unruliness is narrow, based on outworn ideals of romantic love and impoverished notions of female connections across time. Much of what follows in this book considers works that, like *Titanic*, have had wide influence either in the culture at large or among teenage girls, but that may question, often covertly, the unthinking matrophobia that undercuts *Titanic*'s well-intentioned efforts to celebrate female independence.

Because it is difficult to talk about unruly girls and unrepentant mothers without at least touching on the boys and men in their lives, I will lightly trace a second thread through these texts, a character type that showed up in the 1990s and that bears an interesting relation to the unruly girl. This type is the slacker, the male teen or twenty-something who refuses normative adult masculinity, although this age category can extend even higher, as in *The 40-Year-Old Virgin* (2005). While some recent films have explored male fantasies of extreme violence (*Fight Club* [1999], *American Psycho* [2000]), I am more interested in the male turn toward passivity and regression. Hints of the slacker might be seen in *Titanic*'s Jack, but the type appears most vividly in the films of Richard Linklater, Kevin Smith, and Judd Apatow, that are addressed to adolescent males. Slacker cinema may be small in numbers, but its influence is not. It can be found in the cultural impact not only of comics-loving fanboys on blockbuster super-hero movies, but also in the cultural cachet of movies about middle-aged men who flirt with or embrace the slacker syndrome: *The Big Lebowski* (the Coen brothers, 1998), *American Beauty* (Sam Mendes, 1999), *Sideways* (Alexander Payne, 2004), and *Broken Flowers* (Jim Jarmusch, 2005).[42] These films about infantilized boys and men made anxious by strong women exist in interesting tension with recent expressions of female unruliness.

Unruly Girls, Unrepentant Mothers begins by laying out cultural contexts that have influenced both contemporary feminism and popular depictions of mothers and daughters. Chapter one, "Postfeminism and the Third Wave: *Titanic*," considers motherhood in relation to postfeminism, a key determinant in contemporary depictions of girls and their mothers. As seen in *Titanic*, the postfeminist sensibility appears to advance the cause of teen-girl empowerment but simultaneously romanticizes traditional femininity and undercuts the figure of the mother. This chapter also examines Third Wave feminism as both a response to the Second Wave and a politicized articulation of postfeminist values.

Chapter two, "Trouble in Paradise: *American Beauty* and the Incest Motif," digs deeper into the roots of contemporary matrophobia by exploring the psychic drive behind the desire to demonize the mother and drive a wedge between her and her daughter. That drive involves a scenario of father-daughter incest dependant on a trio of character types that appear in both contemporary culture and clinical psychology: the eroticized daughter, a nymphet who is sexually attracted to her father; the long-suffering middle-aged man victimized both by his desire for his daughter and by his strong, castrating wife; and the collusive wife and mother, resented by both father and daughter.

Arguing for the enduring power of comedy as a genre sympathetic to female unruliness, chapter three, "Girl World," studies *Clueless, Mean Girls*, and *The Devil Wears Prada* (2006) as expressions of unruliness for a new age. In these films, Girl World becomes a space in which teen girls explore female pleasure and power. Chapter four, "Final Girls and Epic Fantasies: Remaking the World," examines the more epic and apocalyptic visions possible in such genres as fantasy and horror. Both the *Scream* films and the television series *Buffy the Vampire Slayer* create models of femininity that break new ground. Chapter five, "How Reese Witherspoon Walks the Line," is a case study of a star who captures the contradictions of the postfeminist era. In films as varied as *Election* (1999), *Legally Blonde* (2001), and *Rendition* (2007), Witherspoon has established a persona that combines postfeminism's attraction to traditional femininity with the Third Wave's interest in power.

Unruly Girls, Unrepentant Mothers concludes with works that look more closely at the separation between teen girls and their mothers, make greater use of melodrama, and begin to look outside the white mother-daughter dyad. Chapter six, "Teen-Girl Melodramas," begins with the TV series *My So-Called Life*, which inspired the first major Internet community of teen-girl fans with its sympathetic depiction of teen-girl angst. Whereas its alienated protagonist lives secure in her middle-class family, a decade later the film *Thirteen*, co-written by a girl of that age, locates that angst in a culture marked by downward mobility, fractured families, and the toxic influences of materialism. Here, the rift between a teen girl and her single mother is healed, at least temporarily, by the force of maternal love.

Chapter seven, "Girls of Color: Beyond Girl World," looks at the ways girls of color engage with Third Wave feminism, Girl Culture, and their mothers. The works I examine, from *Love and Basketball* to *Real Women Have Curves*, depict nonwhite girls in vexed but close relationships with their mothers and mother figures, whose responses to racism, poverty, and sexism inspire respect from their daughters for a feminism that is lived, if not owned by name. The chapter concludes with *Saving Face*, a romantic comedy that challenges the boundaries of not only race but also sexual orientation, national identity, and age.

Finally, chapter eight, "The Motherline and a Wicked Powerful Feminism," returns to Dutch director Marleen Gorris, whose film *A Question of Silence* (1982) I discussed in *The Unruly Woman*. I conclude with Gorris's later film *Antonia's Line* (1995) because of its inspiring vision of a feminism built on women's solidarity and love across time. This chapter considers the grotesque power of the old woman and new theories of aging that seek to empower women as they age, rather than diminish them. The route to this utopian vision, however, must begin with a closer look at what has inspired it as well as what stands in its way, and I turn now to a series of films and television shows that have honed the shape of desire for a generation of girls.

Postfeminism and the Third Wave

TITANIC

> It will take a while before feminists succeed enough so that feminism is not perceived as a gigantic mother who is held responsible for almost everything, while the patriarchy receives terminal gratitude for the small favors it bestows. —GLORIA STEINEM

NE OF THE MOST perplexing issues in any discussion of contemporary feminism is why young women disavow a social movement intended to benefit them. In the late 1990s, despite the ascendancy of Girl Culture, feminism became an easy target for women who did not feel that they had benefited from the highly touted economic boom of the decade, and who in fact were working harder than ever to get by, with less time to enjoy the rewards of domesticity and family life. At the same time, while most young women agreed with feminism's basic principles, such as equal pay for equal work, young women of all races and social classes appeared to be uncomfortable with the word "feminism." They had little knowledge of the history of the woman's movement, or of the restrictions on women's lives that fueled it. *Mad Men*, AMC's 2007 hit about Madison Avenue advertising executives, bitingly depicts the humiliations and miseries suffered by women old enough to remember the sexism, racism, and anti-Semitism of WASP culture on the cusp of the social upheavals of the 1960s. But the series's unflinching acknowledgment of gender- and race-based inequities that existed a mere generation ago and linger today is rare in the postfeminist age.

Explanations abound for this apparent turn against feminism. Onc is tied to feminism's Third Wave, an explicitly political movement and body of work that sees itself in relation to the Second Wave. Another involves postfeminism, a term that originated in popular discourse of the 1990s to suggest that in the contemporary era, feminism had lost its relevance. More a cultural condition than a movement, postfeminism has generated a second line of feminist inquiry that overlaps with the first. Both might question why the figure of the housewife/mother morphed from *Roseanne* in the 1980s to *Desperate Housewives* in the 2000s, or why Bridget Jones of the novel and films and the "girls" of *Sex and the City* have become iconic figures of identification for young women in the 1990s and early 2000s. This chapter poses yet another question: What is the connection between ambivalence toward feminism today and ambivalence toward mothers, especially the mothers of the Second Wave?

Backlash and Postfeminism

In 1997, in one of the earliest and still most insightful analyses of the new Girl Culture, Ann Powers described how its icons aggressively flaunt traits such as "prettiness, brattiness, and sexual flamboyance" that were formerly viewed as demeaning by feminists and misogynists alike. The question here is whether girls' interest in these traits reflects a postfeminist naïveté about gender politics or the new manifestation of feminism known as the Third Wave. In order to understand the Third Wave, it is important first to consider why young women felt the need to distance themselves from the feminism of their mothers.

Many have explained the turn from feminism by looking outward from the movement to its social and political context. In 1991, Susan Faludi's *Backlash* popularized the idea that feminism suffered from massive efforts during the 1980s and 1990s to reverse the gains achieved by the women's movement. From this perspective, if young women believe in their unlimited freedom and opportunity as individuals, reject structural analyses of social power, and avoid questioning the unequal effects of economic prosperity, that is because they have grown up in a political environment that closed off any other points of view.[1] During this period, other highly publicized books put feminism back in the popular discourse, but more ambiguously. Writers such as Naomi Wolf, Katie Roiphe, and Rene Denfield may have identified themselves with feminism but according to a new set of definitions based on rhetorically savvy but misleading oppositions: victim feminism vs. power feminism, gender or "difference" feminism vs. equity feminism.

Young, white, and educated at elite institutions, these women conformed to *Time* magazine's choice of TV character Ally McBeal as the face of a new, popularized feminism. Other conservative voices with more established academic credentials, including Elizabeth Fox-Genovese, Camille Paglia, and Christina Hoff-Sommers, joined the chorus.[2] While claiming to refashion a new feminism, however, these writers had not learned the lessons about racial and class privilege so hard won by the old, and their ideas were well refuted in scholarly venues. But the mainstream press embraced them anyway and used them as the basis for sensationalized discussions of contemporary feminism.[3] Concluding that the need for anything resembling old-style feminism no longer existed, the discourse of postfeminism took hold.

By the 2000s, feminist scholars developed increasingly sophisticated explanations of postfeminism's contradictory mixture of feminist and antifeminist notions.[4] According to Angela McRobbie, postfeminism differs from backlash theory because it seems to embrace feminism while at the same time viewing the movement as so outdated that it has become oppressive itself. She argues that postfeminism is less an ideology than a *process* by which popular culture "undoes" feminism while appearing to offer a well-intentioned response to it. Beginning with the premise that individuals are free to choose any life they wish, it makes heavy use of the tropes of boldness, entitlement, and choice, along with the practices of self-surveillance and monitoring fostered by teen magazines and self-help TV and literature aimed at women.

At the same time, postfeminism shows little interest in the inequities that constrain an individual's choice. Nor does it consider the implications of expressing choice largely in the realm of the sexualized body, normative femininity, and consumer culture. Reflecting the eroding sense of social structure that has accompanied the rise of neoliberalism, it teaches young women that they can gain social and sexual recognition only by distancing themselves from feminism. Postfeminism, then, is a sensibility that has characterized contemporary, popular understandings of gender, and the broad discursive field that frames both Girl Culture and the Third Wave.

What's Wrong with Feminism?
And What's Mom Got to Do With It?

The culture of postfeminism co-opted the Second Wave, and substantive ide-ological differences exist between the Second Wave and the Third. But some-thing else also contributed to girls' alienation from feminism, and that is the mother factor.

Feminism has long been riddled with generational tensions or "mama drama," in Deborah Siegel's words, and conflicted attitudes toward figures viewed literally and metaphorically as maternal have contributed to the gap between young feminists and those who preceded them.[5] Indeed, Third Wave feminists have only now begun to think about motherhood *not* from the posi-tion of daughter and to consider how their attitudes toward mothering, moth-erhood, and their own mothers may reflect the culture's ambivalences. For example, while autonomy has been an overarching goal of feminism, even feminists can be ambivalent about selfhood when it comes to mothers (Baum-gartner and Richards 2000, 212). Moreover, because feminism has historically stressed the positive psychological and social aspects of the mother/daughter bond, it has not fully theorized daughters' feelings of ambivalence—or out-right hostility—toward their mothers.

In the West, this daughterly need for distance from the mother cannot be seen apart from the broader ideology of individualism, which has resurfaced with renewed force under the neoliberalism of the 1990s and 2000s. Extend-ing her previous work on the impact of relationship in women's lives, Carol Gilligan suggests that the problems besetting current feminism arise from our culture's pervasive ethos of separation.[6] Gilligan has been roundly criticized for the essentialism of her early work, but she stands as a compelling example of a Second Wave feminist "mother" who has much to offer the Third Wave. As girls mature, she argues, they learn that success requires them to "dissoci-ate" or disconnect not only from their mothers but also from their own per-ceptions and desires. The issue becomes "how to keep our relationships with the power structures of the world while remaining in relationship with one another and ourselves."[7] This tension lies at the heart of romantic comedy, with its delicate dance between female unruliness and domestication.

Girls have other reasons, as well, for retreating from a feminism they asso-ciate with their mother's generation as they approach adulthood. First, young women desire to maintain connections with the existing (still largely male) power structure, especially when that power structure begins to appear within reach. In *Clueless*, young, beautiful Cher, like Rose in *Titanic*, is very close to the peak of her social power. This identification with the status quo is particularly strong for girls already privileged by race, class, sexuality, or education; lesbians and girls of color, for example, are less likely to assume that playing by the rules will give them a fair chance to win.

In addition, while girls at this age develop curiosity about becoming a woman, they do not necessarily want to hear about a previous generation's experiences (Gilligan 1997, 22). Americans notoriously lack historical awareness, and young women are no exception. And so, as teen girls begin to experience the contradictions of female life and increasingly learn to put on a false face to please those who have power over them, their conversations with their mothers typically become more volatile.

Finally, feminism has wrought significant changes in Western society, and its effects, especially on family and domestic life, have been complex. For previous generations of white middle-class women, work represented a longed-for freedom to participate in public life, and family life meant forced confinement within the private sphere. However, for many young women today these categories have come to mean the opposite: work is a necessity, and family life (or their fantasies about motherhood and domesticity) an option or "luxury" that may appear frustratingly out of reach. At the same time, both work and domestic life remain fraught with inequities that continue to weigh heavily on women's shoulders.[8] Drawing on clinical psychology, Gilligan notes that patients often hesitate on the cusp of major transformations. As a result, feminism has become an easy scapegoat for problems originating elsewhere, whether from the economic restructuring brought about by globalization or from the incomplete realization of the feminist project.

The solution Gilligan proposes for feminism and the culture at large is a new model of "relational psychology" that would privilege connection with ourselves, each other, and the world. In *Clueless*, Cher's discovery of her real self coincides with a heightened awareness of her connections with an ever-expanding community that extends to classmates she once scorned and finally to strangers, the victims of a natural disaster nearby. This model provides a psychological and ethical basis for the kind of coalition politics needed to preserve and advance the feminist movement. From the long perspective of history, feminism's current debates should not be troubling in themselves, but only when they are used to prevent or reverse radical social change. As Gloria

Steinem acknowledges, with an apt use of the matrophor, "it will take awhile before feminists succeed enough so that feminism is not perceived as a gigantic mother who is held responsible for almost everything, while the patriarchy receives terminal gratitude for the small favors it bestows" (Walker 1995, xix).

It is hard to quarrel with the fundamental principles of the Second Wave. In addition to the push for workplace and reproductive rights, the movement zeroed in on issues it saw as most deeply implicated in perpetuating patriarchal power: the objectification of women through normative standards of feminine beauty; the oppressiveness of heterosexuality as an institution; the exploitation of women's domestic labor; and popular culture's role in socializing women into patriarchy. The Second Wave also believed the social world could be transformed through collective action and the power of sisterhood—strikes, guerrilla theater, protest, legislation, and consciousness-raising.

Still, many women found reasons within the movement to distance themselves from it. They perceived aspects of the Second Wave as dogmatic, censorious, and out-of-touch with their everyday lives in areas that mattered to them, including sex, romance, the pleasures of domesticity, and popular culture. First, sex. As Carol Siegel argues, many women contemporary with the Second Wave, and even within it, were put off by its prevailing views of censorship, pornography, and other matters pertaining to sexuality. Even though more bohemian or "outlaw" strains of feminism took issue with these views, the Second Wave failed to address sexuality and love, especially between women and men, in ways that most women could relate to.[9]

In some instances, Second Wave feminists have also inadvertently aligned themselves with conservative social forces. According to Catherine Lumby, older feminists have been reluctant to acknowledge their deepening stakes in the establishment, especially in academia, and as a result, have been blind to dramatic changes in technology and popular culture that have transformed the landscape of politics and public life. For example, feminism has been slow to develop theories of technology and new media. And like the Left, the Second Wave has long been suspicious of the easy pleasures of popular culture. When asked in a recent interview whether the Third Wave has replaced politics with play, Elaine Showalter, a major figure of the Second Wave, acknowledged "that you get a feeling for a place and for people by participating in popular culture." Yet, somewhat wistfully, she added that popular culture is a form of women's play, and women have never been allowed the same right to play as men have. "I do not know why I should feel guilty about it" (Gillis, Howie, and Munford 2004, 64).

This guilt is understandable, however, given the taboos not only around women's pleasure but also around the boundaries between high and low culture. As cultural studies theorists have long demonstrated, these boundaries create and maintain hierarchies of social power. Whereas the very existence of high culture has served the needs of the elite, new forms of culture, such as the Internet, evoke anxiety because, like feminism itself, they help destabilize old power structures by shifting the boundaries between the public and the private. Just as the liberation movements in the late 1960s followed the penetration of television into middle-class households in the 1950s, the Internet at the turn of the twenty-first century has become the flashpoint of struggle between those who view access to information as a means to social power and those who wish to restrict that access.[10] Young women and men who do not see themselves reflected in the dominant culture have found vital information and communities online.

Perhaps feminism's deepest wounds and most serious failures have occurred in the area of race. Despite the widespread social realities of homophobia, queer theory has found a place in academic feminism in part because its critique of heteronormativity keeps it within the paradigm of gender as feminism's primary identity category. However, the failures of mainstream American feminism to forge a racially inclusive movement date from its earliest history in the nineteenth century, when Susan B. Anthony refused to support the enfranchisement of black men despite feminism's roots in the abolitionist movement.

In later decades, white American feminism engaged with minority voices, but selectively—the highly intellectual Gayatri Spivak or the "easily digested" Maya Angelou. The resulting tensions came to a head at the 1981 National Women's Studies Association Conference, when women of color, angered by the conference's exclusionary structure, launched a movement they identified as U.S. Third World feminism.[11] Since then, this movement, a coalition of diverse feminisms, has modeled ways of working through identity as well as notions of "difference from/similar to" as a basis for coalition building. U.S. Third World feminism has also been foundational to the Third Wave, which, unlike postfeminism, conceives of itself as a political entity.

The Third Wave

While postfeminism was fostering a nostalgic and apolitical stance toward gender politics, a series of events, including the Clarence Thomas/Anita Hill hearings in 1991, reawakened a widespread and more serious recognition of feminism's unfinished business. In a 1992 article in Ms. ("Becoming the Third Wave"), Rebecca Walker, novelist Alice Walker's daughter, described the stirrings of a renewed feminist movement she named the Third Wave, and a surge of writing followed that embraced the name. Provocative, wide-ranging, and diverse in rhetorical style, this work often combined critique with manifesto and included collections of personal testimonies as well as more academic scholarship.[12]

In seeking to break beyond the racial, class, and national boundaries of the Second Wave, young feminists of the Third Wave have been especially interested in issues related to sex, identity, and culture, and cross-currents flow between Girl Culture, with its reclamation of aspects of traditional femininity, and the Third Wave's theoretical explorations of gender.[13] Consistent with postfeminism, the Third Wave is comfortable with contradiction. But it differs in other important ways from the popularized feminisms of Katie Roiphe et al. as well as from the Second Wave. The Third Wave tends to be more inclusive than the Second, both racially and sexually. It is global and ecological in perspective, with young campus feminists seeing environmental and international labor issues as deeply connected, and the anti-sweatshop and workers' rights movements as central to feminism today. It shows the influence of poststructuralist theory on its notions of identity and subjectivity as fluid, socially constructed categories. It is postmodernist in its orientation toward popular culture and consumer culture, seeing both as affording opportunities for pleasure and self-expression. And it views sexuality as a touchstone issue that mobilizes young women the way Civil Rights and Vietnam mobilized their mothers.

The regulation of female sexuality is deeply ingrained in our culture to hold the structures of patriarchy and heterosexuality in place, with mothers, even feminist mothers who have internalized these lessons, teaching their daughters from an early age to police their sexuality. For Ruth in *Titanic*, Rose's virginity is a commodity that must be protected so it will fetch the highest price. And so, as Third Wavers Nan Bauer Maglin and Donna Perry argue, sexuality has become a "lightning rod for this generation's hopes and discontents (and democratic visions)" (1996, xvi). For them, society's "construction, containment, and exploitation of female sexuality in the 1990s" mirrors women's situation in general and calls up questions of agency or victimization, key topics of debate among postfeminist writers.

Much adult concern about young women and popular culture arises from the depictions of teen-girl sexuality in movies, MTV, magazines, advertisements, clothing, and TV shows, so Third Wavers focus on the relation between sexual politics and cultural production. While the Second Wave generally tied (hetero)sexuality to oppression, the Third Wave is less conflicted about sexuality in any form. In her ethnographic studies of youth subcultures and alternative music, Carol Siegel found an interest in fluid categories of gender and wide-ranging sexualities (or "sexstyles"). This interest challenges power structures that are threatened by sexual practices such as S&M or fetishism that resist the ideological frameworks of both mainstream culture and the Second Wave.

The insistence of young feminists on their right to define their political strategy as "[making] use of the pleasure, danger, and defining power" of social structures critiqued by the Second Wave (Heywood and Drake 1997, 3) may well unsettle older women concerned about girls' vulnerability to exploitation by men or experimentation outside the social norms of heterosexuality. And there are legitimate reasons to fear that sexual freedom has become reduced to one more way of exploiting girls. However, older women need to understand more fully the intention that motivates this strategy. *Clueless* and *Titanic* treat sex as a given for young women as long as it is on their own terms. As Lisa Jones writes of the Third Wave, "We are smart-ass girls with a sense of entitlement, who . . . delight in our sexual bravura, and live womanism as pleasure, not academic mandate" (1995, 251).

Young feminists today resist the positivist epistemology of the Second Wave, which led to divisive universalizing around such categories as "woman." In the Third Wave, "male," "female," "black," "white," "lesbian," and "heterosexual" are not transparent signifiers of "the real." Many Third Wavers are uneasy about the political consequences of abandoning these categories, which may be pragmatic bases for identity politics. At the same time, they see these categories as mobile markers of identity that can be borrowed, performed, and pieced together ironically, playfully, or with political intent, in a mode typical of postmodern culture. And so, if young women reject the label of feminist, that rejection may have less to do with the meaning of the term than with their skepticism about the capacity of language to represent the truth of who they are, a perspective based on a poststructuralist critique of the relation between language and the real.

In Third Wave feminism, popular culture is a natural site of identity formation and empowerment, providing an abundant storehouse of images and narratives valuable less as a means of representing reality and more as motifs available for contesting, rewriting, and recoding. In this context, films such as *Clueless, Scream,* or *Titanic* provide an opportunity to sort out the relation between a highly commodified Girl Culture and the real empowerment of girls.

For youth culture, the appropriation of diverse cultural labels, motifs, or other signifiers expresses an aesthetics and politics of hybridity consistent with its consciousness of racial, ethnic, and sexual diversity.[14] And so young women of all races and ethnicities borrow from hip-hop, the preeminent movement in youth culture today, despite its roots in urban, male, African American culture, in order to align themselves with its politicized stance toward racial injustice (Niesel 1997). Similarly, young women freely engage in masculinity within themselves as well as in male-oriented music and violent action films in order to claim the power our culture still identifies with boys and men. With films such as the *Scream* trilogy, girls rewrite to their advantage the codes of femininity embedded in highly conventionalized film genres.

Yet another puzzle for older feminists is Girl Culture's embrace of girliness because, for women of the Second Wave, the habit of addressing or considering women as girls reflected patriarchy's desire to deny them the status of adults. From the perspective of the Third Wave, however, that stance led to a wholesale rejection of femininity and many of the pleasures of female culture that have long been trivialized by the culture at large, from shopping and dressing up to gossiping. Thus, much as gays and lesbians reclaimed "queer," the Third Wave has reclaimed the term "girl" and its attendant pleasures, and made a reevaluation of femininity central to its concerns. "Girlie girls" include adult women, usually in the mid-twenties to late thirties, such as the authors of *Bust* (founded in 1993 by Debbie Stoller) and *Bitch* (founded in 1996 by Lisa Jervis and Andi Ziesler), who see Girl Culture as a site of feminist agency and resistance. For them, feminism includes reclaiming aspects of female culture, "be it Barbie, housekeeping, or girl talk . . . that were tossed out with sexism during the Second Wave" (Baumgarder and Richards 2000, 400).

The Third Wave is committed to retaining important aspects of the Second Wave, including the critique of beauty culture and sexual abuse. At the same time, both Girl Culture and the Third Wave complicate the older feminist critique of the male gaze as a weapon to put women in their place. The new girl heroes exploit the spotlight as a source of power and energy, and they do not see a contradiction between female power and assertive sexuality. Like Buffy the Vampire Slayer, they can dress in provocative clothing while demonstrating fierce physical prowess or, like the Spice Girls, chant the virtues of female power and solidarity while wearing Wonderbras. Ann Powers's sharpest insight into the new Girl Culture describes its strategy as neither rational nor analytic, like the Second Wave's, but mythic, manifesting itself in the symbols, rhythms, and motifs of a media-infused age.

Titanic and Postfeminism

Because postfeminism places a high premium on sex and romance as an aspect of identity formation, romantic comedy is among the most popular of postfeminist genres. Romantic comedies such as *Clueless* and *Bridget Jones's Diary* treat a young woman's coming of age primarily in terms of finding the right mate, and they always end happily. Melodrama, however, is also well suited for exploring postfeminist themes, especially when cast in terms of rejecting the Bad Mother and her outdated baggage.

The 1990s saw a renewed interest in melodrama, but often in the guise of what Jeffrey Sconce has identified as the "new American 'smart' film." According to Sconce, the smart film, a convergence of the art film, Hollywood, and independent cinema, combines irony, black humor, and fatalism in what *New York Times* film critic Manohla Dargis has described as "the new nihilism." This sensibility can be found in *American Beauty*, the subject of chapter two, as well as in the work of Todd Solondz, Neil LaBute, Hal Hartley, Alexander Payne, and Wes Anderson.[15] As Sconce notes, the smart film is not gender neutral but associated with young white male directors interested in their own status as victims.

In contrast, *Titanic* embraces melodrama with no irony or reserve, going all out to seek emotional heights and surrendering to the pull of an earlier age, both in its historical referents and its narrative use of flashback. It so clearly embodies melodramatic characteristics that Linda Williams, among the most important voices on melodrama since the 1970s, pairs it with Griffith's *Way Down East* (1920) as exemplary of the form (2001). *Titanic*'s enormous popularity suggests that if some audiences in the 1990s were drawn to the irony of smart cinema, larger ones hungered for the emotional intensity offered not only by *Titanic* but by such epic blockbusters as the *Lord of the Rings* films.[16] Williams argues that more than a genre, melodrama is a "major force of moral reasoning in American mass culture" (2001, xv), encompassing most U.S. film genres and shaping America's fundamental sense of its national identity.[17] As she and others have argued, melodrama works through a set of rhetorical conventions designed to generate sensation and moral clarity by setting up dramatic stakes around the yearning for innocence or moral virtue, associated with home. "If emotional and moral registers are sounded," she writes, "if a work invites us to feel sympathy for the virtues of beset victims, if the narrative trajectory is ultimately concerned with the retrieval and staging of virtue through adversity and suffering, then the operative mode is melodrama" (2001, 15).

Melodrama has long appealed to feminist scholars because of the ways it generates pathos around the suffering of women, pushing toward "moral legibility" the injustices inherent in the institution of heterosexuality: impossible dilemmas arising from the imperative for women, especially mothers, to nurture others at the expense of the self.[8] Melodrama can serve progressive ends by tackling real social problems, and like comedy, it expresses utopian impulses. At the same time, it is inherently conservative. While beginning and ending in a place of innocence, it seeks that innocence through nostalgic reconstructions of the past. As Robert Dassanowsky suggests, *Titanic* succeeds in making a class-based society of "rabid inequality" more appealing than today's "faceless bar codes and vague e-mail identities" (20).

Titanic draws on melodrama's dynamic moral oppositions to capture the ambivalences of postfeminism, and draws on its pathos to tap into the volatility of teen girls' emotional lives. With its tintype images and dreamy sequences set under the sea, its voyeuristic probing into the ruins of the great ship, its haunting soundtrack, and its wildly romantic love story, *Titanic* expresses the inarticulate yearnings of a generation of girls for the certainties of an imagined, prefeminist past around sex, gender, and romantic love. In discussing the film's appeal, Dassanowsky compares its reception to the emotional outpouring that followed the death of Princess Diana in August 1997. Both satisfied the need for mass ritual and emotional fulfillment in a time of "relative aimlessness," and both dealt with repressed women when feminism had all but disappeared as a political movement. *Titanic* acknowledges the pain of female adolescence, the shrinking of a girl's self which Mary Pipher's *Reviving Ophelia* identified (and which director Cameron is reported to have read while he was making the film). The film offers strong messages of teen girl empowerment with its smart, independent, and sexually free young protagonist. However, it entangles that message in others based on rescue fantasies about self-sacrificing princes and evil mothers.

Titanic is unique among blockbusters and action films for the role teen girls played in its success, and it catalyzed a shift in entertainment industries toward this demographic group (Gateward and Pomerance 2002). Sixty percent of its viewers were female, and sixty-three percent under the age of twenty-five. Forty-five percent of the younger group were repeat viewers, and girls made its soundtrack the all-time bestseller (Lubin 1999, 8–13). In teen magazines and Internet fan fiction, a huge community developed around Leonardo DiCaprio, already adored by teen girls for *Romeo + Juliet* (1996). As a result, girls were featured more prominently than ever in commercial films across a range of genres, including horror (*Scream*), comedy (*The Opposite of Sex* [1998]), and sci-fi (*Lost in Space* [1999]). They also played important roles in films aimed at adults, such as *The Ice Storm* (1997), *American Beauty* (1999), and *Felicia's Journey* (1999).

This box office power may have been both overestimated and undercut by subtle forms of sexism directed against the "swarms" and "hoards" of girls "flocking" to the film (Lahti and Nash 1999, 83).[19] Nonetheless, it marked a deviation in a tradition that has historically seen male taste as homologous with the mainstream market. In fact, by 2007, fanboys (geeky, sixteen- to thirty-five-year-old males) were heralded for their disproportionate influence as tastemakers. An article in *Time* magazine described fanboys as loving "obsessively" a certain type of movie, typically comic-based franchises and homages to B-movies, from the *Star Wars* franchise to *Grindhouse* (2007) and *Snakes on a Plane* (2006) (Winters 2007). While film critics and the mainstream moviegoing public often don't share these obsessions, studios take fanboys and their tastes seriously, no doubt because some of Hollywood's biggest moneymakers (e.g., George Lucas) were fanboys of an earlier generation. Since 1994, filmmaker Kevin Smith has built his career around a brand (his "View Askewniverse") designed to appeal to fanboys, a cohort that might well be considered in a state of arrested development for retreating from strong women, including their mothers, into homosocial worlds of comic books and similarly obsessed boys.

While DiCaprio appears to have been the driving force behind *Titanic's* appeal to girls, that appeal must also be read in terms of the particular meanings his star text took on within the film and the fantasies that it activated. There he serves as an object of desire for Rose, who is the film's main point of identification and whose voice-over links us to her subjectivity. James Cameron earned his feminist credentials for a history of groundbreaking work on femininity.

He is credited with creating the 1980s and 1990s female action hero, with Linda Hamilton (the *Terminator* films), Sigourney Weaver (the *Alien* films), and Jamie Lee Curtis (*True Lies*) all playing physically powerful characters in his films.[20] Moreover, in *Aliens* and *Terminator 2*, he created worlds seen as extensions of female subjectivity, centered narratively and thematically on maternal love and childbirth. In 2000–2002, he brought his vision of female power to television with the series *Dark Angel*, built around the struggles of a genetically enhanced, superhuman young woman in a postapocalyptic world. Cameron's female protagonists, as Peter Krämer notes, are driven not by professionalism, duty, or selflessness, but by an intense emotional bond with another being (1999, 113)—the kind of individualized understanding of the world consistent with postfeminist culture.

Similarly, *Titanic* endows Rose with mythic proportions, embedding her life in the story of America and modernity itself, seen as examples of technological and imperial grandeur. Rose dramatizes the transformation of a Victorian female ideal into a Progressive Era New Woman, and in fact Cameron modeled her on a real person, Beatrice Wood (1893–1998), a high society girl who ran away at the age of seventeen from her domineering mother to pursue her independence.[21] In choosing this model from an earlier era, Cameron created a new image of woman for contemporary times, reinforcing postfeminism's interest in redefining femininity. Indeed, Rose does not conform to female character types familiar in film history—the victims of melodrama, film noir's *femmes fatales*, the fetishized spectacles of musicals, the "female appendages" of the buddy films, or even the hard-bodied women Cameron popularized in his earlier action and sci-fi films (Liggett 2002).

In the 1990s, teen-girl audiences were interested in exploring a kind of femininity that combined masculine physical prowess with girliness, as typified by Sarah Michelle Gellar in *Buffy the Vampire Slayer*. At the same time, white middle-class girls were obsessed with thinness to the point of physical illness and even death. No wonder Kate Winslet's body appealed to them, with its combination of feminine curves and masculine power and strength. The film displays her physicality in spectacular action sequences that further elevate Rose's story to the stuff of legend. She races through the flooding ship, wields an ax to free Jack and punches characters who get in her way.[22] Smoking cigars and spitting, she rejects codes of passive, ladylike femininity. Yet her voluptuous body is a far cry from the muscled action heroines of Cameron's earlier films and the skinny women of fashion layouts and popular TV shows such as

In the 1990s, teen girls were interested in a femininity that combined physical prowess with girliness. Like Buffy the Vampire Slayer, *Titanic*'s Rose is femininely beautiful and masculinely active.

Friends. As the action progresses, the film increasingly displays her body. While the women around her wear high-necked suits and fussy hats, she is hatless and with exposed decolletage. She poses nude for Jack, and rushes to his rescue wearing a thin, wet dress that clings to her as the ship begins to sink.

While Rose does not display an interest in clothing consistent with the postfeminist reclamation of shopping and fashion, the film displays her in sumptuous feminine attire, beginning with her introduction as a young woman boarding the ship, wearing a low-brimmed hat that covers much of her face. The image recalls a similar one of Bette Davis in *Now, Voyager* (1942), another film about a woman whose journey of self-discovery takes place on an ocean liner. The allusion to Davis places Winslet's character in a line of other unruly women of classical melodrama who battle to free themselves for independent lives.[23] In both films, the broad, angled hats draw attention to the gap between an external reality of confidence and an internal one of turmoil. In *Now, Voyager*, the hat signifies the character's progression from an ugly duckling to a confident woman. In *Titanic*, it conveys the painful division between the outward Rose and the stifled Rose who, as she recounts, was screaming inside. In both films, repressed daughters rebel against domineering mothers by having forbidden trysts in an automobile, the symbol of the new era's mobility, and both protagonists mature to live rewarding lives without the men they love.

Reading Rose in the context of her historical times, she is indeed an unruly girl. She literally moves out of her place by ranging freely throughout the ship, especially to its forbidden lower decks. Her hair, attire, behavior, and language are "loose"; she defies authority; even as old Rose, her red-painted toe nails signify her refusal to become sexless and invisible as she ages. The photographs she travels with document a life lived large, especially for a woman of her generation, and as Peter Krämer notes, her anger carries fierce feminist potential: "Behind the romantic dream of an adolescent girl lurks the nightmare of suppressed female rage" (1999, 119).

However, what does it mean on the brink of the millennium for girls to see feminism in terms of defying one's mother? Or female power as a matter of choosing one's sexual partner? Here the film operates as a postfeminist text, both asserting and undermining feminist principles. Taking feminism as a *fait accompli*, it defines its crucial dilemmas around matters of individual choice in the area of sexuality and femininity, and assumes that a woman's pursuit of freedom and independence can happen on an even playing field. Like the glamorous female protagonists of classical romantic comedy, Rose defines her rebelliousness around her freedom to fall in love outside her class. Unlike them, however, she is an innocent who surrenders to the greater wisdom of her lover. Moreover, the film provides Rose with no female friends or sisters, isolating her in the suffocating emotional confines of her relationship with her mother and two romantic rivals.

By constructing Rose as a charismatic protofeminist who orchestrates her own sexual initiation and redefines her femininity to include behaviors of the male working class, the film covers up the implications of its deeply romantic message about the power of heterosexual love to transcend not only social divisions but time itself. This message is based on a classic rescue fantasy and the seductive appeal of old-fashioned chivalry, with a working-class knight (the film's real gentleman) willingly sacrificing his life to save the woman he loves. It is hard not to understand the appeal of this scenario to girls in the context of such other youth-oriented films as Smith's *Clerks* and *Mallrats* and Linklater's *Slacker* and *Dazed and Confused*, which feature immature young men who are fearful of women, commitment, and simply growing up.

The film's gestures toward feminism are most compromised, however, by its treatment of the mother. It so powerfully condenses its critique of class on her that the reasons for her own suffering as a woman become lost. Structurally, the film resembles a romantic comedy about star-crossed lovers of

Recalling an image similar to Bette Davis in *Now, Voyager* (1942), Rose's introduction in a low-brimmed hat places Winslet's character in a tradition of unruly women battling to free themselves for happier and more independent lives.

In both films, the hats draw attention to the gap between an external appearance of self-possession and an interior reality of distress.

different classes. It even resolves on the tonic chord of comedy, bringing the couple together (if only in fantasy, on the eve of Rose's death) with a kiss performed to the applause of the entire ship. However, unlike comedy, the father is not there. His death has left his family with nothing but a "good name and bad debts" and set in motion the film's chain of events. In the dangerous absence of patriarchal power, Ruth must find a means of livelihood for herself and her daughter. Both mother and daughter evoke biblical archetypes. If Rose's name is associated with the New Testament, her mother recalls the Old Testament figure of Ruth, revered as a figure of loyalty to her mother-in-law and of surrender to the patriarchal tradition of Judaism. Frances Fisher's performance of Ruth imbues the character with intelligence and hints of vulnerability. But because of the character's identification with patriarchy, she cannot escape becoming a phallic mother who stands as the most significant obstacle to Rose's happiness.

The film's overarching theme is the desire for freedom, and its narrative is organized around a conflict between the young lovers who want it and those who stand in their way. This theme resonates in the film's dialogue, imagery, and Cameron's own commentary. In the film's most widely circulated image, which recalls Greta Garbo at the conclusion of Rouben Mamoulian's *Queen Cristina* (1933), Rose stands on the ship's prow, with her arms outstretched, feeling the immense power of the ship behind her as she moves into the wind. Where Cristina is somber, though, facing the real cost of her choice to be free, Rose is euphoric. The obstacles to Rose's freedom arise from both her gender and her class, but because the film establishes its more powerful moral and dramatic oppositions along the lines of class, Rose's liberation becomes a simple matter of replacing one man—a boorish, evil man of wealth—with another, a gallant artist from the working class who dies to save her but lives in her heart forever.

Jack's virtue originates in his working-class identity.[24] He is vital, youthful, artistic, generous, wise—and able to live with no need to think about money and financial security. In some regards, he might be considered a more energetic version of a Gen-X slacker, preferring his freedom to the shackles of convention. Played by DiCaprio with an almost feminine beauty, he also offers an image of masculinity unthreatening to young girls. Winslet's physical presence dominates his, and while he rescues Rose by sacrificing his life for her and instilling in her his will to live, he appears physically vulnerable and in need of rescue by her when she must smash apart the chains that hold him prisoner in the rising waters of the ship. In contrast, the film's most

Titanic's compositions often position Cal (Billy Zane) between Ruth and Rose, exaggerating his villainy by showing him disrupting the relation between mother and daughter.

unappealing characters—Ruth and Cal—share the evil values of their class and are co-conspirators in trying to destroy Rose's happiness. Sequences alternate shots of Rose with two-shots of Cal and Ruth, and compositions position Cal between Ruth and Rose, exaggerating his villainy by literally placing him between mother and daughter.

Three scenes demonstrate the film's failure to extend to the mother its analysis of and sympathy for women's suffering under patriarchy. The first occurs after Cal's violent outburst against Rose. Rose is standing in her stateroom holding onto the bedpost, as Trudy, her maid, laces up her corset, an obvious symbol of women's oppression. The setting is warmly lit to showcase the opulence of Rose's current life—what's at stake in the conversation to come—as well as her physical desirability, or the sexual value her mother wants to leverage to maintain that way of life. Ruth enters from behind, dismisses Trudy and continues the job. During this scene, Ruth explains why Rose must marry Cal, and as her impatience at Rose's resistance mounts, she yanks on the cords with enough force to jerk her daughter's body. She moves aggressively into Rose's space, crowding her against the bedpost. Cameron films the scene to show the women's physical resemblance, with Ruth's red hair and pale skin a faded echo of Rose's more vibrant coloring. But we also see their differences of temperament and age—Rose bare-shouldered, with hair flowing free, and Ruth in a high-necked dark dress, with her hair pinned up. Cameron heightens our identification with Rose by placing her in the

Rose's placement in the foreground with her back to Ruth suggests *Titanic*'s failure to sympathize with the mother.

foreground, well lit and in focus so we can read her facial expressions and share her disgust at her mother's words. Ruth's face is visible behind her, and for most of the scene the two estranged women do not face each other.

The second scene is even briefer, but more telling. It occurs after Rose has decided to obey her mother and cut off her growing attraction to Jack. The setting is the ship's dining room, where Rose sits with her mother and two other women, listening silently to the muted sound of their voices as they gossip about the trivialities of her wedding plans. The camera moves closer, tightly framing the women and centering on Rose, who is in the background but lit more brightly than the others. While they are covered with high necklines, hats, and gloves, Rose's exposed skin glows, offset by a blue dress that conveys her mood. Increasingly the camera moves in to isolate Rose and contrast her with the other women, who internally frame and visually dominate her. A point of view shot then connects Rose to a nearby table, where a mother is teaching table manners to her small daughter. A medium shot of the girl cuts off her head, as she extends her little pinky and pats the napkin on her lap. The young girl is a mirror of her mother, and the scene underlines the mother's role in socializing girls into lives of conformity and repression. The sequence ends with an abrupt cut to the prow of the *Titanic* plowing through the water. Rose approaches Jack, who is posed against a radiant sunset, and tells him she has changed her mind.

Finally, in a third scene, Rose irrevocably rejects her mother. As the life-boats are filling up, Ruth urges Rose to join her but Rose, revolted by her mother's classism, refuses with a definitive, "Good-bye, Mother." By this point, any maternal longing Ruth might have for her daughter has become narratively implausible, and her cries of panic as she disappears below the deck without her daughter are drowned out by the sexier drama of Rose's discovery that she'd rather go down with Jack and the ship than survive with her mother.

ABOVE: As Rose continues to sense her alienation from the women of her social class, the camera shows her isolated and hemmed in by women who internally frame and visually dominate her. BELOW: Rose watches a mother socializing her small daughter into a life of conformity and repression.

Ruth—with her unsentimental views about the place of money, sex, and love in women's lives—survives, but to face a lonely future, estranged from her daughter and the grandchildren she will bear.

These scenes show a sensitivity to the stifling of a girl's spirit that cuts across class lines. However, a more subtle feminist analysis would not evade the ways class complicates women's oppression, for these girls are learning rituals of their social class. It is easy to romanticize the poor and show the rich as emotionally stunted monsters but more difficult to show the consequences of the class sytem on both. A more feminist *Titanic* would also resist targeting mothers as heartless or unthinking tools of patriarchy. It might have made more of the role of Molly Brown (Kathy Bates), who serves as a more sympathetic mother figure in the film, especially in her connection with Jack.[25] Indeed, the historical Brown, who was the daughter of Irish immigrants and later became known as the Unsinkable Molly Brown after surviving the ship's disaster, was a well-known activist on behalf of women's and labor rights. Moreover, Bates's star text resonates with unruliness, from her role as a deranged fan of romance novels in *Misery* (1990) to that of the mother's fun-loving friend in the TV series *Six Feet Under*.

Instead, *Titanic* capitalizes on the distance adolescent girls often establish from their mothers in the process of growing up by putting its most irritating messages about practicalities such as money in the mouth of its insufferable mother. Cameron, in his commentary on the film, berates Ruth for "not protecting her daughter's emotional well-being," a view that shows his limited understanding of the relation between emotional well-being and financial security, or of the economic realities of women's lives, especially during the time the film was set.

Ruth's situation has provided the raw material for untold numbers of novels and films about women—the plight of mothers left destitute for various reasons, and their struggles to find matches that will ensure their daughters a decent livelihood. Ruth answers Rose's protests by replying, "Of course it's unfair, we're women. Our choices are never easy." But unlike such canonical melodramas as *Stella Dallas* (1937), *Mildred Pierce* (1945), and *Imitation of Life* (1934, 1959), *Titanic* musters little sympathy for Ruth, showing her as an arrogant snob who would rather sell her daughter than demean herself by working for a living. Nor does the film allow us to discover how Rose and Jack's romance would have fared in a tenement filled with the passel of children he wished for her.

Finally, the film's treatment of the mother-daughter relation is influenced by the whiteness of its universe, beginning with the fetishizing of the British empire that made possible the opulence of the *Titanic*. The absence of people of color from the film's main characters conveys through omission the role of colonized, enslaved, and otherwise exploited people in enriching the white ruling classes of the U.S. and British empire. In *White*, Richard Dyer explains how the white race identifies itself with the rigors of high altitudes and cold climates, metonyms for the "higher" mental and spiritual powers it attributes to itself. Indeed, the white man's assumed entitlement to rule empires comes from his "enterprisingness," his ability to rise above the mental "softness" and baser physicality of the darker races. Robert Dassonowsky links *Titanic* to the German Bergfilm, which set its dramas among glaciers, precipices, and other natural wilds. *Titanic*, he notes, heightens its own drama—and whiteness, I would add—by embedding the stories of its characters in the "titanic" confrontation between twin mountains of iron and ice. Jack's demise in the icy waters of the Atlantic and Rose's rebirth from them enhance their whiteness, which the film further glamorizes by setting Winslet's porcelain skin and DiCaprio's blond handsomeness against Billy Zane's dark-haired, dark-eyed, black-garbed villainy.

For my purposes, the film is most suggestively racialized in its vision of the mother-daughter relation, where it reinforces the frigid limitations of the white middle-class family and the mother-daughter dyad within it. There is no sisterhood to soften Ruth's desperation as her money runs out or to support Rose through the stormy years of her adolescence. The film is framed by old Rose, a beautiful depiction of an old woman at the end of a full and adventurous life. We learn that Rose eventually became an artist like Jack, an unruly woman who lived her life with the name of one man she loved and the secret fortune of another she despised. Ironically, although she gave away her father's name, she retained the fabulous Heart of the Ocean jewel, the fortune her mother pushed her to accept. The gem is doubly coded. It is a memento of her night with Jack but also of the life she turned her back on. And it remained a safety net for her, one she could toss into the ocean when she no longer needed it, indicating her romantic disregard for money. Rose travels with a devoted granddaughter, but still the film sees her as a daughter. Among the photos documenting her life are no signs of her own children, nor of their grandmother Ruth. There is no motherline in *Titanic*.

Most of *Titanic* is set in the early twentieth century, but the film tells us a lot about the desires of contemporary audiences. The next chapter moves more deeply into those desires, to consider the psychic structures behind *Titanic's* demonization of its mother figure. *American Beauty* is a more modest and realistic drama than this blockbuster epic but it is equally driven by fantasy, and its harsh treatment of the mother even more unsettling.

Trouble in Paradise

AMERICAN BEAUTY AND
THE INCEST MOTIF

ERE ARE A FEW suggestive tales from American popular culture of the late 1990s:

- In the film *American Beauty* (Sam Mendes, 1999), Lester Burnham, middle-aged and middle management, throws off the responsibilities of the comfortable life he has come to despise when he begins to fantasize about having sex with his teenage daughter's best friend. Lester's rebellion brings about his death, but not before he redeems himself through an enlightenment that is at once moral, spiritual, and artistic.
- In *Armageddon* (Michael Bay, 1998), an aging warrior faces down both an asteroid headed to planet Earth and a young hotshot with a romantic interest in his daughter. In the end, the hero softens and gives the young couple his blessing before taking off on a suicide mission to intercept the asteroid and save the world.
- In the White House, a president known for his boyish charisma and a history of extramarital affairs creates a scandal that nearly topples his

presidency when the public learns he has been having a sexual relationship with a young female intern.

At first glance the stylish art film, lowbrow blockbuster, and political scandal appear to have little in common. However, they all captured the American imagination at the end of the 1990s. *American Beauty* swept the Academy Awards and was named best picture of 1999. It also won raves from the arthouse crowd for its cinematic style and satire of American bourgeois life. *Armageddon*, engineered to deliver maximum sensory thrills to summer audiences, was a hit with mainstream audiences, if not with critics.[1] "Monicagate" repelled much of the American public but also provided it with the fascination, titillation, and high moral stakes of a classical melodrama, infused, like *American Beauty*, with black comedy.

All three scenarios involve white men with some affluence or power and the malaise of the American male in midlife. The scenarios also share a similar cast of characters: a middle-aged man, played for sympathy by Kevin Spacey in *American Beauty*, Bruce Willis in *Armageddon*, and Bill Clinton in real life; a young woman who arouses his intense interest; and a working wife/mother, who—like Hillary Clinton in real life and Carolyn Burnham in *American Beauty*—evokes derision, hostility, or pity for her failure to perform the duties of a "good" wife and mother.

These character types, which have been familiar on the U.S. cultural landscape for much longer than the last decade or so, are intriguing in their own right, but even more so when viewed as a configuration: the midlife male, the adolescent female, and a working wife/mother who, more often than being vilified, is erased altogether. The meaning or deep structure of this configuration, which underlies most representations of the mother-daughter relation in mainstream culture, is veiled in *American Beauty* and *Armageddon*, but emerges more clearly in a third film of this period, the ambitious melodrama *Magnolia* (1999). *Magnolia* tells interlocking stories that ruthlessly examine the pathologies of American family life but roots them in male authority run amok. It identifies the ultimate expression of this authority as father-daughter incest, which is the troubling subtext of the scenarios outlined above.

The topic of incest has come out of the closet and entered popular culture in recent years. In addition to its very real existence in the social world, it has emerged as the subject of popular discourse on talk shows, tabloids, teen films, art films, and blockbusters, suggesting a powerful resonance between

Like Bruce Willis in *Armageddon*, Arnold Schwarzenegger in *Commando* (1985) depicts the malaise of the midlife white male. Both men rediscover their masculinity in order to save their daughters.

the cinematic and the political, the symbolic and the real.[2] The definition of the term, of course, is unstable and hotly contested. The subject is also characterized by denial and displacement—processes that Freud named, that undoubtedly shaped his own work on the subject, and that have recurred with a vengeance in the recent debates about memory related to childhood abuse.[3]

Magnolia is unusual in directly linking incest with the abuse of male power. More often, popular narratives disguise incest themes through the process of displacement. When the father's desire is explicit, as in *American Beauty*, the target is displaced onto a daughter substitute. When that desire stops short of overstepping conventional boundaries, it can manifest itself as an intense "protectiveness" of or emotional involvement with the daughter, as in *Armageddon* or any number of melodramas and comedies aimed at teen girls, from *Pretty in Pink* (1986) to *10 Things I Hate About You* (1999).[4] When incest is understood as a representational structure or motif that most often works through displacement, it can be seen in a formidable array of recent films that confront the sexual abuse of daughters and daughter-figures head-on. These

51

Popular narratives often disguise father/daughter incest themes with displacement. In *American Beauty*, Angela (Mena Suvari) stands in for Lester's daughter Jane (Thora Birch).

films, some of which I will return to later in this book, include *Poison Ivy* (1992), *Dolores Claiborne* (1995), *Clueless* (1995), the remake of *Lolita* (1997), *Eve's Bayou* (1997), *A Thousand Acres* (1997), *The Slums of Beverly Hills* (1998), *Election* (1999), *She's All That* (1999), *The Cider House Rules* (1999), and *Girl, Interrupted* (1999), as well as such international films as *Once Were Warriors* (New Zealand, 1994), *The Sweet Hereafter* (Canada, 1997) and *The War Zone* (Britain, 1999). Whenever a film or cultural narrative centers on a midlife male, a young girl who arouses his sexual or intense proprietary interest, and a mother who is missing or otherwise characterized as inadequate, the incest theme is likely to be lurking in the background.

This chapter examines how the motif of father-daughter incest has emerged as a response to several cultural currents. These are the most recent expression of the "crisis in masculinity," evident in various men's movements and popular expressions of nostalgia for the good old days (for example, Tom Brokaw's 1998 bestseller *The Greatest Generation*); the "crisis in the family," attributed primarily but not exclusively to feminism; and the growing presence of Girl Power/Girl Culture, which, since Madonna, has encouraged girls to claim their sexuality at ever younger ages.[5] As men claim their right to "act out" and girls to "act bad," incest provides a discourse or established set of conventions available for examining—and usually reasserting—male authority perceived to be under siege. The threats to this authority are linked to an array of sources, from various liberation movements (feminism, civil rights, gay rights) to the pressures and malaise of an increasingly materialist consumer culture.

Incest provides a narrative structure derived from Freud's work on the subject that ideologically inverts the social realities of white male privilege. This structure redirects sympathy toward beleaguered midlife heroes by portraying them as victims of unhinged and vengeful wives, seductive and manipulative daughters, or both. Not surprisingly, it has been bolstered by continued antifeminist backlash against the working wife/mother. Paradoxically, however, films with this structure also make use of the increased acceptance in mainstream culture of young girls who, under the banner of Girl Power and Third Wave feminism, are claiming the sexual entitlement boys and men have always enjoyed.

Cinema, Freud, and the Nymphet

American Beauty tells the story of the relationship between an apparently precocious nymphet and a father figure described by his daughter as a "horny geek." The cultural resonance of this relationship, despite its perverse undertones, results from its similarities to the classic Western love myth, in which a socially powerful male must compete with a younger and more virile rival for a desirable young woman. This triangular configuration shapes the myths and legends Western culture has created for its most intense expressions of sexual longing and love, from Lancelot and Guinevere to Tristan and Isolde. In some versions of these myths, the love plot is the primary focus of interest; in others it is interwoven with other fundamental narratives such as the coming-of-age plot or the journey/quest.

Because this configuration can be approached from a variety of vantage points, its valence shifts according to whose perspective dominates—the older man's, the younger man's, the woman's, or an overview of the three. Youth invariably trumps old age, as Northrop Frye showed in his now classic studies of narrative structure, and when a plot takes the perspective of youth, it ends happily, as a comedy. When the narrative takes the perspective of the older man, as in *American Beauty*, it assumes the tone of tragedy, melancholy, or loss. But regardless of which perspective a narrative favors, this triangular dynamic is endlessly fascinating because it provides a means of exploring our culture's deepest fantasies about love, sexuality, and social power.

When Freud sought a story on which to rest his theories of the human psyche, he found it in the Greek myth of Oedipus.[6] In this urtext of the dynamic outlined above, the two competing men are father and son, and the woman their wife/mother. By locating the triangle within the family, the Oedipus myth strips away the niceties of the romantic love myth to its incestuous root.[7] Fictional narratives rarely address incest directly because the topic is too explosive. However, the dynamics of incest are present again and again in popular culture through various degrees of displacement and condensation.

Fiction offers us characters that operate as symbolic terms on which we can project incest-driven desires we may not wish to act on or even acknowledge, from the near-literal stepfather of *Lolita* (Kubrick, 1962, remade by Adrian Lyne in 1997) to the more safely distanced teacher of *Election* to Gothic plots, such as *Rebecca's*, that evoke the helplessness of the wife/child in the face of the powerful husband/father. Similarly, the perennially popular jokes about May-December couples enable us to release the psychic energy required to repress our knowledge of the incest dynamic implicit in such relations. These patterns of characterization offered by popular culture limit emotional options for both men and women in ways that are, as Julia Lesage has noted, oppressively perverse.[8]

One of the most notorious images of film history is an advertisement for Stanley Kubrick's 1962 film *Lolita* (based on Vladimir Nabokov's 1955 novel) that shows a bikini-clad Sue Lyon at age fourteen or fifteen, wearing heart-shaped sunglasses and sucking on a lollipop. Lyon as Lolita helped put the word "nymphet" in the popular vocabulary of the sexually liberalizing 1960s. Similarly, Mena Suvari in *American Beauty* combines a blonde all-American girlishness with a sexual ripeness suggested by the red rose petals that coyly cover her body in Lester Burnham's fantasies.

The nymphet, a highly ambivalent term, belongs to a tradition of idealized American femininity rooted in Victorian culture and heightened with the development of cinema a century ago.[9] During the silent era, the Gish sisters and Mary Pickford built prestigious star images that joined girlishness with sexuality. Lillian Gish at the age of twenty-three played the child victim of violence and implied incest in *Broken Blossoms* (D. W. Griffith, 1919), a powerful precursor to *Magnolia* in its linkage of male power and sexual abuse. At twenty-seven, Mary Pickford, known as "America's Sweetheart" and "Little Mary," played twelve-year-old Pollyanna. While Pickford and the Gishes showed that adult women are sexually appealing when they act like girls, Shirley Temple

Sue Lyon's Lolita, like Mena Suvari's Angela, is a nymphet, combining blonde all-American girlishness with sexual ripeness.

showed that little girls are adorable when they act like adult women. Temple was among the top-grossing stars of the Depression, and had a particular appeal to middle-aged men and male clergy. Graham Greene was sued for libel and the magazine he edited was shut down when, in reviews of her films, he noted the "peculiar interest" of her coquetry and her body's "carnal" appeal.[10]

There is no doubt American culture eroticizes little girls who act like women and women who act like girls. This is not to say that young people cannot be genuinely and appropriately sexual, but to consider what stands in the way of such expressions of sexuality. Consider teen idol Britney Spears, who in her midteens combined parochial schoolgirl attire with lyrics that were, at the least, suggestive ("hit me, baby, one more time") and who was rumored to have had breast augmentation surgery at sixteen; or the extremely popular "barely legal" theme in pornography, which uses especially young women as actors and explicitly plays on the taboo of borderline sexual availability.[11] At the same time, U.S. culture resists acknowledging its interest in erotic images of young girls, let alone the consequences of that interest in the lives of real girls. While devouring cinematic images of nymphets, the public professes dismay at directors such as Charlie Chaplin, Errol Flynn, Roman Polanski, and

Woody Allen, who lived out the fantasies they had created on the screen. The public also recoils from the idea of sexual abuse, insisting that it doesn't happen in nice families or in large numbers, although empirical evidence consistently confirms that it does.[12]

This contradiction and massive denial cannot be understood apart from the intellectual history that has shaped the cultural meaning of incest. This history has been dominated by two discourses—psychoanalysis and the myth of the innocent child—which together support the status of the traditional middle-class family. In *The History of Sexuality*, Foucault argues that incest should be viewed less as a particular act than as a discursive category intended to regulate aspects of human behavior.[13] As Valerie Walkerdine suggests in her study of young girls and popular culture, symbolic systems embody social fantasies that are psychic in origin, reflecting social relations that are not timeless and universal, but historically specific "regimes" of meaning and truth (179–181). Thus, while brother-sister incest was a common theme in Renaissance literature and in Gothic texts of the Romantic era, incest in general was not the subject of widespread public concern or regulation until the end of the nineteenth century, when pressure on the nuclear family intensified to socialize children according to prevailing norms of gender and sexuality.[14]

At that time, incest became the focus of several emerging fields of study.[15] Anthropology, for example, made incest its central preoccupation, culminating in Claude Lévi-Strauss's monumental work on kinship. Psychoanalysis, originating from a set of beliefs about incest derived from bourgeois family life in late-nineteenth-century Vienna, evolved into a complex and highly elaborated intellectual tradition that continues to shape our culture's understanding of the motivations and other processes associated with incest. The tenacity of this tradition can be seen in the social and scientific credibility lent to the so-called false-memory syndrome movement that arose in the early 1990s to defend the patriarchal family after widespread reports of incest threatened its claims to virtue and authority. The false-memory movement furthered its conservative social agenda by capitalizing on the moral panic resulting from charges of sexual abuse in day care centers. Despite the fact that in some cases these charges were baseless, it used the fear they aroused to imply that children were safe only in traditional homes.[16]

Briefly, Freud developed his position on incest from conversations with female patients he was treating for hysteria or other neuroses. These patients recounted childhood experiences of sexual contact with family members, often uncles and fathers. Initially accepting these accounts as true, Freud theorized that childhood sexual trauma lies at the root of neurosis. In private correspondence, he even acknowledged that "seduction by the father" was the "essential point."[17] Uneasy, however, about accepting that such "perverted acts" could be as common as his clinical work indicated, Freud revised his position a year later, suggesting instead that his patients were recounting fantasies based on their repressed desires for their fathers. This revision enabled Freud to develop his theories of childhood sexuality, fantasy, and the unconscious, and also of the Oedipal complex, which became foundational to psychoanalysis.

According to clinical psychologist Judith Herman, who, in 1981, wrote the first major feminist analysis of father-daughter incest, Freud's refusal to accept the accounts of his female patients not only covered up the actual occurrence and effects of incest but it also laid the foundation for a modern psychology that has avoided seeking the truth about women. The focus shifted instead to the incestuous wishes of the male child and his rivalry with his father.[18]

This refusal to accept women's accounts of incest in Freud's day led to assumptions that continue to shape the ways current therapists, social workers, and courts treat cases involving incest. Primary among these assumptions is the belief that children and women don't tell the truth about childhood sexual encounters. When incest can be confirmed, it becomes narrativized according to character types that have become as familiar in popular cinema and culture as in the clinical literature: a "seductive" daughter or nymphet desires sex with her father, and a "collusive" mother enables it to happen because of her absence, frigidity, or other shortcomings. The mother, believed to have both the power and the exclusive responsibility to police the family, becomes a monstrous party to the sexual relationship by failing to prevent or curtail it.[19] Finally, the father, who cannot fend off the daughter's seductiveness and mother's collusion, becomes a victim of both, a deviant from a healthy norm and an exception to the rule that the patriarchs heading bourgeois families are pillars of virtue.

Feminism and Incest

From the outset, the most important challenges to this view have come from feminism, both as a movement of social activism and as a theory of gender and social power. Although the power of the father differs significantly according to the race and ethnicity of the family, incest as an issue cuts across class and race lines.[20] Until the growth of feminism in the twentieth century, however, political movements avoided dealing with incest or related aspects of oppression within the family. During feminism's First Wave, between 1880–1930, suffrage movements concerned about the well-being of children campaigned to make incest illegal, leading to the first laws criminalizing incest and establishing the age of consent. The Second Wave's focus on rape and domestic violence shifted the subject of incest from a psychologized framework into the politicized context of power and socialization within the family. As a result, large numbers of women in the 1980s, including many celebrities, made public their histories of incest. These women denied the culture's insistence that incest didn't happen among outwardly "normal" families and that when it did the father was not responsible.[21] Today, voices from the Third Wave, such as musician Ani DiFranco and riot grrrls, continue to proclaim the widespread occurrence of incest and other forms of abuse.

Beginning in the mid-1970s, an influential body of feminist work began to critique psychoanalysis from within. Laura Mulvey, Juliet Mitchell, Jacqueline Rose, Teresa de Lauretis, Jane Gallop, Kaja Silverman, the editors of *Camera Obscura*, and others acknowledged Freud's misogyny but also found in psychoanalysis a powerful set of tools to explain the workings of desire under a patriarchal social order.[22] Janet Walker (1999) has continued this tradition by arguing for a use of Freud that is sensitive to his own ambiguities on the subject of incest and to the ways "real world events and psychic processes, far from being mutually exclusive, are necessarily connected, both in Freud's work and in fact."[23] Similarly, Elizabeth Waites (1993), Janice Haaken (1998), Lenore Terr (1990, 1994), and Susan Reviere (1996) have contributed to the debates about childhood sexual trauma and recovered memories with work that does not dispute the reality of claims of childhood sexual abuse but insists on studying the interrelations of reality and fantasy.[24]

Whereas a psychologized view of incest tends to see it as an individual exception to the rule of paternal authority within the family, feminist theory shows it to be a manifestation of that very rule "carried to a pathological extreme" (Herman 1981, 125). A feminist framework explains why the vast majority of incest cases involve fathers and daughters, not mothers and sons; why feminists view sex between a parent and child as a matter of abuse, regardless of whether physical force was used or the child experienced sexual pleasure; and why the social reality of incest has so long and so vehemently been denied. By placing incestuous relationships in the context of power and its abuse, feminism refutes arguments that defend these relationships on the basis of romantic love, an ideology deeply held by our culture. This defense colors *Lolita*, for example, which normalizes Humbert by depicting him as an obsessed lover who becomes a pitiable victim of his obsession when his love object rejects him.

Feminist research has uncovered patterns in families where incest has occurred that reverberate through the culture at large. Jennifer Freyd and Cindy B. Veldhuis, for example, have shown that incest victims are chosen and "groomed" on the basis of those very qualities of femininity idealized by our culture and taught to daughters in "normal" families.[25] Girls learn that according to our culture's preferred model of sexuality, infantilized women desire Big Daddies who can protect them and thus begin to practice that model with their own fathers, exchanging good behavior (e.g., compliant, obedient, dependent) for tenderness and love. In this way, the father-daughter relationship becomes eroticized as the basis of adult heterosexual identity and desire. In theory, the daughter who successfully resolves her Oedipal transition will channel her sexuality into submissive relationships with older, stronger, more powerful men, just as men will seek younger, weaker, and more submissive females.

When charges of incest are made, the responses they elicit follow a predictable sequence: the person who is accused denies the charge, counterattacks the accuser, and, most perversely, appropriates the role of victim for himself.[26] The intensity of this response suggests the magnitude of what's at stake: core beliefs about the benevolence of patriarchy, the sanctity of the family, and the tradition of romantic love, which is often invoked to defend relationships with incestuous overtones ("We loved each other, I did no harm"). It is no surprise that this mode of response has found its way into films such as *American Beauty*, which tap into similar anxieties and resentments about challenges to the traditional family hierarchy.[27]

Class and the Myth of the Innocent Child

A feminist analysis of the nymphet shows that the desires attributed to her are in fact projected on to her. A class analysis brings richer layers of complexity to this figure. The very existence of the nymphet requires a second child, socially constructed as innocent, in order to conceal the source of the desires projected on her. This child also helps maintain the moral ascendancy of the middle class because, unlike the nymphet, she is one of them. In *Daddy's Girl*, Valerie Walkerdine argues that liberal democracy depends on a belief that its citizens begin their lives in a state of natural innocence and goodness. As a result, it maintains childhood as a place where children should be protected from adult sexuality. This belief denies the erotic interest that adults have in children. Attributing that interest to a small group of adults scapegoated as perverts denies the degree to which their fantasies and desires are in fact widely held.

As Walkerdine shows, the idealized, innocent child is a particularly middle-class type, whose innocence provides a means of defining the boundaries between an upstanding middle class and those who threaten it from below.[28] Childhood innocence is thus considered fragile and easily endangered, and its guardians typically target sex education for bringing sexuality into the school and popular culture (the Spice Girls, Britney Spears, the Internet) for bringing sexuality and violence into the home. The white middle class exorcises violence in its sons and precocious sexuality in its daughters by projecting these qualities onto nonwhites and the working class. For example, news reports and editorials about mass shootings in schools rarely acknowledged that most of these acts of violence have been the work of middle-class white boys.

While no more sheltered from sexual abuse than working-class girls, middle-class girls can afford, literally, an outward innocence of sexuality. Many middle-class parents are likely to prefer that their daughters play with gender-neutral educational toys or dolls associated with a maternal femininity, rather than sexy Barbies who might encourage them to "try on" a femininity that appears prematurely sexual.

In contrast, the nymphet, like popular culture itself, carries class associations that contribute to her allure while putting her at a remove from the innocent middle-class girl. Beauty pageants for little girls are considered unsophisticated or carry working-class associations of kitsch, even when participants in them are from affluent families. For working-class girls, glamour and sexuality are realistic vehicles toward greater social power, through work or attachment to more powerful men.[29] While beyond the age of a nymphet and of the same social class as the Clintons, Monica Lewinsky believed that having sex with the president would advance her social position because, according to her fantasy, he would then marry her. And while her "otherness" arose from her Jewishness rather than her social class, her aggressive sexuality brought a vulgar threat to the first family, polluting the sanctity of the White House, the national home.[30]

Walkerdine's argument is important because it does not deny the reality of childhood sexuality but explains it as a response to the demands of social class and adult sexuality, whether expressed diffusely by cultural fantasies or specifically by older, more powerful figures in children's lives. In other words, when children become sexually precocious, there's a good chance they're doing so out of necessity.

American Beauty and the Incest Motif

American Beauty has received high praise for its cinematography and visual style, its witty script and strong performances, as well as for its critique of materialism, consumer and corporate culture, family relations, and the sexual repression of contemporary American middle-class life.[31] The film speaks pleasurably to audiences of that class because it addresses them as sufficiently rich in cultural capital to appreciate its aesthetic appeal. Like a morality tale, what begins as the hero's amusing midlife crisis becomes a path toward an enlightenment intended to be profound. Under the film's stylish surface, however, lies a reactionary ideology that recycles clichéd notions about working women while evading the privileges of money, masculinity, and whiteness that make the hero's rebellion possible. Updating the tradition of the romantic artist-hero with New Age spirituality in its meditations on the nature of beauty and reality, American Beauty creates a hero with a unique sensitivity that authorizes his transgressions.

Incest drives American Beauty in ways that are typical of contemporary cinema, by using character types that create the incest dynamic and by employing the mechanism of displacement to conceal the more disturbing implications of that dynamic. The plot centers on Lester (Kevin Spacey), a bored middle-aged man who becomes infatuated with his teen daughter Jane's best friend, a flirtatious cheerleader named Angela (Mena Suvari). This infatuation triggers Lester's rebellion against the responsibilities that have defined him. At the same time, Jane (Thora Birch) falls in love with Ricky (Wes Bentley), the drug-dealing boy next door. In the end, just as Lester is about to make his conquest, Angela tells him she's a virgin and he stops. Moments later, he is killed by Ricky's father (Chris Cooper), a closeted homosexual that Lester has just rebuffed.

Incest is explicitly thematized when, in a conversation about Lester's fixation on Angela, Ricky asks Jane if she would prefer that her father were lusting after her instead. However, the film evades the impact of Lester's transgression by displacing the object of his desire from daughter Jane to Angela. At the same time, by conjuring up the incest scenario, the film turns Lester into a sympathetic victim innocent of any wrongdoing that is finally redeemed by his martyrdom. If Angela is the "seductive daughter," Carolyn (Annette Bening) becomes coded as the "collusive mother" ultimately responsible for the incest because of her various inadequacies.

The voices privileged in telling this story conform to the classic incest scenario. The film begins with Jane's voice describing her view of her father's sexual fixation on her friend: "I need a father who's a role model, not some horny geek."[32] This sequence, which is repeated later, establishes a key point of reference for the film, but within moments, Jane's voice is replaced by her father's in voice-over, and the film proper begins. There, the formal devices of plotting, casting, voice-over, and subjective shots support identification with Lester. While we may continue to see him through his daughter's eyes as a "horny geek," the film's formal strategies encourage us to enjoy his transformation into a sympathetic rebel and to interpret his desire for the daughter figure not in the context of exploitation but personal liberation and romantic love.[33] By the end, when the father's voice-over and the image-track combine in a lyrical montage about the meaning of life, the daughter's words have long been forgotten. The story is focalized around the father, and the accusing daughter, as in the incest scenario, is silenced.

The Father as Romantic Hero and Victim

American Beauty polarizes audiences. Among those who like the film are viewers who find it to be contradictory in its attitude toward Lester Burnham: ambivalent but not explicitly critical. Especially in its most stylized moments, such as Lester's fantasies about Angela, the film provides opportunities for a detached and ironic perspective on the character rather than identification with him. At the same time, however, this character cannot be understood apart from the recent cultural focus on masculinity under siege, evident in various men's movements such as the Promise Keepers, the Million Man March, and a new wave of post–Reviving Ophelia books asserting that we should stop worrying so much about girls and start paying more attention to boys.[34] While some films (Unforgiven [1992], Traffic [2000], The Limey [1999], and Moulin Rouge! [2001]) have addressed the responsibilities and failures of older white men, others have been more interested in their angst. These include any number of earlier films starring Michael Douglas (*Falling Down*, 1993), as well as more thoughtful works that have attracted strong followings among hip young viewers—*Fight Club* (1999), which focuses on middle-class young men alienated from corporate yuppie life, and *American History X* (1998), concerned with working-class white men whose racial dominance has been challenged.

American Beauty's use of the incest motif to direct audience sympathy toward the male hero as victim marks a deviation from earlier films dealing with incest. In the postwar period in the United States, single-family dwellings springing up in new suburbs intensified pressure on the increasingly isolated nuclear family. Men in movies who overstepped sexual boundaries within the family were viewed consistently as emblems of individual or social pathology. Kubrick's *Lolita*, for example, acknowledges Humbert Humbert's desire for Lolita as a perversion.[35] In *Chinatown* (1974), incest is symptomatic of another secret corruption that infiltrates the city of Los Angeles through its water supply. In *Taxi Driver* (1976), the twelve-year-old child prostitute played by Jodie Foster bears obvious marks of exploitation and abuse in her eroticized relation with the pimp, played by Harvey Keitel.

Recent treatments of incest have suggested new cultural tensions around male entitlement. On the one hand, some of these films attempt to elicit sympathy for the incest-father. The 1998 remake of *Lolita* loses the earlier film's black humor and critical edge to make Humbert a sensitive romantic hero who, like Lester, is doomed for what is shown more as a fatal obsession than a perversion. Likewise, while retaining the earlier *Lolita's* black humor, *American Beauty* discourages a critical perspective on Lester by portraying him not only as an Everyman but also as an ego-ideal because of his heroic rebellion ("I'm just an ordinary guy with nothing to lose"). Other films, however, attempt to represent incest in the context of critiques of masculinity (*Magnolia*) or by privileging the daughter's voice (*The Slums of Beverly Hills*). Several international films address the issue with unsentimentalized brutality (*The War Zone*) or as an expression of the brutal effects of colonialism on masculine identity and the family (*Once Were Warriors*).

In one regard, normalizing Lester's obsession with the nymphet might have enabled the film to examine incest as an expression of gender norms, including a man's right of sexual access to a child. However, the film uses several means to evade the cultural meaning of Lester's obsession. It makes Angela an apparently willing party to Lester's lust. It celebrates his obsession both

American Beauty discourages a critical perspective on the lust Lester (Kevin Spacey) has for Angela by portraying him as an Everyman and a heroic rebel. Here, he begins to act on his desire to "look good naked."

visually and narratively, creating fantasy sequences about Angela that are among the most beautiful and witty in the film. The rebellion triggered by his infatuation brings him to the ostensible core of the film, his perception of the beauty all around him. And once he has "groomed" Angela for sex, he stops short of having intercourse with her when she tells him she's a virgin.

This aborted encounter is crucial because it signals Lester's ultimate transformation and, through his restraint, enables him to fulfill Jane's wish for a father who acts like "a role model." The *mise en scène* demonstrates his power in relation to Angela and her extreme vulnerability. A high camera angle reduces Lester's size, but his placement in the frame shows Angela to be even smaller and more vulnerable, childlike and prone. The hyperreal lighting on Angela that earlier had emphasized her iconic quality as a nymphet is replaced by the muted tones associated with realism, and she appears with minimal makeup. Lester does not have to complete the seduction to achieve what he sought. He has it both ways. He "possesses" his nymphet, and he gets to act like a good father at the same time, wrapping his jacket around Angela, fixing her a sandwich, and comforting her with paternal sensitivity. When he finally exits the film, he does so "smelling like a rose," as it were.

According to Judith Herman, incest fathers have historically defended themselves with a range of excuses: I did no real harm, so I shouldn't be blamed; only prudes object to sex between adults and minors, since children have a right to sex; incest harms a child only when authorities draw attention to it as a problem; and fathers who commit incest, or are charged with it, are the victims of vengeful women. These justifications are evident in *American Beauty*. While the film might well be read as punishing Lester in the end for his transgressions, it also shows that his obsession with Angela causes her no harm and in fact restores her self-worth. Had she been as sexually experienced as she let on, Lester might have been forgiven for having sex with her. She appeared to want it, and his wife drove him to her.

The slyest justification for behavior, such as incest, that transgresses social standards is perceived membership in a "privileged elite exempt from moral rules of ordinary people" (Herman 1981, 231). Lester belongs to the tradition of the Romantic artist-hero, a figure dating from the nineteenth century, whose unique sensitivity sets him apart from the ordinary and justifies his violations of their taboos. *American Beauty*'s soundtrack identifies Lester's special status when it plays "The Seeker" by the Who.

American Beauty is structured with pairs of characters that mirror and complement each other. Lester is linked with Ricky, the adolescent artist and drug dealer who lives next door and becomes his guru. Ricky also pursues Lester's daughter in a displacement that seals the incest theme. True to the romantic tradition, Ricky is a rebel who supports his need to create art by breaking the laws that govern ordinary Americans. He has a romantic fascination with death—dead birds, dead human bodies. Ricky's heightened sensitivity is both aesthetic and spiritual, and he expresses it in a sequence privileged even more than Lester's nymphet fantasies: silent footage of a bag being tossed around by the wind comes to signify the epiphanies that Ricky and Lester will share. "There's an entire life behind things, a benevolent presence," Ricky says while showing the footage to Jane. This is the "American beauty" Lester will perceive at the moment of his death.

As Julia Lesage has argued in relation to *Broken Blossoms*, capitalism limits the roles it makes available for men. They can participate in the system either as dehumanized workers or powerful bosses, or they can opt out by choosing the life of the artist or intellectual. Neither choice, however, cancels out a man's desire to assert his patriarchal authority through possession of a subordinate female. Lester rebels against the dehumanization of his role as a worker; however, in choosing the role of romantic outsider, he retains his patriarchal right to assert his masculine authority within the family. Indeed, the film explicitly codes his dehumanization in the workforce as emasculation, shifting its origin to social relations of gender rather than those of class.

If Lester begins his transformation seeking a lifestyle vaguely modeled on swingers and adventurers like James Bond ("I want to look good naked"), he soon aspires to Ricky's romantic freedom from the banalities of ordinary life. This shift helps code his transgressions with the cachet of art and New Age spirituality and sweeten them for the sophisticated audience sought by the film. His doubling with Ricky culminates in the film's final moments, when just before his death he repeats Ricky's earlier words about beauty and benevolence. This doubling both transforms Lester into an artist-hero and resolves the incest theme, for although Lester and Angela do not have sex, Ricky and Jane do. In terms of the Oedipal love triangle, Ricky, the youthful lover, defeats the father to win the object of their shared desire.

Through Ricky, the film romanticizes the stalking of women and a relentless, predatory, voyeuristic gaze by linking his behavior with the pursuit of art. Ricky expresses his drive to create by obsessively stalking Jane and photographing her without her knowledge through her bedroom window. Similarly, Lester calls Angela on the phone and hangs up. In shots of him with Angela, he crowds her in the frame, creating a sense of claustrophobia and entrapment. Ricky's identity as a filmmaker thematically and narratively justifies the film's own appeal to the audience's voyeurism in its repeated use of shots exposing the bodies of its two young female protagonists. Ricky ultimately seduces Jane into her proper role in relation to the male artist-hero when she stands before her bedroom window, offers herself to him as a model by exposing her breasts, and eventually runs away with him.

Lester's rebellion is both class- and nation-based, tied not only to matters of gender but to the acceleration of consumer culture in America since World War II and the latent crisis in meaning simmering under the nation's material abundance. Driven by the massive apparatus of advertising evoked by the slick surface of the film, consumer culture creates a hunger for the new and boredom with the familiar, whether cars, jobs, body images, or sexual partners. While Lester derides the expression of these values in his affluent lifestyle, his midlife crisis is driven by the same ideology—a quest for new experience and a sense of entitlement to happiness that is distinctly American.

The film presents itself as a satire on middle-class materialism; however, Lester's freedom to quit his job and take a vacation from his responsibilities is available only to those with the wealth to support such a rebellion. In other words, disavowing an affluent lifestyle is a lot easier for those who are secure in it. Lester's rebellion is financed partly by Carolyn and partly by money he received after he blackmails his corrupt former employer, an even bigger thief, and Lester takes his fast-food job as a lark, not out of necessity. Similarly, Ricky's freedom to pursue his art comes from his romantic vocation as an outlaw. In both cases, the freedom to throw off a conventional lifestyle is not possible without a conventional flow of cash. Both Ricky and Lester share qualities with the slacker, who is typically white and middle class, defined by his rejection of conventional adult masculinity, and usually paired with another buddy.

The Collusive Mother

Lester is absolved of any guilt for his transgressions because his wife Carolyn bears the blame. She stands as a prototypical example of the "collusive mother," sexually unavailable to her husband and emotionally distant from both him and her daughter. Annette Bening's tour de force portrayal of Carolyn's frustration with her family and breakdown at her job carries tremendous resonance for women who have struggled since the 1950s with the combined demands of work and family. Working-class women and women of color, of course, have long been in the workforce, often because their husbands and fathers were not able to get jobs. These women did not pose the same threat to the status quo as white middle-class women, however, who were the primary beneficiaries of Affirmative Action. When women such as Carolyn began competing with men, moving toward economic independence and "abandoning" the home, the stage was set for the antifeminist backlash so powerfully mobilized in the Reagan years and later by the Christian Right.

The film's treatment of Carolyn is painful to watch, despite Bening's knowing performance, because it so relentlessly shows her through the eyes of a husband who blames her for his problems and a daughter who is alienated from her as well. In this respect, Carolyn recalls Shelley Winters in Kubrick's *Lolita*, whose Charlotte Haze is similarly mocked for her lack of self-awareness, her sexual neediness, her desire to better her social position, and her blindness to Humbert's sexual interest in her daughter. The film further mocks Carolyn through her affair with Buddy "the King" Kane, a realtor she sees as instrumental to her own success. Implying that her sexual hunger and ambition come from the same desperate place, the film shows both as monstrously funny.

67

Lester places Carolyn in the position of the all-powerful mother when he infantilizes himself as a bad little boy taking a stand against her. "Mom's mad, I'm in trouble now," he says with glee, as he embraces his rebellion by smashing his dinner plate at the wall, quitting his job, buying a teen-boy fantasy car, smoking marijuana, and indulging in verbal tantrums. The soundtrack blasts "American Woman, stay away from me, American Woman, just let me be" as Lester barrels down the road in his midlife-crisis-mobile. While Lester hurls insults at Carolyn ("You bloodless, money-grubbing freak"), she turns her frustration on herself female-style, slapping her face during an excruciating moment on the job.

As an emblem of the independent woman whose ambition enables her to provide materially for her family, Carolyn bears the resentment of a culture angry about her power and unable to disentangle strong women from frightening images of castrating, phallic mothers. This resentment is tied to our longings for an idealized maternal love, for a mother whose breast is always there and who fulfills our every need. This mother, of course, exists only in fantasy, but the fantasy runs deep. Independent women such as Carolyn—reminders that women can exist apart from their children and the domestic bonds that center on the family—stand as affronts to that fantasy. As a result, such women cannot be assimilated in any easy or sympathetic way into existing cultural narratives.

Noting the fluctuations of Hillary Clinton's relationship with the American public is instructive here. Initially she evoked wariness. The American public was uneasy about her brainpower, education, and ambition, but felt reassured because she was also a mother and had put her husband's ambitions before her own. As First Lady, she soon alienated many men and women when she stated that she didn't want simply to "bake cookies" but to participate as a high-level member of her husband's administration. She was forced to apologize for her cookie remark, and, after failing to bring about a major overhaul of the healthcare system, she retreated into invisibility, eliciting occasional notice from the press mainly for changes in her hairstyle.

Clinton didn't earn her way back into the public's good graces until the Monica Lewinsky scandal broke and she refused to publicly criticize or leave her husband. Some public voices tried to discredit her once again by reading her silence in terms of an unnatural ambition and nasty cynicism. Others, however, grudgingly approved of her for "standing by her man." At last her story became understandable as melodrama, and she became acceptable as the betrayed and suffering wife. Photos of her traveling with her daughter Chelsea during the Lewinsky scandal further normalized her as a good mother. Finally chastened by her public humiliation, she was able to make a successful run for the Senate, a springboard to her campaign for the Democratic nomination for president in 2007–2008.

On that campaign trail, she continually surprised political pundits with her toughness and ability to rebound from repeated setbacks. But even after years in the political spotlight, she remained the subject of ruthless sexism.[36] Early in her campaign, she was attacked for her hearty, unruly laugh, which she usually directed at inane questions from reporters, and it was not until she shed some tears that she became recognizable as a "normal" woman; women's laughter, especially at men, is more threatening than their tears. And as a postmenopausal woman, she had finally succeeded in escaping judgment as a mother. While she lost her bid to become the first female president, she secured a position in the Obama administration as secretary of state, where she has continued to build a public persona increasingly separate from her identity as a wife and mother.

From this book's perspective on unrepentant mothers, Clinton suffered because of her association with Second Wave feminism. She is educated, white, came of age in the 1960s, and spent much of her life working hard to break through the glass ceiling. And she is a mother. These attributes made her appear both out of date and unsexy, especially in contrast to the youthful and charismatic Barack Obama. Obama also struggled to define himself against a set of issues similarly chosen and caricatured by the media and his opponents. But these issues—religious affiliation, patriotism, and race—were more easily digested by young voters and many liberal men. And, the possibility of even imagining a black man as president may have been nudged along by the specter of old Mom in the White House.

In *American Beauty*, Carolyn is similarly punished and pathologized until, in the film's conclusion, we see her redeemed as an image of pathos, stricken with grief and remorse. Just as Lester and Ricky are linked as romantic heroes, Carolyn is linked with Col. Frank Fitts, a repressed homosexual who terrorizes his family and finally kills Lester in shame over having his sexual overture rebuffed. This link between Carolyn and Fitts puts the label of deviancy on her, not Lester. The presence of two attractive, openly gay minor characters suggests that Fitts's pathology doesn't arise from his sexual orientation but his repression of it. Yet, Fitts, like Carolyn, is obsessive, simultaneously controlling and out of control.[37] His insanely violent and abusive behavior toward his wife and son, and his fetish for Nazi memorabilia and guns, further code him as deviant. The pairing of Fitts and Carolyn culminates at the end of the film, when both move toward Lester bearing guns and the intent to kill.

If Carolyn is constructed as collusive and held responsible for the family's dysfunction, at least she is present in the film. More often in media culture of the 1980s and 1990s, the collusive mother is simply missing. This missing mother is not the mother benignly absent from Hollywood for most of its history, but one who is missing in ways that are more visible and charged with ideological significance. *Armageddon*, for example, goes briefly but pointedly out of its way to note the mother's absence then to explain it away in a moment of father-daughter bonding: "She just couldn't love us." In *Stepmom* (1998), the mother conveniently dies so Julia Roberts can take her place. In *Sleepless in Seattle* (1993), the mother dies so Meg Ryan can take her place. In *Juno* (2007), the mother left her daughter to live in the Southwest, sending her an annual cactus that "stings" as much as her abandonment. The missing mother, of course, inverts the social reality of contemporary family life, in which fathers are far more likely than mothers to be missing from the homes of their children.[38]

The mother's absence is especially pronounced in genre films targeting teen-girl audiences, in which her absence often lays the foundation for an incest scenario that guides the daughter to learn the skills of femininity. In some cases (*Clueless, Pocahontas* [1995], and *She's All That*), the mother is missing for the only permissible reason: she died. In others, she has left her family to satisfy her own desires (*Pretty in Pink, 10 Things I Hate About You*). In still others, she may be "present" physically but absent emotionally because of her narcissism and desire for control (*Titanic* [1997], and MTV's *Daria* [1997–2002]). Regardless of why she is gone, her absence is a source of pain and often pathology for her abandoned family. In the *Scream* trilogy (1996, 1997, 2000), the mother's absence unleashes a bloodbath of spectacular proportions.

The missing mother is by definition a guilty mother, a definition supported by a long tradition of mother-blaming in U.S. culture.[39] Mother-blaming facilitates the daughter's passage into an adult femininity that requires her to become male-identified and to sever her connections with other women. Jane Gallop has suggestively described this process as "the father's seduction," the most widespread and damaging seduction of all, as patriarchy lures girls into a femininity based on overvaluing and idealizing men and devaluing women, including themselves (1989). When Jane challenges her father's authority in *American Beauty*, Lester fights back by threatening to withdraw his love for her as he has from her mother: "Watch yourself or you'll turn into a regular bitch like your mother."

In many of these missing-mother teen films, daughters practice the skills of acceptable femininity on fathers who are possessive, weak, or seductive. *Pretty in Pink*, one of a cycle of films by John Hughes that were popular among teen girls in the 1980s, begins with a montage of shots of Molly Ringwald that fragment her body as she is getting dressed, "trying on" her adult femininity. Next she enters her father's bedroom, awakens him with breakfast, coaches him on getting a job, and models her outfit for his admiring eyes. As the film develops, his neediness manipulates her into assuming the role of a caretaking, nurturing wife-substitute.

In *Clueless*, inspired by Jane Austen's *Emma*, Cher (Alicia Silverstone) flirts with her father and manipulates him by playing Daddy's little girl—coy and altogether irresistible to him. In *10 Things I Hate About You*, inspired by Shakespeare's *Taming of the Shrew*, the father, an obstetrician/gynecologist, expresses his desire to control his two daughters by forbidding them to date. He shows his sexual possessiveness by making his daughters strap on monstrous pregnant bellies whenever the subject of boys comes up. The mother's absence is mentioned with resentment once or twice, but not explained.

Not all missing-mother teen films employ incest toward such conservative ends. The 1998 film *The Slums of Beverly Hills* gestures toward incest in its story of a family headed by a middle-aged father struggling to provide for his children, including a teenage daughter discovering her sexuality. The father respects appropriate boundaries with his daughter but makes a pass at his adult niece. Unlike *American Beauty*, the film privileges the daughter's point of view throughout, and the matter is dealt with through the perspective of the daughter and niece.[40]

Good Girls, Bad Girls

American Beauty's final doubling of characters—Angela and Jane—provides an opportunity to study representations of young women in the context of feminism's Third Wave and to hear the voices of girls long-silenced in the incest scenario. Both are unruly girls, but their unruliness is constructed from the father's point of view and in the absence of warm relations with maternal figures. Jane represents the good daughter, the middle-class innocent, social-ized into a nurturing femininity. She expresses her unhappiness at home in the perennial teen-girl mode of a passive sullenness, rather than by striking out on her own as Ricky does. Her sexual innocence supports middle-class notions of a girl's proper introduction to sexuality: she does not appear inter-ested in sex until a suitor pursues her, she waits for sex until she falls in love with him, and she is carried away by him. She gradually accepts then takes pleasure in Ricky's role as artist and hers as his model. In the end, she leaves her family—severing whatever bond remained with her mother—to follow him to New York. Most tellingly, Jane runs off with a boyfriend who is the double of her father and who has seduced her into a femininity that eroticizes her dependence on him. He brushes aside her offer of two thousand dollars (which she has been saving for breast augmentation surgery) because he has forty thousand from his drug dealing, indicating already the economic imbal-ance on which their relationship will rest.

If Jane is the good girl, Angela is the bad girl who, like Monica Lewinsky, has the potential power to expose not only the social pathologies that create nymphets but also the corruption in the normal American family. Although she is not coded as of a lower class than Jane, Angela's vampy dumb-blonde role subtly sets her apart from the bourgeois family life that defines Jane and preserves her sexual innocence. The film depicts Angela in two modes—as a product of Lester's imagination and as a character in her own right, but both are shaped by the father's fantasy. In Lester's fantasy sequences, we see the extent to which the nymphet exists as a projection of male desire. In the first, a point-of-view shot in which Angela morphs from cheerleader to stripper, she is lit with hyperreal intensity and is filmed in slow motion, making her an icon that exists only for Lester. The lighting and camerawork also isolate Lester from his social context, showing his sense of unique visual access to her body. Angela in "real life" as well as in the fantasy sequences appears to legitimize Lester's desire because she controls the tone for the relationship. Until the final moments of the film, she flirts with him and presents herself as sexually experienced, confident, and in control, not as the victim of a seduc-tive older man.

A closer look, however, shows that the film silences Angela as it does Jane. It denies her the kind of family history and motivation given to all of the other characters. Her only character trait is an extreme identification with men and an enthusiastic desire to capitalize on those assets she feels most valued for.

While disdaining weird Ricky because of his predatory attentions to Jane, Angela flirts with weird Lester because she can play Daddy's little girl with him. By presenting herself as experienced at pleasing men sexually, she appears to have absorbed a model of female sexuality that is foremost concerned with pleasing men. On the path from cheerleader to model, she embraces the female exhibitionism that complements Lester's, Ricky's, and even Fitts's voyeurism.

By drawing on the tradition of the dumb blonde, the film invites viewers to laugh at Angela's naïveté and shallow narcissism. However, a feminist reading of her provides a backstory from which the film shrinks away. Whatever her class standing, she has the working-class girl's sense of the material value of her good looks and sex appeal. Lester can seduce her into readiness for sex with him because she has already learned to respond to and participate in the more broadly based sexual fantasies projected on her. And even though she remains a virgin at the end of the film, her obsessive desire to please a father figure, her precocious sexuality, and ultimately her extreme lack of self-confidence mark her as already a victim of abuse. This is not to say that Angela doesn't have sexual desire of her own, including desire for Lester, but to suggest the ways social forces have shaped and directed that desire. Had the film given her the interiority Lester possesses, viewers might have seen in her the kind of psychological division or "dissociation" as well as diminished confidence that Mary Pipher, Carol Gilligan, and Joan Jacobs Brumberg have described in adolescent girls, and that has been linked to trauma and sexual abuse as well.[41] Wrapped in Lester's jacket, she huddles in abjection after her sexual bravado has been exposed as a sad masquerade. The film does not linger on her, however. Once she has performed her narrative function of enabling Lester to rediscover his power, the mantle of victimhood slips from him to her and she disappears.

American Beauty tells the nymphet's story as male fantasy: she exists for him, the power she holds over him is illusory, and under her sexual forwardness lies a helpless little girl. A more provocative understanding of the nymphet, however, comes from feminism's Third Wave, which refuses the victimization implicit in the character of Angela. Books such as Elizabeth Wurtzel's *Bitch: In Praise of Difficult Women* and Paula Kamen's *Her Way: Young Women Remake the Sexual Revolution* cast a politicized light on young women who refuse to play by old rules governing sexual behavior. In music, Madonna led the way, followed by Courtney Love, who made both anger and sex without romantic yearnings acceptable for young women. These women claim the right to be aggressive and self-gratifying, to have multiple partners, and to engage in sex on their own terms. According to Kamen, Monica Lewinsky stands in the mainstream of women of her generation for adopting a sense of sexual entitlement that once belonged only to men.[42]

Since the late 1980s, characters fashioned after these values began appearing in television (*Beverly Hills 90210*, *Melrose Place*, *Sex and the City*) and film (*Poison Ivy*, *The Opposite of Sex*, and *Cruel Intentions*). While these examples contain outrageous models of "bad" girls, other films and TV shows depict young women breaking ideals of feminine decorum in less shocking ways: *Buffy the Vampire Slayer*, the *Scream* trilogy, *Xena: Warrior Princess*, *The Powerpuff Girls*, and *Alias*.

Paradoxically, the emerging presence of sexualized "bad girls" provides a superficial justification for films such as *American Beauty* to use the nymphet in ways that evade the issue of abuse and that elicit sympathy for a victimized father. These girls also trouble some Second Wave feminists who are uneasy about what they see as a misguided emulation of the masculine values of aggression and self-gratification, not to mention a naïve faith in the power of individual agency. Indeed, as Kamen and Wurtzel have noted, young women who lack a consciousness of sexual politics are likely to find that their efforts to live their sex lives like men may well backfire. Lewinsky, despite her sexual bravado, was still sufficiently old-fashioned to fall in love with her partner and long for him to marry her. More to the point, these transgressive young women possess the power to destabilize traditional concepts of gender and family life. Kamen describes them as "superrats" because of the trouble they cause, in real life and on the screen. There is no question that Monica wreaked as much havoc in the nation's symbolic home as Angela did in the all-American household of *American Beauty*.

These examples of sexually adventurous and empowered young women encourage a more complex understanding of sexuality in all of its forms. Sexual desire is often linked to eroticized differentials of power, an insight made explicit in the S&M community and one that raises difficult questions about intergenerational sex and the age of consent.[43] Many would agree that sex between people who bring significantly different degrees of real power to the relationship can only be exploitative and devastating to the weaker party. Indeed, the recent revelations of sexual abuse and cover-up that have rocked the Catholic church seem to support this view, adding new awareness of the potential for abuse of all kinds within hierarchical and tightly closed systems.

Others have been troubled by such easy conclusions on the basis of their own experiences.[44] What's needed is a willingness to look hard at the ways depictions of sexuality in popular culture reinforce or undermine existing social relations.

A recurrent theme among feminist psychologists and psychiatrists who write about incest is the need for continued progress toward families based on egalitarian relationships, with strengthened ties between mothers and their children, especially their daughters. Such families tend to hold paternal authority in check and encourage nurturing and nonexploitative behavior among fathers toward their children. Herman argues that any social changes that benefit women benefit mothers, and any benefits to mothers enhance the well-being of children. Progress toward this end is not enhanced by films that feature collusive mothers and victimized fathers. Such figures may well have satisfied an Oedipal script that reflected the gender relations of the past, but this scenario will not help eradicate incest from real life.

The third term of the incest scenario, however, offers more promise for social change. When the nymphet becomes politicized—and, like the superrat, begins to see claiming her sexuality as part of a broader political entitlement—the entangled structures of power and desire on which abusive relationships long have rested may finally begin to break apart.

Girl World

CLUELESS, MEAN GIRLS, AND
THE DEVIL WEARS PRADA

3

HER, THE PRETTY SIXTEEN-YEAR-OLD protagonist of Amy Heckerling's *Clueless* (1995), is a rich dumb blonde who is a mediocre student at best, and is obsessed with the pleasures of fashion, beauty culture, and shopping. A coy daddy's girl, she pouts and whines when she's frustrated, and her speech is riddled with girly slang. Her universe is filtered entirely through popular culture: she prefers watching cartoons to the news, and she takes pride in the fact that her mother named her after the legendary goddess of pop schlock and excess.

This small film, a piece of apparent cinematic fluff, appears at first glance to represent all that Second Wave feminism opposed, especially the infantilization of women. Yet the film clearly had something to say to a new generation of girls. It became an instant hit, and the slang spoken by its characters spread like wildfire among teen girls, some of its phrases ("whatever," "as if") eventually finding their way into vernacular American English. The film is credited with helping revive the genre of the teen pic, which many thought had died with the John Hughes films of the 1980s. In addition to launching a

TV spin-off of the same name (ABC 1996–1997, UPN 1997-1999), it became the first in a series of teen-oriented romantic comedies that included *Can't Hardly Wait* (1998), 10 *Things I Hate About You* (1999), *She's All That* (1999), *Legally Blonde* (2001), and *Save the Last Dance* (2001).

Clueless's success embarrassed 20th Century Fox, which had owned the rights to the film but dropped its option because its executives were worried about something "so female-oriented," director Heckerling said (Weinraub 1995). "They kept pressuring me to create more of a life for the boys in the film, to create more of an ensemble piece, which didn't make sense to me at all." Heckerling had made her directorial debut with *Fast Times at Ridgemont High* (1982), highly regarded for its unsentimental treatment of a teen girl's coming of age. Shortly before *Clueless*, she had read Jane Austen's *Emma* (1815), which is set among the English gentry, and it inspired her to make a film with a similarly optimistic female protagonist set in a fun-filled world of luxury. Paramount, recognizing that studios had neglected eight- to twenty-year-old females for some time, picked up the film, which cost about $12 million to make and brought in nearly double that amount its first weekend.

In retrospect, it should be no surprise *Clueless* was as successful as it was. Pastiche and the hybridization of genres typify postmodern film and television, and like *Titanic*, which mixes the action film with romantic melodrama, *Clueless* is an inspired hybrid, combining two genres certain to appeal to teen girls: the teen pic and the romantic comedy. This chapter explores that appeal by taking a closer look at *Clueless* and two other films identified with Girl Culture: *Mean Girls* (2004) and *The Devil Wears Prada* (2006). Tapping into postfeminist fantasies, all three take place in white, financially comfortable settings. All exist in an ambiguous relation to feminism, invoking the female unruliness of classical romantic comedy but recoding it in new ways. And all bear the strong hand of female authorship. As a result, these films provide rare and richly rendered views of what girls and young women want in the postfeminist era.

Female unruliness begins with female desire—for power and other pleasures forbidden to girls and women. In these films, that desire unfolds in what *Mean Girls* identifies as "Girl World." While the demographic boundaries of girlhood have expanded well past childhood and early adolescence, Girl World refers to a liminal time and space between childhood and adulthood where girls rule. It had been explored in earlier films, most notably, the dark comedy *Heathers* (1988), but when cultural producers recognized the untapped potential of teen girls as consumers, Girl World found expression in a full range of contemporary Girl Culture texts, including books, magazines and online sites (such as *Bitch* and *Bust*), music, television shows and films addressing girls.[1] Much of the rhetoric of Girl Culture involved Girl Power, which, according to some accounts, soon became a marketing ploy to sell products (D. Siegel, 146).

Girl World is, of course, ambivalent. On the one hand, it is inherently unruly because it places female desire at its core, validating its very existence. In Girl World, girls flex their muscles as they begin to leave childhood behind and test the waters of womanhood. They experiment with Femininity with a capital "F," from fashion to girliness to romance, all mediated through popular culture. They experience close connections with each other through shopping, gossip, and makeovers. While they may obsess over boys and experiment with sex, serious relationships with boys hold less appeal than the idea of them. Most threateningly, Girl World lets girls experience the taboo emotion of anger. Girls let themselves get mean. What matters is girls, who begin to learn about social power by exercising it over each other.

At the same time, Girl World's fantasies are manufactured and constrained by the ideologies of a patriarchal, postfeminist culture, and as girls experiment with social hierarchies, the results largely mirror the adult world. Girl World encourages girls to believe in the enduring rescue fantasies kept alive by films like *Pretty Woman* and *Titanic*, and the expressive fun of fashion and makeup— femininity for the self—cannot be extricated from more insidious lessons that teach girls to please others, especially boys. In Girl World, girls' power tends to stop at the boundaries of normative femininity.

The danger inherent in Girl World becomes clearer when observing the narrative closure of these films, which all end by domesticating their young protagonists. Jane Austen's novels typically explore how an independent-minded young woman negotiates the requirement of making a good marriage if she wants a good life. Austen's interest in the tension between female desire and a conservative social order may explain why film and television adaptations of her works have proven so appealing to the postfeminist sensibility.[2] Because her perspective is comic, her narratives eventually reconcile individual and social desire through marriage.

Today, happy endings for young women may no longer assume marriage, at least right away, but in the teen-girl films, unruly girls leave Girl World behind for a femininity that is less focused on other girls and the self than on gracefully acquiescing to a social order still largely defined by patriarchy and capitalism. And so, postfeminist films tell the stories of daughters still more identified with their fathers than their mothers. Andy in *The Devil Wears Prada* turns from the heady and glamorous power available to her in an adult version of Girl World toward the safety of working with a male mentor in the dark and tweedy corridors of "Man World." Mothers may be more present in these postfeminist films than in classical Hollywood's romantic comedies, but fathers remain their daughters' emotional touchstones.

Because of these entanglements and ambivalences, Girl World evokes mixed reviews from adults. One perspective—a misogynistic one—sees only its narcissism and superficiality, traits long projected on women in a culture that condemns female desire as inevitably narcissistic and female pleasures as superficial. *Sex and the City,* beloved by many teen girls and young women for its forthright discussions of female sexuality and powerful depiction of female friendship, has received especially intense criticism on those accounts.[3] Another perspective, rooted in the Second Wave, views Girl World with genuine concern about its complicity in patriarchy and consumerism. Indeed, most films that engage with Girl World hint at its dark side, and some, such as *Thirteen,* show its potential to create devastation in the lives of girls and their mothers.

A third view acknowledges the taboo pleasures of Girl World, the pleasures of self-indulgence, anger, and a power that soon must be moderated. This view, tied to the Third Wave, accounts for the pleasures so many teen girls and young women experience in the female-oriented media texts of recent popular culture, from *Clueless* to *Sex and the City* to *Bridget Jones's Diary.* These works offer fantasies—of love, power, female friendship, fabulous shoes—that are irresistible to many girls coming of age in a culture that sends them endlessly mixed messages about what it means to be a woman.

Clueless

Of the three films I write about in this chapter, *Clueless* creates the most sympathetic picture of Girl World, which its protagonist Cher rules with innocence and charm. The film closely follows its literary source in creating Cher as "handsome, clever, and rich," in Austen's words, a spirited but spoiled young woman who has little interest in romance herself but takes great pleasure in matchmaking for others. Like Emma, Cher has a protective father and a

Postfeminist films like *Clueless* show daughters identifying more with their fathers than with their mothers.

somewhat older male friend, who alone among her circle challenges her and who becomes her proper match once she has matured enough to recognize that she loves him. In *Clueless*, which is fully anchored in the comic vision, power is never really dangerous, whether it is wielded by Cher, her rivals, or her intimidating father.

The film draws on the basic conventions of the teen pic typified by Hughes's more melodramatic films: high school as a microcosm of the (white middle-class) social world, with ruthlessly exclusive cliques; token nonwhite and/or gay characters; silly adults; a prom or wild party where "the truth" comes out; pop music often performed diegetically; and teen-originated slang. Teen films also show a strong interest in sex, but diffuse the focus on the couple found in the classical romantic comedies by placing the romantic leads within a peer group of other well-defined characters. Teen media is also densely intertextual, with abundant references to television, film, music, advertising, and other aspects of consumer culture. *Clueless* (and even more so *Scream*) shows how these forms of media flow seamlessly into one another, and into teen life itself. The film begins with a series of conventionalized scenes of teen life, followed by Cher in voice-over chastising the viewer for mistaking the montage for a Noxzema commercial.

From romantic comedy *Clueless* draws its unruly female protagonist, and Cher's voice-over anchors the film in her subjectivity. Throughout, she asserts her authority as narrator, speaking directly to us with affectionate tolerance for our ignorance of her universe. The film's *mise en scène* consists of high-school classrooms, bedrooms, and shopping malls, where the dramas of Girl World unfold. Other formal devices, including point-of-view shots, close-ups, and music, guide viewers to see the excesses of her life—the motorized racks in her closet, her blithe ignorance of current events—with tolerance and amusement.

In Girl World, fashion is not a trivial diversion but an essential means of establishing one's social identity, and a surprising number of female-oriented films and TV shows place protagonists in some relation to the fashion industry (the TV shows *All-American Girl* [1994] and *Ugly Betty* [2006–present], and the films *The Devil Wears Prada*, *13 Going on 30* [2004], *Real Women Have Curves* [2002]). Like *Pretty in Pink* and *The Devil Wears Prada*, *Clueless* begins with the ritual of Cher dressing for the day, and cliques in her social world identify themselves by clothing and other markers of style. Teen films often include slow motion shots of the girls who rule Girl World as they parade in tight squadrons, drawing the gaze of both film viewer and awed characters within the diegesis. While Cher and her best friends clearly attract that gaze, *Clueless* establishes Cher's unruly independence by wittily reversing its gendered convention. Over a slow-motion shot of a phalanx of high school boys wearing baggy, hip-hop clothing and backward baseball caps, she explains that she has no interest in high school boys because their fashion sense is incomprehensible.

Teen films deal with coming of age, and *Clueless* is no exception. Its plot centers on Cher's quest to discover who she is: her journey from giving makeovers to her teachers and friends to giving one to her "soul," and from faulting others for their cluelessness to recognizing and overcoming her own. Because the film is a romantic comedy, her passage to adulthood is tied to her gendered identity—to learning what it means to be a woman. The film's casting and comic tone set us up from the outset to view Cher as an inherently kind-hearted person whose superficiality is an amusing trait, and whose cluelessness is a product of her immaturity. Nonetheless, to create narrative drama, she must face and overcome obstacles to her discovery of who she is. The film places these obstacles in areas central to Girl World—sex, romance, and a femininity defined around girlish pleasures.

Clueless's Cher (Alicia Silverstone) demonstrates that in Girl World, fashion is an essential means of establishing one's social identity.

As in the classic romantic comedy, Cher's primary familial relationship is with her father. Her mother died years ago (during "routine liposuction"), and Cher performs the household role of stand-in wife. She fusses over her father, adjusts his tie, and generally lavishes loving attention on him. Other teen comedies, such as *10 Things I Hate About You* and *She's All That* as well as *Pretty in Pink*, place daughters in similar mock husband-wife relationships with their fathers, where they practice the nurturing skills that will be expected of them as women. Whereas these films create father-daughter relationships that are uncomfortably intimate, *Clueless* defuses the incestuous potential of Cher's relationship with Mel, her father. Played for comedy by Dan Hedaya, Mel shows no signs of undue interest in or emotional dependence on her, and his gruff personality keeps him at an appropriate distance from her.

Most important, *Clueless* does not demonize the missing mother, unlike other teen-oriented films where a mother's absence weighs heavily on the abandoned family. In *Pretty in Pink*, Andie's caretaking role arises from her father's emotional devastation from being left by her mother. In *10 Things*, Kat, the elder daughter, accuses her father of punishing her because her mother

Unlike many other teen films, *Clueless* celebrates Cher's dead mother rather than blaming or vilifying her. Says Cher: "Wasn't my mom a Bette?"

left, and when her younger sister accepts her mother's pearls, she remarks bitterly, "It's not like she's coming back to claim them." In contrast, Cher's dead mother is beloved by both father and daughter. A large portrait of her hangs in the foyer of their house, where she benignly watches over their comings and goings. In the film's most tender moment, Mel reassures Cher of her goodness by telling her, "I have not seen such good-doing since your mother." And so, while *Clueless* still depends on the primacy of the father-daughter relation, Cher's quest to discover who she is takes her back to her mother.

Clueless negotiates the landscape of postfeminism with a canny sensitivity to teen-girl desire, showing that girls can rule and still embrace pleasurable aspects of femininity that went underground, at least for many feminists, with the Second Wave. Cher's unruliness continues the tradition of the dumb blonde, where characters played by Judy Holliday, Marilyn Monroe, and more recently Reese Witherspoon (in the *Legally Blonde* franchise) expose the limitations of a masculinity that takes itself too seriously. Her character also has much in common with Susan (Katherine Hepburn) in *Bringing Up Baby* (1938) who is also a terrible driver, wreaks havoc with language and other people's property, and brings a revitalizing chaos into the rigid, lifeless world of her professor love-interest.[4]

Cher's namesake is one of the most unruly women of popular culture and since the 1960s shocked and entertained television audiences with outrageous costumes that played up her statuesque and exotic beauty. Wearing sequins, feathers, and headdresses, as well as harem pants and halters, the singer Cher notoriously exposed her midriff and navel well before Madonna began mainstreaming such styles. Later, as an actor, she eventually came to portray new models of unrepentant motherhood in such melodramas as *Mask* (1985) and *Mermaids* (1990).

Like the real-world Cher and *Pretty in Pink*'s Andie, *Clueless*'s Cher uses fashion as a creative performance of her identity in a culture increasingly consumed with surface and commodity. Her fashion choices tend toward postmodern expressions of little-girl styles—Mary Jane shoes, over-the-knee socks, miniskirts—yet she also wears sophisticated sheaths for evenings out. Her vacillation between these styles suggests the ambivalence of teen girls drawn to adulthood but uneasy about its costs and thus happy to linger over the less complicated pleasures of girlhood. In this context, the mall becomes a postmodern version of public female space where girls gather for recreation and where shopping becomes a cover for the more important work of tending to friendships.

Because Cher's most important growth happens in the context of her relationships with her girlfriends, the film both de-emphasizes the place of romance in her life and reinforces the importance of female friendships. But, as in most mainstream teen comedies, white protagonists dominate the action, with supporting roles played by actors of color. Cher's best friend is Dionne, played by racially mixed Stacey Dash, and the new girl they befriend, Tai (Brittany Murphy), is coded as "East Coast ethnic." Both intensify Cher's blonde, white desirability through contrast, normalizing the subordination of characters of color while participating in the "multiculturalizing" of popular culture.

While *Clueless* does not break new ground with race, one of its most appealing aspects is its treatment of female sexual autonomy. Heckerling showed similar sensitivity in her 1982 film *Fast Times at Ridgemont High*. Cher has nothing but disdain for the immature boys who swarm around her. She is a virgin, not for reasons of abstinence-only morality but because of a self-confidence and maturity that belie her apparent cluelessness. In this way, the

Clueless reinforces the importance of female friendships. Cher's most important growth happens in the context of her relationships with her girlfriends.

film counters the assumption (depicted in *Thirteen*) that girls agree to casual sex knowing little about their own sexuality or right to sexual pleasure.[5] Instead, Cher controls her sexuality. When stylish Christian shows up on her scene, she sets the stage for him to seduce her. Her failure to recognize he's gay becomes an opportunity for the film to poke gentle fun at her innocence. At the same time, it gives Christian the opportunity to show his physical prowess and bravery by confronting a group of boorish straight guys who are threatening Tai.

Given the conventions of romantic comedy, Cher must find her way to Josh (Paul Rudd), but before she does, the match must overcome initial obstacles. The first is a slight whiff of the incest avoided in Cher's relationship with her father: Josh is not only older than Cher but is her ex-stepbrother. Moreover, in the postfeminist age, young women no longer inevitably assume that a young woman cannot find herself without finding "Mr. Right." Experience taught Rose in *Titanic* that Mr. Right does exist, even if there are no guarantees he'll be around for long. Yet feminist viewers of *Sex and the City* squirmed about Carrie's marriage to Mr. Big (Di Mattia 2004). However, *Clueless*'s awareness of itself as a conventionalized and thus unrealistic film softens these ideological concerns. Moreover, *Clueless* draws on classical romantic comedy's gender inversion to tip the balance of power in favor of its female protagonist.

From the outset, Cher and Josh squabble over their differences. Like most romantic male heroes, Josh is bland. And in the tradition of the "professor hero," a common counterpart to unruly female protagonists in romantic comedy, he is an overly serious, bookish nerd. He can't dance, which sends a worrisome message in movie-code about his virility. But his virtues come into sharp relief when contrasted with the snobbishness and sexual entitlement of his rival Elton, also a member of Cher's social class. In fact, Josh is a prince waiting in the wings to inherit the kingdom from Cher's father, a ruthless, wealthy litigator. Moreover, Josh's interest in environmental law matches Cher's inherent "good-doing" and establishes him as a gentle but real corrective to the abuses of Cher's social class. Despite these qualities, he needs Cher's vitality and sense of fun. And so, even if the film does not match *Bringing Up Baby* or *Ball of Fire* (1941) in moderating an overly serious masculinity, it puts its romantic protagonists on equal footing.

As Heckerling understood, Cher's wealth, an enduring convention of romantic comedy, enables the film to offer its viewers satisfying fantasies of abundance, much like the sophisticated comedies and musicals of the Depression era. Indeed, *Clueless* culminates in a closing image that is almost Shakespearean in its tone of festive celebration and social renewal. The film flanks its bridal couple—the formerly lovelorn teachers—with three other couples, including Cher and Josh. The genre's conventions require that Cher be domesticated by the end, and much of the film affirms qualities long ascribed to women but not men—the selfless care of others that she, like her mother before her, performs with such ease. There's an easy slippage in the film between the affirmation of caretaking as a quality that is desirable in all people and one that is especially desirable in women.

However, like her unruly antecedents, Cher is a girl on top whose point of view has controlled the film from its opening frames to its conclusion. She is an innocent, an unusual trait among sympathetic characters in teen pics, but she is not dumb. She understands, if imperfectly, the workings of power in her universe. Her unruliness results from her rare combination of confidence and goodness, and from a moral virtue that arises not only from her "doing goodness" but also from her charisma, compassion, and imagination. In Cher, girliness does not mean a surrender of power, but an insistence on pleasure and a holding off of premature adulthood while developing her capacity to understand herself and outgrow the self-absorption of youth.

Mean Girls

If *Clueless* takes an affectionate look at Girl World, *Mean Girls*, less than a decade later, comes to very different conclusions. *Mean Girls* acknowledges the intensity of girls' anger, their attraction to power, and the ways sisterhood—the mantra of the Second Wave—still goes sour in the age of the Third. Like *Clueless*, this fast-paced, witty, and girl-friendly film shows the hand of female authorship. While directed by a man (Mark Waters), it is based on Rosalind Wiseman's *Queen Bees and Wannabes* (2002), which helped shift the focus of popular discourse on female adolescence from the victimization underlying *Reviving Ophelia* to the ways girls use and abuse power. Tina Fey, the first woman to head the writing team of NBC's *Saturday Night Live*, adapted the nonfiction book for the screen and plays the role of Ms. Norbury, a wry and savvy math teacher wise to the ways of girls. (Fey went on to become executive producer, writer, and star of the NBC sitcom *30 Rock*.) *Mean Girls* is a rallying cry for female solidarity, or at least for a turn from the ways girls often misdirect their anger toward themselves and each other.[6]

Like *Clueless*, *Mean Girls* uses familiar tropes of the teen film, including slo-mo promenades of popular cliques, a wild party, makeovers, and the protagonist's quest to discover who she is. And once again, the film takes viewers inside a teen girl's consciousness with the on-going voice-over of its protagonist Cady (Lindsay Lohan). Raised in Africa and home-schooled by her professor parents, Cady is ideally positioned to investigate Girl World from an anthropologist's perspective, which enables an on-going joke about how the savagery of Girl World exceeds common stereotypes about African wildlife. North Shore High School is ruled by three girls known as the Plastics: Regina, the aptly named Queen Bee, and her two sycophants, Karen, a dumb blonde, and Gretchen, coded as Jewish. As in *Clueless*, the popular girls adopt the new girl on campus to amuse themselves, not realizing that she has already been befriended by Janice and Damian, two "Art Freaks" who encourage her to go undercover with the Plastics and share her findings with them.

What Cady discovers there is a social world governed by a set of rules rigidly enforced by a small group of girls and followed by the rest out of a perverse mixture of fear and desire. In one scene, the girls show their sheeplike emulation of the Plastics when they cut breast holes in their T-shirts to copy Regina, after the Art Freaks cut holes in hers in an act of intended sabotage that backfired. The Plastics are "dumb, rich, and evil," in Janice's words, but they represent power, and girls want to be near power if they can't have it themselves. In postmodern culture, power exists simply through being visible, and the Plastics succeed in drawing the gaze. While Cher is at the center of power in *Clueless*, that power in *Mean Girls* has become dangerous.

The subtitle of Wiseman's book—*Helping Your Daughter Survive Cliques, Gossip, Boyfriends, and Other Realities of Adolescence*—identifies the most treacherous areas for teen girls as "boyfriends" (sex and/or romance), "cliques," and "gossip" (other girls). In *Mean Girls*, the Art Freaks note that the Plastics' power rests on three related pillars: "man candy," a "hot body," and an "army of skanks." Clearly, the reclamation of girly femininity and sexuality may not be as uncomplicated as it seemed in the Spice Girls' upbeat anthems of female friendship and power.

The first requirement, man candy, keeps girls locked into old dependencies on male validation and fantasies of romantic love. The second, a hot body, reinforces girls' unhealthy belief that their worth is based on unattainable goals of physical beauty while encouraging them to limit their sense of identity to the sexual. The third, the army of skanks, teaches girls to follow rather than lead and to internalize misogynistic and hypocritical attitudes toward themselves and each other. The Plastics label girls they don't like "skanks" yet use Halloween as an opportunity to "dress like sluts" themselves and get away with it.

Indeed, the "army of skanks" suggests the mixture of disdain and desire that defines female hierarchies and relationships in adolescence. As Cady observes, all fighting in Girl World has to be sneaky because girls must not acknowledge anger or express it directly. In one scene, a split screen shows Regina's adept use of three-way phone connections to manipulate one friend into offending another. And so the Plastics rule through intimidation and manipulation, false rumors and gossip. Here, *Mean Girls* shows that when girls foster suspicion and distrust among themselves, they are doing patriarchy's work. Janice's rage at the Plastics originated when they started a rumor that she is gay. The label of "lesbian," of course, has long been used to control women who seem to care too much for other women.

As in *Clueless*, the plot turns on Cady's need to discover who she is, and her biggest obstacle is her own vulnerability to being seduced by power. When Cady begins to enjoy her new role as Queen Bee, the film shows the appeal of power to teen girls, even at the expense of their own integrity. One of Cady's most distinguishing traits is her talent in math, and Ms. Norbury tries to recruit

Mean Girls shows that when girls foster distrust among themselves, they are doing patriarchy's work. Here, Cady overhears Regina manipulating the other Plastics to betray each other.

her for the Mathletes. Yet when she falls under the spell of man candy, another bland, good-looking guy, she plays dumb to attract him, suggesting that Girl Culture has not yet succeeded in redefining femininity to include braininess, let alone braininess in math.

Like most teen films, *Mean Girls* has its share of incompetent adults, including the hypocritical coach who teaches abstinence-only sex education but chases after young students. Regina's mother (Amy Poehler) is an older Plastic, the target of visual jokes for her rock-hard fake breasts, which are so immune to sensation that she doesn't feel her designer dog gnawing on them. She describes herself as "not a regular mom, a cool mom," who wants to be "best girlfriends" with her daughters and pushes them into precocious sexuality. Cady's parents are generally sympathetic, although the film falters in its feminism when it undercuts the mother by describing her as fearful of her daughter. Once again, the teen girl's ally and confidant is her father.

It is Ms. Norbury, the math teacher, who gives the girls the tough guidance they need to break the pernicious cultural pattern of pitting girls and women against each other. "This is not a self-esteem problem," she announces, challenging Mary Pipher's victim-oriented analysis of female adolescence. It's about "girl-on-girl crime." She tells the girls that when they call each other "slut" and "whore," they give guys permission to do the same. Then she guides them through an "attitude makeover" in which they agree to stop seeking power by putting other girls down. In this role, Ms. Norbury serves as a stand-in mother, a voice of adult female authority to help girls learn a femininity that begins with respect for themselves and other girls. Her pivotal role in the narrative shows that girls cannot reach their potential without the guidance of older women. Children and teenagers may often believe they can raise themselves, but they can't, nor should they have to.

By the film's conclusion, Cady has evolved from a "jungle freak" to "shiny plastic" to an "actual human being." She has accepted her braininess and won the state competition for the math team. She is also queen of the requisite prom, where she accepts the tiara while wearing her Mathlete team jacket. The tiara is plastic, however, and she breaks it in pieces and tosses to the crowd to signal the dawn of a new age of female respect and solidarity. In a coda, we see Regina playing a fiercely physical lacrosse game, having learned to channel her aggression in healthier ways. We also get an ominous glimpse of a new generation of Junior Plastics strutting onto the scene. In voice-over, much like Cher's at the end of *Clueless*, Cady reassures the viewer not to worry: the older girls will guide the younger ones into the new femininity they have learned. In this small way, *Mean Girls* models empowering relationships between female generations.

Through Ms. Norbury (Tina Fey), *Mean Girls* shows that girls cannot thrive without maternal guidance and support.

Mean Girls is important for shining a critical light on sentimental depictions of Girl Culture and for exposing old ideologies of femininity that linger in new ones—celebrations of sexuality that are still sexist, and the tendency to teach girls that they are valued more for their bodies than their minds. It also exposes the enduring contradiction that girls and women should not express anger or aggression, but at the same time they should not trust each other. Most important, through Ms. Norbury, *Mean Girls* shows that girls cannot achieve real power without maternal guidance and support.

The Devil Wears Prada

The three films studied in this chapter have followed a downward spiral in their attitudes toward the excesses of Girl World, seeing these excesses first as "clueless," then "mean," and finally "devil-like." Admittedly, *The Devil Wears Prada* is as fascinated with its devil as it is appalled by her, but the film takes an even darker look at Girl World than *Mean Girls* does. Moreover, it ups the ante of the previous two films with more mature protagonists, sumptuous costumes, romantic settings in New York and Paris, and the star power of Meryl Streep, who plays Miranda Priestly, a fictionalized version of *Vogue* editor Anna Wintour. In doing so, the film enters the more complex territory of postfeminist ambiguity.

Like the male-oriented slacker comedies of Kevin Smith and Judd Apatow, *The Devil Wears Prada* sends a cautionary message about women's power. After flirting with the pleasures of Girl World, it refuses them and closes on a note of conservatism. At the same time, that conservatism is trumped by Streep's performance as well as the guilty pleasures of a fully realized Grown-up Girl World which viewers experience through her. The film offers the rare spectacle of a woman in her fifties wielding power while wearing wonderful clothes, and it is she, rather than the mild character played by Anne Hathaway, who embodies female unruliness. Most intriguingly, the film concludes with the suggestion that its Prada-wearing devil can also be a generous, unrepentant mother.

The film is based on Lauren Weisberger's best-selling novel about her experiences working for Wintour. The screenplay was written by Aline Brosh McKenna, who is credited with giving added dimension to the novel's characters, especially Miranda. In her hands, Miranda becomes not simply a monstrous boss but a working mother doing her best and having to pay personal costs for her success that men with wives rarely have to.[7]

The Devil Wears Prada depicts the rare spectacle of an attractive over-fifty woman wielding unruly power.

The Devil Wears Prada tells the story of Andy, a brainy young woman from the Midwest who gave up a scholarship to study law for a career in journalism. As in *Mean Girls*, her journey of self-discovery involves a detour into the alien territory of Girl World but here adult-style, which she experiences working in the office of *Runway*, a top fashion magazine. With yet another opening montage of young women dressing for the day (to the pop tune "Suddenly I See" ["what I want to be," the lyrics continue] by KT Tunstall), the film foreshadows yet another makeover, but less like the ones of character and attitude depicted in *Clueless* and *Mean Girls*. Andy will morph from being a "smart, fat girl" (in Miranda's words) into a glamorous player in the highest echelons of fashion culture.

Overtly, Andy appears to face a struggle between two opposing worlds of journalism. She won awards as a college journalist for stories on serious social issues, such as janitors' unions. When she can't get a job at a "respectable" newspaper, she finds herself working for Miranda, the frightening but fascinating editor of *Runway*. Initially she knows nothing about fashion and views it with amused condescension. The film makes only one reference to feminism when Andy later defends Miranda's ruthlessness on feminist grounds, but Andy's skepticism about fashion recalls the Second Wave's critique of the male gaze. At the same, Miranda's cool embrace of the spotlight is consistent with the values of postfeminist culture and aspects of the Third Wave. The film thus undercuts any simplistic effort to tie the Second and Third Waves to biological generations rather than to political positions and values.

The film's narrative depends on the premise that Andy can't succeed in her career or personal life until she experiences the temptations of Girl World, and not only the pleasures of fashion most notoriously celebrated by *Sex and the City* but also real power wielded by women.[8] After putting Andy down for her smugness ("You take yourself too seriously to care what you wear"), Miranda defends the fashion industry on the basis of its cultural influence by pointing out that even though Andy may believe she freely chose the frumpy sweater she is wearing, in fact its color was chosen for her. Nigel, Miranda's loyal gay lieutenant, explains how great designers outrank great artists because they create art that is lived in.

When Andy's father visits her from the Midwest, he is concerned that her involvement in her job means she has forgotten her intellectual aspirations, but even Andy's serious-minded friends understand the appeal of Miranda's world: when Andy pleases them with luxury items of "swag" as gifts, her gay friend Doug explains that fashion isn't about utility but self-expression. Her friend Lily adds, "and it's pretty." The film makes its case most effectively with its spectacles of striking clothing and accessories used for runway shows and photo shoots, and, most engagingly, for character exposition.

Miranda is a true heroine for the postfeminist age in that her charisma comes from a potent mixture of femininity and power. The film introduces her with a kinetic montage that links her mastery of fashion with the thrill of power. To the accompaniment of driving nondiegetic music, the sequence crosscuts between office workers scrambling to get ready for her arrival and her approach to the office. The montage begins with a close-up of her feet as she steps out of a car, her high heels connoting a femininity that is both retro and aggressive, old and new.

At first, Andy takes a condescending attitude toward *Runway*, assuming that her journalistic credentials are enough to ensure her success there. Once she realizes that she needs to take her new job more seriously, she embarks on a makeover that is both outward and inward, and the film's ideological confusion becomes more apparent. On the one hand, we see a maturation that now enables her to meet her challenges head on, and the film lovingly photographs her in many stunning outfits that signify her transformation. But when she quietly downsizes from size six to four and the sympathetic Nigel applauds her, the film also exposes the postfeminist values of dangerous self-

The Devil Wears Prada poses ambition and a happy personal life as incompatible for women. Here, Andy (Anne Hathaway) tries to make amends for working late and missing her boyfriend's birthday.

surveillance and body obsession. Through Emily, the bitter fashionista whom Andy finally replaces as Miranda's top assistant, the film mocks the starvation young women undergo in seeking their image-based goals.[9]

Yet, as Andy becomes increasingly unavailable to her boyfriend Nate, the film uses the postfeminist discourse of choice to judge her unsympathetically. Her friends remind her that she is freely "choosing" to answer Miranda's calls at all hours, to miss Nate's birthday, and so on. When Nate accuses her of becoming what she used to disdain, she disingenuously tries to separate her appearance from a deeper reality—"same Andy, better clothes."

It is not Miranda's glamour that tempts Andy, however, but her power, and as the film progresses, we begin to see that the real choices it offers are not between two kinds of journalism but between ambition and a satisfying personal life, which the film poses as incompatible, especially for women. The film's turning point occurs when Andy sees Miranda after her most recent husband has left her, and her naked eyes, often veiled by designer sunglasses, are red from crying. Miranda observes, with her usual breathy flatness, that the press will crucify her as a "dragon lady" or "snow queen" who can only drive men away. The film now makes clear that underneath the facades that Emily, Nigel, and even Miranda wear lies loneliness.

Still, Miranda makes a strong argument that power is its own reward. When she offers Andy the keys to her kingdom and Andy demurs, Miranda replies,

"Don't be ridiculous. Eveyone wants this, everyone wants to be us." Moreover, Miranda refuses to pretend that power can be wielded without dirtying one's hands. She reminds Andy that she has already dirtied hers by climbing over Emily to satisfy her own ambition.

The film resolves its conflicts with choices that postfeminism would applaud as evidence of Andy's freedom, though these choices ring hollow. Throughout Andy's experience at *Runway*, Nate, who aspires to be a chef, has resented her absorption in her work and her decreasing availability to him. Andy reconciles with him by admitting that he was "right about everything" and that she "turned her back on everything, and for what?" When he answers, "Shoes, belts, jackets, shirt," he diminishes her desire for power into a girlish infatuation for pretty things. Indeed, by linking pretty things with power in the figure of Miranda, the film warns girls to beware of their interest in either.

Meanwhile, Andy has taken a new job at the kind of newspaper she had first aspired to work at. Its environment is dully masculine, with drab brown tones, wood paneling, and subdued lighting, and she is now dressed in dark sensible clothes, including a businesslike black turtleneck. The film implies that by choosing the male establishment, untouched by girly femininity, Andy will be immune to the corruption that taints power held by women. In this new job, Andy won't let pretty things trick her into giving up her personal life for power, and with a sleight of hand the film resolves its fundamental conflict.

Not surprisingly, Andy's romance with Nate is barely convincing. Only narrative convention makes her reconciliation with him plausible, as open-ended as it is. And her flirtation with Christian, the handsome editor who offers to mentor her, mainly enables her to fulfill the fantasy of a sexy fling in Paris. The film's real romance, of course, is between Miranda and Andy. By the end of the film, Miranda has come to recognize her own intelligence and drive in Andy. The typical girls who worship *Runway*, she sighs, are vapid, always "disappointing." Two-shots of the women riding in Paris as its landmarks fly by give aesthetic weight to Miranda's choice of Andy as her heiress apparent.

Miranda is the mother of young twin daughters, and earlier we saw her distressed because she had to miss one of their recitals. This incident was a sign that she does her best to be a good mother and that she pays a dear price for achieving her potential in her work. Streep's brilliant performance never allows Miranda to appear simply monstrous or even only comic, and as the film progresses, we are drawn to her, first by her power and style but then by

Meryl Streep's performance never allows Miranda to appear simply monstrous or even only comic. Her private smile here shows her pleasure in having helped Andy achieve her goals.

subtle shadings of her character. By the film's conclusion, she has taken on the gravitas of a mother who recognizes the talents of a daughter figure she wants to nurture. She finally shows herself to be a generous benefactor when she uses her influence to ensure that Andy will be hired at the newspaper where she truly wants to work.

Finally, some time after the two women have gone their separate ways, their paths cross again and their eyes meet. Andy smiles, but Miranda doesn't acknowledge her. Moments later, a cut takes us to a close-up of Miranda in the privacy of her car, where she removes her sunglasses, drops her impassive composure, and indulges in a rare smile. This image, which concludes the film, suggests an intriguing model of generational connections among women, relations defined by separation but also support. Miranda, a cool, detached, and unrepentant mother, does not punish Andy for going her own way. In fact, she paves that way for her. And, we can hope that as Andy matures, she will grow to more fully recognize and value those parts of herself she shares with Miranda, including confidence, a drive for excellence, and the desire to be fully who she is.

What do these films tell us about teen-girl desire today? What fantasies does Girl World tap into? Girl World is a postfeminist phenomenon, largely based in the white middle class. It attempts to create a new vision of femininity that retains the social and political gains achieved by the Second Wave while recovering aspects that were lost along the way—the pleasures of time and space devoted to aspects of life traditionally associated with girls and women. These aspects have historically been limited to women's sexual identities, and so for teen girls, "female time" revolves around the rituals of courtship, and for women, the routines of family and domestic life.

It is clear from Girl World's presence in popular culture that these aspects of femininity have not lost their appeal. Indeed, girls have turned their desires for them into expressions of unruliness—a rebellious insistence on pursuing what they want, with or without the approval of their mothers. However, beauty culture, for example, can be embraced in more or less healthy ways, and there is no question that fantasies of bodily perfection marketed to girls have had devastating effects on them. Those effects continue as women age and become vulnerable to new insecurities in a youth-obsessed culture. Similarly, fantasies of eternal romantic love, if not outgrown, leave young women unprepared for the realities of adult relationships. The emotional and financial security of a happy marriage is not likely to be destroyed by natural disasters such as an iceberg, as in *Titanic*, but by the more mundane turns of ordinary lives.

And so whether the unruly desires of Girl World are compatible with the gains achieved by the Second Wave is not clear, as the contradictions in these texts suggest. These contradictions turn in part on the unstable position of the mother, and maternal figures loom in the background of these films as benign (*Clueless*), nurturing (*Mean Girls*), or powerful, seductive, and frightening (*The Devil Wears Prada*). Girl World tends to be daddy-identified, a bittersweet recognition that outside it's still a man's world.

Final Girls and
Epic Fantasies

REMAKING THE WORLD

Popular culture is the politics
of the twenty-first century.
——GALE WEATHERS, *SCREAM*

OR SOME UNRULY Third Wave girls, the genres of laughter—
the romantic comedies or comedy/melodramas inspired by
Clueless (1995)—could no longer contain their desire, and the
dangers of the world as they perceived it could no longer be
represented by the verbal and emotional warfare of Girl World.
Film and TV genres hybridized and mutated to accommodate female action
figures that kickboxed, slugged, and slaughtered enemies, both mortal and
demonic. The romantic comedy/action film *Mr. and Mrs. Smith* (2005), with
Angelina Jolie and Brad Pitt as its sexy, sparring lovers, pushed the limits of romantic comedy by replacing wordplay with gunplay as foreplay. Indeed, Jolie,
especially in the Lara Croft franchise, came to typify the protagonist of what
Marc O'Day has described as "action babe cinema"—a figure who combines
the toughness of Second Wave–inspired protagonists (such as those played
by Sigourney Weaver and Linda Hamilton) with the old-fashioned beauty and
sex appeal aspired to by many girls and women in the postfeminist age, dished
up with a big dose of ironic playfulness.[1] Not surprisingly, this explosion of action cinema and television, often featuring a female detective or crime-fighter,
has inspired a wealth of feminist scholarship.[2]

At the same time, the rise of action heroines coincided with an impulse to remasculinize men by keeping women vulnerable and weak. As Carol Stabile argues in an incisive analysis of the Terror Warrior in the age of market fundamentalism (or, neoliberalism with a religious twist), U.S. masculinity justifies (white) male violence by invoking the need to protect women and children from (dark) outsiders (2007). The attacks of 9/11 reactivated this narrative, which, in addition to its other racist and sexist assumptions, requires that women be unable to defend themselves. If women's safety were truly desired, women would be encouraged to defend themselves and their children by bearing arms, learning martial arts, and so on. But this does not happen. Women must be weak to justify male aggression and to allow men to be men.

Girl Culture has not accepted this narrative. While *Titanic*'s popularity with girls suggests that the rescue fantasy persists, the film's appeal also rests on a young protagonist who combines normative femininity with physical prowess. Still, *Titanic*, like *Clueless*, was limited by the constraints of realism. Other TV and film genres were needed for more fantastic explorations of femininity and for conflicts pitting girls and women against enemies of a far different order than *Mean Girls*' Plastics: killer boyfriends, patriarchal institutions, or the unknowable forces of evil. With stylistic and emotional excess ripe for parody, horror is well suited to the teen sensibility and to hybridization with other genres, such as the gothic melodrama, the slasher film, romantic comedy, the action film, and the epic. It is also ideally suited to capturing the mythic dimensions Ann Powers saw in Girl Culture.

This chapter considers the *Scream* film trilogy (Wes Craven, 1996, 1997, and 2000) and the TV serial *Buffy the Vampire Slayer* (Joss Whedon, 1997–2003, broadcast on WB, UPN, and Fox), with a short postscript on *Twilight* (2008). Like *The Da Vinci Code* and *The Lord of the Rings* blockbusters, *Buffy* is obsessed with arcane mythologies, but like the *Scream* trilogy, it offers a radically different vision of female power. These works are teen-girl answers to the female helplessness required by the cultural narratives of violent masculinity.

Both the *Scream* films and *Buffy* deal with expressions of female desire—especially anger and violence—that exceed the ideological possibilities of genres, such as the romantic melodrama or comedy, that are rooted in realism. Richly intertexual and postmodern, both *Scream* and *Buffy* expanded into franchises that vastly exceeded their original texts. Both draw on the conventions of the horror film, especially the Final Girl, who in the past survived the final bloodbath only by remaining a virgin.

As in most postfeminist texts, both show daughters struggling to find their way to adulthood despite their mothers, not with their support. But both provide suggestive models for reimagining the use of female power to change our cultural narratives, if not the world itself. In *Scream*, the path toward that power moves back in time, toward the lost mother. In *Buffy*, it moves ahead, toward a utopic global sisterhood. Combined, these visions of connection— one based on motherhood and the other on sisterhood—make a powerful package.

Scream

If any recent popular text works on a mythic rather than rational level, it is the *Scream* trilogy, which is as drenched in generational guilt, excess, violence, and sexuality as any ancient Greek or Renaissance drama, while also exemplifying the postmodern aesthetic and cultural values of its time. And if any popular text joins the issues of power, danger, anger, and desire for girls of the 1990s, it is *Scream*. Understanding the place of these issues in girls' lives today provides a helpful context for assessing the meaning of sensational material in these films that women of the Second Wave and other adults might well find disturbing. Indeed, the *Scream* films demonstrate the potential of Girl Culture's highly commodified popular texts to yield meanings consistent with Girl Power. Like popular culture itself, the trilogy is built on familiar old narratives, but in addressing new audiences, it bends those narratives in new ways.

The first *Scream* film, like many current teen movies, is set in an affluent, bucolic, and predominantly white community being preyed on by a masked serial killer. The movie begins with the violent murder of a teen girl named Casey, then shifts its attention to another girl, Sidney, who has been left alone by her father and becomes the killer's next target. Still grieving for her mother, who was raped and murdered a year ago, Sidney has resisted her boyfriend Billy's pressure for sex. Meanwhile, Gale, a TV newscaster, pursues the story of the new killings. The subplots come together at a party during which Sidney decides to have sex with Billy and the killer lays siege to the gathered teens. After a violent battle, a wounded and battered Sidney learns that the killer is Billy, who killed her mother because her affair with his father broke up his family. With Gale's help, Sidney kills him.

The *Scream* trilogy taps into issues of particular concern for teen girls: (1) sexuality and virginity; (2) adult femininity and its relation to agency and power; (3) identity as it is shaped by the narratives of popular culture; and (4) identity as it is shaped by the family of origin—in particular, a daughter's relationship with her mother. The *Scream* trilogy confronts each of these issues head-on, resolving them in powerful and innovative ways that allow a teen girl to occupy center stage, defend herself, and define her identity according to her own desire.

Scream zeroes in on sexuality as a source of anxiety for young women. It does not shrink from the realization that sex is tied to violence and power and thus is dangerous. Sex can cause a girl or woman to lose not only her reputation ("Your mother was a slut bag," Sidney hears throughout the trilogy) but her life. The enduring cultural myths of heterosexual romance, evident in *Pretty Woman*, *Titanic*, and most disturbingly *American Beauty*, perpetuate female fantasies of Prince Charming boyfriends who will rescue them. *Scream* radically revises that myth.

Recent work on female adolescence, such as Mary Pipher's, explores how coming of age "kills off" young girls' confidence and strength, implying that for them, the boyfriend (or desire for a boyfriend) is a "killer."[3] *Scream* literalizes the metaphor. Drawing on literary and cinematic traditions of the Gothic, it captures a heterosexual girl's sense of boys as mysterious and unknowable entities who, like the killer, can wear masks that disguise their true identity. For the generation that gave a name to date rape, *Scream* shows how easily a trusted friend can become a potential rapist. The high school principal, cleverly cast as former teen idol Henry Winkler ("the Fonz" from the 1970s sitcom *Happy Days*) touches Sidney to reassure her but in a way that conveys a creepy sense of entitlement. Heterosexuality can be deadly for growing girls, and adult masculinity is not only mysterious and unknowable, but also capable of manifesting itself in ways that are potentially psychotic. Sidney doesn't know who the killer is, and—as the film-savvy character Randy reminds the other teens—everyone in the film, including her absent father, comes under suspicion.

Undercurrents of danger run through Billy's efforts to seduce Sidney, who is a virgin when the film begins. In one scene, he climbs uninvited into her bedroom, a metaphor for his desire to penetrate her body—at first sexually, then with a knife—and thus reenact the violence he inflicted on her mother. Sexual urgency and aggression are implicitly tolerated or even valued in teen males, and we don't know until the film's final moments whether Billy's edginess merely reflects that urgency or is something more threatening. Yet the film also acknowledges the ambivalence of female desire for the sexual other, and the fine line that divides the crazed killer of *Scream* from the brooding, bodice-ripping romantic heroes of women's pulp fiction. However, like Cher in *Clueless* and Rose in *Titanic*, Sidney remains in control of her own sexuality and chooses when to have sex with Billy. The film does not romanticize or sensationalize this rite of passage, showing only her cool agency in initiating it and its unexceptional aftermath.

Scream's treatment of sexuality arises from its identity not only as a teen film but also as a horror film, a genre which since *Halloween* (1978) has increasingly absorbed the concerns (and audiences) of the teen flick. The horror genre has generated a tradition of important scholarship in film studies, particularly by feminists who have used its graphic excesses to explore cultural connections between violence and sexual difference.[4] This scholarship, exemplified by Carol Clover's influential *Men, Women, and Chainsaws* (1992), maps out a generic tradition that both anchors *Scream* and highlights its departure from it. According to Clover, horror films, like fairy tales, provide raw and unmediated glimpses into unconscious fears and desires, especially around sexual difference. The killer is typically male, like Billy, and his victims female—young, beautiful, and sexual, like Casey. A "Final Girl" eventually kills the killer. Like Sidney, the Final Girl is boyish in name and demeanor, using an active, male gaze to study the situation and hunt the killer. However, unlike Sidney, the typical Final Girl remains a virgin. In effect, she is allowed to kill the killer because she has not yet discovered her most dangerous power, which is her sexuality. For Clover, the horror film is primarily a male discourse, with the Final Girl a point of identification for the male adolescent viewer. However, other critics, such as Isabel Pinedo in *Recreational Terror* (1997), see in the genre the potential for female and feminist appropriation, a potential that *Scream* develops.

Scream, like *Clueless*, depends on an easy familiarity with the generic conventions from which it is built, and the trilogy's most noted formal characteristic is its self-reflexivity. The films are filled with in-jokes about popular culture, from the conventions of the teen slasher film to debates about violence in the media and trends in pop sociology ("Teen suicides are out this year. Homicide is healthier"). This self-reflexivity increases as the trilogy progresses and the films begin to build a dense layering of narratives within narratives and intertextual references. In the first film, the killer repeatedly quizzes his victims on their knowledge of the horror film. "Do you like scary movies?" he

Halloween's Laurie (Jamie Lee Curtis) is the prototypical virginal Final Girl. *Scream's* Sidney (Neve Campbell) updates the formula by losing her virginity while her friends watch *Halloween* downstairs.

taunts. Sidney and Billy describe the degree of their sexual intimacy in terms of movie ratings (Sidney struggles to keep their relationship "PG-13"), and when they have sex, the scene is intercut with shots of their friends watching movies downstairs. The trilogy finally highlights the place of popular culture in teen lives by making knowledge of it the defining characteristic of those who live and those who die. Indeed, in today's world, it is hard to dispute the implications that understanding media is a crucial survival skill.

The self-reflexivity of these films marks them as hip, ironic, and contemporary, and they reinforce subcultural bonds among their teen audiences by highlighting their shared knowledge of a film genre less familiar to their parents. In the 1990s, the *Scream* films became popular fare for slumber parties, and like the *Titanic* phenomenon, reinforced the place of cinema and video as a communal experience and social ritual for teen girls. *Scream* depicts that ritual by showing teens picking out videos together then gathering around the TV to watch them. This communal viewing becomes an occasion for social interaction and shared commentary. The trilogy also uses self-reflexivity to interrogate its own generic conventions, examining in particular how those conventions are tied to cultural ideals of femininity and masculinity. At one point, a flippant teen notes that in movies, "there's always some reason to kill a girlfriend," foregrounding the misogyny of American culture as it is reflected in Hollywood film.

If retro, girly femininity raises red flags for some older women, *Scream*'s apparent approval of violence in the hands of teen girls raises others. This violence cannot be understood, however, apart from the narrative and generic conventions that give it meaning as well as the frame of reference young fans bring to these films. Teen viewers are likely to approach director Wes Craven as an auteur whose films have consistently challenged dominant ideologies of gender and bourgeois family life (*The Hills Have Eyes*) as well as race (*The People Under the Stairs*).[5] The first *Scream* is structured around two very different types of female leading characters whose differences lead to radically different narratives. The female protagonist in most narratives plays a familiar and unchanging role: she is the passive object of the active male hero's quest or the prize at the end of his journey. The slasher film exaggerates this passive/active opposition according to its own highly stylized requirements: blonde female victims ("some big-breasted girl" as one character in *Scream* observes) and male psychopaths. Male fear of female sexuality becomes encoded in the slasher convention that only female virgins can survive—a convention that *Scream* notably rejects.

Scream begins with a graphic and exaggerated display of those conventions in order to undermine and rewrite them for the remainder of the film. Its first joke on viewers' expectations is its witty casting of Drew Barrymore (the film's biggest teen star attraction) as Casey, only to kill her within the first fifteen minutes.[6] In the film's most sustained sequence of suspense and gory violence, Casey is ruthlessly trapped by the killer's threatening taunts, as well as by the camera's complicitous, voyeuristic gaze. Most important, the film hinges her death on her ignorance of popular culture: when the killer quizzes her about slasher films she falters, and her ignorance of the rules—where the killer is hiding, how to elude him, and so on—takes her right to his knife. By killing off this character so decisively, the film also kills off a certain model of femininity—dumb, passive, dependent, victimized—in order to replace it with another that is more knowing, less glamorous, and a lot more capable. Sidney, played by Neve Campbell, a lesser-known model and TV star, understands the rules but resists them, and in the end she usurps the masculine role by unmasking and killing the killer herself.

The film constructs Sidney's character with quiet visual references to icons of Girl Power, such as the poster of the Indigo Girls in her bedroom, and shows her techno-confidence when she signals for help via her computer. Like Buffy the Vampire Slayer and Xena the Warrior Princess, she is physically active, strong, resourceful, and capable of taking care of herself. She has sex on her own timetable, not her boyfriend's, and the loss of her virginity doesn't mean the end of the story for her, as it does in the traditional slasher film. Instead, her sexual initiation marks the beginning of her real power as an adult woman. She doesn't depend on male authorities to rescue her, whether the school principal, the cop, her father, or her boyfriend.

One of the film's most telling moments occurs in a brief moment of calm when the battle to kill Billy and his partner has apparently ended. One of the surviving teens—Randy, the film buff—warns Sidney that the killer always rises once again from apparent death, and Billy lurches up to attack one last time. "Not in my movie," Sidney claims, before killing him for good. With that remark, she claims her place not only as a new kind of female protagonist, but as the auteur of her own movie, or, in fact, her own life, in an age where the movies and life are indistinguishable. As the killer says, "It's all a movie, just pick your genre." The happy ending of this script does not require the union of a heterosexual couple, the Hollywood staple reinforced in *Titanic* when the fated lovers are reunited in Rose's memory, but instead *Scream* blasts the couple apart, leaving the teen-girl heroine independent and unattached.

According to the logic of realism, *Scream* might well be seen as endorsing violence in the hands of a teen girl. But when viewed in its cinematic context, the film, like the slasher genre in general, provides an opportunity to examine cultural and individual fantasies as they relate to gender and power. The film's particular revision of the genre invites female viewers imaginatively to sample a model of femininity more suited to young women of the Third Wave. Moreover, its generic license for excess and exaggeration enables it to make its points with bold strokes: the boyfriend can literally be a killer, the girl can boldly defend herself and take on power formerly off limits to girls. Interestingly, our culture has rarely provided girls the opportunity for such utopic imaginings in the genres of realism, which continue to limit them to traditional roles. Supergirls like Buffy, Xena, Sabrina the Teenage Witch, and Sidney remain thinkable mainly in the realms and genres of fantasy.

Teen films from *Rebel Without a Cause* to *Clueless* have traditionally addressed issues of generational tension, but this tension takes on a new dimension in the 1990s when it is played out against the social backdrop of divorce, single-parent homes, and houses empty after school. Indeed, the empty house signifies more than an opportunity for a wild party, but has become an occasion for terror. And parents no longer stand as towering figures of authority against which to rebel, or even neutral absences, but become haunting specters

"Not in my movie!" says Sidney, claiming her place not only as a new kind of female protagonist but as an auteur in an age when movies and life are indistinguishable.

of impotence and loss. *Scream*'s title, taken from Edvard Munch's famous Expressionist painting of 1893, evokes the inarticulate anguish of an alienated age, and the killer always wears a mask bearing its image. However, the *Scream* trilogy uses this image to capture the angst of its own historical times, where it expresses deep-rooted fears about changes in the family and the desire to blame women for the consequences of these changes, especially as they relate to boys and men.

The film establishes these themes in its opening sequence when Casey is home alone. Her parents return, but too late, as she is near death. In a horrific image of botched communication and the limits of technology to substitute for genuine contact, parents and child scream at each other into wireless phones but cannot connect even though they are in close proximity. Similarly, Sidney's father has left her alone and put her at risk. By also rendering him a suspect, the film taps in to heightened cultural awareness of violence and sexual abuse in the home and fathers as figures of potential risk to their daughters. He returns during the siege, but is unable to help his daughter. In an exaggerated image of paternal weakness, the killer ties him up with duct tape, rendering him even more powerless until Sidney rescues him. Indeed, the film's critique of idealized figures of masculinity is as telling as its reconstruction of femininity. All male figures whom a girl should trust—father, school principal, boyfriend, cop—are suspicious, silly, or weak. As the trilogy progresses, the cop develops stature as a new and gentler model of masculinity, but in the first film the only male who is both trustworthy and able to approach the killer on his own turf is Randy, the teen cinema buff who draws on his vast knowledge of pulp film to provide a metacommentary on the unfolding events.

Despite the presence of failed father figures, however, it is absent mothers who provide the foundational narrative enigma in the *Scream* trilogy. The first segment of *Scream* concludes with Casey gasping "Mom" as she dies, and the remainder of the trilogy becomes an investigation of the mystery of Sidney's mother's life and death. This mystery is only heightened when the killer discloses his motives, and we learn that Billy lost his mind when he lost his mother—all because of *Sidney's* mother, whose affair with his father drove his mother away. The film highlights the depth of Billy's obsession with his mother by having him refute current conventional wisdom about what creates violence and all other contemporary social ills: it is not movies, he insists, but mothers; movies only make killers more creative. Quoting pop psychology, he informs Sidney that "maternal abandonment creates psychopathology." This abandonment sends him on a rampage to punish all mothers and potential mothers.

Maternal abandonment triggered by maternal sex lies at the core of the *Scream* films, and both evoke powerful cultural taboos. Our culture likes its mothers "immaculate" and maternal sexuality unacknowledged and unrepresented, so Sidney's mother has ensured her own violent punishment and death by having sex outside marriage. (The same rules, of course, do not apply to fathers, and Billy's father doesn't warrant a mention for his role in the affair.) Throughout cinema history, a mother shown as sexual, especially outside marriage, is certain to suffer, possibly lose a child, and probably die by the end of the film. The 1990s have been particularly fixated on the missing mother, who, like feminism itself, becomes a scapegoat for the malaise of a generation brought up with divorce, low economic expectations, and empty houses. However, a more careful look at the trope of maternal abandonment exposes it as a stark ideological inversion of the social reality of teen lives, where in cases of divorce and blended families, it is more likely to be the father, not the mother, who is missing from the home.

Initially, the films provide very little information about Sidney's mother. Billy accuses Sidney of being a "slut . . . just like [her] mother," and Sidney acknowledges her own confusion about who her mother was and her fear of turning out like her. This fear suggests her vulnerability to the power of the double standard, especially as it applies to mothers. Her struggle, like that of

Gale Weathers (Courteney Cox) is a displaced maternal figure who literally saves Sidney.

all girls, is to know her mother not only as her mother but as a person in her own right, and as the trilogy advances, the focus intensifies around Sidney's quest to understand her own identity in relation to her mother's.

The trilogy takes its first step toward that understanding with the relationship between Sidney and Gale Weathers, played by another popular TV star, Courteney Cox (who played Monica on the long-running sitcom *Friends* [1994–2004]). Gale combines stereotypes of bloodthirsty tabloid TV and the ambitious woman, like the mother in *American Beauty*, both of which are targets of derision in our culture. *Scream*, however, succeeds in redeeming this unpopular figure without domesticating her. Gale is allowed the film's only successful romance when she falls in love with Dewey, a dim but endearing cop. She, not Sidney, was right in her suspicions about the first trial, concerning the murder of Sidney's mother, which left the real killer at large and an innocent man in prison. And by the end of the film, it is Gale, not any of the film's well-intentioned but helpless boys and men, who comes to Sidney's aid.

An accomplished woman a decade or so older than Sidney, Gale stands as a displaced maternal figure, a target for the conflicted feelings teen girls often have toward their mothers. This is clear when Sidney punches her the first time the two face each other early in the film, and again when they meet in *Scream 2*. Sidney's relationship with Gale, however, not only paves the way for her to renegotiate her more complex relationship with her mother but also models a kind of solidarity among women who can unite toward common goals despite their differences. In the first two films of the trilogy, Sidney and Gale never manage to like each other. But they do develop an uneasy alliance as they recognize they both want to survive, and in that way they suggest a kind of coalition politics for the Third Wave.

Scream 2

Scream 2 takes place a year later, in a college town where Sidney is studying drama and attempting to put her past behind her. She has a new boyfriend and a close girlfriend who is encouraging her to join a sorority. She is also preparing for her role as Cassandra in the college production of *Agamemnon*, the Greek tragedy of violence and revenge within the family. Like the *Scream* films, *Agamemnon* hinges on issues of maternal adultery and rebellion, the primacy of mother-daughter bonds, and the struggle between patriarchal and matriarchal orders. The film begins in a movie theater with the opening of *Stab*, a film based on Gale Weathers's book about the Hillsboro slayings. This film-within-the-film triggers a series of copycat killings that end when Sidney, once again, kills the killer after learning that it is Billy's mother Mrs. Loomis, who has been seeking revenge for the death of her son.[7]

Scream 2 is moodier and darker than the first film, with Sidney and other returning characters bearing the emotional scars of the events of the first film. It is also more ambitious in scope, making bold claims for popular cinema as a serious means of enacting a culture's most profound anxieties and myths. Most dramatically, with its use of Greek mythology and drama it links the teen horror film of today with a long tradition of respected dramatic and narrative antecedents. Popular audiences have always been drawn to sensationalistic treatments of highly charged subject matter on stage, page, and screen, from the tragedies and comedies of antiquity to the violent dramas of the Jacobean stage, the melodramatic novels of Dickens, and the action-packed, emotionally charged films of Spielberg.

Following the rule of sequels (spelled out in an early scene set in a cinema studies class), not only are the stakes higher in *Scream 2*, but the film's self-reflexivity even more layered and complex. *Scream 2* includes overt allusions to such classics of the genre as *Nosferatu* (1922) and *Psycho* (1960). *Stab* replays the events of the first film with its characters played by yet another set of actors. At its theatrical opening, an unruly audience surrounded by *Stab* posters and brandishing fake *Stab* knives (reminiscent of *Star Wars* light sabers) points to the ways popular culture commodifies real life tragedies by turning them into entertainment. The first characters introduced by the film are a young black couple who argue over Hollywood's racial politics. The woman, a cinema studies student, criticizes the horror genre for its exclusion of blacks and its violence against women. As if to underscore her point, the couple becomes the new killer's first victims, violently reasserting the genre's, and Hollywood's, narrative privileging of white characters. The casting delves even deeper into teen culture, drawing more stars from TV teen hits such as *Dawson's Creek* and *Felicity*, in addition to teen icons Tori Spelling playing Sidney in *Stab* and Sarah Michelle Gellar, the star of *Buffy*, cast against type as a defenseless sorority girl.

Masks—both literal and figurative—become an even more prominent narrative and visual motif worn to sinister effect not only by the killer but in the two spheres of Greek culture within film: actors performing *Agamemnon* according to traditional dramatic style, and the Greek social world of campus sororities and fraternities, with their celebration of outmoded styles of femininity and masculinity. The sorority girls put on femininity as a mask of silliness, superficiality, and the desire to please men at all costs. "Everyone thinks sororities are just about blow jobs, but that's not true," one vacuous-sounding girl explains to an unconvinced Sidney. The fraternity boys exemplify a masculinity defined by animal house carousing, violence, and loyalty to the exclusive all-male group at all costs. They wear actual masks when they abduct Sidney's new boyfriend Derrick, one of their brothers, to discipline him for giving a charm bearing his fraternity letters to his girlfriend. Derrick represents the possibilities of an evolving masculinity that must be excluded from the older order, and his ritual punishment by his "brothers" leaves him carved and bloodied, strapped crucifixion-style on a stage prop suspended high over the stage.

With Billy's mother, Mrs. Loomis, as the new killer, the trilogy deepens its investigation into motherhood, suggesting once again that even before the movies could be blamed for kids gone wrong, there were mothers. Hovering over the trilogy is Clytemnestra, the tragic queen of *Agamemnon* who is remembered for her many transgressions: her rebellion against her husband for killing her daughter, her eventual adultery, her death at the hands of her son, and the curse he bore for killing her. "I'm sick of everyone saying it's all the parents' fault," Mrs. Loomis rages. Then she acknowledges that the weight of that blame falls more heavily on mothers than fathers: "I was a good mother," she says. "You don't know what it's like to be a mother."

To be a mother is not an easy task in a culture where mothers can be blamed for loving too much or not enough, for being too present or not

Sidney as Cassandra: a powerful image of a new girl hero with not only the wits and physical courage to defend herself but a growing capacity to understand the cultural scripts that would define her.

present enough, for leaving their homes to work if they are middle class or for staying home to care for their children if they receive public assistance. Played by Laurie Metcalf with the controlled hysteria she brought to her role in the sitcom *Roseanne*, Mrs. Loomis doesn't collapse in despair over her losses but rears up as a demonic fury who becomes legible and even sympathetic within the horror genre.[8] A crazed Clytemnestra seeking revenge for the loss of her child, she is neither pitiable nor weak but a figure of superhuman strength who refuses to be a victim. Muscling herself to the center of the narrative, she usurps the place of the villainous male serial killer and stands face to face with the new Girl Power hero.

In *Scream 2*, Sidney also develops into a more mature and complex hero for the Third Wave. By casting her as Cassandra in the production of *Agamemnon*, the film identifies her with a figure of mythic stature, described by Sidney's drama teacher as one of the "great visionaries of literature" who was fated to see the truth but not to be believed. As in the first film, Sidney battles her own demons, which would wall her off from other people as a result of her emotional trauma. When Sidney attempts to beg out of the production, her drama teacher refuses to let her do so, reminding her and the film audience that she is a fighter, someone who has the courage to "face her fate" and embrace it. In a intense scene from the play within the film, a crimson-clad Sidney as

Cassandra stands out against the masked chorus, a powerful image of a new girl hero who not only has the wits and physical courage to defend herself but also a growing capacity to understand herself and the cultural scripts that would define her. This time when Sidney defeats the killer, she puts an extra bullet in Mrs. Loomis's head for good measure, and walks away with cool self-assurance.

Scream 3

The ghost of Sidney's mother, a structuring absence in the first two films, becomes the focus of the final film, which zeroes in on the mystery of Maureen Prescott's life and its meaning for Sidney. And if Scream 3 appears to lose some of the momentum of the earlier films, it brings the trilogy to a satisfying conclusion.

Scream 3 finds Sidney isolated once again in a bucolic setting where she takes calls for a women's crisis center. Meanwhile, Stab 3, based on the Windsor College killings, is in production in Hollywood. On the studio set, the masked killer strikes again, leaving photographs of a young Maureen Prescott, Sidney's mother, with each victim. When the killer starts calling Sidney, she travels to Hollywood where she begins to learn about a missing chapter in her mother's life: when her mother was her age, she had appeared in several horror films under the name of Rena Reynolds. In her final showdown with the killer, Sidney learns that he is Roman Bridges, who is both the director of Stab 3 and her half-brother.[9] He tells her that their mother ended her career after she had been raped and left pregnant by studio executives. Roman tracked her down four years ago, only to have her reject him as the child of someone who no longer exists. In rage, he turned on her and Sidney, the daughter the mother acknowledged, and masterminded the murders to follow. Sidney puts an end to the horror by killing him, and then returns to the mountains to take up her new life.

As the mother's story moves into the foreground in Scream 3, so does the story of Hollywood with which it is so closely intertwined. As if to signal the scope of its critique, the film begins with a helicopter roaring over the "Hollywood" sign in Los Angeles. And the film's self-reflexivity deepens to include practices within the film industry itself. Like the earlier films, Scream 3 abounds in references to other films and most of its action takes place on a Hollywood studio set that recreates the settings of the earlier films. Randy, the video buff who died in *Scream* 2, addresses the characters on a videotape to let them know that the final chapter of a trilogy differs from a sequel in its inevitable return to the beginning. Like Freud's return of the repressed ("The past will come back to bite you," Randy warns) and the great dramas of antiquity, film trilogies uncover past secrets and "unexpected backstories."

In a more subtle variation on this theme, a detective new to the story explains to Sidney that Hollywood is "always about death," a statement resonating with the very essence of film according to classic theories of cinema.[10] Indeed, *Scream* 3 is more a ghost story than a horror film, haunted as it is by Sidney's dead mother. Maureen Prescott appears as a narrative device in photographic images, as a ghostly hallucination in Sidney's mind, and as a key to Sidney's identity finally to be faced. Throughout she appears as a monstrous ghost, expressing the daughter's ongoing struggle to reconcile her conflicting ideas about who her mother was. On one hand, Sidney experienced her as "the perfect mother" at the heart of a "perfect family." On the other, she has learned about her mother's extramarital affairs, heard her judged a slut, and discovered that she had a secret life. This monstrous mother is the mother as seen and judged by the social world and the woman Sidney fears she will become. However, the film eventually provides a backstory to that judgment that redeems the mother and points an accusing finger where it belongs.

Sidney's final discoveries about her mother occur in a sequence that imagistically returns the viewer to the maternal body. Her struggle with the killer in the paternal mansion takes her down secret passageways evoking the birth canal, and she and Roman confront each other in a dark, womblike room. The real villain, it turns out, is not Roman, but John Milton, the powerful studio mogul and emblem of the patriarchal power Roman both exposes and desires.[11] As a legendary director of horror films, Milton made millions on young women like Maureen only to destroy them. Sidney learns that he was renowned for hosting wild parties for powerful men and young women seeking careers in the movies. At one of those parties, "things got out of hand," and Maureen ended up leaving Hollywood for good. Other references to the casting couch add weight to the film's critique of Hollywood's sexual politics and imply that they continue to the present. Carrie Fisher in a cameo role says her famous part of Princess Leia in the *Star Wars* films went to another actress who looked like her but agreed to have sex with director George Lucas. And the young woman playing Sidney in *Stab* 3 bitterly acknowledges having had to sleep with Roman to get the part.

By unmasking Milton as the real killer, Roman emerges at this point not so much as a monster but as the male victim of a cruel and exploitative gender system, an Orestes figure driven by the patriarchal order to commit the sin of matricide. The film portrays Sidney's killing of her brother as yet another chapter in her life that deepens her character, and the two clasp hands as he nears death. By linking his mother's later sexual history to the sins inflicted on her by a paternal figure who gave away her innocence, Roman demystifies the term slut. "She never got over it," he says of her Hollywood experience. And so Hollywood is "about death" not only in the effects of its flickering, ghostlike images, but also in the costs of putting those images on the screen. As Milton said in trying to defend himself, Hollywood is "not the city for innocence." While focused on Hollywood, however, the *Scream* trilogy points to the very essence of a culture in which women, from Monica Lewinsky to the sorority girls of *Scream 2*, see sexually servicing men as their most immediate route to power or even their only means of survival.

Maureen Prescott/Rena Reynolds is not only the victim Roman describes, however, but a rebel and a fighter like her daughter. "The bottom line is, Rena Reynolds wouldn't play by the rules," Milton says. Just as Sidney refused to follow the script of the classical horror film in *Scream*, her mother resisted the script for success in Hollywood. Moreover, Rena succeeded in rewriting her post-Hollywood identity in order to create a new life for herself—one that represented success for a woman of her generation. By the end of the film, and the trilogy, Sidney has completed a horrific journey into her own past and put the ghost of her mother to rest. The knowledge she has gained enables her to redeem her mother's life and expose the systemic injustices that had brutalized her.

The trilogy concludes at Sidney's mountain retreat, where shots of Sidney walking alone in a setting bathed in golden light return the film to an Edenic beginning. Dewey and Gale are present, along with the golden retriever who was Sidney's only companion at the beginning of the film. When Gale accepts an engagement ring from Dewey, the film reconstitutes the lost nuclear family, replacing the family of origin—with the repressed secrets and horrors implicit in the very structure of the nuclear family—with one that has battled openly and hard for its rewards. Sidney has conquered her demons of isolation, and leaves the door ajar, signaling her openness to a new life.[12]

For director Craven, the moral center of contemporary culture lies with girls, and in this trilogy Sidney has been assaulted on all sides by corruption and compromise.[13] By locating Sidney's most dangerous threat within her family and requiring her to commit fratricide to survive, the film creates a devastating portrait of female isolation and vulnerability. Female adolescence is a lonely place, especially for young women such as Sidney who develop an awareness of what it means to be a woman in our society. The trilogy's success in capturing that loneliness suggests one reason for its appeal to young female audiences. Sidney as a Final Girl is a figure of identification for girls, not boys, and in that way the trilogy stands firmly outside the tradition of horror Carol Clover documented. As with all Hollywood films, the ending reasserts the ideological promise of the perfect family, at home in a rural paradise. But the *mise en scène* renders the resolution surreal after the weight of the darkness and horror that have preceded it. In its generic context, the open door connotes not only Sidney's new security and openness to life but the possibility that some new ghost can rise up again to cause yet another chapter in the story. No happy endings are permanent, no closure guaranteed.

In Hollywood, collective histories are always retold as personal stories, and *Scream's* saga of the missing mother might well be seen as the repressed history of the women's movement itself and the injustices that brought it about. Sidney's journey forced her to face the historical realities of her mother's life when they erupted as horrors in her own. The trilogy suggests that history must be faced because to fail to do so threatens the present. The subtle erasure of historical consciousness is the surest way to take the teeth out of any liberation movement. Without knowing and remembering the world of their mothers and grandmothers, young women remain vulnerable to having to fight old battles once again. *Scream* explores the bonds that connect generations of women, but does so without sentimentalizing a daughter's acceptance of her mother. Instead it shows a daughter growing in her own strength through her experiences with the maternal figures in her life.

Buffy the Vampire Slayer

In 1992, a few years before *Scream*, a small movie appeared about a petite, pretty Valley Girl who discovers her special powers to slay monsters. The film, *Buffy the Vampire Slayer*, was created by Joss Whedon to challenge the horror film convention of the "little blonde girl who goes down a dark alley and gets killed."[14] The film did not attract much critical or popular attention, but in a few years, its themes of teen girl empowerment through violence returned with a vengeance, not only in *Scream* but also in the television series inspired by the earlier film. The television series *Buffy the Vampire Slayer* ran for seven seasons, produced the spinoff *Angel* (1999–2004) and spawned hundreds of tie-ins, from novels and comics to video games.

Buffy also helped usher in the era of post–network TV because, while its weekly audience of four to six million viewers was small by major network standards, it was enormous for the minor networks that carried it as their flagship program. *Buffy*'s fan base made up in intensity what it lacked in numbers, setting new standards for Internet-based creative and interactive engagement with media texts through blogs, fanfic, and vidfic, as well as exchanges with Whedon who, as executive producer and often writer and director, participated in online discussion groups.[15] The series's reach also extended into academia, where it inspired a score of academic books from a range of disciplines, including sociology, philosophy, and psychology.[16]

Envisioned by Whedon as a combination of *My So-Called Life* (1994–1995), the groundbreaking TV melodrama of teen angst to which I'll return in chapter six, and *The X-Files* (1993–2002), a cult series about the paranormal, *Buffy* interweaves the lives of its core characters, mainly teens from the Southern California suburb of Sunnydale, with dramas emanating from a vast universe of vampires, witches, and other nasty supernatural creatures. Buffy Summers, a cute, blonde teenager, discovers, to her dismay, that she has been chosen to become a Slayer, a destiny that falls to one girl in every generation. Despite its cheery name, Sunnydale exists on top of the Hellmouth, a passage to the underworld, so vampires and monsters of all sorts frequent the place. Buffy is guided by Giles, a middle-aged, British librarian who has been appointed her Watcher. She is also helped by her friends, a small group of fellow outcasts who include Willow, a brainy girl who eventually discovers her own powers as a witch. Buffy's circle also includes Angel and Spike, two vampires who are her major love interests. The series ends when Buffy, with Willow's help, activates an army of Potentials, or latent slayers, by sharing with them the power that had been limited to her. Together they defeat legions of demons in an apocalyptic battle that destroys Sunnydale and closes the Hellmouth.

Buffy's aesthetic and thematic impact begins with its identity as a television program. As television scholars long have noted, television lacks the aesthetic impact of film, but it has its own powers of seduction, which have continued to evolve as technological advances and economic changes alter how we consume moving images. Television is a domestic medium, a familiar presence in the home. Like commercial radio, from which most American television developed, it breaks stories into small segments typically interspersed with commercial breaks. Melodramatic cliff-hangers often precede these breaks to bring easily distracted viewers back to the story.

The distinction between the TV series, with its self-contained episodes, and the serial, connected narratively from episode to episode, has eroded in recent years, with many shows, like *Buffy*, achieving partial closure in each episode while carrying longer story arcs across many. In contrast to the feature film, television's serials know no limits of time, only those imposed by their ability to hold the interest of their viewers and the support of their sponsors. This format enabled *Buffy* to return week after week, year after year, expanding its universe with incremental layers of narrative interest and psychological complexity. And by bringing its horrors into the home, it demonstrated that vampires and other horrific monsters lurk everywhere, including where we feel most safe. Eventually *Buffy* included 144 episodes that spanned seven years and spilled into the online Buffyverse. As a result, it was able not only to follow its characters from adolescence to early adulthood, but also to endow their actions with mythical significance limited only by its writers' imaginations.

As with the *Scream* films, Buffy's protagonist is an ordinary teen girl who discovers her extraordinary strength when she is on the cusp of womanhood. Her drama is played out against the family romance gone bad, with flawed parents who do not protect her. Like *Scream*, it makes abundant references to popular culture. Both address themes of isolation and loneliness as their teenaged protagonists begin to absorb the sober realities of adulthood. But *Buffy*, fully embracing fantasy, ventures even further into literalizing its metaphors. *Scream* confronts the existential question of what it means to be human by using masks to allow characters to release their monstrousness, but the characters still remain human. In *Buffy*, sympathetic characters morph from human to monster then back in an instant, demonstrating the fragility of the boundaries between human and nonhuman. Buffy laments her isolation throughout the series, how she is set apart from all others, not "normal." However, the isolation most teens feel is in fact normal, and her discovery of it part of growing up. Through her doomed love for Angel, then her later romances with Riley and Spike, Buffy loses her innocence by facing adult truths: the reality of evil, and the insurmountable solitude of human existence.

Like *Scream*, *Buffy* is driven by the mysteries of sexuality, and the mixture of desire and fear it arouses in young women.[17] As *Scream* demonstrates, the boyfriend can be a killer. In *Buffy*, he's a vampire, which is even more frightening because his human form is so beautiful and his ways so seductive. The vampire embodies the connections between sexual surrender and death, and thus carries inescapable eroticism in shadings from the baroque to camp. With the dark and brooding Angel, *Buffy* offers its young female viewers the guilty pleasures of bodice-ripper romantic fiction. For a girl, the awakening of sexual desire means discovering that she will have to negotiate her sexuality within social structures meant to police her desire.

Buffy develops these themes through various aesthetic and formal means. First is the grotesque, long available for explorations of excess, liminality, and transformation, especially within the genres of horror, the slasher film, and the Gothic. In *Buffy*, vampires' bodies morph from the classical to the grotesque. Angel and Spike, in particular, capture the ambivalence of the grotesque because, alone among their species, they have the human ability to love. Hellmouth is a threshold, a permeable boundary between realms of the human and the monstrous. The series's *mise en scène* and cinematography use conventions of horror and film noir (moody, low-key lighting, a moving camera, off-screen space) to heighten suspense and horror.[18]

However, comedy is also associated with the grotesque, and *Buffy*, like *Scream*, tempers its visual violence with verbal humor—Buffy's clever send-offs to the monsters she slays, the sarcastic putdowns among the teens, and witty repartee between monsters and humans. This tone enables the series's fantastic elements to be read as tongue-in-check, an acknowledgment of its fans' sophistication in recognizing the demons on the screen as fabrications or metaphors for the real monsters of human life the series explores.

Like *Titanic*, Buffy is also deeply indebted to melodrama, which magnifies the experience and significance of the conflicts faced by its protagonist. In Buffy's world, there is no lack of moral clarity. Even though the affairs of demons and humans are hopelessly entangled, good and evil are clearly defined and opposed to each other. Steeped in arcane lore, *Buffy* recalls Peter Brooks's famous description of melodrama as the moral occult of a modern, desacralized age. This framework enables the series to elevate an average American girl's concerns, typically dismissed as trivial and inconsequential, to an apocalyptic level. The stakes are indeed high for this California teen, who, in episode after episode, notes with irritation or resignation that she must skip her homework *again* to save the world.

Buffy has inspired an abundance of writing, not only in the Buffyverse of fan fiction and commentaries, but in academia. Much of this writing praises the series for its treatment of female power, and its protagonist is built from two cultural traditions well-suited for postfeminist visions of Girl Power: the superhero and the dumb blonde. Whedon, Buffy's creator, was inspired by the character Kitty Pryde from the Marvel Comics series *X-Men*. The dumb blonde, such as Cher in *Clueless* or Elle in *Legally Blonde* (see chapter five), uses her power while maintaining, and often exploiting, her girly identity.[19] However, other scholars have questioned the series's complicity in conservative ideologies of class and gender, and its use of a straight, white, suburban middle-class environment to connote "normal."[20] For my purposes, *Buffy* falters most in its treatment of mothers.[21] The series reinforces cultural notions that teen girls are better supported by adult males than by their mothers, who have very little to offer them. As J. P. Williams notes in "Choosing Your Own Mother," "Buffy is overfathered and undermothered." The series's only reliable adult figure is Giles, a fantasy father whose bookishness codes him as largely asexual, removing the threat of incest that hovers over many father-daughter relations in Girl Culture and beyond.

Buffy's well-meaning mother Joyce quotes pop-culture authorities on parenting but is insecure as a single mother. Buffy initially keeps her new identity as a Slayer from Joyce, whose inability to see the changes in her daughter's life makes her appear foolish to both characters and viewers. As Williams notes, ideology expects mothers to instinctively understand their children. In "Becoming: Part 2," (season 2, episode 34), Buffy finally tells her the truth about her identity as a Slayer, but patronizes her at the same time: "Open your eyes, Mom. What do you think has been going on for the past two years?" This exchange anticipates a similar one in the film *Thirteen*, when the daughter rages at her mother for giving her the emotional space she has demanded. In another *Buffy* episode, "Helpless" (season 3, episode 46), Joyce is further infantilized when she is kidnapped by Zachary, a monster who hates women, especially mothers. The episode mocks the culture of mother-blaming and narcissism masquerading as self-improvement when Zachary says, "I have a problem with mothers. I'm aware of that." Yet, in a role reversal that typifies their relationship, Buffy has to act as the protective adult and rescue Joyce.

Other episodes suggest that Zachary's "problem" with mothers extends to the series. "Gingerbread" (season 3, episode 45) shows Willow's mother as even more self-absorbed and blind to her daughter than Joyce is to Buffy. In this episode, both she and Joyce are so threatened by their daughters' superhuman powers that they attempt to burn the girls at the stake, stoking the fire with piles of library books. This image associates the mothers with centuries-old practices of ritually burning perceived threats to a community. In Europe

Buffy the Vampire Slayer portrays mothers as fearful of their daughters' powers. Here, Buffy and Willow's mothers try to burn their daughters at the stake—the traditional method of executing witches.

and the American colonies, women who seemed to have undue sexual or supernatural power were burned at the stake as witches. And dictatorial regimes worldwide, including the Nazis, burned books to purge threatening ideas. The episode suggests that teen girls should fear their mothers, who are likely to be threatened by their emerging power as women. Recall, in *Mean Girls*, the father explaining to his daughter Cady that her mother is afraid of her.

In "Normal Again" (season 6, episode 117), Buffy vacillates between two apparent realities—one, her vampire-slaying life in Sunnydale, and another, her confinement to a mental hospital, where she has been diagnosed with schizophrenia for her "delusions" of power. Buffy cannot tell which life is real, especially since her parents insist that her reality—the monsters she fights, the weight of her destiny—is an illusion. This episode dramatizes the waning self-confidence many girls experience as they move through adolescence and learn to trust others more than themselves. While Joyce ultimately urges Buffy to believe in herself, she also appears as a gentler, more tender version of Rose's mother in *Titanic*, teaching her to submit to a patriarchal social order that will squelch her nascent efforts to assert her power.

Through Joyce, the series dramatizes the tensions between feminism's Second and Third Waves. Joyce's backstory associates her with the Second Wave. She came of age in the 1960s, participated in the civil rights and women's movements, works full time, and divorced Buffy's father. She represents what Buffy is defining herself against, especially the victim status the Third Wave often attributes to Second Wave. As Irene Karras argues, Joyce's anxieties about Buffy's independence suggest that when Second Wave mothers view their daughters as politically apathetic, they are mistaken. It is not politics generally, but another generation's politics, that hold little interest for young women. From this perspective, Joyce also represents an older generation's frustration at their daughters' haughty confidence that this time they'll do feminism right.

Joyce finally seems most important in the series as an idea, or a structuring absence. One of *Buffy*'s most acclaimed episodes is "The Body" (season 5, episode 94), wherein Buffy finds her mother dead and discovers that her superpowers can't bring her back. In his DVD commentary, Whedon notes his regrets that he forgot to include Joyce in opening shots of Buffy and her posse happily gathered around the Summers' dining room table. Joyce is off-screen, in the kitchen preparing food for them, and the sequence is meant to prepare viewers for the grief that will follow when she is gone. However, the omission is telling. If not by design, then by default, mothers drop out of the picture. Similarly, author Jess Battis, in *Blood Relations*, omits Joyce from the mini-profiles of nineteen key characters from *Buffy* and *Angel* that open his book on families in *Buffy*.

Rather than a fully realized exploration of a single mother's struggles to parent her teen daughter(s), Joyce comes to represent mortality, which Buffy must acknowledge as part of her growth as a superhero. Mothers, once again, seem incapable of escaping their archaic associations with life and death. In that way, mothers share some of the taboo around the mythic creature of the vampire. Both mothers and vampires intermingle life, death, and sex. Vampires don't die but they also don't really live (they are "undead"). Mothers, in giving life, also give death. It is not until Joyce dies that Buffy truly comes into her own, mature enough to fully assume her destiny as protector of her sister Dawn, her classmates, and the world. While the series attaches elements of the maternal to Buffy's role, its treatment of biological mothers or female elders mutes any suggestion that a girl's power might be enhanced with that of her mother and foremothers behind her.

The *Buffy* saga concludes with a postfeminist rallying cry about the power of individual choice, but it frames this choice as a collective one, recalling the Second Wave's insistence on sisterhood.

Interestingly, while evading the issue of mothers, *Buffy* reaches its fullest feminist power when, in its final season, it embraces the ideal of sisterhood, the rallying cry of the Second Wave. In "Chosen" (season 7, episode 144), the series's last episode, once again, the world must be saved, this time in a battle to end all battles. As armies of Ubervamps gather, Buffy calls together her own army of "slayers in training," girls whose power remained dormant "all because a bunch of men a long time ago decided it was so." The episode begins with Buffy wielding the feminine symbol of the scythe and splitting her evil enemy Caleb in half, from the crotch up. As the potential slayers gather before the battle, Buffy cuts her hand and they all cut theirs, bonding in a ritual of shared bleeding. The metaphor of blood, now evoking menstruation, has shifted from the vampiric sucking of life to the female power to reproduce it. Meanwhile, Willow gathers her powers to release the spell that has always limited the Slayer's power to one girl. In the climactic moment of transformation, power surges through Willow, who gasps in ecstasy "Oh, my god—dess," as her red hair glows white. A montage follows of girls worldwide, jolted as their latent power is unleashed. The ensuing battle ends in victory, and a new era of female power begins.

The episode's title "Chosen" and Buffy's key speech to her potential army invokes many levels of feminist and postfeminist discourse. When Buffy rallies the latent slayers, she says, "Make your choice. Are you ready to be strong?" conveying a postfeminist confidence in the individual's power to "choose" and the Third Wave's refusal of victimhood. At the same time, that choice is presented as a collective one, recalling the Second Wave's insistence on sisterhood as the basis for both individual and social change. Throughout the entire series, Buffy has bemoaned her destiny as something she never chose. Yet in this episode, Buffy embraces her fate as an act of volition. When she surrenders the power that has isolated her, she becomes part of an army of slayers who choose to claim theirs.

A Postscript on Vampires: *Twilight*

The vampire is an enduring and suggestive metaphor with a long history in folklore, literature, and cinema, and, as *Buffy* demonstrates, it has continued to exert its appeal in the postfeminist era. In 2008, Alan Ball, *American Beauty*'s screenwriter, created and produced HBO's *True Blood* based on *The Southern Vampire Mysteries*, a series of books by Charlaine Harris that follow the character Sookie Stackhouse. While *True Blood* has attracted attention for its rich mix of sex and violence, Stephenie Meyer's *Twilight* quartet, named after the first novel in the series (2005), has become a cultural phenomenon because of its devoted fan base of girls and women. The quartet has sold more than forty-two million copies worldwide and been translated into thirty-seven languages. *Twilight* became the bestselling book of 2008 and was adapted for film that year by Catherine Hardwicke, who, in 2003, directed *Thirteen* (chapter 6), another bold venture into teen girl desire.

Twilight (2008) uses the same tropes of vampires and the supernatural that *Buffy* does, creating a moody visual beauty with its spectacular Pacific Northwest setting and exploiting the region's Native American cultures for exoticism and mystery. But unlike *Buffy*, *Twilight* takes its Gothic darkness straight. And, unlike *Buffy* and *Scream*, franchises that were created by men, it bears the strong hand of female authorship. Hardwicke and Meyer, who was a Mormon housewife before earning celebrity and wealth with the quartet, clearly have their fingers on the pulse of what many girls want. On the basis of *Twilight*, that appears to be a femininity that is even more nostalgic than the fantasies played out in *Titanic* just over a decade earlier.

Twilight shares several conventions of the Girl Culture text. First, it puts female desire at its center, beginning with teen protagonist Bella's voice-over. It also recreates the family romance around a missing mother. Bella is the daughter of divorced parents. She lives with her mother and appears to be close to her, but she also sees her as "erratic and harebrained." To give her mother time alone with her new husband, Bella decides to move in with her quiet, distant father, who lives alone in the Northwest. Finally, like *Buffy* and *Scream*, the boyfriend is a (potential) killer, thus exploring girls' and women's attraction to the bad boy as well as their wish to believe that, at heart, he is good.

Unlike the other Girl Culture texts, however, *Twilight* teaches girls to live with unfulfilled desire. *Twilight* resurrects the horror film's convention of the Final Girl, rewritten in *Scream*. The film doesn't indicate whether Bella is a virgin, but her survival depends on her willingness to resist her passion for Edward, her beautiful vampire boyfriend; if Bella and Edward consummate their love, he may lose control of his vampire instincts and kill her. Desire always intensifies when its gratification is withheld, of course, but in *Twilight* gratification is never a possibility.[22] The film compensates for this by intensely eroticizing Bella's self-denial, but as long as she loves Edward and wants to remain human, she must remain in her liminal state of chastity, suspended between childhood and adulthood.

Edward rescues Bella whenever she is in any kind of danger, and the fantasy of a male lover with superhuman strength appeals not only to girls but adult women. Edward, in fact, is the ideal lover with a love that is strong enough to protect Bella from her own vulnerability to him. However, as Carol Stabile reminds us, the cult of masculine strength depends on a corresponding need to keep women weak. Bella has none of Buffy's or Sidney's physical bravery and strength but is clumsy and awkward. Her only strengths lie in her ability not to fear Edward and in her willingness to surrender to him and become a vampire. And more than *Buffy* and *Scream*, *Twilight* places its female protagonist in a world devoid of not only available maternal figures but close female friends. In gloomy *Twilight*, the pastel Girl World of gossip and prom dresses is a distant and surreal distraction from Bella's all-consuming love for Edward.

Once again, for a woman, love is all that matters. As Bonnie Mann writes (2009), recalling Simone de Beauvoir's classic treatise on femininity *The Second Sex* (1949), love is not merely an enrichment to a woman's life but existential, bringing her into existence. Mann also notes that as women have made gains in the public sphere, pressure has mounted to keep them dependent on men in the private. And so *Twilight* brings to light another dark side of postfeminism: the temptations of a femininity based on childlike passivity and frailty, and the tired notion that femininity and adulthood are mutually exclusive.

The *Scream* film trilogy and the *Buffy the Vampire Slayer* TV series, which have been the subject of most of this chapter, spin bloody tales of epic proportions. While the epic typically evokes nostalgia for an imagined time of wise fathers and noble causes (consider the blockbuster *Lord of the Rings* films), the *Scream* trilogy looks back on that time with anger, and *Buffy* looks forward to a new era when the authority of an elite old council of British males has been unseated by a "Revolution Girl Style Now!" in the words of riot grrrl band Bikini Kill.[23]

Feminism is never mentioned in the *Scream* trilogy, and only in passing in *Buffy*, but both address head-on the issues of representation, power, and sexuality that speak to Third Wave audiences. Like the Girl Power phenomenon, *Scream* and *Buffy* operate in the realm of myth rather than rationality, acting out scenarios of female desire, pleasure, and anger. Both abound in female characters who refuse to play by rules that would diminish them, from Maureen Prescott to Gale Weathers to Sidney in the *Scream* films, to Buffy, Willow, Faith, and the army of slayers in *Buffy*. If *Twilight*'s Bella acknowledges the tug of the old, these figures model a new femininity for Third Wave audiences: a girl who can protect herself through physical resources, who can claim power over her own sexuality, and who can express rather than repress her rage. This new girl hero knows her culture, from the legends underpinning its institutions to the popular culture and technology of her own generation, and uses the tools it offers as a means of rewriting old narratives that no longer serve her. Most important, she provides a suggestive model for contemporary feminism, combining *Scream*'s saga of a daughter's struggle to come to terms with her mother and *Buffy*'s utopian insistence on the possibility of sisterhood writ large.

How Reese Witherspoon
Walks the Line

5

My grandmother was one of the biggest
inspirations of my life. She taught me how
to be a real woman, to have strength and
respect, and to never give those things away.
—REESE WITHERSPOON, ACCEPTING
ACADEMY AWARD FOR BEST ACTRESS,
2005

Man, I don't like her.
—KEVIN SMITH, *SILENT BOB SPEAKS*, 2005

EVIN SMITH, the enterprising creator of *Clerks* (1994), *Mallrats* (1995), and other films popular among Generation X males, can't stand Reese Witherspoon. He devotes a chapter of his book *Silent Bob Speaks*—"The Unholy Tale of Greasy Reese Witherspoon" (53–61)—to his fantasy of egging her house because he finds her insufferable. "She's *faux* erudite as all hell, and condescending to boot," he writes (54). He knows this about her because he saw her snub one of his friends, and she appears not to think very much of his work. Not surprisingly, Smith takes an ironic tone, ensuring that his remarks will be read as tongue-in-check. However, that irony is also a bit *faux*, failing to conceal a subtext that demands a closer look. Why does Smith feel so strongly about her? Why does he feel compelled to take aim, in the essay's title, at her image of tidy blonde perfection? There's something about her that has touched a nerve. And not only with him.

By 2007, Witherspoon was commanding $20 million per movie and was ranked among the world's highest paid female stars.[1] This achievement should not have surprised anyone who had been paying attention to her since 1999, when *Election* established the essence of her ambivalent appeal in a culture made anxious by pretty, ambitious women. Even before that, she showed her exceptional talent and versatility as a teenager in indie dramas (*The Man in the Moon* [1991]) and dark comedies (*Freeway* [1996]). In 2001, she hit the big time with *Legally Blonde*, and then *Legally Blonde 2: Red, White, and Blonde* in 2003. In 2004, at the age of twenty-nine, she won an Academy Award for her performance in *Walk the Line*.

And yet, as Smith's sour tone suggests, Witherspoon's star text is not uncomplicated. Like Roseanne in the late 1980s and 1990s, she elicits strong responses, both positive and negative, suggesting her ability to tap into some of the deepest social anxieties of her time. Spanning the years of Girl Culture, Witherspoon's career dramatizes the contradictions of postfeminist culture and the limits it imposes on female unruliness. Encompassing elements of the protagonists from the preceding two chapters, her persona is an original. Sunny but vaguely menacing, it fits uneasily in old genres that cannot accommodate her combination of old-fashioned femininity with a fierce refusal to be anyone's victim.

These contradictions can also be found in related pop-culture trends involving men and boys, including the rise of Kevin Smith's slacker-centered empire (his "View Askewniverse" of films, blogs, books, and speaking engagements), the influence of fanboys in creating comic book–based franchises aimed at boys and young men, and the emergence of a new version of the venerable genre of romantic comedy, traditionally a sympathetic site for female unruliness.

New Yorker film critic David Denby identified this new romantic comedy as the "slacker-driven romance" and outlined its characteristics in his astute essay on Judd Apatow's *Knocked Up* (2006), a film he described as becoming a cultural event after receiving mostly raves from critics and grossing more than $90 million in its first three weeks.[2] In *Knocked Up*, a beautiful young career woman gets pregnant after a one-night stand with a chubby young man who spends his days with his buddies getting stoned and avoiding work. She decides to keep the baby and try to develop a romantic relationship with its father. By the time the baby arrives, the couple has fallen in love, the father has taken some steps toward adulthood, and the mother is now helping him with his fledgling business managing a pornography-rating website. One year after the film was released, Apatow topped *Entertainment Weekly*'s list of Hollywood's fifty smartest people for his inspired new formulation of comedy, notable not only in *Knocked Up* but *The 40-Year-Old Virgin* (2005) and *Superbad* (2007). Interestingly, Witherspoon, one the world's highest paid female stars, was not among the twelve women on the list.[3]

Typified by such films as *High Fidelity, Failure to Launch,* and *Wedding Crashers,* as well as others by Smith, Richard Linklater, and the Farrelly brothers (*There's Something About Mary*), the slacker romance rejects romantic comedy's belief in the equality of the sexes, retreating from battles of the sexes played by well-matched adversaries into fantasies driven by male fear of female ambition.[4] In the slacker romance, the female love interest is smart, accomplished, attractive, and serious, and the male protagonist desires her for all of these reasons. But he also fears her and the challenge she presents to his immaturity.[5] In most of today's Peter Pan films, young men refuse to grow up, or older men revert to adolescence. And if boys don't cry, these men do, often out of self-pity. And so the slacker hero takes refuge in a prolonged adolescence he shares with his buddies, similarly inclined fellows who, like him, may be poorly groomed, physically unappealing, and lacking in drive, but they're fun. As Denby writes, "It's as if Romeo and Mercutio had left the women and all that mess in Verona behind and gone off to practice their swordsmanship."

The slacker romance eventually maneuvers the male into growing up by fulfilling his fantasy that the woman with good looks and good sense loves him even if he has nothing comparable to offer her. As in *Knocked Up*, she may even lighten up enough to join him and his buddies in their juvenile pursuits, despite her commitment to her career and the responsibilities of mother-hood.[6] This scenario, of course, inverts the traditional pattern in which an unruly woman liberates the repressed male protagonist.

Focalized around male desire, these works evade the question of what attracts their female protagonists to such infantilized men, despite the small degree of charm or lovability some of them may possess—for example, the characters played by Hugh Grant in *About a Boy* (Chris and Paul Weitz, 2002), or Steve Carell in *The 40-Year-Old Virgin*, or even Paul Giamatti, suffering a midlife crisis in *Sideways* (Payne, 2004). In *Knocked Up*, women exist primarily as "bedmates and babysitters" (A. O. Scott 2007), kids are sentimentalized, and there are no credible models of adult masculinity. Even worse, when the fearful males are accomplished yuppies, these films often take a darker tone and resolve in tragedy (*American Beauty*) or madness (*American Psycho*). It would appear that appealing adult men have disappeared from the cinematic landscape, only to be replaced by hobbits, slackers, and psychopaths.

This chapter argues that Witherspoon's cultural power arises from her ability to capture the contradictory fantasies about women that are evident in the slacker romance and postfeminist culture in general. Her star text reads as both (conventionally) feminine and feminist, traditional and modern, the girl-next-door and a powerhouse high-achiever. Yet Witherspoon is not among the stars—Drew Barrymore, Cameron Diaz, Jennifer Aniston, Kate Hudson, Sarah Jessica Parker, Katherine Heigl—typically cast in the slacker films. Nor is she the "new Meg Ryan," as some reviewers claimed after *Legally Blonde*. The independent, ambitious, unruly feminist side of her star persona, established early in her career, lingers too insistently.

Witherspoon began her career playing a fierce Final Girl with the survivor skills of such Third Wave protagonists as Sidney of *Scream* and Buffy the Vampire Slayer. With *Legally Blonde*, she complicated her persona by adding a layer drawn from the postfeminist ideals of Girl World. This layer softened her "attitude" with girlish charm and her intelligence with the attributes of the dumb blonde. As she matured and became a wife and mother, her persona began to reflect the increasing conservatism of American culture in the wake of 9/11, as well as the persistent ideological pressure to force unruly girls into conventionality with motherhood. Finally, she became among the most powerful female actors in Hollywood by playing June Carter in *Walk the Line*, a role that transformed her toughness and strength from Girl Power into "Good Woman Power," that is, the power to stand by, and behind, her man.

Witherspoon as Postfeminist Star

The most important traits that define Witherspoon's persona are intelligence and ambition—traits that carry an unstable ideological charge because they are positive in a male but more threatening in a female. Before turning to the most important films of her career, here is a look at the other traits that emerge from a survey of her biography, major works, and the popular discourse around her.[7]

Intelligence: Witherspoon is the daughter of two accomplished professionals. Her father, a surgeon, graduated at the top of his class at Yale, and her mother is a professor of pediatric medicine. Witherspoon has been described as "acutely intelligent," and a prominent feature of her biography is that she spent a year at Stanford as an English major.[8] She is considered an outstanding actor of great versatility and professionalism, the recipient of numerous awards, and a possible successor to Meryl Streep as Hollywood's most talented female actor.[9]

Class: Witherspoon was raised in Nashville by the contemporary equivalent of Southern gentry, and her Southernness reads as both classy and trashy. On the one hand, it links her with tradition and social aristocracy. Her ancestor John Witherspoon, a Scot, was a signer of the Declaration of Independence and president of Princeton. She attended an all-girls' prep school and was a debutante.[10] Despite Kevin Smith's jab at her, she is considered well mannered. On the other hand, stereotypes of Southerners as "white trash" and "rednecks" undercut her pedigree, and in many interviews she says her Southern roots prevent her from being taken seriously.

Ambition: Witherspoon is known for maintaining tight control over her career and her image. The *New York Times* film critic Elvis Mitchell described her as "the most determined actress of the twenty-first century," and the *Daily Mail's* Paul Scott described her as "hiding a Machiavellian mind behind a Monroe countenance." At seven, she appeared in a TV ad, and at ten was modeling and acting part-time. In 2007, she made her first endorsement, for Avon Products, because of the company's involvement in research on breast cancer and domestic violence, and its use of a home-based, freelance sales staff of women. In her Academy Award speech and elsewhere, she speaks of her desire to do something that "matters," thereby enhancing her image as a woman of seriousness and purpose.

There is a strong correlation between her public persona and the characters she plays, most of whom hold themselves to high standards. After her success in *Election*, she turned down a number of roles in teen horror films. She currently runs a production company known as Type A Films, rumored to refer to her childhood nickname ("Little Miss Type A"). Witherspoon says the name came from her ability as a child to understand complicated medical terminology, but in claiming it, she also claims its connotations of obsessiveness and the desire for control.

Self-possession, confidence, and righteousness: In the words of one reviewer, Witherspoon has "all the confidence to play nasty girls and demon insurrectionaries. But you don't get $15 million a time for those outsiders" (Thompson 2007). And so, as her career has advanced, she has increasingly played characters who are positive, optimistic, and on the "right" side of moral conflicts. These characters don't achieve their goals through physical prowess like the Final Girls and action heroines that embody Third Wave ideals, nor do they use the more traditionally feminine means of sexual wiles. Instead, they survive, and often win, through character and will. Witherspoon's persona models a kind of female power based on tenacity and optimism. But like intelligence and drive, these qualities are ambivalent in women. Her tenacity can be read as frightening, and her optimism condescended to, especially in an era that favors the irony of *Scream* and *Buffy the Vampire Slayer*. But her talent for comedy tempers her righteousness while enabling her to play characters that painlessly score points against their enemies.

Beauty: Popular accounts of Witherspoon's appearance describe her with some inconsistency. Most call her beautiful but not glamorous, and while her blondeness conforms to racialized ideals of physical beauty, she is not associated with the kind of narcissism of blonde celebrities such as Paris Hilton. She is petite, with a "pixielike" or "elfin" face and "perky demeanor." Like Julia Roberts, her smile is often described as "megawatt," reinforcing a wholesome girl-next-door quality that moderates the threat of her intelligence and ambition. And though her eyes sparkle with an intelligence that contrasts with the vacant gaze of Britney Spears, her blondeness recalls the "ditzy blonde" stereotype which she used to propel her to stardom in the *Legally Blonde* films.

Femininity: Witherspoon's combination of normative femininity and ambition makes her the quintessential postfeminist star. She was a cheerleader as a teen, and cultivated a traditional image of domesticity by marrying (actor Ryan Phillippe) at twenty-three and having two children before she was thirty. (Before Phillippe, she had romantic relationships with Jeremy Sisto, Chris O'Donnell, and Mark Wahlberg.) Conservative columnist Michael Medved credits her box-office power to her cultivation of "distinctively feminine strengths" rather than the "sweaty brutality" of female action figures (2005). At the same time, Witherspoon credits her success to the strong, intelligent women in her life, especially her maternal grandmother, who instilled in her a love of reading but suffered from depression, which Witherspoon attributes to the few opportunities available for her to express her talents.

Sexuality: Sexual freedom is high among the values of the Third Wave, and as Ariel Levy argues, "hotness" now is as conventional a value for girls as niceness once was (2005). As a result, sex no longer carries the transgressive charge it did in the years leading up to Madonna's superstardom. Early in her career, Witherspoon played sexually precocious nymphets and she was once listed as one of "the world's sexiest women," but she has not cultivated a sexy image."￼ Indeed, one reviewer noted that "she's always been a somewhat prissy, demure, bloodless presence" (McGill 2004). Her star text offers the intriguing possibility of self-possessed female sexuality that is not based on danger (the *femme fatale*), vulnerability (the victim), or playing to the male gaze (the sexpot).

A rescuer, not a victim: Witherspoon is the quintessential Third Wave star in her refusal to appear a victim. She is the antithesis of Princess Diana, and despite one description of her as combining Katherine Hepburn's toughness with Goldie Hawn's vulnerability, she has rarely been associated with vulnerability. She has avoided the conventional celebrity misadventures in drugs, alcohol abuse, and multiple affairs that might leave her looking vulnerable, like Lindsay Lohan, Britney Spears, or Drew Barrymore. Men do not rescue her in her films. Bad things happen to the characters she plays, and they make mistakes, but they come out on top. Moreover, her characters often rescue other characters, or, increasingly, major institutions in need of reform, such as the legal system or U.S. intelligence operations.

Ordinariness: Witherspoon has avoided typical star scandals, but her brother's alcohol abuse and arrest for sexual battery in 2006 dented her appearance of perfection, as did the dissolution of her marriage in 2007, when she joined other female stars whose marriages fell apart soon after they won an Academy Award.[12] Rather than diminishing her star power, these events have only enhanced it, for, as Richard Dyer argues in his classic works on the subject, stars must seem not only extraordinary but like us (1977, 1997).

Phase 1: The Final Girl

Witherspoon began her career with a series of films that established her toughness, confidence, and frank sexuality, traits that later softened but remain essential elements of her persona. At fourteen, she delivered a remarkable performance in *The Man in the Moon* (Mulligan, 1991), a beautifully realized family melodrama. The film, the first of several that take advantage of Witherspoon's southern roots, develops a rare, unsentimentalized portrait of an imperfect but loving family. It is told through the point of view of Dani, played by Witherspoon, who enjoys a tender relationship with her older sister based on sharing secrets about the mysteries of their awakening sexuality. Displaying equal ease with comedy and drama, Witherspoon plays several types in *The Man in the Moon* that would become part of her persona, including the tomboy and the girl next door, but above all, she shows a centeredness and feistiness beyond her years.

Witherspoon's next major roles bring the confidence of her character in *The Man in the Moon* to a new level by pitting her against a series of men who appear normal but in fact harbor intense fear of or desire to control women. These films, which include *Fear* (1996), *Cruel Intentions* (1999), and *American Psycho* (2000), explore the desire of male protagonists across the spectrum of class to subject women to extreme forms of punishment. Far more than the slacker films, they show the male psyche confronting gender challenges it can manage only through violence, and Witherspoon's presence in them brings to her star persona a strong association with her refusal to appear a victim.[13]

The most riveting of these films is *Freeway* (1996), which was released the same year as *Scream* and has achieved cult status among fans of raw indie cinema. Whereas *Scream*'s Final Girl begins as a well-mannered middle-class teen, *Freeway*'s fifteen-year-old protagonist lives in an environment of drug abuse, prostitution, and foster care, her anger fueled by her knowledge that the social system is guaranteed to make her fail. Her nemesis is a child psychologist who is recognized as a pillar of the community but is really a serial killer. The film dramatizes the conflict between Witherspoon's character, who simply refuses to accept the killer's judgment of her social class as "garbage people," and a smug establishment that identifies with the killer more easily than with his victims, the girls he preys on from the underclass. *Freeway* never achieved the currency among teen girls that the *Scream* franchise did, but it deserves a place in the canon of Girl Power cultural texts for its exhilarating depiction of teen girl fury.[14]

Director Matthew Bright categorizes *Freeway* as "art-sploitation," and indeed, the film echoes John Waters's classics of grotesquerie *Female Trouble* (1974) and *Pink Flamingos* (1972). *Freeway* retells the Grimm's fairy tale of Little Red Riding Hood, emphasizing, according to Bright, its latent smuttiness. Witherspoon's character Vanessa lives with her mother and stepfather in a cheap motel off a freeway in Los Angeles. When her mother is arrested for prostitution, Vanessa decides to seek refuge with her grandmother. Along the way, she meets Bob Wolverton, the serial killer. When he attacks her, she shoots him and leaves him for dead, but he survives, grotesquely disfigured. She is sent to prison, escapes, and continues her journey till she faces Wolverton again at her grandmother's house and kills him.

The film's power, and fun, arise from its shocking juxtapositions of tone and content. Vanessa is an illiterate, gum-chewing, foul-mouthed teenager who wears her blonde hair in a tidy girlish braid that accentuates the openness of her face. She's "a Lolita with killer bees in her underpants, . . . but also a God-fearing innocent," in the words of one reviewer (Thompson 1999). "As played—spectacularly—by Reese Witherspoon," in the words of another, "Vanessa is an utterly flabbergasting mixture of propriety and bluntness. She's both naïve and wised-up, quick-tempered and unflappable, tough but not unappealingly hardened, ripe without ever going soft" (Taylor 1996). While ferocious enough to physically attack a detective who goads her with crude innuendo, she retains enough innocence to give Wolverton a chance to make his peace with Jesus before shooting him in the head. Her emotions, even more than those of most teenage girls, are labile and uncensored. She can enjoy a voluptuous kiss with her boyfriend, or sell sexual services in a businesslike way, or weep when Wolverton manipulates her into describing how her stepfather forced her to give him oral sex.

Above all, she is disarmingly honest, and she refuses to let adults insult her intelligence by assuming she can't see through their hypocrisy. As Wolverton reminds her, the law exists to protect people like him, not her, and the film proves him right. The press and legal system rally around him and his wife, played by a campy Brooke Shields, and the court sends Vanessa to a prison run by more sadistic authority figures, including a predatory lesbian matron straight from a classic B-movie. When the detectives assigned to her case badger her to change her story, she loses her patience with trying to explain the obvious: the truth is eternal, she says, and besides, if she didn't stop Wolverton, he'd kill some other poor girl, and then how could she live with herself?

Freeway exposes overlapping forms of oppression, showing common ground between poor whites and middle-class blacks. During her interrogation she admits to having been arrested for solicitation, and Detective Breer, who is black, accuses her of only "doing what comes naturally." She responds with a barrage of racial epithets and physical blows, forcing him to experience the same kind of prejudice he showed toward her. Already impressed by her record of petty crime, Breer develops even more regard for her when he discovers that her boyfriend, who died after giving her his gun, was black.

Throughout the film, Vanessa exhibits power over Wolverton that emanates from her confidence in herself. In one especially grotesque sequence, the detectives visit the hospital to question Wolverton, his face swathed in bloody bandages. The camera takes Wolverton's point of view as he looks up at a doctor and Detective Wallace, their faces distorted by a wide-angle lens. The sound track plays exaggerated sounds of Wolverton's life-support systems while he blubbers and sobs, just as he did when Vanessa was holding the gun to his head. Now he weeps because he will have to have a colostomy. When one of the detectives thrusts a photo of Vanessa in his face, the camera takes Wolverton's point of view so we experience her impact on him. He looks up to her eyes twinkling with mirth, her mouth in a grin, and her tongue protruding, a grotesque image that only intensifies his misery. Even in a silent photo, she mocks him, her self-possession only heightening his self-pity. The sequence concludes with Bob's wife in the foreground berating the detectives, and Bob continuing to wail while someone performs a degrading procedure on his backside.

In contrast, Vanessa never seeks pity, despite the hardships of her life. One of the film's most satisfying scenes occurs in the courtroom when Vanessa and Wolverton meet for the first time after their bloody encounter on the freeway. Wolverton, now totally helpless, is wheeled in with a bizarre contraption around his head, one eye swollen shut, and his drooling mouth wrenched into a crooked grimace. Vanessa turns to meet the gaze of his single eye, then rises in disbelief, recognizing the miracle she has accomplished: she has made Wolverton's formerly nondescript appearance reflect his inner monstrousness. She greets him with a shriek: "Holy shit, look who got beat with the ugly stick! Is that you, Bob? I can't believe such a teeny-weeny gun could make such a mess out of someone." Intimidated by neither him nor the legal system, she taunts and ridicules him. "You are *so ugly*, Bob!" she howls, showing no fear. Wolverton licks his lips in suppressed rage as she goads him to think of her every time he has to empty the "big old shit bag" he now has to carry around. A police officer quiets Vanessa, but her outburst has only convinced the judge of her guilt. Vanessa refuses to show remorse for an action that saved her life. But the court cannot conceive that a girl who is so fearless and spirited—who so violates the ideology of good girlhood—could be innocent. *Freeway* proves Wolverton right.

"Little Red Riding Hood" tells of a girl's journey to her grandmother's house, intended in *Freeway* to be a refuge from a terrible social system. But by the time Vanessa reaches her destination, Wolverton is waiting for her, along with grandma's grotesque corpse. Again, Vanessa does not need rescuing. She arrives ahead of the detectives and battles it out with Wolverton by herself. The film concludes with Vanessa killing Wolverton and winning over the two cops, who have learned, through her, about their own prejudices against white working-class girls.

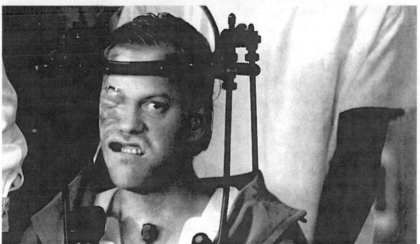

ABOVE: Reese Witherspoon's portrayal of Vanessa in *Freeway* adds to the toughness of her persona. Here she taunts Wolverton in the courtroom: "Holy shit, look who got beat with the ugly stick!" BELOW: Vanessa has turned Wolverton's world upside down by rendering him physically grotesque and totally helpless.

There is no motherline to protect girls in this universe—or, for that matter, in the fairy tale. Even if Vanessa had been able to save her grandmother from Wolverton, it is not certain what kind of maternal care her grandmother could have given her. As Vanessa explains, her grandmother and mother were estranged because of a past incident in which one threw acid at the other's face.[15] In *Freeway*, the villain isn't a big bad wolf but a social system that creates environments so beset by violence and poverty that the vulnerable prey on each other.

While in prison, Vanessa finds a friend in Mesquita, a Mexican girl who tried to bully her and ended up with a broken nose. Mesquita eventually escapes with Vanessa and voices the film's most explicit message of Girl Power, couched in postfeminist disavowal: "I don't wanna get all feminist and shit, but one thing I learned in jail is, girls gotta help other girls—especially convict girls—or they'll be dead." Sisterhood is powerful, and the girls help each other out. But Vanessa survives because of other attributes closely associated with Witherspoon's star persona. She is smart and resourceful. She refuses to be a victim despite the harsh circumstances of her life, and instead becomes a rescuer herself. She is willing to stand up for the truth and to fight to protect not only herself but Bob's other potential victims. She is not intimidated by authority, and she defends herself verbally and physically. She is on the right side ethically, righteous without being self-righteous. And, as she notes during the prison sequence, all she needs to survive is her will.

In the same year as *Freeway*, Witherspoon performed another extraordinary venture into male pathology with two men locked in a perverse and violent battle over control of her character. In the thriller *Fear*, she plays Nicole, the sixteen-year-old daughter of divorced parents. She moves in with her father Steve and his new, younger wife, and falls in love with David (Mark Wahlberg), a good-looking but troubled young man with a dangerous streak of possessiveness and violence. An Oedipal battle ensues between Steve and David, who then lays siege to the family house with his lowlife friends. After a prolonged and violent battle, Nicole drives a stake through David's back.

Fear recalls many of the films and TV shows already discussed in this book—Nicole dispatches David with a Buffyesque blow, and David's childhood resembles Vanessa's in *Freeway*. Most intriguingly, the film brings the incestuous dynamic of *American Beauty* into the open, barely veiling the sexual motivation behind the father's desire to protect his daughter. *Fear* literally removes the mother from the scene—she is three thousand miles away—and replaces her with an inadequate substitute, clearing the way for an explicit triangle between father, daughter, and the daughter's boyfriend. The film ensures that we're on the father's side by proving him right about the boyfriend. But by taking the daughter's point of view, it shows the father to be less upstanding than he first appears.

Like *American Beauty*, *Fear* shows the affluent, almost perfect family to be troubled from the outset, with the patriarch's façade of confidence, virtue, and physical strength beginning to crumble. Trouble erupts when even a weak patriarch leaves town, but the family is already endangered because the mother's absence has left a vacuum waiting to be filled by uncivilized maleness. The film opens with Steve charging toward his house, gasping for breath, after a jog that has pushed him nearly beyond his limits. Later, when Nicole's boyfriend goes bad, Steve is powerless to help her. During the siege, he becomes as impotent as Sidney's father in *Scream*, and, like him, ends up bound in duct tape while his daughter battles for her life. He also resembles the teacher in *Election*, losing his authority because he has compromised his morals. Eventually Steve breaks free and sends David flying out the window, but only after Nicole has delivered the decisive blow.

In *Fear*, Witherspoon's character displays key traits of the Third Wave protagonist. She shows the same physical prowess she did in *Freeway*, fighting David and his scary friends with ferocity. She also shows a ripening sexuality that will continue to be part of her persona for the next several years. Straddling innocence and experience, she is confident beyond her years. She receives David's sexual attentions with steady control, resisting them until she is ready, then welcoming them with casual self-possession. Like other Witherspoon characters, Nicole is no innocent victim. She plays an active role in creating her troubles and she stays with David in part to rile her father. But she creates her own solution as well. The "fear" of the film's title refers to the terror of a wealthy family facing an assault by a crazed and wounded figure of working-class masculinity. But it also refers to the anxiety of the middle-aged male, no longer able to control his daughter.

Phase 2: *Election*, or the Final Girl Goes Establishment

Alexander Payne's *Election* (1999) is the urtext of Witherspoon's star text, and of Witherspoon's major films, it most clearly lays out the tension at the heart of both her star persona and the slacker comedy—the anxieties women with ambition, intelligence, and drive raise in men who are struggling to redefine masculinity in the postfeminist age.[16] Based on a novel by Tom Perrotta, *Election* was partially inspired by the 1992 presidential race, and London film reviewer David Thompson described Witherspoon's character, the high-school overachiever Tracy Flick, as the "young hard bud of Hillary Clinton in the making" (1990). The film was resurrected during the 2008 presidential campaign in "Hillary's Inner Tracy Flick," a video in the online journal *Slate* V. The video mocked Clinton by intercutting scenes from *Election* with clips from her campaign and that of her opponent Barack Obama, whose casual charisma, as he romped in the surf, contrasted with Clinton's matronly drive. The montage emphasizes the obsessiveness and wounded sense of justice shared by Clinton and Tracy Flick, who believe they deserve victory because they work so much harder than their more popular opponents. In the video, both Tracy and Clinton come across with an intensity that borders on hysteria.

Witherspoon's earlier films delivered uncomplicated entertainment by casting her as characters who survive freakish circumstances because of their feisty determination. That determination becomes more ambivalent when a perky blonde teenager in a Midwestern high school aims it at a political process considered to be the foundation of the American way of life. *Election* tells the story of teacher Jim McAllister and his battle of wills with his student Tracy Flick, who wants to become student body president. Jim tries to stop Tracy by rigging the election results but is exposed and loses his job. Years later, Jim is still struggling to rebuild his life, but Tracy has become a polished political professional in Washington, DC.

Many reviewers read *Election* as a gender-neutral exposure of a certain kind of political animal, unlikable but unbeatable. The film spares none of its characters, including Jim, played by Matthew Broderick thirteen years after his role in the teen classic *Ferris Bueller's Day Off*. Yet the film aligns its viewers' wry sympathies with Jim more than Tracy. Tracy carries the weight of the film's satire of both the U.S. political system and mainstream America's suspicion of excellence, and it matters that she is a girl and that the character who wants to bring her down is a bland and ordinary man. In *Election*, there is no mistake that girls with the will to win run the risk of becoming male-devouring monsters. Ruthless in her pursuit of power, entitled, unsentimental about sex, Tracy behaves like a man. And worse, she turns her male victims into women—weeping failures at both love and work, defenseless against the Tracys of the world, their only refuge in passivity and other aspects of slackerdom.

The DVD menu image of *Election* captures the key tension in Witherspoon's star persona: men's anxieties about being "devoured" by newly empowered women.

Despite its setting in a high school, then, *Election* is not a teen film. There is no depiction of Girl World here, or exploration of Tracy from the perspective of other girls or her classmates in general. Instead, *Election* tracks with fascination the impact of a powerful girl on the men around her.

The DVD's menu graphically establishes the film's stakes: Tracy's cheery face appears in a big, open-mouthed grin. Her eyes are bright. Her gaping mouth, colored with red lipstick, surrounds a small image of Jim's face. *Election* does not construct Tracy as sexy, but this vaguely demonic image evokes the vagina dentata and sexualizes the danger she presents to her male teachers. It also recalls the photograph of her character in *Freeway*, an image that tormented the man who tormented her. With this exception, the film never fragments Jim's body or manipulates it with cinematic special effects, but it uses many stylized techniques, including freeze-frames and composite images, to render Tracy visually grotesque. Flattened images of Tracy's head cut off from her body haunt Jim's sleep and enter into his sexual fantasies, where he hears her saying, "Fuck me, Mr. McAllister." Freeze-frames hold her face in unflattering poses while Jim expounds on her in voice-over. *Election* gives voice-overs to several characters, including Tracy, but Jim's voice opens and closes the film, in contrast to the Girl World comedies that privilege the perspectives of their female protagonists.

Defining the two characters who will dominate the film, the opening cred-it sequence begins with the rhythmic off-screen sound of an irrigation system mechanically pumping an arc of water across the school field, suggesting the film's interest in masculinity, if not male sexuality. (In a related image of a mu-seum display toward the film's end, Jim asks, "What happens to a man when he loses everything?" over a medium shot centering on an early proto-human man's penis.) Jim is running in the field, and he will soon be on the run from Tracy's drive and the consequences of his own weakness. This workout se-quence recalls the opening of *Fear*, as well as the scenes in *American Beauty* that show another middle-aged man channeling his frustration, rage, and lust into physical exercise.

The tension created by the sound of the irrigation system returns moments later with yet another barrage of rhythmic sounds. In a series of rapid shots, Tracy's hands slide across metal poles that look like weapons as she snaps the legs of a card table into place. With mock-ominous nondiegetic music playing and the credits continuing to roll, she drops sticks of gum into a glass bowl, taps the points of her pens, and one by one places three legal pads on the table, nudging them into perfect order. An overhead shot holds long enough for viewers to read the happy faces on the top of each pad, followed by "Tracy Flick for President." Throughout the film, images such as these—tightly com-posed, often symmetrical and internally framed—convey Tracy's excessively controlled character.

Jim embodies the film's sense of male victimization and impotence, a sen-sibility articulated more explicitly in the slacker films. He is unable to get his bored wife pregnant, and his first attempt at an affair leads to catastrophe. Wherever he turns, he finds the world out to get him, from the vending ma-chine that eats his money to the bee that stings his eyelid while he waits for a tryst that never happens. The sting finally renders him as grotesque as Tracy, but unlike her, he appears pathetic and defeated. He is not entirely a victim, however, but knowingly and mock-tragically creates his own misery. He ac-knowledges a fundamental immaturity in people like him who are attracted to teaching high school. He says in voice-over, "They teach because they never wanted to leave high school in the first place," while the image track shows him playing in a garage band with male buddies. Like the slacker, he does not want to grow up. Above all, his description of himself as an expert on "moral and ethical situations" ensures that he will soon be exposed for his hypocrisy.

Jim's fate is sealed when he observes Tracy's effect on his best friend Dave

Novotny, another teacher, who had an affair with her. The film introduces Dave with his direct address to the camera about Tracy—"Her pussy gets so wet you won't believe it!"—establishing in an instant his lack of ethics and Tracy's "excessive" sexuality. From the outset, the film portrays Dave, not Tracy, as the victim of an exploitative situation he initiated. Dave's seduction of Tracy unfolds without eroticism or portentousness, in contrast to the aborted seduction in *American Beauty*. Tracy concedes that she may have been vulnerable to Dave because she grew up without a father, but—again, no victim—she dismisses the idea, and treats their relationship with nonchalance. Adult men play no serious role in her life. Dave, on the other hand, falls pathetically in love with her. When he starts trying to look like a playboy, he appears ridiculous. And when he's caught, he tries to justify the affair with sobbing declarations of his innocence ("We're in love!"). In the end, he loses his job and his wife, and leaves town to move in with his parents, another adult man who can't function in a world with girls like Tracy.

Tracy triumphs, even though the odds are stacked against her. She is young, female, and has none of the class advantages of her opponents in the school election, or of her classmates at Georgetown, who are smart and ambitious like her but "spoiled little rich kids." Often, the camera draws attention to Witherspoon's tiny size. One shot through a wide-angle lens shows her diminutive form at the end of a long corridor. Another shows her behind the wheel of a car, her face barely visible above the steering wheel. However, she makes up in will for what she lacks in size, and the film endows her with a demonic energy that is evident not only in her grin but in her childlike explosions of emotion—when she hops for joy, or rips down her opponents' posters with such force that she bloodies her hands. When Jim tries to expose her, she out-intimidates him. "Are you lecturing *me*?" she asks him, then reminds him of the hypocrisy of teachers who lust after their students and lets him know that Dave created his own misery by getting "all mushy" about her, "like a baby." Jim can't stand Tracy not only because she beats him at his own game, but because her very personality is an affront to him. Her lack of irony and cynicism, her hand raised so insistently because she knows she has the right answer, are a rebuke to his own mediocrity.

If an ambitious girl is dangerous on her own, she is even more so in league with other women, and *Election* completes its depiction of men on the run by showing women's treachery when they join forces. Tracy lives in a rare movie household in which the missing parent is the father, and mother and daughter

In *Election*, Tracy indulges in childlike explosions of emotion. By making her energy appear demonic, the film pathologizes her drive.

are not at war with each other. Tracy says she loves her mother because she supports her drive to excel. Indeed, the film implies that it is the absence of the father that makes Tracy strong. Her mother, who tells her, "girls have to work twice as hard as boys," wears the face of feminism in the film. But that face is subtly discredited by her Nietzschean view of human nature ("the weak sabotage the strong") as well as the suggestion that she is over-involved in Tracy's life. Nonetheless, Tracy and her mother make a powerful pair. Similarly, Dave's wife Linda not only rejects Jim after having sex with him, but she tells his wife about it. When Jim sees the two of them at his home and his wife closes the door on him, he doesn't even try to explain himself to her.

By the end, Tracy has shown some small vulnerability. She notes that she has no friends and is perplexed about why, given all that she has done for her class. Yet this loneliness doesn't motivate her to change, and she moves confidently along her path to success. Jim hasn't changed either. When he sees her from a distance in Washington, DC, he tries to convince himself that he is no longer angry at her, and that he even feels sad about her "pathetic life." As his voice rises, however, the anger he has had toward her from the outset erupts: "Who the fuck does she think she is?" he says, and throws a soda can at her limo, in a juvenile effort to strike back at her once again. When the limo stops, though, he makes a hasty retreat, showing that he is as weak as ever.

Phase 3: *Legally Blonde*, or Girl World Changes the World

It is unlikely Witherspoon could have achieved the stature she did by continuing to play tough and scrappy characters like Tracy, and in his review of *Election*, David Thompson asks what will happen to her when she is too old to play "high school Medusas" (1999). One answer is the *Legally Blonde* films, in which she plays a character who continues Tracy's path to power, first to Harvard Law School then, again, to the nation's capital. In the postfeminist era of sexual freedom, women's threat to men arises less from their sexual power than from their access to places like Harvard. To defuse that threat, Witherspoon creates a character that retains the optimism and confidence she has established in her persona but softens its hard edge.

As Elle Woods, she plays an adorable, ultra-femme sweetheart with broad postfeminist appeal. Whereas phallic Tracy reinforced the corruption of our society's institutions of power, Elle redeems those institutions with a beautiful and radiant femininity much like Cher's in *Clueless*. A sorority girl from Southern California, "Elle" is the eternal "she," uncomplicatedly feminine. At the same time, Elle retains a vague echo of Tracy's phallicism with her surname "Woods." In a quintessential postfeminist move, *Legally Blonde* uses a minor character, activist Enid Wexler, to depict the Second Wave as amusingly passé, while allowing Elle to have the best of both worlds. Elle sets high professional goals for herself while considering *Cosmopolitan* her Bible.

As Elle Woods in *Legally Blonde*, Witherspoon shifts her persona from horror's Final Girl toward comedy's effervescent woman on top, whose radiant femininity redeems patriarchy's corrupt institutions.

Legally Blonde follows Elle after her boyfriend Warner dumps her before he heads to Harvard Law School. She decides to win him back by getting admitted to Harvard herself. The film tracks her increasing confidence as she discovers her intelligence, overcomes numerous obstacles, and gains the love of Emmett, a lawyer who respects and values her. In *Legally Blonde 2: Red, White, and Blonde* (2003) Elle is now practicing law in Boston. In planning her wedding to Emmett, she finds her dog Bruiser's mother held captive in a cosmetics testing facility. She launches a successful campaign to ban animal testing, and in the process inspires a jaded Washington to remember its idealism.

Like *Clueless*, the *Legally Blonde* films place a sympathetic depiction of Girl World within the narrative structure of romantic comedy, showing yet again the feminist potential of the genre. By moving toward romantic comedy, Witherspoon's persona shifts from horror's Final Girl to comedy's effervescent, unruly woman on top, who brings a revitalizing energy and style to the bleak, repressed world of male-dominated institutions. But even more than *Clueless*, these films subordinate the romantic love plot to another that follows the female protagonist's discovery of herself. In fact, the films' titles are a pun on "legally blind," suggesting Elle and those around her have yet to see past her dumb blonde exterior to the intelligence within.

Elle's power begins with her identification with Girl World, where she developed the skills and the network of support to take on the stuffy and corrupt institutions of the establishment. Here, Girl World is a utopian place with none of the meanness of *Mean Girls* or cutthroat ambition of *The Devil Wears Prada* but many of the values of the Third Wave, including the pleasures of normative femininity and female culture. The tension between Girl World and the establishment is heightened by a West Coast/East Coast opposition. In L.A., Elle basks in an ever-sunny setting of movie star sightings, swimming pools, and squealing girls who live in a sorority house that is a vision of pink fluffiness. Despite their apparent superficiality, the sorority sisters become formidable when they join forces to help Elle prepare her application. Later, in Cambridge when her life begins to fall apart, Elle finds similar support in the female space of a beauty parlor. She bursts in and asks for an "emergency" manicure, and within minutes she and Paulette, the manicurist, are bonding over intimate confidences. Elle is restored by the comfort of physical touch and the common language the women share, along with the kind of warm human contact nowhere to be found at Harvard.

The pleasures of the manicure also suggest the transformation of Witherspoon's persona into an icon of glamorous femininity. Throughout, Elle wears fashionable outfits, almost all in shades of pink, and her long blonde hair is styled in at least forty different ways. Especially after her move to Cambridge, glamour lighting highlights her radiance against the dreary backdrop of dark, wood-paneled rooms. Warner tells her he needs a "Jackie, not a Marilyn," linking her with the dumb blonde, and she constantly fights the assumption that she is neither smart nor serious because she is cheerful and blonde. This, of course, is a joke on Witherspoon's star persona, already encoded with an intelligence that Elle begins to show when she scores four points higher than she needed on her law boards. Elle can begin the film as a dumb and shallow girl because, played by Witherspoon, we know she's not. Elle displays other aspects of Witherspoon's star persona in her refusal to be a victim. She follows Warner to Harvard, but she doesn't chase him when she's there, and eventually she dumps him. Nor does she let herself appear vulnerable, despite the many humiliations she suffers. "I am not afraid of a challenge," she asserts in class, when Warner's new fiancée begins to sabotage her.

From Elle's point of view, Harvard Law falls short for many reasons. It's "serious, boring, ugly," in her father's words. Even worse, it's a corrupt bastion of male privilege, as Elle discovers when her male mentor pressures her to trade sexual favors for professional advancement. Later she learns that Harvard admitted Warner because of his family connections, despite his lack of qualifications. Most of all, the institution of the law fosters an ideology of competition that teaches individuals to sacrifice others to get ahead.

What the law needs—as does the government, in *Legally Blonde*'s sequel—is a major dose of Girl Power, exemplified by Elle. That means values traditionally associated with the feminine: intuition over reason, everyday knowledge over book knowledge, cooperation over competition, and idealism over cynicism. The film's dramatic climax comes when Elle defends a former sorority sister, a fitness guru, against a murder charge. She wins the day by putting these values into action. She trusts her intuition (women who exercise have high levels of endorphins so they don't want to kill their husbands). She uses her everyday knowledge about beauty regimens to expose the guilty party for lying ("The rules of hair care are simple and finite"). She displays integrity over cynicism (she honors the confidence of her sorority sister even though she has reason to betray her). And rather than pursuing the case alone, she brings in the resources of friends who have come to trust and admire her.

While *Legally Blonde*'s celebration of Girl Power is a valuable perspective in the postfeminist age, the film can be charged with sentimentalizing sisterhood in ways that recall the Second Wave. As embodied in the sorority system, sisterhood seems untroubled by differences of class. This absence can be explained by the same conventions of romantic comedy that influenced *Clueless*, and the depiction of the beauty parlor seen as an effort to imagine a utopian space of class-free female intimacy, where a Harvard law student can become best friends with a middle-aged manicurist whose ex lives in a trailer. The film's treatment of race is less successful, however. Nonwhite characters are almost invisible until a sequence in the beauty salon when Elle teaches a group of women the "bend and snap" move for getting a man's attention. As the demonstration shifts into a production number, several African American women rise from their seats to dance with abandon, reinforcing stereotypes about African Americans as natural entertainers. *Legally Blonde 2* places more black characters in supporting roles. But in fetishizing Witherspoon's blondeness, the films also fetishize her whiteness and, like *Titanic*, the WASP establishment they overtly skewer.

Most interestingly, however, *Legally Blonde* models a strong connection between the Second and Third Waves. The final sequence of the film, which is set two years later, suggests a model for intergenerational feminism by showcasing the bond that has developed between Elle and Professor Stromwell (Holland Taylor), who exemplifies the Second Wave feminist. Commanding and confident, Stromwell has succeeded in the male bastion of Harvard Law School by accepting it on its own terms. She initiated Elle into the cutthroat competition of law by humiliating and expelling her from class for being unprepared. In contrast to Meryl Streep's Prada-wearing devil, she wears understated attire that minimizes her femininity, and her career has probably cost her a personal life. However, when Elle was ready to return to California in defeat, it was Stromwell who stopped her, in the female refuge of the beauty shop. Stromwell's stern, maternal admonition was really an expression of confidence that helped Elle rediscover her own determination.

With obvious affection and warmth, Stromwell introduces Elle to the graduating class as their elected speaker. "I am sure we're going to see great things from her," she says. The two embrace, then Elle begins her speech with an anecdote about her first class at Harvard, when Stromwell—a "very wise professor," she says—quoted Aristotle to define the law as "reason free from passion." In a point-of-view shot, Elle looks off-screen to Stromwell, who bows her head and smiles. Elle continues—"with no offense to Aristotle"—by making the case for passion, in law as well as life. Her point is less important here than the fact that Elle has not only learned crucial lessons from her elder but has made them her own, and with Stromwell's blessings.

Legally Blonde's Professor Stromwell (Holland Taylor) is a tough but supportive maternal figure. Through her relationship with Elle, the film models a strong connection between feminism's Second and Third Waves.

With the optimism characteristic of Witherspoon's persona, Elle urges her class to have "faith in people. And most importantly, you must always have faith in yourself." These words suggest a postfeminist endorsement of individual power over political action. However, in the film's context, they should be read as Elle's own success in transcending the low expectations she internalized as a pretty blonde girl. Elle discovers the new rewards of using her intellect to support values she believes in. And she does not have to outgrow Girl World, as *Clueless* requires of Cher, or reform it, as in *Mean Girls*. Instead she takes it with her to change the "serious, boring, ugly" world of the male establishment.

Legally Blonde 2, the first film produced by Type A Productions and Witherspoon's first major-studio star vehicle, continues the project of *Legally Blonde* and offers many of the same pleasures. But with Elle now a successful lawyer, the first film's "fish out of water" premise is more strained, and the sequel relies more on romantic comedy to motivate its plot and bring it to closure. It also relies on the feel-good message of the first film—"Have faith in yourself, have faith in others, and together we can make the world better"—but now aimed even higher. Using the values of Girl World, Witherspoon takes on the role of rescuer, saving not only the animals she has targeted in her bill but also a system of government that has lost its idealism. Elle, once again, is successful in rallying the support she needs, and the film ends with her delivering a motivational speech to Congress about why citizens should engage actively in the political process: "Speak up, America. And remember, you are beautiful!"

At this point, Witherspoon's star text is continuing to take on power. In the film's penultimate shot, as Elle and Emmett drive away from their wedding, Emmett asks her where she would like to live now. She turns to the White House, and winks at the camera. But that persona has already begun a subtle domestication. Pink Power prevails, but only in the service of the Red, White, and Blue.

Phase 4: *Walk the Line* and Beyond, or Unrepentant Motherhood

Three years before *Walk the Line*, Witherspoon appeared in *Sweet Home Alabama* (Andy Tennant, 2002), a romantic comedy that, like *Walk the Line*, draws on Witherspoon's Southern roots. It took in over $100 million, and at the time it was released it was the biggest September opening ever, making Witherspoon the first megastar of the twenty-first century. But that stature came at the expense of her unruliness and her righteous invulnerability. Humiliating her character and requiring her to apologize repeatedly, *Sweet Home Alabama* comes painfully close to the sensibility of the slacker romance in its repudiation of female ambition.

The film tells the story of Melanie, a fashion designer whose boyfriend Andrew (Patrick Dempsey) is New York's most eligible bachelor. Andrew wants to marry Melanie, but, unbeknownst to him, she has "white trash" Alabama roots along with a husband, Jake, who won't divorce her. The film's conflict centers on the values associated with the two men who love Melanie. Both are romantic and appealing. But Jake, we learn, is the right choice because he knows and loves the "real" Melanie, who leaves Andrew at the altar for a "sweeter" life with Jake back in Alabama.

"New York Melanie" is sophisticated and successful at her career in a high fashion world like those of *The Devil Wears Prada* and *Ugly Betty*. Yet the film undercuts her New York life in many ways. To succeed there, Melanie lied about her roots and her marriage to Jake, indicating the moral corruption attached to female ambition. Andrew's mother Kate (Candice Bergen) is the mayor of New York City, and mothers play an unusually important role in this romantic comedy by helping Melanie decide who she wants to be. Kate epitomizes the ambitious woman, and she is a "hoity-toity Yankee bitch," in the words of one of her Alabama counterparts. Although Kate is politically powerful, the film judges her primarily, and harshly, for her failures as a mother, implying that she is Melanie's future if she stays with Andrew. In contrast, "Alabama Melanie" thrives on the pleasures of home, where beauty pageants and football are revered, men amuse themselves with Civil War reenactments, and women stay in kitchens wearing aprons and making jam. Not incidentally, that environment is steeped in racism, and the film's title recalls not only the notoriously evil plantation in Toni Morrison's novel *Beloved* but also a song by Lynyrd Skynyrd rebutting Neil Young's anti-KKK anthem "Southern Man."[7]

Much of the film's dramatic tension comes from screwball bantering between Melanie and Jake, whose role is to advocate for Melanie's real self. By suggesting that "Alabama Melanie" is really wilder and more unruly than her New York self, the film works hard to manage the tension between the independence of Witherspoon's star persona and the case it wants to make for traditional gender roles.[8] Jake forces Melanie to remember the self she has forgotten: "The girl I knew used to be fearless," he says, reminding her of when she accidentally blew up a bank at the age of ten. Meanwhile, the film subjects "New York Melanie" to an escalating series of humiliations that bring her to her senses. She behaves badly, drinks too much and vomits in public, then begins an interminable series of apologies—to the postal clerk she treated rudely, to a gay friend she outed, to another friend who is now a mother of four, and even to her dead pet dog ("You never left my side, and I just left you"). "I've been pretty selfish lately," she admits, as her speech reverts to its Southern accent and her dress becomes more casual.

The plot resolves when its two good, traditional mothers—Jake's and Melanie's—conspire to bring the sparring couple together. At the wedding, Melanie switches grooms at the last minute, and when Kate objects out of wounded pride, Melanie dispatches her with a punch, signaling that in Alabama she will recover her real, feisty self. The film concludes with images of Melanie's future life with Jake and their children, steeped in nostalgia for the traditional family living on a country homestead.

This domestication of Witherspoon's persona continues in another romantic comedy, *Almost Heaven* (2005), which tries even harder to punish her character, a successful physician, for working too hard. The film was not well received. *Sweet Home Alabama*'s success may have resulted from its timing—it debuted shortly after 9/11—and the popular appeal of its fantasy of cheery redneck life in a largely white south. The failure of the second film, however, confirms the problematic fit between Witherspoon's persona and romantic comedy, at least in the age of the slacker romance. Her most successful performances have not been in romantic comedies—"romantic" is not a word associated with her—but in genres that have depended more on her toughness and will.

Walk the Line (James Mangold, 2005) capitalizes on those elements of Witherspoon's star persona, harnessing its force, not to change public institutions such as Harvard or Congress, but to support her man, a larger-than-life icon of American masculinity. The film also moves Witherspoon into the new territory of the unrepentant mother. As June Carter, she plays her first fully adult role, a mature woman who acquired over her lifetime a major career, three children, and three husbands. And the film draws on three genres. As a biopic, it dramatizes the stormy years of Johnny Cash's early life. As a musical, it enables Witherspoon to showcase yet another side of her talent by successfully performing several numbers herself. And as a melodrama, it taps into similar anxieties to those of the slacker romance, especially around strong, active women and wounded, passive men.

The film portrays Cash (Joaquin Phoenix) as a man whose suffering nearly prevents him from realizing his talents. His paralysis does not arise from fear of strong women, however, but from the brutal impact of patriarchy on the sensitive male, a theme that was common in the family melodramas of classical Hollywood, such as Douglas Sirk's *Written on the Wind* (1956), and that appears in the more recent slacker-friendly films. In fact, it is June's strength of character that rescues Johnny. June's career eventually takes a backseat to Johnny's—not, in the logic of the film, for ideological reasons but because his talent is greater than hers. And so the film walks the postfeminist line by celebrating female strength—but mainly when that strength is used for unthreatening ends.

Walk the Line begins in Folsom Prison, moments before a performance that defined Cash's star persona. The sound track plays the unmistakable opening bars of "Walk the Line," accompanied by the sound of hundreds of prisoners clapping and stomping to the beat, as they await Johnny's appearance on stage. A shot of his hand on a saw blade in a woodshop backstage cuts to a long flashback that comprises the body of the film and establishes its key conflict: Johnny cannot realize his destiny until he overcomes the weight of his cruel father's judgment on him, as well as the early death of his idolized older brother. It is within this Oedipal framework that June's story unfolds, as she gradually replaces the stern patriarch with her tough but nurturing maternal love.

Walk the Line celebrates female strength as long as it doesn't threaten the status quo. As June Carter, Witherspoon stands by— and behind—her man, whose guitar occupies the image's foreground.

Johnny is a classical romantic hero whose suffering fuels his art and helps define his star persona around a mythical identification with society's most alienated men. When the opening sequence, which alludes to the brutality of the prison system, flashes back to Johnny's boyhood, the film connects the institutions of the family and the prison with abuses of male authority. Johnny's tyrannical father destroyed his confidence, and restoring that confidence becomes the film's dominant narrative goal—a goal ideally suited to Witherspoon's persona. Johnny's brother dreamed of becoming a preacher so he could save people, and Johnny aspires to the same goal. But as his first producer tells him, music that saves people begins with conviction. "I don't believe you," he tells Johnny when he hears him sing a Gospel song. "It ain't got nothing to do with believing in God, Mr. Cash. It has to do with believing in yourself." As Johnny struggles with his self-doubts, the film tracks his simultaneous rise to fame and descent into self-destructiveness.

Through cinematic and narrative means, the film creates June as both an elusive goal for Johnny and the "woman behind the man." She enters the film as the disembodied voice of a child star singing on the radio, while Johnny as a boy listens raptly. Next we see Johnny studying her image on magazine covers while he is stationed in Germany as a young soldier. Later, her voice on the radio returns as a reproach to Johnny, when his wife Vivian tells him he'll never sound as good as she does. Framed photos of June provoke an irrevocable split between Johnny and Vivian when he insists on displaying them in their home.

June's first actual appearance in the film occurs at a concert, when Johnny catches sight of her kissing her husband backstage. The long shot indicates the distance between them that he will struggle to overcome for most of the film. As usual, she's wearing red, a sign of her spiritedness, which contrasts with Johnny's signature black. In her eagerness to begin her own performance, she charges into him, entangling her dress in his guitar strings. She rips free, but he retains the swatch of torn fabric, and from that point on their lives are joined. While both characters repeatedly watch the other perform from backstage, June more frequently watches Johnny, taking on her role as observer of his career. And when the film returns at the end to the framing device of the Folsom Prison sequence, a singing Johnny dominates the foreground of the frame, with her in the background standing literally "behind her man."

June pulls together Witherspoon's most enduring star traits and the ones that most strongly identify her with the postfeminist age. She is both unruly and traditional. Like the female protagonists of the slacker romances, she is highly disciplined. Johnny taunts her with the charge that she won't do anything that "ain't written" on her calendar, and he accuses her of not wanting to marry him because she fears losing control and living in his "big shadow." She is a spirited survivor. Like Johnny, she suffered during her childhood, in constant comparison to her siblings in the musical Carter family, but she responded resourcefully, developing "personality" and "sass" and a talent for "giving it her all." She also learned to be funny in order to have "something to offer" her family. This sense of purpose resonates with Witherspoon's persona, and her sass with female unruliness.

"Ring of Fire," the title of a song written by June, alludes to the ways she suffers from her love for Johnny ("It burns, burns, burns"). But she does not suffer passively. In the scene that depicts the origins of the song "Walk the Line" (as well as the film's title), June finds a drunken Johnny carousing with a group of musicians—an apparent brotherhood of slackers—gathered on a stage littered with empty beer bottles. She turns to leave, but when he taunts her, she hurls bottles at him in rage, and he and his pals dive for cover, joking about "surrendering." Here the film identifies Johnny's retreat into drugs with the juvenile behavior of men whose idea of fun is getting drunk, taking drugs, and setting off bombs in trees.

June is both wife and mother to Johnny, showing him tough maternal love by hurling bottles at him when he squanders his talent by drinking.

June's most important role in the film is a maternal one, and for the first time, Witherspoon plays an unrepentant mother. While her daughters aren't central to the film's action, they are an important part of June's character and add to the taboo attached to her because of her divorces and her position as the "other woman" in Johnny's life. Indeed, one of the filmmakers' challenges was to create sympathy for June while not demonizing Vivian, a task made easier by Witherspoon's associations with the moral high ground. Like the other characters Witherspoon has played—in *The Man in the Moon, Fear, Cruel Intentions,* even *Election*—June pursues her desire freely and without apology, and accepts the consequences of her decisions.

These consequences include the harsh judgment of many of her fans, hard-line Christians who believe she compromised herself when she divorced her first husband. In one sober scene, set ironically in a brightly lit variety store, a woman berates June for her divorce. June carries "a world of judgment" on her, she says, and it is clear that, as a woman, she has paid in her career for her perceived moral shortcomings, while Johnny, as a man, has built his career on his. And yet she bears these judgments with dignity. She also resists Johnny's advances for most of the film, until viewers are convinced that the couple has earned the right to be together. The role of June also adds a layer of softness and vulnerability to Witherspoon's star persona. These qualities seep in through Witherspoon's performances of June's songs, such as the plaintive ballad "Wildwood Flower," her mother Maybelle's favorite song, or "Ring of Fire," which she sings with tears in her eyes.

Most important, June directs her maternal drive toward the man in her life, playing midwife to a reborn Johnny. This role draws on Witherspoon's history of characters whose optimism inspires others. Both *Legally Blonde* films deliver motivational messages about believing in oneself. Early in her relationship with Johnny, she gives him a copy of Khalil Gibrans's *The Prophet*. When he responds by attempting to kiss her, she stops him—but encourages him to take credit for trying. The use of extreme close-ups during their conversation, especially on June, signals the importance of what she tells him: rather than explaining his look, his sound, and even his attempt to kiss her as having "just happened," he should start taking credit for himself. Later, during his recovery, she again tells him, "You're not nothing, you're a good man," prodding him to take advantage of the second chance he has now earned.

The film offers matriarchal power as an alternative to the patriarchal social system that drives men and women to prisons of all kinds. In a key scene, June stands on the front porch of the Carter house, with her mother and daughters by her side, while Johnny, still in the throes of his addiction, stands on the ground before them. A low-angle shot adds stature to the three generations of women, implying that June's strength comes from a strong bond with the women of her family. Mother Maybelle supports June, and Johnny too, because she knows that June loves him. And when a drug pusher shows up to tempt Johnny, Maybelle stands right behind her own man, June's father, both of them armed with shotguns to protect their family. Close to the end of the film, Maybelle tells June to go to Johnny when he is wrestling with his demons in the form of a tractor lodged in the mud. This gentle nudge to follow her heart enables June to rescue Johnny one more time and, as a bringer of new life, to turn his near-death from drowning into a baptism.

The film concludes by reasserting the priority of the Oedipal narrative, now happily resolved. In the film's penultimate sequence, as Johnny descends the stairs to the dock, he engages in a respectful conversation with his now-chastened father. The scene is blocked to place Johnny between his father in the background, and June, at some distance away, fishing from the dock. Johnny moves away from his father and toward her, with their gazes joined in an eyeline match, and the film freezes on a medium shot of his face, finally at peace. This shot is followed by a coda that brings June and Johnny together in the frame one more time, singing and laughing on stage, but this time the voices we hear are those of Johnny Cash and June Carter. At this point, the film not only restores June to a more prominent narrative place but it also joins the symbolic with the real, disclosing its artifice in a gesture consistent with the image of transparency Witherspoon has cultivated in her star persona.

In 2007's *Rendition*, Witherspoon plays Isabella, a mother who is even more explicitly unrepentant than June, and a brief look at this film suggests that the maternal may increasingly be absorbed into her star persona. The film is a powerful melodrama about the illegal practice of extraordinary rendition, or imprisoning suspects without legal process and delivering them to locations abroad where they can be tortured with impunity. The United States began this policy during the Clinton years, and despite international outcries, has practiced it on a much larger scale since 9/11. *Rendition* is not interested in motherhood per se—indeed, it shows us very little of Isabella's life as a mother. Instead, it uses motherhood as a symbol to achieve its melodramatic goal of depicting the consequences of rendition on its victims, their families, and our political institutions. The film received generally positive reviews, but, not surprisingly given its bleak view of American policy, it did not find a big audience.

The film begins with Isabella, a young soccer mom who is nearly nine months pregnant, kicking a ball around with her young son on the lawn of their suburban Chicago home. The film then tracks multiple storylines around the disappearance of her husband Anwar, who has been abducted and transported to North Africa for interrogation. There, Anwar is tortured by Abasi Fawal, a police chief whose family suffers tragedies of its own. Isabella travels to DC for help finding Anwar, and after an emotional confrontation with Corrine (Meryl Streep), the implacable head of the rendition operations, she goes into labor. Anwar is finally released and returns home to his family, which now includes an infant.

As Isabella, Witherspoon draws on key aspects of her persona. Isabella is confident and fierce in her determination to achieve her goals. She is a rescuer. She stands on the moral high ground. And she refuses victimhood. At the same time, the ideology of motherhood tempers some of Witherspoon's earlier unruliness. Isabella's pregnant belly inscribes her sexuality on her body, but in a way that falls within the bounds of normative femininity. Even more than in *Walk the Line*, motherhood requires her to channel her drive into taking care of her family. In her relentless efforts to rescue her husband, she uncovers information that sows doubt about his innocence, but that does not deter her

This promotional image for *Rendition* shows Isabella's pregnant belly "advancing" on the Capitol, suggesting that the nation's well-being is inseparable from that of the family.

from her quest to find him and free him. Her efforts to expose the corruption of our nation's institutions recall similar exposures in the sassy *Legally Blonde* comedies, and even in the "art-sploitation" *Freeway*.

Concerned fundamentally with the right of habeas corpus, the film uses bodies—Anwar's tortured body and Isabella's pregnant one—to concretize and personalize its abstract moral conflicts. Ultimately, states render justice, or not, on real bodies. Isabella's body, semiotically distilled around her pregnant belly, makes visible the human stakes in upholding the abstract principles of law, while Anwar's battered and degraded body shows the consequences of disregarding them. Indeed, the film uses the authority of the pregnant, un-repentant mother to make its case. Several shots frame Isabella in silhouette against the backdrop of familiar Washington landmarks. Through repeated invocations of family in both Isabella's storyline and Abasi's, *Rendition* binds the well-being of the family with that of the larger social order.

As Linda Williams argues, melodrama wants to resolve itself in a place of innocence, and *Rendition* ends by returning us to where it began, the bucolic lawns of suburbia, where we want to believe that soccer moms can play with their children, secure in the safety of their families. That confidence, of course, has been shattered by the end of the film, the final notes of which seem to evoke innocence only to underscore its loss.

Witherspoon's star text captures the essence of unruly femininity in the post-feminist age, as well as exemplifying many Third Wave ideals. On the one hand, she appears comfortable with the ultrafemininity of Elle Woods, even if she wears it ironically. But a persistent undercurrent of unruliness gives a feminist charge to her persona, as evident in slacker guru Kevin Smith's antipathy toward her. Thus, despite her star power, she has not fit well into the variation of romantic comedy that has been most popular during her ingénue years: the slacker romance, which treats the ambitious woman with suspicion.

Blondeness is a fetishized aspect of her persona, which has subtly reinforced racialized notions of female beauty and done little to advance the Third Wave agenda regarding race. However, that persona has also incorporated the key tropes of female desire during the era of Girl Power. *Election*, the film that most defined her star text, brings the Final Girl of *Scream* and *Buffy* into a more realistic setting and examines her through the eyes of the threatened, slacker-type male. The *Legally Blonde* films retain the ambition of her earlier star persona and combine it with the normative femininity embraced by Girl World. Finally, while advocating for female desire like Rose in *Titanic*, Witherspoon's characters have avoided the matrophobia and obsession with old-fashioned romance that undermine that film's feminist potential.

As Witherspoon moves toward more mature roles, as in *Walk the Line* and *Rendition*, motherhood figures more prominently in her star persona. Ideally, she will be able to resist the ideological pressure to play mothers as victims or monsters, but instead as unrepentant figures of female desire.

Teen-Girl Melodramas
MY SO-CALLED LIFE AND THIRTEEN

I need Angela's emotions . . .

—AN ONLINE FAN OF *MY SO-CALLED LIFE*

LLISON ANDERS'S indie film *Gas Food Lodging* (1992) begins with its young protagonist Shade, played by Fairuza Balk, sitting in the Sunn Cinema, a rundown old theater in a lonely corner of New Mexico. She is alone, and her eyes are riveted to the screen, brimming with tears, as she gazes at a Mexican melodrama featuring the fictional star Elvia Rivera. In voice-over, she describes that whenever Elvia's films come to town she comes alive, her emotions awakening against the desolation and flatness of her hometown. The scene is a compelling image of cinematic suture and teen-girl cinephilia. Inspired by Elvia, Shade decides to find a man for her single mother, and in the process, of course, finds herself. *Gas Food Lodging* predates by a few years the big texts of Girl Culture, but Shade anticipates the sensitive girls of the melodramas of this period, and her wry, long-suffering mother, wonderfully played by Brooke Adams, remains one of cinema's most sympathetic unrepentant mothers.[1]

This chapter considers media texts that follow *Gas Food Lodging*'s lead in taking advantage of melodrama's interest in mother-daughter relations and the unrepentant mother. After a short look at the television melodrama *My So-Called Life* (ABC, 1994–1995), it turns to a more extensive discussion of the film *Thirteen.*[2] *My So-Called Life* is centered on the character of fifteen-year-old Angela Chase, played by Claire Danes. The series was canceled after only one season because of low ratings, but it acquired legendary status in Girl Culture for its role in creating the contemporary teen-girl fan. Six months before *Romeo + Juliet* (1996), which also starred Claire Danes, and two years before *Titanic* (1997), *My So-Called Life* galvanized its fans to develop an online community around the series and to organize national protests when it was cancelled.[3]

Less than a decade later, *Thirteen* (2003), directed by Catherine Hardwicke, became the first feature film to bear the authorial hand of a teen girl, Nikki Reed, who co-wrote the screenplay when she was thirteen and plays a major role in the film. While overwhelmed in the popular consciousness by blockbuster epics of the early 2000s, it attracted critical attention for its authenticity and emotional power. *Thirteen* pushes into intense melodrama the dark side of Girl Culture considered more lightly in *Mean Girls*. It dramatizes the impact of neo-liberalism's unraveling social institutions on single mothers and their daughters, and the necessity of strong mother-daughter relations in a world that is as dangerous as ever for girls.

The two texts discussed in this chapter share important similarities. In addition to their melodramatic tone, both focus on sensitive girls who move toward adulthood by creating distance from their parents, exploring friendships outside their former social circle, and experimenting with their sexuality. Both girls develop passionate friendships with wilder girls who lure them away from the protected confines of their homes, and both have stormy relationships with their mothers, who are unrepentant in their own ways. Marshall Herskovitz, one of the creators of *My So-Called Life*, describes a teen's experience of school as essentially unchanging. The social world may change with time, he says, but "it's the same clock you're staring at."[4] Nonetheless, the two texts depict vastly different universes. In *My So-Called Life*, the middle-class family remains a stable and viable foundation for its teen-girl protagonist as she explores her identity through close relationships with troubled teens on the fringes of her secure world. In *Thirteen*, that foundation has disappeared, leaving the teen girl with few defenses against the pressures of a world defined by consumerism, alienation, addiction, and precocious sexuality. Both texts use melodrama to show that as daughters begin to move away from their parents in the process of growing up, they still need their mothers.

My So-Called Life: Second Wave Feminism and
the Unrepentant Mother

My So-Called Life is set in an ordinary, middle-class suburb of Pittsburgh at a time when women wore their hair big and their shoulders padded and teen girls concealed the signs of their maturing bodies with baggy flannel shirts and Dr. Martens boots. Neither postmodern, postfeminist, nor "about" popular culture, it has an aura of nostalgia when viewed today. And even when it first aired, it had more in common with the John Hughes melodramas of the 1980s than with Beverly Hills, 90210 (1990–2000) and Melrose Place (1992–1998), the two series that competed with it for teen audiences. Whereas those "money soaps," with their slick settings and perfect characters, offered the fantasies of a sexy, consumer-oriented postfeminism, My So-Called Life was imbued with a moody realism. Just before the rise of Girl Culture, this show depicted a social world wrestling with the impact of the Second Wave on the family. The mother is the family's main breadwinner, and the father, between jobs, is the more domestic parent. The materialism and girly femininity of Girl Culture are nowhere to be found, and the identity issues its characters grapple with have less to do with navigating the social divisions of high school than with exploring the self and surviving the impact of broader social forces on their lives.

My So-Called Life is noted for creating one of television's most memorable teen-girl characters. Recognizing the opportunity provided by the lack of media attention to teen girls, writer Winnie Holzman developed the series around Angela, a sensitive and introspective girl whose diaristic voice-over defines the consciousness and tone of the series.[5] In the words of Ginia Bellafante (2007), Angela captured a "slouchy, endearing neurasthenia that seemed to befit the indolent mood of the mid-'90s." The series was recognized for its artful production values, including single-camera filming, atmospheric lighting, and slow-motion cinematography suited to Angela's lassitude and melancholy, and it was praised for treating issues such as teen homelessness, homosexuality, and alcoholism with a focus and depth rarely sustained on network TV. My So-Called Life also benefited from a quirk of casting. Holzman, along with producers Marshall Herskovitz and Ed Zwick, did not conceive the series as primarily for teen girls. Because Danes was only thirteen when she won the part of Angela and fourteen when she played it, child labor laws limited her time on set. Thus the writers were challenged to enrich the series by developing interesting plotlines around other characters, such as Angela's parents

Patty (Bess Armstrong) and Graham (Tom Irwin), as well as her friends, the biracial, openly gay Rickie Vasquez (Wilson Cruz) and Rayanne Graff (A. J. Langer), a wild girl teetering out of control.[6]

My So-Called Life also played a groundbreaking role in defining the contemporary teen-girl fan, anticipating the online fandom and "participatory spectatorship" of the Buffyverse. At the time the series appeared, girls were largely alienated from popular television. Even in shows such as *Beverly Hills 90210*, teens were played by actors in their twenties and the storylines were adult-oriented. As Susan Murray argues, teen-girl fandom differs somewhat from that of teen boys. Girls don't catalogue textual detail, as boy fans tend to do, but extend their "bedroom culture" through the Internet to form relationships with other fans and express their emotions to them.

As with Shade's attachment to Elvia Rivera in *Gas Food Lodging*, *My So-Called Life*'s fans believed they came alive through Angela. They invested deeply in the series, using it to experiment with their own identities and their ambivalence toward encroaching womanhood. Viewing Angela as an ideal or symbolic self, many dyed their hair red, wore flannel shirts, and called themselves "Lifers." When word came that the series would be canceled after its nineteen episodes, they organized a campaign to save the show (and "Angela's life"), an expression, according to Murray, of their deeper anger about girls' invisibility in popular culture and lack of control over their representation.

Taking full advantage of the open-endedness of television's narrative forms, *My So-Called Life* developed Angela's relationships with her parents in unusual depth for media popular with peer-oriented teens. Moreover, it characterized those relationships as more traditional than those in the other film and TV shows popular with teens then and now. Recall the mother in *Mean Girls*, who identifies herself as "cool Mom" to her daughter's friends, the Plastics. In *Gilmore Girls* (2000–2007), mother and daughter are best friends and relate with the easy familiarity of sisters close in age.[7] In *My So-Called Life*, adults impose rules and engage with young people in ways that are frustrating but still meaningful. Adults and teens may live in different universes, but they are parallel ones fraught with similar anxieties. As a result, the possibility exists for transgenerational empathy and communication. In the pilot episode, Angela dyes her hair red to experiment with her developing self, and in the next episode, "Dancing in the Dark," her mother Patty cuts hers as she takes on new responsibilities in the family. Patty's haircut follows warnings from her female friends that men don't like short hair and her knowledge that Hillary Clinton's

My So-Called Life introduced Angela Chase, one of television's most memorable teen-girl characters. Claire Danes was cast for the part because of the unformed, tentative quality she conveyed.

stature had suffered from trivial attention to her hair. At this point Patty cannot accept Angela's red hair because she cannot accept what it signifies—the impending changes in their relationship. Yet she and her daughter are struggling with similar issues of self-definition and change.

Many of the series's characters push quietly but consistently at traditional gender ideologies. Normative masculinity does not sit easily on Graham, Rickie, and even Jordan Catalano, Angela's love interest, a low-achieving proto-slacker more notable for his beauty and passivity than his masculine drive. And Patty is clearly a woman on top, too busy taking care of business to even think about the lost pleasures of pre–Second Wave femininity, including domesticity. But, unlike *American Beauty*, the series handles these characters with evenhandedness and restraint.

Graham's passivity evokes the slacker's uneasiness around traditional adult masculinity as well as newly empowered forms of femininity. He does

In *My So-Called Life*, both mother and daughter struggle with similar issues of self-definition and change. Here, Patty (Bess Armstrong) has signaled a change in her life by cutting her hair short, just as Angela dyed her hair red.

not define himself by how well he provides for his family, and yearns to express himself through cooking, an area associated with femininity. As Patty explains to her mother, Graham is "emotional about food." He identifies with the young through shared taste in music, and shows his rebellious side by bonding with Rayanne over the Grateful Dead. But he feels anxious about Patty's lack of confidence in him. The episode "Self-Esteem" begins with the Chases' younger daughter Danielle asking Graham how to spell "mediocrity," and later in the episode, Patty's judgmental, old-fashioned father sharply criticizes him for "sponging off" his wife. ("You deserve better," he tells Patty.)

Graham begins the series working for Patty, who is running her father's printing business. He is unhappy with this work, however, and communicates his unhappiness through passive aggression until Patty fires him, forcing him to take action to realize his dream of becoming a chef. Patty is also more sexually assertive than he, initiating sex between them and trying to lure him into more adventurous behavior. Despite the clear gender reversals within their marriage, however, Graham and Patty work through their conflicts and remain committed to each other.

Similarly, in an episode titled "Father Figures," the series acknowledges the ways daughters idolize their fathers without romanticizing the relationship. Patty suffers from her own father's lack of respect for her ability to run the family business, and she battles him for cheating on his taxes. Meanwhile, Angela overhears Graham in a compromising phone call with another woman and begins to withdraw from him. As a father, Graham lets Patty do the dirty work of reining in Angela, while he enjoys his role as the easier parent. That role has already been shifting as Angela physically matures. She notes wistfully in voice-over that her growing breasts have come between them. When Graham becomes distraught about Angela's withdrawal, Patty comforts him by explaining that Angela is merely pushing him off his pedestal, "on schedule," so when she's an adult she won't suffer like her mother, who is still seeking her father's approval. Despite the emotional intimacy between father and daughter, the viewer never worries that Angela's private moments with Graham, such as the late night snacks he fixes for her ("Food never tastes as good as what my father cooks for me," she says), will move into taboo territory.

The series struggles harder with the character of Patty, who at times appears to be a caricature of an overbearing mother and a Second Wave feminist, at once excessively feminine ("hysterical") and phallic. The allusion to Hillary Clinton is no accident; there are few models in popular culture of women who combine authority with a femininity that reads as familiar and appealing. As in most shows about teen girls, Patty is alien and unbearable to her daughter. "I can't even look at my mother without wanting to stab her repeatedly," Angela says in the pilot episode, recalling Rose's disgust at her mother in *Titanic*.

We often see Patty sitting in bed with papers strewn around her, indicating that her role in keeping the family's affairs in order has invaded the intimate space of her marriage. She talks constantly, often to herself, sighs heavily, and is ignored by her husband and children. (Graham interrupts one of her off-screen monologues by asking her, "Is this a private conversation, or can anyone join?") In the painful episode "Weekend," she humiliates herself by getting drunk at a restaurant from fear that Graham is considering an affair with his attractive new business partner. Patty is wracked with self-doubt, but she is the only consistently adult person in the household.

The series's ambivalence around Patty is no clearer than in the episode "Other People's Mothers," which contrasts Rayanne's family life with Angela's, and shows Patty in relation to her own mother Vivian. The episode unfolds around the premise of parallel parties, which test Angela's divided loyalties and highlight different models of motherhood. Rayanne receives a gift of money from her absent father, but she doesn't want to keep it because of their troubled relationship. She decides to use it to throw a huge party. At the same time, Patty feels she must host a party for her parents' forty-fifth anniversary.

The episode begins by establishing Patty as impossibly controlling and Rayanne's mother Amber as warm and fun. When Patty catches Rickie with a beer, she begins a litany of threats she recognizes as clichéd even as she makes them: "I will not tolerate . . . Under no circumstances . . . There are certain rules." Later Rayanne mocks her for her orderliness ("Have you seen her vegetable bin?"). Rayanne decides that she, Angela, and Ricki will hang out at her house instead because her mother, Amber, isn't "that strict." Angela meets Amber for the first time, entering the apartment through veils of beaded curtains to the sound of ethnic flutes and wind chimes made of shells. Amber, played by Patti D'Arbanville as a New Age earth mother, rises from her bed, fruity cocktail in hand, opens her arms, and invites Angela to "come to mama." After her own mother's orderly vegetable bin, Angela is mesmerized by Amber's exotic allure. Amber further seduces her with a tarot reading that identifies Angela as someone who hides her feelings, then covers her card with the Moon card, which she reads as a "deadly mother." "Like a wicked witch?" Angela asks. Amber knows that the party will take place while she's at work, and that the teens will be drinking, but her main concern is that her neighbor not complain about noise.

In contrast, Angela's grandmother Vivian reflects, in exaggerated form, her own daughter's overbearing qualities. Even though Patty is adopted (the source of her "abandonment issues," as Angela confides to Amber), she and her mother appear cut from the same cloth. Vivian wears short hair and a masculine power suit almost exactly like her daughter's. When she arrives at the Chase house, she upsets Patty by rearranging the décor and sending passive-aggressive messages about Angela's presence at the party. Yet Patty is as helpless around her mother as she is with her father. In her compulsive desire to be a "good girl" and take care of everyone, she models the pathologies of normative femininity rejected by the Second Wave. She wears a robotic smile that reassures others but masks *her* real feelings. Observing her mother at the anniversary party, Angela deepens her understanding of her: "Sometimes I think if my mother wasn't so good at pretending to be happy, she'd actually *be* happy."

After Patty saves Rayanne from an overdose in the episode "Other People's Mothers,"
Angela sees her mother through new eyes, and the gap between them briefly closes.

Not surprisingly, Angela's romantic view of Amber is short-lived. Rayanne overdoses at the party, and a panicking Angela calls Patty, whose ability to take charge of the situation saves Rayanne's life. Angela now sees how Amber has failed Rayanne by refusing to give her the strong and clearheaded parenting she needs, and when Amber falls apart at the hospital where she finds her daughter under Patty's steady care, Angela's new judgment is confirmed. Once the crisis is over, Angela and Patty share a sober moment in the family car. Angela, still shaken, asks Patty how she knew what to do, and Patty explains that she once had a best friend who was a lot like Rayanne but did not survive. Once again, the series briefly closes the gap between the generations, and Patty and Angela reach a tentative truce. Patty accepts the fact that she can't break up Angela's friendship with Rayanne, but she also recognizes that Angela deserves her trust. When Angela leaves the car to join the anniversary party, Patty, finally alone, weeps. The episode ends with Angela reflecting on what she has learned. Folded back into the embrace of her family, including her difficult grandmother, she names the characters of her life according to Amber's tarot deck: her grandmother is the Empress, her father the Magician, her little sister the Fool, and her mother Strength.

Remarkably, the series creates in Patty a mother who is far from perfect, yet it does not banish or demonize her. The show respects her for the strength that sustains not only her but also her husband, her children, and even her parents. Moreover, it demonstrates that mothers and daughters, despite their differences, need to remain close. In the emotional Christmas episode, titled "So-Called Angels," Angela befriends a homeless girl. "I'm no different from her," Angela insists to Patty, who at first refuses to accept this reality. But the episode forces Patty to confront her denial of her own daughter's vulnerability as well as the racism and homophobia lurking under the surface of her liberalism. The homeless girl, revealed later to be an angel, died after an irreparable estrangement from her mother.

The aspects I have highlighted in *My So-Called Life* may suggest that the series is moralistic and conservative, idealizing rigid rules and white, middle-class, two-parent, heterosexual families with all-sacrificing mothers. Instead, I would argue that it portrays how the new social order aspired to by feminism will not be achieved overnight but take generations to enact. During this time of social instability and transformation, women and men will continue to love each other and parent their children with varying degrees of success. Patty, flawed as she is, is an unrepentant mother, still taking care of everyone else and often resenting it, but also learning to hold her own ground and take care of herself. In her strength and dynamism, she is a model for her daughters.

Thirteen: The Perils of Postfeminism

In the decade or so before *Thirteen*, a handful of films took on the subject of teen-girl angst and the mother-daughter relation by focusing on single, often "zany" mothers and their teenage daughters. These works, which include *Mermaids* (1990), *Tumbleweeds* (1999), *Anywhere But Here* (1999), and *White Oleander* (2002), cast strong unruly women in middle age (Susan Sarandon, Cher) as the mothers. Among them, *White Oleander* (directed by Peter Kosminsky), based on the novel by Janet Fitch, stands out for its portrait of one of cinema's fiercest and most difficult mothers and for its unsentimentalized depiction of a daughter's struggle for independence.

Michelle Pfeiffer plays Ingrid, a charismatic artist with an unshakeable sense of her own uniqueness and autonomy. In a fatal act of vulnerability, she lets herself fall for a man. He dumps her, she kills him, and then is sent to prison for life, leaving her fifteen-year-old daughter Astrid (Alison Lohman) to fend for herself. Prison agrees with Ingrid. It's kill or be killed, she says, and everyone knows the rules. Astrid's new life in the foster care system, though, proves more difficult.

Through letters and rare prison visits, Ingrid continues to try to instill in Astrid her own values: "Don't forget who you are," she tells her repeatedly. "You are my daughter, and you are perfect." Indeed, the mother and daughter, both blonde beauties with Nordic names, evoke a superiority based on race— "We're the Vikings, remember," Ingrid tells Astrid when admonishing her not to show weakness. Astrid, however, grows increasingly angry over Ingrid's efforts to control her. The film concludes in a wrenching act of separation, when Ingrid finally lets go of Astrid, accepting that her daughter's needs are in conflict with hers and that she must put her own aside. As Astrid heads off to her own life, she indicates in voice-over that the rage she has felt toward her mother has given way to a more nuanced recognition of who she is: "No matter how much she's damaged me, no matter how flawed she is, I know my mother loves me."

Whether Ingrid's sense of her own exceptionality is grounded in reality or not, *White Oleander* shows how fine the line is between resisting the norms of femininity in socially tolerable ways and slipping into deviance, criminality, or even insanity. "I don't want to be redeemed," Ingrid says in defiant unrepentance. "I regret nothing." However, while the film unflinchingly explores mother-daughter "passion and rupture," to recall Adrienne Rich, Ingrid remains opaque, in part because we see her only through her daughter's eyes but also because characters like her are extremely rare in popular media, except as monsters.

In contrast, *Thirteen*, another film about a girl coming of age in Southern California, creates a mother who is notable for her ordinariness and vulnerability rather than for her sense of superiority. And while privileging the point of view of its teen protagonist, the film also gives more narrative and cinematic attention to her mother. *Thirteen* is a difficult film to watch, beginning with its pre-title sequence. Directed by Catherine Hardwicke and released in 2003, it opens with its young protagonist Tracy (Evan Rachel Wood), staring with a woozy smile at the camera in medium close-up. "Hit me," she says. "I'm serious, I can't feel anything, hit me! Again, do it harder! . . . This is awesome!" The camera pulls back to a two-shot of her and another girl, and we watch them slug each other until they're bleeding. The film doesn't get any easier, as it flashes back four months to follow Tracy's ecstatic, horrific path to this moment—self-mutilation, casual sex, drugs, petty crime, failing at school, depression, and rage.

My So-Called Life did not shrink from wrenching social issues and their impact on teens, but as this sequence indicates, *Thirteen* takes its viewers deep into a world that seems significantly different from that of the earlier TV series. The film is set in Los Angeles, but the fantasies of wealth evoked by the Reagan era's *Beverly Hills, 90210, Melrose Place,* and the more recent *The O.C.* have disappeared. Even the security of middle-class life is slipping away for the film's struggling single mother. Adults are largely impotent in the lives of their children, and the institutions of family and school are incapable of nurturing them. In *My So-Called Life,* high school students read literary classics like Shakespeare's sonnets and take them seriously, and they glimpse into history with books such as *The Diary of Anne Frank.* Traditional bodies of knowledge and culture still hold value for them. In *Thirteen,* the cultural past has vanished from a landscape of advertisements and the easy sensations of schlock culture. The white nuclear family is no longer intact, a mother's need to work is a given, and feminist issues around the family now concern living-wage jobs for single mothers and child support from missing fathers—issues long familiar to women of color but not to white middle-class women. *Thirteen*'s protagonist Tracy lives to join the popular girls, but Girl World has become a place even more treacherous and deadly than its comic realization in *Mean Girls.*

Both *My So-Called Life* and *Thirteen* register changing attitudes towards sex. In *My So-Called Life,* girls used clothing to conceal their emerging sexuality. The series is driven largely by Angela's sexual desire, which awakens through her obsession with the beautiful but vacant Jordan Catalano. As Ginia Bellafante notes (2007), his name still stirs women who came of age watching the series. For Angela, stolen make-out sessions awaken her eroticism, and she indulges in rhapsodic reveries about them—"There are only two realities: kissing, and not kissing." But she remains a virgin. In *Thirteen,* teen girls flaunt their developing sexuality with playful appropriations of porn style meant to shock, but there is little sense that they have yet experienced for themselves the sexual desire that grips Angela. Girls engage in casual sexual behavior, and Tracy's offhand sexual initiation is no more or less significant than piercing her navel or shoplifting.

I was eager to see *Thirteen* when it was released because of advance publicity about its co-authorship by Nikki Reed, who not only co-wrote it but also stars as Tracy's best friend Evie. I expected the film would hold great interest to teen girls and their parents alike, and when I showed it in a class on teen-girl culture, it left the students, primarily young women, in silence, many in tears. However, I soon discovered that many of the other people I thought would be interested in it—friends and colleagues who have daughters—did not see it, and frankly admitted that they didn't want to. Rather than surprising me, this avoidance confirmed one of the film's most insistent concerns: the refusal or inability of adults to see uncomfortable realities unfolding in their midst. Indeed, *Thirteen* links the numbness, denial, and disconnectedness of its characters with a larger, free-floating anxiety and pain—conditions, in fact, familiar to life in contemporary America, especially in the years following 9/11.

Thirteen attracted mixed reviews and widely varying critical readings. Praised by many for its authenticity, rawness, and emotional power, it won several awards, including the Sundance Film Festival's Dramatic Directing Award for Catherine Hardwicke and an Oscar nomination for Holly Hunter as best actress. Others criticized it for being heavy-handed in its treatment of the perils of growing up female. Still others questioned its treatment of race, as well as its cautionary messages about teen-girl sexuality and the disintegration of the nuclear family.[8]

Despite these diverging points of view, *Thirteen* is an important film that engages with the crucial issues of its times. Produced by Antidote Films, it exposes an array of cultural toxins particularly deadly to girls today, who are shown to be easily poisoned by a nearly irresistible brew of consumerism, drugs, and precocious sexuality, with little help from adults who are as distracted, tormented, and lost as they are. According to the film, there is not much new and improved about growing up female today except that girls experience the perils of femininity at ever-younger ages and with less help from adults. But the film also offers an antidote to these poisons by using the moral force of melodrama to argue for the imperfect but atavistic power of maternal love.

Like the best melodramas, *Thirteen* personalizes the political, registering through the suffering of its protagonists the impact of wider social forces on their lives. In its depiction of female adolescence, the film explores themes associated with postfeminism: sexuality as an expression of empowered femininity, and the pleasures of consumerism as a means of self-expression. However, it poses a sobering critique of the sexism, superficiality, and materialism implicated in postfeminist recuperations of traditional femininity. Depicting heterosexuality as a vortex that "catches" girls at ever-younger ages, it asks difficult questions about when girls are ready for sexual activity and under what conditions. With its focus on female-headed families, it considers the consequences of conservative economic policies on single mothers and a largely female working class struggling in the media-saturated landscapes of the New Economy. And with capitalism penetrating ever deeper into the psyche, it looks at the implications of the individual freedom celebrated by postfeminism and neoliberalism when that freedom is pursued primarily at a shopping mall. In response to these conditions, virtually every one of the film's characters struggles with addictions of one kind or another.

This is the stuff of melodrama, and in a cinematic environment that has banished sympathetic mothers from the screen for decades, *Thirteen*'s use of melodrama enables it to foreground its central concerns and its simple but urgent message: We may no longer believe that children are innocent, or that they ever were. Nor do we believe that adults have much power to protect them from a predatory world drained of moral purpose. But as girls enter the perilous time of adolescence, there's something to be said for a caring woman's tight grip on them when things fall apart. As melodrama, of course, the film offers a solution that is more satisfying emotionally than politically or intellectually. But it also brings into sharp relief the impact of larger social forces its characters are unable to articulate. And it demonstrates the importance for girls and women of stories about female rites of passage, friendships, and the relationship of mother and daughter—stories that are rarely told in other genres but that urgently need telling.

Global/Local

Briefly, *Thirteen* depicts a few tumultuous months in the life of Tracy Freeland, a sensitive, poetry-writing thirteen-year-old, who lives with her older brother Mason and divorced mother Melanie (Holly Hunter). Tracy's father, a businessman, is largely absent from their lives. He drives a nice car but doesn't always make his child support payments. Melanie is a high school dropout and recovering alcoholic who tries to make ends meet by running a hairdressing business out of their home. She has a boyfriend, Brady (Jeremy Sisto), a decent guy who gives her companionship and sex but is in fragile recovery from his own addiction to cocaine. The narrative follows Tracy's friendship with the charismatic Evie, who is being raised by her cousin Brooke, a bartender and part-time model with a drinking problem of her own. After Evie moves into the Freeland household, Tracy makes a rapid decline into angry, self-destructive behavior, and the cutting she had already begun intensifies. When Mel can no longer ignore the situation, she kicks Evie out, reasserts her maternal authority, and the film closes almost literally with a new dawn.

Thirteen takes place in Los Angeles, a setting rich with connotations of American culture. For the past century, Hollywood has manufactured fantasies that speak to viewers around the globe. The city also connotes the "noir" side of those fantasies, the costs of an obsessive pursuit of personal freedom, and material enrichment associated with the American Dream. Similar themes are evident in other films that use L.A. as more than a convenient setting: *Chinatown* (1974) and *Magnolia* (1999), both of which dramatize, like *Thirteen*, the vulnerability of daughters to corruption that seeps into the family and the powerlessness of mothers to protect them. In the earlier films, the threat, explicitly sexual, comes from powerful fathers. In *Thirteen*, the patriarch's power is dispersed, opening up space for a more optimistic vision of maternal power.

With its large population of immigrants, many of them from Latin America, Los Angeles is also a gateway city. This status has become particularly charged in the past decade, as the U.S. government, in the name of free trade, has opened its borders for the flow of capital south but has also increasingly fortified them against the flow of labor north. Much of the government's rhetoric around borders since 9/11 has conflated fears about illegal drugs, terrorism, and immigration from nonwhite countries. That rhetoric suggests deeper anxieties about the loss of social and economic security in a nation increasingly mired in debt and floundering in ill-conceived wars against not only specific nations but also "terror," an amorphous, free-floating enemy that renders the real threat of terrorism into something even more elusive and terrifying.

This *mise en scène* provides a crucial backdrop for *Thirteen*, which displays an obsession with borders and boundaries of the self, the body, and the home, and which frames its story of female adolescence within not only the persistent structures of patriarchy but also those of multinational capitalism. Tracy's family name—Freeland—comments ironically on both the rhetoric of political freedom so relentlessly promoted by the U.S. government in its post-9/11 military adventures and the unregulated, unsupervised freedom that characterizes Tracy and Evie's lives.

Like its opening scene, much of *Thirteen*'s drama centers on the ways a girl's body becomes a stage for the most consuming dramas of her life as she enters adulthood. It is the place most targeted by the related discourses of consumer culture and (hetero)sexuality. The film shows Tracy's sudden awareness of the dawning power of her own maturing body with a point-of-view shot of Evie and her girlfriends showing off their butts in tight, low-slung jeans. The film's *mise en scène* is plastered with images of a commodity culture aimed at women. Billboards advertise expensive clothing brands such as Armani. Posters promote a brand of cosmetics with the tagline "Beauty is Truth" and an image of a glamorous, unblinking eye that returns the gaze of the film's characters. In these ways, the film makes explicit the panoptical gaze of consumer culture, especially on girls and women, who cannot escape the pressure to spend money and expend effort in cultivating their physical beauty. Both Mel and Brooke have pink-collar jobs that depend on women's desire to meet certain standards of beauty. Brooke suffers the misery of plastic surgery to retain her work in a business that rewards her for looking sexy.

The film's interest in bodies extends beyond characters caught in the cult of female beauty to others in the throes of addictions of all kinds. Drugs are evident in every aspect of the film's narrative, including its shocking opening sequence, when Tracy and Evie are high from huffing aerosol cans. We see a flashback of Brady overdosing on cocaine. Mel pleads for time away from her responsibilities at home to attend Alcoholics Anonymous meetings. Brady says he needs to "get loaded" when Tracy's anger becomes more than he can bear. Brooke swills beer in midday and offers it to Evie and Tracy. Tracy's brother, Mason, smokes pot daily. Tracy and Evie experiment with drugs of all kinds, which are widely available to them to casually buy and sell. Tracy's most dangerous addiction is not to drugs but to cutting and the film connects the two habits by crosscutting between a flashback to Brady's episode of overdosing and the first time we see Tracy cutting herself.

In some scenes, such as one in which a group of teens gets high on a summer night, characters appear to use drugs to experience the euphoric pleasures of group connection; as the teens play in the water from a sprinkler system, the sequence encourages us to see them as children indulging in a harmless pastime. Soon, however, these sequences are replaced by others shot with surrealistic distortions pointing to the darker causes and consequences of drug use. Tracy giggles, "I can't feel a thing," in the opening sequence, suggesting the broader, social numbness the film exposes, as its characters seek to escape the difficult pressures in contemporary life, from making a living and supporting a family with low-income jobs to raising teenagers in single-parent families. *Thirteen* suggests that these circumstances make its characters vulnerable to a

Thirteen exposes an array of cultural toxins particularly deadly to girls today. Tracy (Evan Rachel Wood) releases tension by cutting herself.

host of other addictions cultivated by the social world itself: to money, material goods, youth, beauty, popularity, social approval.

Thirteen is not explicitly "about" addiction or the economic hardships of its characters, both familiar tropes of melodrama. But by avoiding psychological or moralistic judgments of drug use and other addictions the film invites a more social and political consideration of their causes. It is difficult not to see in *Thirteen* the marks of an extensive array of economic and social forces that are shaping the material conditions of women's lives and their gendered subjectivity. Postfeminism is usually discussed in the context of neoliberalism, a discourse that underpins not only the conservative economic policies behind globalization but also the rise of militarism and expansion of empire pursued by the U.S. government, especially since 9/11. These policies—and the widespread denial of their consequences—have contributed to the anxiety that colors the atmosphere of *Thirteen*.

In her preface to the second edition of *Of Woman Born*, Adrienne Rich acknowledges that gender has receded as feminism's fundamental target for analysis and activism (xvii–xviii). Instead, feminism must confront the ways economic forces destroy the personhood of all human beings. This argument has long been made by women of color, and it is central to the postcolonial and transnational feminisms of Chandra Mohanty, Ella Shohat, and others. As Shohat writes, "The global nature of the colonizing process, the global flow of transnational capital, and the global reach of contemporary communications technologies virtually oblige the multicultural feminist critic to move beyond the restrictive framework of the nation-state as a unit for analysis" (1998, 47).

Most of these analyses concur that under globalization, state power has receded in favor of multi- or transnational corporations that operate across national boundaries with little or no accountability to elected governments. Eric Cazdyn (2006) offers a perspective that is particularly suggestive in relation to *Thirteen*. For Cazdyn, access to *legal* drugs is a crucial index of globalization's power over the lives of ordinary people. In global capitalism, he argues, the human body is no longer an object primarily of political control but of economic control, which is exercised most insidiously by pharmaceutical giants. These corporations, with little accountability to state institutions, determine who lives and who is condemned to premature death.[9] As the injustice of this situation becomes increasingly apparent, it produces psychic distress that in turn triggers a desire to "forget" that is evident in a series of recent films dealing with themes of amnesia or acutely fragmented consciousness.[10] That fragmentation and distress may explain why efforts to reform the American healthcare system continue to be met with a degree of hysteria and fear that seems irrational.

For some theorists of decolonization, the entire project of modernity has been a steady march to the kind of devastation *Thirteen* registers, more obviously on the victims of colonialism outside the borders of industrialized nations but increasingly on those within.[11] One example of the penetration of capitalism ever deeper into personal life is It's Just Lunch, a dating service advertised online and in in-flight magazines. It's Just Lunch offers its services to young professionals who want to have a romantic relationship but work too much to meet people. Serving one hundred cities worldwide, It's Just Lunch lures lonely and overworked professionals with the trendy language of globalization: "Outsource your personal life," its ads beckon.

Recent studies have also pointed to increasing social and psychological pathologies in the United States. An alarming one quarter of American adults now meet the criteria for having a mental illness, suggesting that the United States is poised to rank number one for mental illness globally (Weiss 2005).

American girls have now surpassed boys in drug use, and the rates of teen pregnancies are rising, despite efforts by social conservatives to depict boys as victims (of a triumphant feminism) (Connolly 2006). And, for the past two decades, Americans have drawn emotional support from fewer close friends than ever, from three to barely two (Hartsoe 2006). These developments may not be causally related to global capitalism, but they are signs of disorder and alienation within the social body.

Thirteen registers the economic, social, and psychological costs that these worldwide shifts of economic power have wrought within American borders. Some accounts of globalization emphasize the benefits that have accompanied the astonishingly easy flow of information worldwide made possible by the Internet. However, while *Thirteen* shows occasional use of cell phones, its *mise en scène* is tellingly empty of characters using computers or other high-tech communications devices, suggesting that these benefits are not uniformly available, especially to members of the working class. In fact, Mel's phone service and cable TV have been shut off because she hasn't been able to pay the bills. As *Thirteen* suggests, the consequences of frayed communities, families in flux, and unraveling social institutions weigh particularly heavily on working-class women and children.

Mel's situation represents the financial vulnerability of mothers who are divorced in this economic climate, as well-paying jobs for the working class have been replaced by minimum-wage jobs in the service sector. While her ex-husband drives a new car and appears to be upwardly mobile, he defaults on his child-support payments, leaving Mel barely able to maintain herself and her children in the middle class. Without even a high school diploma, she has few prospects to better her financial circumstances. Similarly, Brooke—a "model-slash-actress," in Evie's words—earns her living tending bar, dressed in attire so sexually provocative that she appears clownlike in a red fright wig and a bra stuffed with "cutlets."

Tracy's path to adulthood requires her to participate in a consumer culture shown to be both trendy and trashy. After *Thirteen*'s opening sequence, a flashback shows Tracy before her transformation. In one moment, she is reading Mel a poem she has written, expressing herself through an act of personal creativity. Under Evie's tutelage, however, she soon learns the social power that comes from wearing sexy clothing bought—or, better yet, shoplifted—from boutiques on Melrose Avenue. Mel, meanwhile, struggling with the pressures of her own life, is too distracted to pay attention to Tracy, foreshadowing the costs eventually to be paid for her unavailability. Later, Tracy demands expensive jeans so she can fit in with Evie's crowd, and throws away the clothing, dolls, and stuffed animals of her girlhood. When Mel offers Tracy inexpensive jeans she has hand-decorated ("for only seven dollars"), the well-intentioned gesture exposes her naïveté about her own diminishing capital in comparison to Evie, the hottest girl in school.

Cinematic Toxins and the Melodramatic Fix

Thirteen offers itself as an antidote not only to social toxins but to cinematic ones, including aspects of several genres that have dominated cinema screens in the millennial years. These include the epic, which enjoyed a surge of popularity during the Bush presidency, as well as the teen pics that have been popular with young women since the 1990s. Whereas teen romantic comedies, such as *Clueless*, push the pleasures of shopping and romance, *Thirteen* depicts consumerism not as harmless "retail therapy" but as a manic mode of rebellion and identity formation. And while exploring the lures and dangers of young sexuality, *Thirteen* has little interest in heterosexual romance itself, focusing instead on intense female-to-female relationships.

Most importantly, *Thirteen* asserts melodrama's ability to activate a sense of moral clarity and meaning at a time when the social order has lost its bearings. American culture appears to be experiencing an accelerating malaise and crisis of purpose, evident not only in a rise of fundamentalist religion but also in a taste for films in the melodramatic mode. Indeed, even well-respected ironist Art Spiegelman (author of *Maus* [2006] and regular contributor to the *New Yorker* magazine) has called for a turn from postmodern irony to a new seriousness and engagement with the pressing issues of our times, a stance he describes as "neosincerity." *Thirteen*, with its emphasis on relationships and its lament for lost innocence, depends on classic strategies of melodrama. But unlike other popular melodramatic films, including the "smart" melodramas Jeffrey Sconce identifies (2002) or melodramatic epics such as *The Lord of the Rings* that celebrate the power of its male saviors, *Thirteen* draws on the form's sympathy for the weak, the powerless, and the inarticulate, or those victimized by social forces impossible for them to resist or even understand.

Thirteen's melodramatic excess centers on the suffering of girls facing what it means to become a woman today. As Angela McRobbie notes, "*Thirteen* depicts a world where the fashioning of a credible female self brings with it

Thirteen examines how the primal mother/daughter bond must be restored before Tracy can move toward independence.

incalculable injuries and loss, and the requirement to become a 'real girl' gives rise to unfathomable rage" (2003, 8). Moreover, although the film is focused more around Tracy than her mother, *Thirteen*'s exploration of the relationship of mother and daughter identifies it as a *maternal* melodrama of the first order. Melodrama has not had much traction for young women in the postfeminist 1990s and beyond. But after a decade or more of films obsessed with relationships between fathers and daughter figures and films that treat mothers with little sympathy or interest, the most suggestive antidote *Thirteen* offers to the alienating chaos of its world is an imperfect but gritty maternal love.

Structurally, the film is organized around a melodramatic struggle to return to the innocence of the primal mother-child bond, which has been threatened by invaders on all fronts and must be restored before Tracy can begin to assert her own independence. The challenge then becomes shoring up and sorting out a series of boundaries against these invaders—boundaries of the self, the body, the home. Indeed, the film's rampant addictions are symptoms of inescapable anxieties around boundaries of all kinds, in an environment where the need for meaningful human contact is countered by fears of violation, invasion, and unwanted penetration. For Tracy, this means closing the door to her mother emotionally and literally as she begins her differentiation into adulthood. For Mel, it means learning when to let go of Tracy—but also when to bang down the door and hang on.

Doors are a recurring visual motif of this film. Slamming doors and strained verbal exchanges through closed doors literalize the boundaries that are at stake for the film's characters. The drama is played out on the grounds of a middle school, in the shops in Melrose Avenue, on the streets of Hollywood—but most of all, within the often chaotic space of the Freeland household. The escalation of chaos within this space occurs with successive intrusions into it by a series of people with varying claims on its members. Two characters eventually destroy the fragile equilibrium between Tracy and Mel by literally moving into the house and offering taboo pleasures to each. Evie insinuates herself between Tracy and Mel by cultivating Mel's maternal feelings for her. Repeated scenes show her visually intruding between mother and daughter, and in one scene she slyly follows Tracy's rant against her mother by planting a kiss on Mel's lips. Brady, the second intruder, brings misery to Tracy, who does not want to share her mother with him, or probably anyone.

When Mel's friend Birdie and her child move in while she awaits the arrival of a check, Mel can no longer hold the household together. Tracy, like most teen girls, views her bedroom as her sanctuary, where her best friend is welcome but her mother is not. However, it too becomes violated when she finds Birdie's child and the family dog sleeping in her bed, which has been soiled with urine. These examples suggest an uncertainty over interpersonal responsibilities and obligations, especially concerning emotional limits. Does Mel have a right to the companionship and sex Brady offers if her daughter doesn't want him in the house? Should she agree to Tracy's plea to have her best friend move in, even if she is uneasy about the girl? Mel struggles to strike a balance between giving Tracy the increasing freedom and privacy she needs, while also retaining her authority to impose limits on her behavior. She is startled by her new view of Tracy in more "sexed up" attire, but also accepts it. Yet she draws the line after one of Tracy's particularly brutal verbal attacks on her and insists, "That's not how I raised you."

Tracy ultimately retreats to the bathroom, where she can be alone and relieve her stress by cutting herself. For Tracy, piercing her tongue and navel are important but relatively harmless acts of rebellion that mark her as sexually adult. More troublingly, her cutting suggests her inability to deal with the very pressures that led to the piercings. (Evie's body, too, bears scars that she attributes to an abusive uncle.) The film shows Tracy cutting herself three times. The first time, she has just seen Mel and Brady beginning a sexual encounter, and she realizes that Brady has returned to her life. The second time, Evie leaves the bed she is sharing with Tracy and climbs out the window to have sex with a teen boy. The third incident occurs after Mason tells her that Mel wants to send her to live with her father. The first two episodes suggest Tracy's sensitivity to sex as an early adolescent, especially as a virgin. In all three instances, males threaten to violate the space between Tracy and the females who are most important to her life, her best friend and her mother.

Boys on the Side: Girlfriends, Mothers, Daughters

The film begins explicitly focused on Tracy. In a long take, in medium close-up, she gazes directly at the camera, indicating that what follows will be her story. But this sequence also shows the importance of her relationship with Evie. Initially off screen, Evie soon shares the frame with Tracy and will for most of the film, until its final shot, when Tracy once again commands the screen alone. Evie is the plot's instigator and the object of Tracy's desire. It is through this relationship that the film explores central issues a girl must confront in her passage to adult femininity: control over her body, understanding her sexuality, relationships with family, and how to find a place for herself in a world that is filled with exciting sensory stimuli but lacking in clear direction or purpose.

Thirteen captures the intensity of teen-girl friendships and their place in preparing girls for strong affective bonds outside the primary family. Indeed, it shows the relationship as a romance of sorts, especially for Tracy, who literally sets her sights on Evie when she observes her popularity and sexual power. Tracy aggressively courts Evie, and as the friendship intensifies, she abandons her best friends Noel and Yumi, quiet, studious girls, for an exclusive relationship with Evie. Tracy's former life, which consisted of babysitting, dog-walking, doing school projects, and writing poetry, offered her few incentives not to model herself on Evie, who is an object of awe in the socially competitive world of middle school. Meanwhile, Evie seduces Tracy with her flamboyant sexuality, confident style, and the thrills of breaking rules.

Along with the exhilaration, shrieks, and squeals that accompany their transgressions, the girls also share moments of tenderness, especially as they lie together in Tracy's bed. At one point, the camera plays a cinematic joke by pulling back from a close-up of Tracy reclining in bed after her sexual encounter with Javi, a young man in Evie's circle who has shown interest in Tracy. We expect to see Javi lying behind her, but it's Evie, who has returned to Tracy's bed after her own sexual encounter with Javi's friend. Evie caresses and kisses Tracy before they both drift into a postcoital sleep. The tactile nature of their intimacy recalls the physicality of Tracy's relationship with her mother at the beginning of the film, when Mel could dissipate Tracy's irritability simply by stroking her hair. However, as Tracy's physical closeness with Evie deepens, she recoils from her mother's touch and even her gaze, at one point forbidding Mel even to look at her.

Thirteen treats its unruly "bad girl" Evie with a certain sympathy. Tracy was ripe for rebellion before she met Evie, so viewers cannot blame her for Tracy's undoing, although the film's characters do. Nonetheless, Evie is difficult to read. She is brilliantly manipulative and a convincing liar. But we also see the circumstances of her life. If the film suggests, as I believe it does, that girls in early adolescence need not only loving attention from adults but also a firm hand as they make the transition to the freedom of adulthood, Evie gets neither from Brooke. Brooke is a catastrophe, and the toxins of patriarchy that poison Mel and Tracy have even more deadly effects on her and her charge Evie. In a film that side-steps the moral polarizations of melodrama, Brooke's characterization comes closest to melodramatic excess. If Mel's hands are stained by her labor in beauty culture, Brooke's face is ravaged by cosmetic surgery she underwent for similar reasons. If Tracy's father fails her by leaving and then neglecting the family, Evie says her uncle sexually abused and burned her when she was nine and Brooke's boyfriend hits her. If Tracy's mother has had bouts of alcohol abuse, Evie's mother died of an addiction to crack cocaine. Because Evie lies, we never know how much of this is true, but in the logic of the film, her accounts are plausible. Brooke is Evie's future.

Complicating the film's portrait of Evie is her identity as a Latina. *Thirteen*'s social environment appears casually multicultural, with classrooms, school grounds, and city streets racially mixed. Tracy's closest friends, before she meets Evie, are Noel (Vanessa Hudgens), who appears Asian American, and Yumi (Tessa Ludwick), who is also dark-skinned. Evie is so well assimilated that her Latina identity is evident only through her last name, Zamora. However, even an independent film such as *Thirteen* does not escape the racialized conventions of mainstream media by centering its story on a young white girl

As a Latina, Evie (Nikki Reed) mediates between black and white, guiding Tracy, the white virgin, to sex with two African American teenage boys.

and fetishizing her blonde beauty by surrounding her with darker-skinned friends. As the plot progresses, the film conveys the downward spiral of Tracy's life with an increasingly desaturated palette. Tracy's radiance turns to pallor, indicating the decline of her physical health, the effects of her emotional turbulence, and possibly the blood loss from her cutting. But even then, she remains an emblem of racially idealized female beauty.

Bad girls such as Evie typically transgress by acting out sexually. Explicitly dramatizing the film's concern with unstable boundaries and their danger to young women, Evie comes on to every character she meets, her precocious sexuality and promiscuity suggesting that she is telling the truth about her history of sexual abuse. She makes suggestive remarks to Brady and Mason, tries to seduce Luke the neighbor, and performs oral sex on Javi after he has paired up with Tracy.

Because Evie is a Latina, her character also draws on racial stereotyping of Latin sexual "heat," and her role is consistent with that of other Latina figures, from Rita Hayworth to Jennifer Lopez, who are positioned to mediate between black and white (Ovalle). Evie guides Tracy, the white virgin, not only toward drug use but also to sex with Javi, an African American teenage boy, a minor but likeable character who is probably at least a few years older than

Tracy. Tracy remarks with naïve sincerity that interracial sex would end prejudice in one generation. However, the film suggests that for girls like Evie and Tracy, having sex with nonwhite men has less to do with rebelling against racism than with making a fashion statement and appropriating the coolness of hip-hop and other forms of black culture now reigning in youth-oriented fashion and music.

The film raises several difficult questions about sex for girls in early adolescence. Third Wave feminism has defined itself in part by prioritizing the right of girls and women to experience sexuality on their own terms. The defiant reclaiming of the word "slut" by riot grrrls in the 1990s, for example, struck a blow against the double standard and helped advance the Third Wave beyond the perceived Puritanism of the Second Wave. In *Thirteen*, girls pursue boys. They have little interest in emotional attachments to them, indicating a desire to experience sex for its own sake. In fact, the girls casually engage in sex play by practicing kissing together, and while they don't pursue sexual feelings for each other, their emotional attachment is intense. *Thirteen* liberates the sexuality of its young protagonists from the ideology of heterosexual romance, and one of the film's most important elements is its demonstration that coming-of-age stories about teen girls need not revolve around the pursuit of boyfriends.

The Third Wave's affirmation of sexual agency, however, assumes a teen girl's ability to experience sexuality in circumstances not characterized by exploitation or unequal social power. Unlike Angela in *My So-Called Life*, who lived for her make-out sessions with Jordan Catalano, Tracy appears to have little awareness of her own desire or capacity for sexual pleasure. Tracy typifies the situation Joan Jacobs Brumberg describes in *The Body Project*, where she argues that although girls today mature physically at ever-younger ages, their emotional maturity lags behind. As a result, they are ill equipped to express their sexuality with responsibility, let alone a nuanced understanding of sexual politics. Tracy's sexual initiation involves performing fellatio on Javi, an act that she appears to do because he expects her to. Ultimately the experience is yet another opportunity to bond with Evie, with whom she's linked by eyeline matches early in the encounter and who joins her in bed when it is over.

According to Carol Siegel (2006), *Thirteen* falls into the reactionary trap of arguing against women's sexual freedom by employing imagery and rhetoric from the New Right's abstinence movement; moreover, it naturalizes domesticity as the only refuge for women and girls.[12] However, if Tracy's heterosexual initiation appears disturbing, it is not because the film argues against teen sex per se. Rather, it argues against teen sex under the circumstances it depicts. By depersonalizing the encounter and downplaying its drama, *Thirteen* shows how easily a teen girl can be drawn into traditional scripts about what the culture idealizes in female sexuality. *Thirteen* asks how girls can be supported in exploring their sexuality in a culture that continues to teach them that their primary value is as sexual objects for men. At what age are girls mature enough to wear panties with "I ♥ cock" printed on them and T-shirts that read "Porn Star" as affirmations of their own desire, rather than as signs of their unthinking acceptance of sexual ideologies based on female objectification?

Perhaps Tracy's best hope with regard to her sexual development lies in what causes her the most distress: the model of her mother as a sexual being whose life does not revolve exclusively around her identity as a mother. Here, the film considers not only the economic costs of divorce, but the emotional ones as well, which weigh heavily on Tracy. While Tracy resents Brady's claims on her mother's attention, what most pains her is that Mel is no longer having (invisible, parental) sex with Tracy's father. In Mel, *Thirteen* offers a sympathetic portrait of a mother who is comfortable with her own sexuality as well as her daughter's. Tracy calls Brady a loser and hints that Mel has been used by men in the past, and when she accuses Mel of having let men "fuck her over" before, she shows a dawning awareness of sexual politics. But Mel, by not acceding to Tracy's wishes that Brady not move in, displays a rare confidence in her own right to companionship and sex, to be "something else besides a mother."

Moreover, in an era of films about missing mothers who bear the blame when families fall apart, *Thirteen* takes a hard look at the consequences of missing fathers on the lives of their children. In early adolescence, when girls begin to imagine themselves as adult, sexual beings, they often cathect more powerfully on their fathers than on their mothers. Tracy needs to feel the paternal love of an adult man, but her father has a new wife and baby, and a new job that requires him to travel. The film shows his emotional absence when, during a short visit with Tracy, he repeatedly interrupts their conversation by accepting business calls on his cell phone. In a further slight to Tracy, he tries to extricate himself from the calls with the clichéd excuse of being "with a client." When Mason pleads with him to step in to help Tracy, the father is unwilling to take the time to learn about her problems and demands an explanation "in a nutshell." This busyness is yet another sign of the penetration of work into private life, but it also indicates the persistence of gendered structures that forgive men for their shortcomings as parents. Tracy's father makes time to surf with Mason, an easy teen, but he does not have the emotional maturity or commitment to be a father to his troubled daughter, and it is hard not to see Tracy's feelings of paternal rejection as part of what fuels her unhappiness.

Eventually, Brady must recede, and Evie be evicted, before Tracy's self-destructive descent can be turned around and her recovery begin. This occurs during the film's most cathartic sequence, when Mel, Brooke, and Evie confront Tracy about her stealing, drug use, and other transgressions. Filled with emotional excess and the spectacle of suffering, the sequence most fully realizes the film's melodramatic potential. Tracy, cornered, tries to escape through the bathroom window, but fails. A tumultuous showdown follows, with screaming, tears, and accusations, but "just in time" (a classic melodramatic convention), Mel sees through the frightful barriers that have separated her from Tracy. Then, when Brooke turns on Tracy and accuses her of corrupting Evie, Mel finally sees the truth and kicks them both out of the house.

Mel's misrecognition has finally given way to recognition of her daughter's vulnerability and of her own responsibility to rescue her, yet another melodramatic trope. As Tracy shrinks weeping on the floor, Mel embraces her and discovers the cuts on her arms. Tracy rages, "Get off me," but Mel continues to hold her, kissing her wounds and refusing to let go. The drama is heightened by details of *mise en scène* that remind us of Mel's earlier agony on that kitchen floor, when she ripped up its cheap vinyl flooring in despair. The camera does not cut or rush away from a long take as Mel rocks Tracy and kisses her, restoring the tactile intimacy so evident in the film's opening. Then, a series of dissolves shows Mel and Tracy asleep in Tracy's bed, the intruders gone and the primal mother-child unit restored.

The sequence, like the film itself, is a powerful antidote to the cinematic demonization or erasure of mothers, especially single mothers. Here, Hunter's performance recalls her role as Ada in Jane Campion's *The Piano* (1993), another mother similarly struggling for a life of her own that includes sexual passion and artistic expression, while she is tightly bound to a headstrong daughter. It is easy to blame Mel for not seeing what was going on sooner, or for bringing a weak boyfriend into the household, or for being too trusting of Evie, or for being too nurturing of everyone else around her. She can also be criticized for falling victim to the pressure to look younger than she is, and for trying to take care of Tracy by acting more like a sister than a mother. (Evie flatters her by describing her as "the hot older sister.") These criticisms have merit. But they also remind us of how easily mothers get blamed when things go wrong with their children.

Thirteen is a powerful antidote to cinema's familiar erasure or demonization of mothers, especially single mothers. When the film's conflicts are resolved, Tracy sleeps in Mel's (Holly Hunter's) protective arms.

Thirteen neither sentimentalizes nor demonizes Mel, and instead ties her, like her daughter, into a web of impossible expectations and demands. We do not know why she became an alcoholic, but we do know she works hard and tries to do her best. Indeed, Mel represents the perfectly socialized woman in a world still governed by patriarchal values, a caretaker who is concerned about maintaining her attractiveness to men and who can't say no to anyone in need. The film asks us to see Mel as imperfect but ultimately strong enough to do what needs to be done. Siegel (2006) reads Mel's embrace of Tracy as a suffocating and overbearing assertion of maternal control, perhaps like Ingrid's pernicious hold on Astrid in *White Oleander*. However, in asserting her right to touch her daughter—even as her daughter pushes her away—Mel touches viewers to the core, for in this instance at least, she is right. Once again, her touch eases her daughter's pain.

Thirteen's concluding scene shows Tracy alone, with neither Evie nor her mother close by. Ultimately, she will have to make her way in the world drawing on her own strengths, making her own choices. As in the opening sequence, she is the focus of the camera, but the angle is wider and the setting is outside in a park. Recalling François Truffaut's *400 Blows* (1959), another film about growing up that also ends with a freeze frame on the face of its young protagonist, she begins to spin on a circular ride, which propels her outward toward a larger world. But she is holding on now with a secure grip. She lets out a long scream, which, unlike the numb and manic shrieks of the opening sequence, suggests the beginning of her release from the forces that had entangled her. *Thirteen* has not returned her to that place of innocence so close to the heart of melodrama, and her future is at best unclear. But she is poised for her first tenuous steps toward adulthood, and the color that had been draining from the film during its most despairing moments has begun to return.

Both *My So-Called Life* and *Thirteen* feature sensitive girl protagonists who enter adolescence with a healthy desire to leave the sheltered environment of their homes. *Thirteen*, in particular, exposes the limits of teen-girl unruliness in a world that poses new dangers to girls and young women. In seeking new experiences, both girls distance themselves from their mothers—credible and sympathetic characters who struggle not only with their daughters but also with issues of their own related to money, sex, work, and aging. Both works demonstrate that girls need their mothers. Mothers need their children, too. This is a simple message—after all, these are melodramas—but one that resonates literally and symbolically. *Thirteen* and *My So-Called Life* remind us of the power of melodrama to put urgent social issues in the public consciousness, and the ability of maternal melodrama to draw our attention to the lives of girls and women related generationally to each other.

For at least the past decade, feminism has wrestled with its own issues of generation in an effort to find productive connections between its "mothers" and "daughters." At the same time, despite its pro-family rhetoric, the U.S. government has pursued policies that have undermined our collective commitment to future generations by abandoning the weakest among us, pushing war and materialism at the expense of social and economic justice, and pursuing environmental policies that are recklessly shortsighted. As Joan Jacobs Brumberg argues, strengthening intergenerational relations between girls and women is an obvious place to begin to help girls survive the storms of adolescence and mature into confident adults.

Girls of Color

BEYOND GIRL WORLD

What my mother showed me is that
sometimes, we improve our lot as women
together and through each other.
——CECILIA BALLI

ABC'S UGLY BETTY was inspired by the Colombian telenovela *Yo Soy Betty, La Fea* (1990–2001), but for North American viewers knowledgeable about popular culture, the hit series's most immediate debt is to *The Devil Wears Prada*. Beginning with its pilot episode, *Ugly Betty* makes abundant references to the film and to other well-known examples from Girl Culture. Betty, a smart but somewhat overweight and fashion-challenged young woman, accepts a job at the fashion magazine *Mode*. There, like Andy in *The Devil Wears Prada*, she encounters Girl World, again grown up and camped up. However, she responds to it in significantly different ways than Andy. Betty is from a working-class Mexican American family, and the Girl World of mainstream U.S. culture does not hold the same kind of allure for her as it does for many middle-class white girls. At work, Betty scrutinizes the excesses of the *Mode* universe with curiosity, but she returns home each night to a parallel universe defined by struggles around such basic necessities as finding money for medicine and rent. Girl World awakens desire in her, but not to make herself over in its image. Betty directs her unruly desire elsewhere.

This chapter considers films and television series that feature young women of color who, like Betty, are determined to achieve their desires. For them, however, Girl World is not a site of unruliness but is instead complicit with other forms of oppression. Instead of seeking to belong to the popular clique, or to find Mr. Right, or to play with ultrafemininity, these smart, focused, and serious young women want access to the highest levels of athletics and education, or recognition of their sexual identity, or acceptance of a body that doesn't conform to racialized standards of beauty. These aspirations harken back to feminism's earliest insistence on a woman's right to full enfranchisement as a citizen, and they remain especially compelling to girls of color, who, in seeking to achieve them, face obstacles related not only to gender but also to race, ethnicity, national identity, and often class.

These girls may also face unexpected resistance from their mothers, often strong-willed women who are devoted to their families but committed to traditional ideologies of femininity and fearful of the costs their daughters may pay for abandoning the values that have given meaning to their own lives. Thus, in these works, we see daughters challenging their mothers and breaking from them, if necessary, in order to pursue opportunities that were not available a generation ago. The African American protagonist of *Love and Basketball* (Gina Prince-Bythewood, 2000), for example, refuses to succumb to her mother's pressure that she abandon her desire to fulfill her athletic potential. *Real Women Have Curves* (Patricia Cardoso, 2002) similarly dramatizes the conflict between its Latina protagonist and her mother over the daughter's refusal to lose weight and her determination to attend a prestigious college across the continent.

These works acknowledge the tension between mothers who are unrepentant about their own identity and daughters who express their unruliness by rebelling against them. Drawing on melodrama more heavily than the mainstream Girl Culture texts do, they offer a rare representational space in which the relationship between mothers and daughters is neither sentimentalized nor trivialized but recognized for its intensity and complexity. In their own ways, these works also push at the claustrophobic dyad that structures representations of white mother-daughter relationships in the dominant culture and that severely limits imaginings of cross-generational relations among girls and women.

This chapter also looks at how girls of color negotiate their passage to adulthood in a culture shaped by the values of postfeminism. In *Ugly Betty*, America

Ferrera brings her unruly persona from *Real Women Have Curves* to the world of high fashion, which she dissects through the eyes of a working-class Latina teen. In contrast, in the ABC sitcom *All-American Girl* (1994–1995), Girl World is a site of desire for the protagonist, played by Korean American comedian Margaret Cho, whose enthusiastic embrace of its values signals her assimilation into American culture. Finally, *Saving Face* (Alice Wu, 2004), taking full advantage of romantic comedy's inclusivity and comfort with unruly women, rewrites the genre to give equal weight to a young lesbian woman and her mother, who is unwed and pregnant in middle age. This wonderful film, set in a New York community of Chinese immigrants, offers a model of generational relations by finding a place for femininities and pleasures of all kinds.

In considering these works together, I don't intend to reinforce the exclusion of the communities they represent from the dominant culture, which is the subject of most of this book. The percentage of mainstream films and television shows that focus on girls and women of color is extremely small, and this grouping acknowledges the ways the dominant culture still privileges whiteness and heterosexuality. Throughout this chapter, I place these works in conversation with the media texts I discuss elsewhere in the book.

Nor do I wish to minimize the differences among these groups or within them. Identity can never be reduced to a single determinant, and multiple factors influence the ways girls of varying ethnic and racial identities relate to the dominant culture, not to mention to feminism. For example, the notion of belonging means something quite different to a Latina girl like Betty, who fears her father will be deported, than it does to girls of any race who are secure in their citizenship. Working outside the home, as well, has rarely been a "lifestyle choice" for women of color in this country but instead an economic necessity, influenced, once again, by a range of variables, from class (*Love and Basketball*, set in the black bourgeoisie) to the easier assimilation experienced by members of a "model minority" (*Saving Face*).

Nonetheless, common threads run through these texts. These include the strong hand of female authorship in most of them, as well as similarities in how nonwhite girls define themselves in relation to both feminism and the dominant culture. I trace these threads in the spirit of learning to find commonality and strength in difference. Success in building theoretical and political strength from difference eluded the Second Wave, the failures of which can be heard in the voices of the American Third Wave feminists of color I now turn to.

(Not So) Close Encounters: Girls of Color and the Third Wave

The Third Wave fully embraces the messiness of contradiction. In its desire to respect individual difference, it presents itself as comfortable with diversity of all kinds, including modes of writing. For example, the anthology *Colonize This!* (Hernandez and Rehman 2002) gathers writings of young women with diverse racial and ethnic identities and national backgrounds, refusing to shape their stories onto a totalizing narrative. Still, themes recur throughout these writings and others that shed light on both representations of mothers and daughters from communities of color and on the relation of girls of color to feminism.

Not surprisingly, the matrophor figures differently for young women of color than it does for young white women in influencing their attitudes toward feminism. For some young black women, as Joan Morgan notes, a mythic black mother feminism holds as little appeal as the ideal of the "STRONGBLACK-WOMAN," which they see as damaging to both women and men (1999, see especially 56–62). Nor are these women interested in "inserting" themselves into the Third Wave paradigm, despite the prominent role feminists of color, such as Rebecca Walker, have played in naming and establishing the movement. Instead, as Kimberley Springer suggests, some have preferred to continue the work of generations of black "race women" who were also concerned with gender (2007, 19). Indeed, many young people of color discover their political identities through first identifying with their racial or ethnic group, then finding their way to a feminist consciousness.[1]

Frequently these young women see their mothers as powerful feminist role models, even if the mothers don't identify as feminists. For these daughters, the mother-daughter relation enhances the power of both rather than impedes their autonomy. This perspective offers an important contrast to the fraught mother-daughter relationship described in much white Third Wave discourse (Henry 2004, 173).

Other young women of color first encounter the contemporary women's movement in women's studies classes, where they may find an academic model that not only has little obvious relevance to their lives but also remains painfully marked by the racism and classism that estranged their mothers from the Second Wave.[2] In her essay "Heartbreak," Korean-born Rebecca Hurdis describes her high hopes for the book *Manifesta*, which marketed itself as "*the* text for the third wave of feminism," and her outrage and grief in discovering that it reconstructs the history of feminism as "the specific story of white [privileged] women" (2002, 286–287). She continues, "I found it astounding that there is no extensive discussion of women of color feminism," nor any acknowledgement of how works such as *This Bridge Called My Back* (1981) or *Sister Outsider* (1984) were groundbreaking for Gen-X women of color.

This "classroom feminism" often bears little relation to the "real-world, everyday feminism" these young women see in the lives of their impoverished, hardworking mothers. For Siobhan Brooks, the daughter of a poor African American mother, the feminism she grew up with was missing from her classes: "The women had the theory but not the practice," she writes of the teachers and authors she encountered (2002, 115). Bushra Rehman and Daisy Hernandez "wondered how it could be that, according to feminist thought, our mothers were considered passive when they raised six children; worked night and day at stores, in factories and at home; and when they were feared and respected even by the bully on the block" (2002, xxiii). Paula Austin, born in Guyana, adds, "I have felt left out of feminism mostly because it leaves out women who look like my mother—traditionally feminine, of color, poor, powerful despite the impact of oppression on her psyche . . . It leaves no room for women who find their power through a perceived powerlessness" (2002, 167). According to Florence Maatita, noting the ways young Chicana feminists are ignored in the academy, the Third Wave will not attract them or other women of color until it speaks to their family relations and traditions (2005, 26).[3]

Others describe encountering white women who express liberal guilt but fail to acknowledge the ways poverty and racism shape the lives of women of color. As Mary Thompson argues, issues relating to motherhood have been foundational to the First and Second Waves. But rather than working toward structural solutions to the problems of motherhood, Third Wave feminism has often redefined those problems within the framework of consumer culture, excluding mothers without the means (or desire) to ease their burdens by purchasing goods or services. The new momism, for example, defines success at motherhood through the endless self-surveillance and well-informed consumer decisions associated with postfeminism.

Moreover, the discourse of choice so familiar in writings from the Third Wave has often failed to consider how a history of oppression has restricted the choices available to women of color, who have been subjected to racist constructions of their sexuality and excluded from choices available to white women. Regular access to birth control, artificial insemination, abortion, and adoption all require a level of means many mothers do not have. The discourse of choice also establishes categories of "good choice-makers" and "bad choice-makers," which reinforce the belief that motherhood is the earned privilege of the middle class. Punitive public policy and welfare reforms judge nonwhite women as bad decision-makers who are not entitled to care for their children or make decisions about them because they are too poor and/or got pregnant too young or too often.

Estranged from academic feminism, the young women quoted above value the weapons of critical thinking and theory they have learned in the classroom and do not hesitate to challenge the patriarchal values they see internalized in their mothers. But they also speak of other feminisms more rooted in their own experiences. As Hernandez and Rehman write, "While college may have given us the theories, many of us return home for a working definition of what it means to be a feminist—whether that means learning lesbian femme tactics from a mom who did sex work or taking after a fearless auntie who owned a brothel in Colombia" (xxvi). Their views challenge contemporary feminism in crucial ways, showing how continued failures around race and class influence its positions on motherhood.[4]

Darice Jones's moving account of her discovery of feminism models how women of all ages and races might negotiate the challenges of difference. While describing the institutionalized white privilege she encountered in women's studies classes (2002, 117), Jones's essay is above all a love letter to her mother, who raised her daughter under extraordinarily difficult conditions, including mental illness and extreme poverty. Anticipating a moment in the film *Saving Face*, which I will return to later, Jones recounts her yearning for her mother to accept her lesbianism. Her mother could not do so. And yet Jones herself learned a powerful lesson about acceptance when she recognized her own integrity and strength as gifts from her mother. "More deep and motivating than any books on feminist theory, I'd spent my entire life face to face with a feminist powerhouse who offered neither explanation nor apology," she writes, in words that capture her mother's unrepentance and well-earned pride. "She taught me an abiding love for self and humanity—and she taught by example. So I went to work," she writes (323–324).

Love and Basketball: Learning to Fight

Produced by Spike Lee, America's most successful African American film-maker, *Love and Basketball* brings a keen political perspective to its exploration of ongoing pressure on girls to see competitiveness and femininity as mutually exclusive. If *Clueless, Mean Girls,* and *The Devil Wears Prada* follow their protagonists into various versions of Girl Culture, *Love and Basketball* sets its drama in the world of sports, where the stakes for competition are more explicit and no one can succeed without a strong drive to win. Whereas *Mean Girls* studies the ways ordinary girls torment each other when not given healthy outlets for their aggression, *Love and Basketball* zeroes in on the challenges faced by competitive, athletic girls with little interest in old-fashioned femininity—girls who want to compete not only with other girls in girly matters but with boys, on male turf.

Love and Basketball is a serious film, but it is also an immensely enjoyable one. It offers the emotional satisfactions of melodrama, enhanced by an expressive soundtrack of popular tunes as well as the cinematic pleasures of watching dynamic sequences of basketball played to high emotional stakes. It also follows romantic comedy's trajectory to a happy ending signified by the union of two appealing characters. While girls are still encouraged to believe that female ambition cannot be reconciled with romance, the title of this film suggests otherwise. Monica, its unruly protagonist, manages to make a life for herself that includes love and basketball.

The film, the first feature by African American writer and producer Gina Prince-Bythewood, tells the story of Monica and Quincy, who have lived next door to each other since they were eleven and share a common passion for basketball. Quincy, the son of a famous professional player, is marked for a basketball career of his own and has been groomed to compete and excel. Monica, on the other hand, has to fight hard not only to pursue her love of basketball but for everything else she desires. By anchoring their stories in their family backgrounds, the film treats its overt subjects—love and basket-ball—with added emotional and political nuance. Monica's relationship with her old-fashioned mother is strained, and Quincy faces a difficult hurdle when he learns that the father he has idolized is a philanderer.

The film carefully interweaves race and gender as factors shaping the lives of its characters. Racial difference is an obvious source of conflict well suited to the structure of romantic comedy, but interracial romances are still rare

Love and Basketball's unruly and competitive protagonist Monica (Sanaa Lathan) has little interest in old-fashioned femininity, but manages to make a life for herself that includes romantic love and basketball.

in mainstream cinema and TV.[5] All of *Love and Basketball*'s major characters, including its romantic couple, are African American, and so the film avoids the tensions that have traditionally surrounded an interracial love story. Even so, as Prince-Bythewood notes on the DVD commentary, mainstream media rarely shows love scenes with black characters. Despite their restraint and sensitivity, Quincy and Monica's sex scenes attracted more attention for their eroticism than they probably would have if the characters had been white, and Prince-Bythewood had to tone them down in order to avoid an R rating.

Through the subplot based on Quincy's father Zeke (Dennis Haysbert), the film shows the consequences of white America's obsession with and exploitation of black male athletes. Because of racist constructions of the black male body, sports and entertainment remain the most obvious routes to the American Dream for black men, and racist constructions of black male sexuality make black men objects of white fear and desire. Zeke achieved fame and financial rewards as a basketball star, enabling him to take masculine pride in keeping his wife in "Gucci and gold." However, that fame has its costs. Not only must he travel much of the time, but he is never free from the aggressive pursuits of women who make him the target of their sexual and racial fantasies. Indeed, Quincy is already experiencing the heady pleasure of having girls offer him sex just because he is a sports star. The film treats Zeke as a dignified and devoted father undone by temptations that are difficult for a talented and ambitious black man to avoid. Aware of his own vulnerability, he is eager to guide his son to a better life and urges Quincy to focus on his education rather than early fame.

The film's most overt political message concerns Monica's struggle to pursue her passion for basketball. She faces many obstacles, which the film attributes primarily to gender.[6] The film is not about Title IX, however, which it takes for granted, but about the prejudices girls continue to face when they assert their competitiveness. As *Mean Girls* and other teen films show, girls hold back, whether in academics or sports, especially when they are competing with boys. Girls who compete hard for a goal, like Tracy Flick in *Election*, are seen as too hungry for success rather than as simply wanting to be their best. Quincy plays in stadiums packed with fans, newscasters, and scouts, in contrast to Monica's games played to small crowds in the boys' gym. These differences are not lost on Monica. At one point, she tells Quincy that an emotional outburst from a male player earns him a pat on the rear, while a female player would be told to calm down and act like a lady. Yet the film implies that women will never assume their full power until they are willing to fight for it.

In creating Monica, Prince-Bythewood wanted to dispel the stereotype associating athletic girls with lesbianism. Monica is continually accused of being "different," and she is, but not because she is gay. She embodies a heterosexual femininity that exudes physical power, mental toughness, and a beauty based on nonwhite and non-"plastic" standards. She avoids makeup and feminine attire, and her body language is masculine. On the rare occasions she dresses up—for the first day of school, or her high school prom—she appears to be wearing "girl drag." She refuses to cover up her often-angry moods with ingratiating smiles (the "disease to please," in Oprah's words), and remains a loner even among the girls on her team. And yet, she is beautiful, especially when she is doing what she does best—competing in a game that requires aggression and intimidation as well as physical grace and skill. Much of the film's power arises from its realism and the effects of the intensive training actor Sanaa Lathan, who previously did not play basketball, underwent for the part.

If Quincy's parental distress comes from his father, Monica's comes from her mother Camille (Alfre Woodard), who cannot understand her daughter's tomboyish ways and instead wants to groom her for success as her generation of black women understood it. Camille shows her disapproval of Monica by not attending her games and putting continued pressure on her to become more feminine. But in Monica's eyes, Camille is weak. Monica accuses her of never standing up for herself, and of shutting down her catering business to make her husband feel more like a man. Indeed, Camille appears to combine elements of the stereotypical "STRONGBLACKWOMAN" (Springer 2007) with the pre-Friedan suburban housewife. She is still imprisoned by old ideologies of femininity newly romanticized by postfeminism, and through her, the film makes the Second Wave's case for the crippling effects of excessive domesticity on women—a canny warning to girls caught up in postfeminism.[7]

Yet Camille's behavior is shaped not only by gender but also by race and class. She understands the heightened scrutiny her daughters will face in the white world and the unstated benefits they will gain from bearing themselves with dignity and style. She also understands the particular challenges to his masculinity her husband faces as a black man in the United States. In a powerful showdown, Camille accuses her daughter of being ashamed of her for being "nothing but a housewife," but she takes on the stature of an unrepentant mother when she refuses to apologize for who she is. Most poignantly, after years of unresolved tension between the two, she shows her understanding and love for Monica by urging her to fight for Quincy. The film suggests that the presence of a strong mother in a girl's life may not always be easy for the daughter but it is still foundational to her well-being. Camille can't support Monica's desire for basketball, but she can push her toward something she understands better, and that is love.

The film's affirmation of romantic love may well counter its more radical resistance to the traditional pleasures of Girl World—shopping and flirting with boys rather than challenging them in contact sports. But the film's view of love is consistent with its view of basketball. Here it is not the boy who wins the girl, but the reverse. Throughout their lives, Monica and Quincy have played one-on-one to work through the attraction and tensions between them. Just before the film ends, Monica challenges Quincy one more time, this time for his heart. They both know he can beat her if he wants to. But after years of floundering in the wake of his father's weakness, he lets Monica win because her toughness and desire have inspired him to discover his own.

The film concludes a few years later. Monica is playing ball, and Quincy watches her from the stands, holding their little daughter. A final shot shows

Camille (Alfre Woodard), an unrepentant, traditional mother, opposes Monica's passion for basketball, but she still remains an important presence in her daughter's life.

the child dressed in feminine finery, playing with a basketball. *Love and Basketball* does not orchestrate a festive comic ending with all family wounds healed. Camille and Zeke are missing from the young new family watching Monica play. But the film does suggest that romantic love can survive women's empowerment, and that when girls remain faithful to their dreams, those dreams just might come true.[8]

Real Women Have Curves: **Learning to Leave**

Real Women Have Curves deals with another talented teen girl with little interest in Girl World, and another mother who wants to hold her daughter close to traditional notions of femininity. This heartfelt film puts boys even farther on the side than *Love and Basketball*, focusing instead on the charged and difficult relation between a headstrong mother and her daughter, and the inevitable separation between them that must occur for the daughter to fulfill her potential. Based on a play by Josefina Lopez, directed by Patricia Cardoso, and filmed on location in the Latino neighborhood of Boyle Heights, Los Angeles, by a mostly Latina crew, the film captured numerous awards and helped propel its young star America Ferrera toward the lead role in ABC's hit *Ugly Betty*. The play originated from Lopez's frustration at being told all her life she would be "so beautiful" if she lost weight. Both she and Cardoso were eager to create dignified Latino characters to be played not by white actors but by Latinos, who are more often cast as gardeners, maids, and gangsters. In casting calls, they sought "real women"—not skinny ones—who identified themselves as actors, and they had difficulty finding them.

The film begins with Ana, about to graduate from high school, at a crossroads in her life. Her teacher is pushing her to apply to a top university, but her mother Carmen (Lupe Ontiveros) expects her to join her and her sister Estela working in a small dress factory. Ana receives a scholarship to Columbia University, but her mother refuses to allow her to go. Ana begins to work in the factory and to date a white boy. Eventually, her father intercedes in the standoff between Carmen and Ana, and Ana leaves for her new life in New York, without her mother's blessing.

The film shares many thematic similarities with *Love and Basketball*. Both feature a talented, moody teen protagonist so focused on her goals that, unlike Cady in *Mean Girls*, she is immune to the temptations of Girl World. Both protagonists pursue their ambitions despite little support from within or outside their community. Each experiences encouragement from her older sister and father but disapproval from her more traditional mother. Both girls set the stage for their sexual initiation, and both face maternal pressure to bring their appearance more in line with conventional (white) standards of female beauty. Both films make significant use of melodrama, especially in their treatment of the mother-daughter relationship, but *Real Women Have Curves* incorporates more comedy because of its refusal to generate pathos around its characters or view them as victims, despite the hardship of their lives.

Mixing lyricism with realism, *Real Women Have Curves* allows viewers to experience Ana's world through her eyes and ears. Tracking shots create the visual texture of her life by following her movement from her neighborhood, with its brightly colored murals and signs, to her school across the city in Beverly Hills. The film's opening sequence includes a shot of a toothless old woman in a garden singing "O Sole Mio" directly to the camera. The woman, who appears again at the film's end, anticipates the visual motif of birds, both caged and in flight, that recurs in the film and suggests a tender side of harsh Carmen as well as Ana's need to fly. The soundtrack's use of traditional acoustic Latin music reinforces the film's lyricism, while its mixture of Spanish and English dialogue contributes to its realism. Characters speak in both languages, depending on their relationship, and more than a third of conversation is in Spanish.

As in many teen-girl films, Ana's relationships with the men in her life are easier than her relationship with her mother, and she is surrounded by nurturing men who care about her—her teacher Mr. Guzman; her grandfather, who helps her slip out to meet her boyfriend; her father, a dignified man who works as a gardener in a wealthy neighborhood; and her boyfriend Jimmy, a white boy whose desire for her helps her to see her body through new eyes. These male figures provide the backdrop against which Ana fights her titanic battles with her mother. While it is gratifying to see Latino male characters presented so sympathetically, however, once again the father becomes the daughter's ally against the mother.

Carmen and Ana match each other's stubbornness and intensity. They have ample reasons to fight simply because of their temperaments, but they have more specific reasons as well, based on their different attitudes toward assimilation. Carmen, rooted in traditional Mexican culture, believes Ana should follow in her footsteps, learning from her the skills she feels are essential for a woman: how to sew, take care of a husband, and raise her children. Ana, who is fully Americanized, wants to take advantage of the opportunities and freedoms that feminism won for white women but that have been less available for women of color, both because of their ties to traditional communities and persistent inequities of race and class.

Carmen is an unrepentant mother, neither sentimentalized nor monstrous, but a complex character whose desire to control Ana is understandable given her cultural roots and her personality. "We are a family, and we are going to stay that way," she insists to Mr. Guzman. Much of the film's humor comes from Carmen's self-dramatizing ways, her hypochondria, and her love for telenovelas ("See what happens when a daughter doesn't listen to a mother!"). The film's most comical and poignant subplot concerns her insistence that she is pregnant because she has missed several periods. At first, this seems to be a ploy to manipulate Ana, but when her doctor tells her she is entering menopause, she seems genuinely surprised.[9] Here the film helps us understand that Carmen's desire to keep Ana as a baby and to be a grandmother comes from her grief at losing what she most values about herself. "It's over," she wails. "I'm no longer a woman."

Women of color are subject to racialized standards of beauty and racist constructions of their sexuality, whether as the "hot-blooded" Latina, the "animalistic" black woman, or the Asian woman fetishized for a delicate and passive femininity. While the cult of skinniness has had devastating effects on white girls, the ideal of a female body without full breasts and hips is even more unattainable for many Jewish, African American, Native American, and Latina women. Thus Ana's most dramatic expression of independence and confidence arises from her attitude toward her body, and her refusal to accept her mother's insistence that she lose weight or remain a virgin so she can attract a husband. "I happen to like myself," she tells her mother.

When Ana is undressing to have sex with Jimmy, she asks him to keep the lights on while she stands before the mirror. The lighting is warm, she is back-lit and internally framed, and the camera holds on her as she intently studies her reflection. In this intimate moment, Jimmy approaches her from behind, embraces her, and says, "What a beauty!" Ana's loss of her virginity marks a milestone in her increasing ability to live fully and confidently in her body. Later, when Jimmy asks if she wants to continue the relationship when he's in college, she declines, a mature acceptance of their short romance for what it was. She does not need to be rescued by a white boy.

Despite her confidence in herself, though, Ana remains innocent of realities about her community that she needs to grasp before she is truly prepared to leave it. Ana's summer at the factory teaches her the kind of "real-world" feminism the writers of *Colonize This!* describe in relation to their mothers. In an inspired critique of the cult of fashion recuperated by postfeminism, *Real Women Have Curves* exposes the invisible and underpaid labor that fuels the fashion industry and the cost of the fantasies marketed by magazines such as *Runway* in *The Devil Wears Prada* or *Mode* in *Ugly Betty*. Ana already has a political understanding of how her sister, mother, and the women in the factory are exploited. Yet her understanding remains limited because it does not keep her from arrogantly looking down on them for participating in a system that exploits them.

Ana's time at the factory grounds her abstract political knowledge in the everyday lives of her mother and sister, as she discovers their dignity and pride in their work as well as the emotional richness of their relationships with each other. She sees how Estela, who owns the dressmaking business, suffers from straddling two worlds—she is a failure in her mother's eyes because she has not married, yet she can barely keep her business afloat because she is so

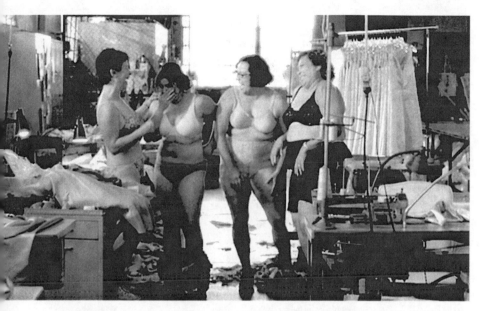

In *Real Women Have Curves*, Ana (America Ferrera) and her co-workers take a break from their work in the sweat shop, strip down, and celebrate their bodies. Ana's disapproving mother is missing from the scene.

poorly paid for her product. Finally, Ana begins to understand the realities of poverty and racism that her mother's lifetime of labor on her behalf has sheltered her from. That labor began with the act of bringing her into the world. When Ana asks her mother about the source of the scar on her abdomen, Carmen answers, "You." A sobered Ana notes how big it is, and Carmen agrees. The scene acknowledges that one cannot become a mother without suffering. Ana's real-world education crystallizes in the film's most celebrated scene, when, on an exceptionally hot day, Ana takes off her shirt and encourages the other women to join her. One by one, her full-figured co-workers, with the exception of Carmen, strip down to their bras and panties, drop their modesty, laugh, and dance. "How beautiful we all are," Ana says, sharing with them the freedom and confidence she feels in her own body.

This festivity does not last long, however. On the day of Ana's departure for college, Carmen closes herself in her bedroom and refuses to say goodbye. Her ambivalence is palpable as she studies photographs of Ana as a young girl and stares through the window as her daughter drives away. Ana looks back in pain, but a gauze curtain blocks their view of each other.

It is tempting to judge Carmen harshly for not reconciling with Ana before she leaves, but the film challenges its viewers to accept this difficult lack of closure because it springs from each character's determination to remain true to herself.[10] Mothers and daughters cannot always agree or avoid hurting each other. This ending recalls Darice Jones's acceptance of her mother's inability to accept her lesbianism. Carmen's intransigence comes from her love for Ana and her inability to support her in an action she truly believes is wrong. What matters is that Ana has the strength to leave, and that she gained that strength from her mother. In the film's final image, Ana emerges from a subway station onto a busy New York street. With her hair free, head high, and arms swinging, she strides toward the camera no longer shuffling but walking tall and proud, "like a lady," as Carmen had prodded her to do earlier.

Ugly Betty: "Ana in Manhattan"

Three years after *Real Women Have Curves*, America Ferrera appeared in *The Sisterhood of the Traveling Pants*, with a considerably larger budget and box office.[11] One year after that, the prime-time comedy/soap opera *Ugly Betty* (2006–2010) made its debut on ABC. Co-produced by Salma Hayek, the series has since become a worldwide hit and has garnered awards, parodies, and even a commendation from Congress for casting a positive light on Latino and Hispanic communities. By the end of its first season, *Time* magazine named Ferrera to its annual list of the one hundred most influential people for her work in defying stereotypes. The show racked up other awards as well, including an Emmy for outstanding lead actress in a comedy series for Ferrera, the Outstanding Comedy Award from the Gay and Lesbian Alliance Against Defamation, and a Peabody Award for storylines exploring "clashing concepts of beauty, class, race, and footwear with intelligence, warmth and wit."[12]

In the final episode of the first season, Betty sits defeated in her orthodontist's chair. Henry, the accountant she has pined over for months, is about to fly out of New York with his former girlfriend, who has told him she is pregnant with their child. The sympathetic dental assistant, who has heard Betty's story and admiringly described her life as "a chick flick," unwittingly exposes the girlfriend as a fraud. Betty, shocked, grabs her phone to call Henry, but the assistant stops her in disbelief: "Would Reese Witherspoon leave a message on his cell? Would Drew Barrymore? This is *your* movie, Betty!" There is only one thing to be done. Betty must race to the airport, force her way onto the plane, reveal the truth, humiliate the "whore," and passionately kiss Henry to an eruption of applause from the passengers. Betty hesitates, and the assistant shrieks, "*Drew Barrymore!*" This sends Betty flying out of the office to fix yet another of the ludicrous but entertaining disasters that have filled the series since its first episode.

Ugly Betty is not a chick flick, but in the twenty-three hour-long episodes of its first season, it shares, expands, and complicates the preoccupations and themes of Girl Culture's canonical films. "East Side Story," the first season's final episode, alludes both to romantic comedy, as characters prepare for two weddings, and to melodrama, when it creates a ludicrous number of coincidences and disasters that end the season with a cliffhanger. The final sequence cuts between unfolding catastrophes, including a car wreck, a shooting, a drug overdose, and a prison break, as Betty's young gay nephew belts out "Something's Coming" from *West Side Story*.[13]

Ugly Betty not only offers the pleasures of Girl Culture, beginning with its focus on a young female character working in the world of high fashion, but it also enriches these pleasures with a critique of classism, racism, and homophobia, not to mention ageism. This critique is overt, and, in the tradition of female unruliness, funny. Betty the "ugly" is heavy and clumsy, and wears thick glasses, braces, and dreadful clothes. But contrary to Girl Culture conventions, she has no makeover. Nor does she want one. She is also a "good girl," not because of a crippling desire to please but because of her core values. Smart, confident, and strong, she pushes the Third Wave—with its ambiguous relation to postfeminism and its imperfectly realized commitment to racial inclusivity—toward a Fourth.

The series's first season begins when Betty Suarez is hired as personal assistant to the new head of *Mode* fashion magazine, playboy Daniel Meade (Eric Mabius). His father, Bradford, hopes that because Betty is so plain, Daniel will concentrate on learning how to run the company. Betty lives in Queens with her widowed father Ignacio, her sexy older sister Hilda, and Hilda's young son Justin. She soon earns Daniel's trust because of her intelligence and integrity, but she is the laughing stock of the superficial and deceitful *Mode* staff, which includes the bubble-headed receptionist Amanda and her gay partner-in-intrigue Marc.

Ugly Betty conveys much of its thematic content through dense intertextuality, with abundant references to the films and personalities of Girl Culture, including Sarah Jessica Parker, Candace Bushnell, *Sex and the City*, *Bridget Jones's*

Diary, All My Children, Queer Eye for the Straight Guy, and Martha Stewart (in a nod to older viewers). Ignacio coaches Walter, one of Betty's love interests, on how to patch up a quarrel with her by referring to *Pretty Woman,* Betty's mother's favorite film, and the series continues the critique of the "Plastics" of *Mean Girls* by mocking the vapidity and meanness of fashion- and diet-obsessed young women through the hilarious character of Amanda. The parallels to *The Devil Wears Prada* are evident in the first episode, which contrasts virtuous Betty with her nemesis Wilhelmina, a glamorous and ruthless middle-aged female executive who wants to take over the company.[14]

Unlike most mainstream media texts, however, *Ugly Betty* does not relegate people of color to supporting roles. Betty is Mexican American, and archvillainous Wilhelmina is played by former Miss America Vanessa Williams, who is African American. Indeed, an important subplot shows the extreme vulnerability of immigrants who have entered the United States illegally. Ignacio has resided in the country for thirty years, but must ingratiate himself to immigration workers when his status is discovered. His humiliation escalates when an unbalanced and lonely woman pretending to be a caseworker tries to manipulate him into marrying her. Here, with African American Octavia Spencer in the unruly role of Constance, the tone combines high comedy with serious indignation.

Much of the series addresses the question of belonging, and of how it shapes social hierarchies. Where do "ugly" people belong? Dark-skinned people? Illegal immigrants? Transgendered people? The film stages these conflicts by moving between two distinctly different worlds: Queens, where Betty lives, and Manhattan, where she works. Queens generally connotes the admirable values of family loyalty and personal honesty. In Betty's household, family members talk to one another, argue, celebrate holidays together and care for each other. Its *mise en scène's* bright, often-clashing colors, warm lighting, and décor indicate the family's Mexican origins. The neighborhood is noisy and cluttered, with bustling activity on the sidewalks spilling out from bodegas and bars. Daniel is drawn to Queens for a taste of a family life he never had and for an image of the more responsible person he might become. In contrast, the *Mode* offices are sleek and ultramodern, decorated in orange, white, and blue, and shot with cool lighting and symmetrical compositions.

The fashion business signifies all that is most corrupt about wealth and social status. However, Betty is drawn to Manhattan despite the cruel exclusion she experiences at *Mode* because, as in many films set in New York (e.g.,

Unlike most mainstream media texts, *Ugly Betty* does not relegate people of color to supporting roles. The series's arch villainess Wilhelmina is played by Vanessa Williams.

Saturday Night Fever [1977]), Manhattan signifies a better future for her. The series dramatizes this tension with her competing love interests: Walter, the whiny shop clerk from her old neighborhood, who—like Nate in *The Devil Wears Prada*—cannot accept her upward mobility, and Henry, a Clark Kent accountant from *Mode* who is smitten by her. Walter heightens Betty's awareness of her own difference from the world she aspires to, especially in subtle matters of *habitus*. He wears his working class taste with pride, and Betty's traditional family pressures her to marry him simply because he loves her.

The vivid contrasts between these two environments heighten the divisions of class and ethnicity that Betty must negotiate. The Meades live with unthinking entitlement to power, glamour, and money, while Ignacio struggles to pay for the medicine he desperately needs. Queens, which Marc describes as "the lost city of Hoochieville," is also a place of racial otherness. When Betty, a college graduate, finds herself without a job, she has to work as a "chip chick" at a local taqueria, where she carries chips and salsa on her head in a huge sombrero. Her sister Hilda, a hairdresser, constantly reminds Betty that the good things she aspires to don't happen to "people like us—unless you're

J.Lo." Indeed, the series shows through the Meades and their circle how the privileged classes depend on the unseen labor of "people like" the Suarezes—poor, nonwhite, hardworking, and in Ignacio's case, a noncitizen.

Despite frequent moments of poignancy, the series is generally comedic in tone, and even its melodramatic moments are often played tongue-in-check. This mixture of tone arises from its wholehearted embrace of camp. Excess, one of the hallmarks of camp aesthetics, permeates every aspect of the series, beginning with its opening credit sequence with its highly saturated colors and bold graphics. Digitized special effects, especially in transition shots of New York City, enhance familiar images with heightened color and luminosity. Plotlines are inventively convoluted and melodramatic, and dialogue is dense and witty (Marc to Betty in disbelief about something she has said: "Have you been smoking one of your ponchos?").

The series often uses grotesque imagery to expose the excesses of fashion, beauty, and celebrity culture, from the effects of Wilhelmina's Botox-like treatment gone bad, to fashion-shoot props of ugly baby dolls dressed in chain mail. Wide-angle lenses distort the faces of even its beautiful characters, such as Amanda, when they are in distress. Exaggerated performance styles and behavioral tics help define each character. When under stress, Betty pushes her glasses up her nose, Marc puffs on his asthma inhaler, and Amanda shovels anything that's edible into her mouth. Consistent with this grotesquerie, the series does not shrink from stereotypes. Amanda is the slutty dumb blonde. Hilda is the fiery and flamboyant Latina, whose greatest pride is her nails, followed by her cleavage. Ignacio, on the other hand, challenges stereotypes of Latin machismo. He is usually dressed in an apron, cooking, feeding his family, fussing in the kitchen—a feminized man who is also a figure of dignity and authority.

The camp sensibility, rooted in gay culture, queers the series in interesting ways. Queer theorist Alexander Doty defines queerness as a ubiquitous position that challenges straightness of any kind (1993), and nonstraight characters figure prominently in Ugly Betty, from Wilhelmina's assistant Marc to Hilda's eleven-year-old son Justin, who loves musicals and whose knowledge of fashion rivals that of Mode's most obsessed fashionistas.[15] In one episode, a handsome male designer masquerades as gay to get a foot in the door of the fashion industry, which is closed, he believes, to straight men. One of the first season's most important enigmas concerns the identity of a mysterious, veiled woman plotting with Wilhelmina to take over the company. This woman turns out to be Bradford's other son Alex, who returns in a later episode as the stunning woman Alexis (Rebecca Romijn).

Coming from a community more grounded in "real-world" values than the *Mode* universe, Betty is well equipped to weather the challenges around appearance and popularity that structure most Girl Culture texts. However, she is vulnerable to another tension familiar to most women—the conflict between her ambition and the tug of romance or other personal ties. Once again, as in *Love and Basketball* and *The Devil Wears Prada*, brains and ambition seem to run counter to a woman's desire to have a personal life. This conflict is intensified by the very nature of Betty's job, which requires her to take care of her boss around the clock.

Emotional caregiving, of course, is classic female labor, and Betty, like Cher in *Clueless*, is a born caregiver. In an episode titled "Four Thanksgivings and a Funeral" (a reference to the chick flick *Four Weddings and a Funeral*), Ignacio, a world-class caregiver in his own right, tells Betty, "You've been taking care of us since your mother died. Maybe it's time for us to stop relying on you." Soon, however, her desire to succeed at her job makes her unavailable to her family or her needy boyfriend Walter. In another episode, reminiscent of *The Devil Wears Prada*, work keeps her from her father's birthday. In yet another, she cannot perform her traditional duties of shopping for the family's Thanksgiving dinner. Betty's romance with Walter is lukewarm, but she is still vulnerable to his pressure to curtail her ambition. More confined than Betty by social class, he reminds her of the difference between the world she comes from and the one she aspires to. When she gets her first chance to write for *Mode*, she takes Walter along to an expensive restaurant she plans to review. She approaches its small servings and artful presentations of food with curiosity, but he has no use for any of it, and embarrasses her by loudly insisting on a burger and fries.

As with *Clueless* and the *Scream* trilogy, Betty's quest to know who she is requires her to learn the story of her lost mother. Ignacio is the series's prime model of maternal nurturing, but a rich array of other mother figures remind viewers of the key role older women play in the lives of younger ones. Most of these women are outrageous and unrepentant, and some are downright bad. A model tries to advance her daughter's career by "selling" her to Daniel. Marc's mother turns her back on him when he comes out to her. And the queen-diva Wilhelmina can't send her daughter away to boarding school fast enough.

More often, however, *Ugly Betty*'s mothers remain sympathetic even when they do not conform to ideologies of the good mother. Hilda became pregnant

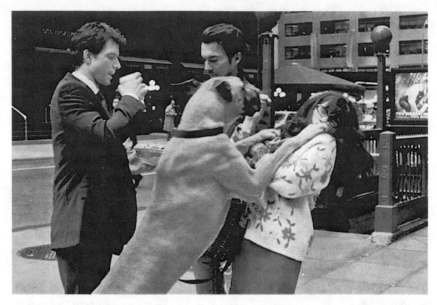

Ugly Betty shows how Betty's ambition bumps up against expectations that she take care of everyone in her life.

on her prom night, a matter she treats without shame, and she unquestioningly supports Justin's gayness as just who he is. When another mother accuses her of being a bad mother because she dresses provocatively, she briefly covers up her décolletage. But her son insists that she not change her old style, so she returns to it, thereby undercutting the taboo on maternal sexuality.

Daniel's tough and glamorous mother Claire (Judith Light) is a powerful, unruly "postmaternal" figure, to use a concept I will return to in the next chapter. Not only is she an alcoholic who does not want to recover but also she was convicted of killing her husband's long-term mistress Fay, and at the series's end she is in prison for the crime. She is also cagey enough to rival Wilhelmina for control of *Mode* magazine. Yet, unlike Bradford, she accepts Alex's metamorphosis into Alexis, and she wants her children to get along. She even gives Betty good motherly advice about following her heart with Henry: "If your mother were here, she'd want you to be happy, and you're not happy," she tells her.

Betty's mother Rosa is missing from the outset, and her absence is an undercurrent throughout the first season. Betty keeps her memory alive at Thanksgiving by making one of her favorite dishes, and at Christmas the family remembers her through her handmade ornaments. Her story remains a mystery until the penultimate episode of the first season, and even then she remains a shadowy figure. In the pilot episode, we learn that she died some time ago. We also learn that Betty has inherited her most defining qualities from her mother: "You're strong, determined, optimistic—just like your mother," Ignacio tells her, when her confidence wanes. The pilot establishes the mother's importance by basing a crucial plot point on a photo of Betty as a young girl with her mother. Betty uses the photo to inspire a new approach to selling cosmetics with a pitch that is not based on spectacular images of unrealistic people and events, but on "little moments" in the lives of ordinary girls and women. The idea saves the day for Daniel, and marks the beginning of Betty's rise at *Mode* not only because of her loyalty to Daniel but also because of her creativity and brains.

The mystery of Betty's mother continues to unravel in "A Tree Grows in Guadalajara," when the Suarez family returns to Mexico to sort out Ignacio's immigration woes. At a family reunion, Betty's Aunt Mirta (Rita Moreno) notes how Betty resembles her mother. Ignacio finally explains his silence around her mother's family. They disapproved of him because of his lowly station in life, so Rosa married another man. But that man beat her, and so Ignacio returned to rescue her. Because he had to kill him, Rosa's mother disowned them both. As the episode continues, it takes on the look of magic realism, with unnatural lighting and surreal appearances by Henry, who is really back in New York, riding a bicycle through the landscape. Betty finally finds an old woman sitting silently in a small house. The woman is her grandmother, who lights up from a reverie and mistakes Betty for her mother Rosa when she greets her. "You've come back," she says. "Forgive me for what I said. I've always loved you."

By pursuing her desire to know her mother's story, Betty has healed the thirty-year rift that fractured her family. She has also gained invaluable insight into what she must do to mature into her own adult identity. "You are brave, my Rosa," her grandmother says. She also says, "Fight for the man you love," a coded message for Betty to follow her heart toward Henry despite all the obstacles that have stood in their way. As in *Love and Basketball*, a traditional maternal figure pushes a young woman to fight for the object of her desire.

Once again, it appears a young woman's rites of passage are inextricable from romantic love. However, it would be a mistake to dismiss *Ugly Betty* for its traditionalism in this regard. Indeed, Betty's desire for Henry is bound up in her quest to know where she came from, especially on her mother's side. As in the *Scream* trilogy, a daughter cannot move securely into her own adulthood until she knows her mother's story. Moreover, many of the series's most powerful female characters, from Wilhelmina to Sofia, played by Salma Hayek, to the high-powered attorney played by Lucy Liu, violate the conventions of normative femininity with their ease in divorcing their emotions from their sexual desires. Indeed, Sofia, author of the self-help book *Girls Like It On Top*, uses Daniel's addiction to sex to exploit *him*. With Henry, Betty discovers her own desire, and her right to pursue it.

Betty is not perfect. She has lessons to learn about forgiving others who disappoint her. But she refuses to be tempted by values that undermine her, and her unruliness lies in her comfort with herself. Throughout the series, characters speak of Betty's strength, and like most of the female protagonists in the key texts of Girl Culture, she is smart and good. But none of those protagonists matches Betty in her geekiness and clumsiness, which are heightened by Ferrera's gift for physical comedy and her willingness to put a different kind of face on television. Betty knows that she is no Hilda. But she flirts with a makeover only once, when in the second episode she turns herself over to her sister to design a new look for her. While the results attract whistles in "hoochieville" Queens, Betty appears only more grotesque to the *Mode* crew in her big hair, clanging jewelry, and platform shoes. The episode underlines the fact that beauty is measured by class- and race-based norms that are out of reach for most women. It also points to the series's deeper content: Betty is fine as she is.

All-American Girl: Margaret Cho Does Girl World

Both *Love and Basketball* and *Real Women Have Curves* show how girls of color use unruliness to resist cultural and familial expectations that weigh heavily on them, and each film's protagonist faces a defining developmental task. So does Wilhelmina in *Saving Face* (2004), which is the final film examined in this chapter. But before turning to this exceptional work, set in a Chinese American community, I would like to detour to the 1994 ABC sitcom *All-American Girl*, which featured the nation's first Asian American family on network television—with an unruly girl, no less, as its central character.

Margaret Cho, who plays the all-American girl, is best known as a standup comedian with an angry, funny persona, a political and often raunchy bent to her humor, and a strong fan base in gay and lesbian communities. Elements of this persona formed the basis of the series's premise, the ongoing generational and cultural conflict between tradition-minded, Korean-born parents and their assimilated daughter. While leaving behind the bisexuality and assault on homophobia of Cho's standup act, *All-American Girl* designed "Margaret Kim" to be Cho's age, gender, ethnicity, and to retain her unruliness.

Margaret lives with her parents, who run a bookstore; her older brother, a physician; and her grandmother, who is addicted to American TV. While her brother conforms to Asian American model minority stereotypes, Margaret's big personality challenges stereotypical notions of passive, refined Asian femininity.[16] In creating her vulgar, all-American character, Cho draws on the Girl Culture emerging in the 1990s as a goldmine of material for ethnic- and generation-based humor. Margaret works at the mall, selling perfume at a cosmetics counter. She wears miniskirts and fuzzy sweaters, speaks slang, and has no interest in Korean culture.

Indeed, Margaret is a poster child for postfeminism, with her sexual bravado and girly love of fashion and popular culture. She has two girlfriends who share her interests in chasing boys and playing "Charlie's Angels" when work gets dull.[17] Margaret and her friends emulate the sexy action heroines with big hair and guns, suggesting the appeal of adventure, violence, and feminine good looks to a generation of girls forming fan communities around *Xena: Warrior Princess*, *Buffy the Vampire Slayer*, and *Scream*. "We must fight crime, while showing off our cute butts," she says. "This is how life should be," she adds. "Three gals, cool clothes, saving children's lives every week. And when they're not working, they go on the Love Boat."

Like Cher in *Clueless*, Margaret may appear superficial, but she never hesitates to challenge authority when it gets in her way, or to use the weapons of Girl Power—sex and popular culture—to her advantage. In an episode titled "Booktopus," she rescues the family bookstore from a corporate takeover with an unruly performance of bluster and sexual manipulation. In "Educating Margaret," one of her professors, a pompous, older filmmaker, develops a romantic interest in her because she has "passion and opinions."[18] Like Cher in *Clueless*, she challenges him over a grade, and, while munching on Milk Duds, defends her argument on behalf of films that are truly popular—*E.T. The Extraterrestrial* and *Indiana Jones*—over the canonical works of European art cinema he reveres. Not surprisingly, the romance fizzles.

The series plays out its cultural and generational clashes most consistently in Margaret's relationship with her elegant mother Katherine (Jodi Long). Through Katherine, a figure of repression, the series displaces generational

On *All-American Girl*, Margaret (Margaret Cho) and her friend play *Charlie's Angels* while on the job selling perfume at the mall. Postmodern femininity is built from icons of popular culture.

difference onto cultural difference to strengthen its case for the superiority of American culture. Katherine is determined to find a suitable (that is, Korean) match for her daughter and to turn her into a respectable lady like herself. In "Submission Impossible," Katherine arranges a date for Margaret with Raymond, an attractive but conservative Korean American. Before he arrives, Katherine criticizes Margaret's flashy attire as suitable for "dining with [her] pimp." On the date, Margaret tries to act like a submissive Korean girl, stifling her opinions and laughing at Raymond's bad jokes, but she cannot sustain the masquerade.

The series's heart lies in Margaret's affectionate relationship with Grandma, a character played with exuberance and flair by Amy Hill. Large, loud, outspoken, Grandma was especially well liked by Korean audiences. Interestingly, one would expect Grandma to be the least assimilated member of the family due to her age. But because she watches American television obsessively and indiscriminately (from *Power Rangers* and *Baywatch* to pornography and commercials), she rivals Margaret in her assimilation. Planted in her television chair, she fills the family's living room with her presence, giving running commentaries in heavily accented English on what she sees. Recalling Ana's relationship with her grandfather in *Real Women Have Curves*, Margaret is closer in spirit to her unruly grandmother than to her mother, suggesting that age does not inevitably determine cultural or political affiliations. In "Exile on Market Street," it is Grandma who literally throws her weight around to rescue Margaret from jail and helps her face her real desire at a moment of crisis around her future. Because of Grandma's support, Margaret commits to a career doing creative work rather than one in the law, which her parents would prefer. Young women, the series shows, can only benefit from strong intergenerational connections.

All-American Girl was canceled after eighteen episodes, doomed, according to Cho, by the network's ignorance of Korean American culture and its uncertainty about its vision of the series. According to her DVD commentary, Cho was pleased that the show provided jobs for Asian American actors and challenged stereotypes of Asians and Asian Americans. But she was frustrated by the network's efforts to make her both more and less "Asian." This matter highlights a fundamental conundrum around identity politics: while ethnic identity has no basis in biology, its cultural significance is real. "Margaret Kim" may have shed her Koreanness to become all-American, but that Koreanness still matters, especially to people who remain identified with it or who cannot see past physical markers of difference.

Cho was particularly critical of the series's producers for manufacturing the conflict between Margaret and her mother. That conflict, mediated by an even-tempered, wise father (a classic sitcom Dad), is consistent with American films and television, but not, according to Cho, with Korean American families: "We're not familiar with fighting within the family." Cho's mother figures prominently in her comedy acts, not because she and Cho disagree but because the mother's accent and ignorance of American ways make her an irresistible subject for comedy. It is in those acts where Cho delivers her most devastating comments about her experiences on *All-American Girl*, describing how she was pressured to lose weight rapidly so she could look "more like herself." She was hospitalized after losing thirty pounds in two weeks. Ironically, the series has lived long past its cancellation because of Cho's success in standup comedy, where she has used it to expose the racism and cynicism of media industries.

Ultimately *All-American Girl* could not overcome a fundamental instability in Cho's star text, the gap between Margaret Cho the radical comedian and Margaret Kim, the all-American girl. Trying to reconcile the two was an ambitious goal that the series could only partially achieve. However, *All-American Girl* put an Asian American family on prime-time television and showed the political potential of Girl Culture. In the persona of Margaret Kim, dressed in miniskirts and wielding perfume atomizers as make-believe weapons, Cho stands as a sign of Girl Culture's early reach beyond mainstream whiteness.

Saving Face: Learning to Love

Ten years after *All-American Girl* was canceled, *Saving Face*, by first-time director Alice Wu, put another Asian American family, this time Chinese, on the big screen. Wilhelmina, the focal point of the film, is not a teenager but an accomplished doctor in her late twenties and thus falls outside even a generous definition of girlhood. But the film warrants a close look here because of its unusual use of romantic comedy to explore the mother-daughter relation. Wayne Wang's melodrama *The Joy Luck Club*, based on Amy Tan's best-selling 1989 novel, had already brought the subject of Chinese American mothers and daughters to American film audiences in 1993.[19] However, *Saving Face* pushes romantic comedy to new limits with examples of female unruliness seldom seen in mainstream film or television.[20]

The film tells the story of Ma (Joan Chen), a forty-eight-year-old widowed beautician, and her daughter Wil (Michelle Kruisiec), a hardworking surgeon. Ma wants to find a husband for Wil, but Wil has no interest in dating men. At a dance in the Chinese American community, Wil meets Vivian (Lynn Chen), a ballerina, and the two fall in love. Wil refuses to come out, however, so Vivian leaves for a new life in Paris. Wil finally tells Ma she's gay, but Ma cannot accept this. Meanwhile, Ma, who lives with her parents, is pregnant but won't name the father, so Grandpa banishes her from their home and she moves in with Wil. Despite their initial wariness, Wil and Ma learn to understand each other, and eventually each takes decisive action to ensure the other's happiness.

In interviews, Wu describes *Saving Face* as a "lesbian comedy of manners" and "an old-fashioned screwball romantic comedy," and the film makes a fitting conclusion to this chapter by recalling the importance of *Clueless* in Girl Culture.[21] Both films are heavily indebted to romantic comedy's tradition of joining female unruliness with social renewal and transformation, and *Saving Face* goes straight to one of the thematic cores of romantic comedy—the power of romantic or sexual love to deepen our understanding of who we are. For this reason, self-knowledge is a common theme of the genre, which often deals—like *Saving Face*—with characters finding the courage to "face" who they are and "come out" to themselves and those they love. The film explicitly addresses Wil's need to drop her mask or masquerade as heterosexual, despite the disapproval she will face. Thus masks are an important visual and thematic motif in the film, which opens with a shot of Wil wearing one of the cosmetic masks Ma sends her. We often see Wil wearing surgical masks, as well, and in another short scene, her African American neighbor Jay wears a light green facial mask, a sly allusion to whiteface consistent with the Third Wave's sympathy with the idea of identity as performance.

Saving Face moves beyond *Clueless*'s white heteronormativity, however, by tracking not one but two taboo romances—a young woman's with another woman, and her mother's with a younger man. Both unfold in the context of a third, a rarely told love story between an unrepentant mother and her daughter. Like *Real Women Have Curves*, the film takes place in an ethnic community where the pursuit of individual desire involves more risks than in mainstream American culture because of more deeply held claims of family and tradition. The conflict between the mother and daughter involves the ways both are caught between East and West, and so the film adds national identity to the genre's familiar interest in differences of class, gender, and temperament.[22] Wu resisted pressure to rewrite the film for greater commercial success by eliminating its Chineseness; its producers wanted to consider Reese Witherspoon and Ellen Burstyn for the roles of daughter and mother (Busack 2004).

Saving Face's charm arises from its carefully calibrated mixtures of tone, genre, and style, arising in part from Wu's admiration for Spanish director Pedro Almodóvar, another gay director known for his love of female actors and characters. His influence can be seen in the film's visual style, especially its use of saturated colors and its interweaving of comedy and melodrama. Strong elements of melodrama appear in the film's entangled family relations (Wil works for Vivian's father) as well as moments of pathos aroused by Wil and Ma's suffering and Grandma's unexpected death. That pathos is countered, however, by comically understated performance styles and a postmodern soundtrack that conveys the subtext of a globalized world with popular songs such as "Brazil" and "Love is Strange," played with samba and tango rhythms and light instrumentation. While nearly half of the dialogue is in Mandarin, these international musical motifs subtly convey a tension between the insularity of the communities where the older characters such as Grandpa and Grandma live and the cultural mobility of the younger ones such as Wil and Vivian.

Saving Face tracks several taboo romances, including the rarely told love story of an unrepentant mother and her daughter.

The film incorporates familiar elements of postfeminist teen films, often to highlight the role reversals Ma and Wil undergo as they begin to reveal themselves to the other. Ma occupies the unruly-teen role and, like Grandma in *All-American Girl*, she watches lots of television, mainly Chinese soap operas and pornography. Her friends are middle-aged versions of the Plastics from *Mean Girls*, a chorus of small-minded gossips who ostracize her when she breaks the rules of Chinese Girl World, grown-up style. Dressed in St. John's designer suits and lined up against the walls of the dance hall, these women exert their power not by drawing the gaze of others, like the dynamic divas of the teen-girl films, but by being active gazers in their own right.

Teen-oriented romantic comedies also support the fantasy that true lovers knew each other in childhood, perhaps a consolation to young adults not yet ready to leave their childhood behind. Just as Cher and Josh from *Clueless* first knew each other as stepsiblings, both Monica in *Love and Basketball* and Wil knew their lovers as children. Similarly, birthdays carry heavy significance as rites of passage. Like Andy in *The Devil Wears Prada* and Betty in *Ugly Betty*, Wil misses an important birthday, ostensibly because of the demands of her job, although in this case, she uses work to avoid the pressure she feels from her love for Vivian to come out.

With the character of Ma, the film brings the missing mother of so many teen-girl comedies to life and to center stage. Ma and Wil develop an uneasy intimacy evident in two-shots of them in bed together, silently watching soap operas and sharing late-night snacks. At first, neither can comprehend the other, but things change. Eventually each rescues the other: Wil blocks Ma's ill-conceived marriage to the older Mr. Cho, and Ma intervenes—not once but twice—to bring Wil and Vivian together. While the film privileges Wil's point of view, Ma's story rivals hers in narrative weight not only for its scandal quotient but because the enigma about her baby's father remains a mystery until almost the end.

Ma epitomizes the complexity of mothers from a daughter's point of view—over-involved and difficult, but a revelation once each begins to really see the other. At one point, after preparing Ma for a date, Wil looks at her with wonder and says, "Ma, you're beautiful," and she is. Moreover, she is an unrepentant mother. She raised Wil alone. She likes sex but doesn't like babies. She is having an affair in middle age, and with a man much younger than she. Most of all, she refuses to buckle to fierce pressure to name her baby's father. She makes a halfhearted attempt to find another husband, but it is clear she is prepared to keep her baby and raise it alone or, to Wil's dismay, with Wil.

Saving Face dramatizes the conflicts immigrant communities experience in balancing the desire to assimilate with the desire to retain essential aspects of their cultural identity. Indeed, Wil's daily commute from Flushing to Manhattan recalls Betty's trips from Queens in *Ugly Betty* and Ana's to Beverly Hills in *Real Women Have Curves*. Both Wil and Vivian conform to model-minority expectations for successful assimilation, but Wil especially testifies to the success of the Second Wave in opening up opportunities for girls and women in formerly all-male fields.

While Wil's community supports her ambition in the public sphere, it has less tolerance for deviation within the private. Grandpa's banishing of Ma seems unduly harsh, as does Ma's denial of Wil's lesbianism. Yet, recalling director Cardoso's comments on Carmen, the stubborn mother of *Real Women Have Curves*, Wu explains that Grandpa's actions are understandable given his cultural identity. He believes Ma needs someone such as Mr. Cho who can help care for her and her new child and restore her place in the community, an essential component of a good life. Ma's life in Wil's apartment bears him out.

She is lonely—"totally depressed, humiliated," as Wil tells Grandma. The soap operas she begins to share with Wil, and the porn she watches surreptitiously, suggest the emotional and sexual toll of her isolation.

Ironically, despite her own unruliness, Ma cannot accept her daughter's, and she shows herself to be her father's daughter when she refuses to accept that Wil is gay. The film carefully locates this failing as much in her personality as in her community by contrasting Ma with Vivian's mother, who has accepted her daughter's lesbianism. For Ma, Wil presents an irreconcilable contradiction, a sign of her maternal failure: "I am a good mother. You are not gay," she says. Both mother and daughter suffer from a traditional culture that cannot tolerate expressions of female sexuality that fall outside narrowly defined boundaries.

As in *All-American Girl*, the grandmother plays a crucial role in the film, suggesting the ways women can nurture each other through intergenerational connections. Grandma counters Grandpa's sternness by taking care of Ma through Wil. She is particularly close to Wil, and follows Ma's criticism of her daughter's unfeminine appearance by casually complimenting her on her butch boots ("like what we wore in the Revolution"). In the hospital, Grandma impatiently banishes her husband and the loyal Mr. Cho in order to have an intimate conversation with Wil about Ma. Her unexpected death, the film's most melodramatic moment, advances the narrative by forcing Grandpa, Ma, and Wil to put aside the conflicts that have divided them.

Wu says she made *Saving Face* in order to film a single shot, when Wil and Ma finally face each other as two women, mother and daughter, without masks. In a film so characterized by emotional restraint, this shot provides a hard-earned resolution to the tension between the two characters. The sequence takes place at the airport, a classic site of romantic comedy crises. Wil has just broken up Ma's wedding to Mr. Cho, which has prompted Ma's handsome young lover Little Yu to identify himself as the father of her baby. Ma then races Wil to the airport to keep Vivian from leaving for Paris. They arrive just in time, but Wil cannot bring herself to give Vivian the public kiss she asks for, so Vivian walks away. The shots that follow are wordless, with slow editing that allows enough time for viewers to read and absorb the emotions on Ma and Wil's faces. Ma, in medium close-up, leans on the cab, huddling in the heavy jacket she's wearing over the dress from her aborted wedding, waiting for Wil to emerge from the airport with Vivian. Behind her, parking ramps and cars connote that we are in liminal space, on the edge of movement. Ma looks up with expectation on her face, only to see Wil exiting from the airport alone.

Filmmaker Alice Wu made *Saving Face* to film a single moment: when Wil (Michelle Krusiec) and Ma (Joan Chen) finally face each other as two women, mother and daughter, without masks.

Through film aesthetics, the sequence conveys the powerful emotional pull between Wil and Ma. As Ma opens her arms, the coat falls open, exposing, in effect, her heart. A cut shows Wil in long shot, with downcast expression on her face. Eyeline matches connect Ma and Wil's gazes, which they hold, communicating silently, in an eight-second shot. A long shot from a side angle then shows them both at some physical distance, with Ma internally framed by the curve of the airport structure overhead, a visual embrace that prepares us for Vivian's walk into her mother's arms. The camera maintains a discreet distance as the two hold each other. There has been no diegetic sound, only the film's love theme on the soundtrack, but when the camera comes in closer to show Wil and Ma's faces, we hear Wil's sobs. Framed to contrast her maternal strength with Wil's vulnerability, Ma holds her daughter, then opens the cab door and ushers her in before they drive away.

The intertitle "Three Months Later" introduces the sequence that will resolve the film. Wil, finally in harmony with her mother, has grown into her own identity. Dressed in a bright coral sweater, she enters the warmly lit environment of the dance hall with her mother. The stage is set for a conclusion in full-blown romantic comedy style: music, dance, food, the promise of sex.

Brought together by their mothers, Wil and Vivian finally share a public kiss in the embrace of their community.

In a series of subjective shots, the camera takes Wil's gaze as she surveys the people, then notices Vivian, who is with her own mother. Wil, who is chewing on a snack, freezes and then Vivian sees her. The two stare at each other, but dancers' bodies intercept their gaze.

As the ambient sound drops away and romantic music rises, a moving camera advances on Vivian from Wil's point of view. At last, Wil—once paralyzed with fear at the airport—now moves toward the object of her desire. Cutaways to both mothers show them watching anxiously from the sidelines, but then everyone drops away to show Vivian and Wil alone in a shot/reverse sequence that keeps them both continually within the frame. The music stops, and Wil asks Vivian to dance, again as an active agent of her own desire. A moment of tension (Vivian replies, "I can't") is resolved by a joke ("There's no music"), the two begin to sway together in silence, and when the music returns they finally share a long, public kiss.

After the misbegotten efforts at matchmaking by Ma, Grandpa, and Wil, it is the mothers finally who have orchestrated this happy ending, and they exchange smiles and a thumbs-up when their daughters are together at last.

Even Grandpa, despite his high standing in the community, is powerless before the combined force of the mothers to bring the right lovers together. The formation of the new couple is also witnessed by their community, giving their relationship the social affirmation Vivian yearned for when she prodded Wil to come out of the closet.

The festive reconciliation is not total. The old biddies leave in disgust, and Grandpa and his old pal mutter on the sidelines. But the rest of the community dance around Vivian and Wil, and the film proper concludes with an overhead shot of the couple encircled by other couples. The community is now sufficiently expanded and renewed to include not only lesbian love but the unconventional romance of Ma and Little Yu, both also now out of their closet—although Ma won't let Little Yu move in with her because she is enjoying her new independence too much.

The film completes its swift transition from melodrama to romantic comedy with a brief montage that interrupts the credits to dissipate any remaining emotional intensity. We see the film's characters eating and commenting on the events that have transpired. Grandpa succeeds in reentering his family while retaining his gruff personality when he announces that he'll frequently visit the new baby, a girl, to counteract the corrupting influence of the child's mother and sister.

With its delicate balance between sentiment and skepticism, *Saving Face* testifies to romantic comedy's enduring capacity to stage questions of female desire while pushing at the ideological limits of how that desire can be imagined. The final shot shows the two unruly couples drinking champagne together, with Ma and Vivian now in league to improve Wil's butch fashion style. As the camera moves in closer, first Little Yu, then Vivian fall away, until mother and daughter share the frame in a two-shot, asserting the primacy of their bond. When Ma tells Wil to start think about having a baby herself, Wil spits out the champagne in disbelief, ending the film with the promise that mother and daughter will remain present in each other's lives, providing each other a comforting mixture of irritation, frustration, and love.

As this chapter has demonstrated, girls of color are not immune to the allures of Girl World. Hilda in *Ugly Betty* and Lena in *Love and Basketball* are confident and comfortable with their manicured nails and stylish hairdos. And *Saving Face* encourages viewers to believe not only that happiness is rooted in finding the right romantic partner, but also that love can triumph over social convention, parental disapproval, homophobia, and the tug of individual ambition. More importantly, however, all of these works show unruly girls of color steadfastly going their own ways—in sports, education, or love—even against the wishes of their equally strong-willed mothers. Along with demonstrating the power of love among women, these works remind us that our fulfillment as individuals begins with our willingness to know and accept who we are, and to challenge our families and communities to do so as well.

The Motherline and a
Wicked Powerful Feminism

ANTONIA'S LINE

Mother's Voices, Daughter's Voices

THIS BOOK HAS BEEN filled with the voices of unruly girls. From *Titanic* to *Clueless*, *Ugly Betty* to *Thirteen*, in comedy, melodrama, and horror, the daughters of the postfeminist era have made their presence felt throughout media culture. However, that has not been so true for their mothers. Reviewing the last seven chapters for the voices of mothers, I hear few rising with unrepentant power. It would seem that Rose's salvo to her mother in *Titanic*—"Oh, Mother, shut up!"—magically silenced the mothers who followed, or rendered them unworthy of a sympathetic ear. Recall the mothers of *American Beauty*, one hysterical and the other catatonic; the idealized but dead mother of *Clueless*; the tainted, murdered mother of *Scream*; Reese Witherspoon's uncertain hold on her unruly persona as she moves toward more maternal roles. Even films and TV shows that treat mothers with more even-handed interest—*My So-Called Life*, *Thirteen*, *Love and Basketball*, *Saving Face*—still present them through the eyes of their daughters. Where in contemporary media culture can one find an engaging look at mothers, especially mothers in relation to their daughters?

I began my book *The Unruly Woman* with a study of Dutch filmmaker Marleen Gorris's extraordinary *A Question of Silence* (1982). When I turned to U.S. culture for the rest of that book, I could find little within our borders that matched *A Question of Silence* in laying out the issues that absorbed me at that stage of my life—how women come to feminist consciousness; how feminist women can live good lives within the institutions of patriarchy, including heterosexuality; how they can use the radical power of female laughter and other behavior considered taboo for women for political ends—thus my interest in comedy, including romantic comedy. Today the issues that most concern me have shifted to reflect not only the current state of feminism but also my own situation as a woman past sixty, and as the mother of three daughters, all now well into adulthood. I wonder about the invisibility of mothers, especially as we age, and the stunted depictions of mother-daughter relations in popular culture. I think about the generational tensions within academic feminism, and their relation to the larger failures of the movement to mobilize around the forces that most threaten the well-being of women and men today—the intensifying global convergence of militarism, neo-imperialism, and late capitalism.

Once again, Gorris has provided a film as well suited to conclude this book as *A Question of Silence* was to begin my earlier one. *Antonia's Line* was released in the United States in 1996, the same year as *Scream* and within a year of *Clueless* and *Titanic*. With cultural weight of its own after winning the Oscar for best foreign-language film, *Antonia's Line* offers an important counterpoint to the teen-girl films of its time, giving voice to the mothers (and grandmothers and great-grandmothers) suppressed in them.[1] Like *A Question of Silence*, *Antonia's Line* is a fable, moving from the moment of unresolved possibility that concluded the earlier film to a fully realized feminist utopia centered on a line of unruly girls and unrepentant mothers. Like *Titanic*, *Antonia's Line* unfolds within a frame story that begins and ends with its female protagonist as an old woman, very close to death. But the two films attach very different meanings to their lives and deaths. Whereas *Titanic* falls back on the clichés of romantic love, *Antonia's Line* is a somber but lyrical meditation on unresolved issues in contemporary feminism. Interweaving feminist fantasy with realism, the film expresses the possibilities embedded in the mother-daughter relationship for new understandings of mothering, aging, and a feminism built on connections across space and time.[2]

In the early years of the new millennium, motherhood remains as ideologically charged as ever, both in the culture at large and in feminism. On the
one hand, it has become a source of increasing anxiety for women who came
of age during the postfeminist era. White, middle-class women in particular,
having postponed pregnancy until their thirties or later, now face fears about
infertility. On the other hand, the postmaternal mother, age theorist Margaret
Morganroth Gullette's term for mothers past the reproductive age, continues
to be invisible in the dominant cultural narratives. Maternal subjectivity was
"discovered" in the 1970s and again in the 1990s, but not the postmaternal.[3]
Indeed, ambivalence toward mothers only increases as they age, when ageism compounds the effects of sexism. In *Titanic*, the shock of seeing Rose at
ninety—beautiful still, and still emplotted as a daughter despite the presence
of her granddaughter—testifies to the cultural pathology that renders most
old people, but especially old women, invisible. And as with matrophobia,
this pathology has seeped into feminism itself.[4]

But first, the daughters. As I noted in chapter five on Reese Witherspoon,
Judd Apatow's film *Knocked Up* (2007) has been recognized as a cultural event,
drawing on the cultural cache of the slacker to rewrite the sexual politics
of the traditional romantic comedy. The film is significant also for its treatment of unwanted pregnancy, a theme that has recurred in *Waitress* (2007),
Bella (2006), and *Juno* (2007). *Juno*, like *Knocked Up*, became a cultural sensation when it unexpectedly attracted four nominations for Academy Awards,
including best picture.[5] In *Knocked Up*, a thirty-something career woman becomes pregnant after a one-night stand with man she would not consider dating if she were sober. In *Juno*, a precocious teen girl gets pregnant after losing
her virginity with her best friend, in an act of "premeditated sex." In *Waitress*,
the only one of these films to consider the impact of unwanted pregnancy on
poor women, a woman gets pregnant after getting drunk and having sex with
her abusive husband. In general, these movies treat safe sex and contraception
with offhandedness or indifference, and abortion as barely thinkable. They
romanticize pregnancy and sentimentalize babies and small children.

Not surprisingly, this cluster of films helped set off a cultural debate around
sex education and reproductive choice that reached new levels of intensity
with the nomination of Alaska Governor Sarah Palin as the Republican candi-
date for vice president in fall 2008. Chosen to reignite the culture wars for her
appeal to the religious Right, the former beauty queen based her persona and
her credentials to lead the nation on her identity as the unflappable mother of
five, including an infant with Down syndrome and an unmarried, pregnant

seventeen-year-old daughter. Like one of Girl Culture's "mean girls" grown up, Palin proved immensely skilled at fanning the fires of the mommy wars, and she used her family to frame herself visually and ideologically as "just another working mom."[6] Todd S. Purdum noted in *Vanity Fair* the "pheromonal reality" of her candidacy, given that she was not only good-looking but also "the first indisputably fertile female to dare to dance with the big dogs." This appreciation was surely enhanced by Palin's contrast with the postmenopausal Hillary Clinton.

News reports soon named Palin's pregnant daughter "Juno from Juneau," capitalizing on the convergence between "reel life and real life." Not surprisingly, the real-life drama proved messier than the movies. The young couple split, and their families began feuding over custody of the baby. These events put pressure on Palin's image as an opponent of reproductive rights and progressive sex education, and she receded from the political spotlight until she startled the nation in summer 2009 by resigning from the governorship. Throughout this period, she remained a topic of tabloid interest because of the family melodrama that continued to unfold around her grandchild.

Most obviously, the unplanned-pregnancy films tap into the understandable anxieties of women in their thirties feeling the pressure of the biological clock and of marketers eager to tap into the spending capacity of a new generation of financially comfortable mothers.[7] But these films also expose an uncomfortable convergence of opposing ideological perspectives. As columnist Ellen Goodman wrote, "On the one hand, liberals who want teens to have access to contraception and abortion don't want to criticize single mothers. On the other hand, conservatives who want teens to be abstinent until marriage applaud girls who don't have abortions."[8]

Class, of course, not to mention race, further complicates these positions. The implications of carrying an unwanted pregnancy to term are vastly different for poor women and for women of means. While entertaining and offbeat, these films are finally conservative, rallying support around their pregnant protagonists by rewarding them with happy Hollywood endings for having their babies. Even more insidiously, they foster generational conflict not by validating the desire of women to have babies but by setting up a false opposition between that desire and the achievements of feminism. In *Knocked Up*, the only person who encourages the pregnant protagonist Alison to consider an abortion is her brusque ("feminist") mother, who makes a brief appearance then disappears. Alison's confidante is her sister, the attractive mother of two charming little girls.

Juno is considered the female answer to *Knocked Up* because it builds its narrative around a smart, independent girl, and it demystifies the potential adoptive father, a slacker uncomfortably close to middle age but too immature to take on the task of parenting. Yet like so many films that target teen girls, the film seems unwilling to place Juno in a loving relationship with her mother, who is divorced from her father, lives far away in the desert, and sends her daughter an annual gift of a cactus, which Juno says stings her as much as her "abandonment" and devotion to her new "substitute kids." Juno's confidante is her father, nicely backed up by his second wife, and both support Juno in her decision to have her baby and give it up for adoption. Only *Waitress* can imagine its pregnant protagonist in a loving relationship with her mother, who is dead but taught her the pie-making skills that bring her both personal fulfillment and a livelihood. These films imply that those old feminists, who insisted on reproductive and workplace rights for women, got it wrong. Nice women want to be mothers, period.

An even more explicit example of generational tensions around motherhood is *Baby Love*, a 2007 memoir by Rebecca Walker, one of the most influential voices of contemporary feminism. The book's subject is Walker's pregnancy and the birth of her son. Its theme is ambivalence. And its subtext is her anger toward her mother, Alice Walker. No one can dispute Rebecca Walker's claims that as the biracial daughter of a famous mother, she endured hardships growing up. But, writing as part of a generation of women with unprecedented freedom to choose motherhood or not, she agonizes over the burden of that freedom. She blames her ambivalence on her mother, whom she resents for her on-going failures to mother her and, in advance, her unborn child. Alice Walker thus becomes the target of a double-barreled blast of criticism aimed at her both as a mother and as a (Second Wave, "anti-maternal") feminist. The attack is ironic, given Alice Walker's legacy of proposing "womanism," which includes men and family, as a more evolved alternative to Second Wave feminism.

Baby Love shows Rebecca Walker as unable to claim an identity differentiated from that of her mother. "Until you become a mother," she writes, "you're a daughter" (2007, 47). In her account of her decision to become a mother, Rebecca Walker reduces her child to a means of freeing her from an undesired fusion with her mother and, as in *Knocked Up*, having a baby appears to be the only avenue to adulthood. But even as a new mother, she writes as a daughter—and not as an adult daughter who can acknowledge her mother as a postmaternal subject in her own right, but as a daughter still absorbed in a child's sense of entitlement. From that perspective, mothers can only disappoint their children.

One of the book's most controversial assertions is that biological motherhood creates a more powerful bond with a child than motherhood through commitment—that is, through adoption or surrogacy. Yet in the context of the personal grief that permeates the book, that assertion appears to be as much a reproach to her own mother as a thoughtful position on a challenging topic. Ultimately, *Baby Love* is a missed opportunity for a respected Third Wave voice to explore her love for her child in the context of a more measured analysis of the social forces behind her ambivalence. Alice Walker has maintained silence about the book and her relationship with her daughter, yet another example of the challenges faced by a postmaternal mother, even of her stature, to find a place from which to speak.

Rebecca Walker, of course, isn't alone in her difficulties with her mother. The strained motherline between them dramatizes feminism's need to find new narratives that leave behind the Oedipal model that has shaped so many of our cultural discourses.[9] Feminism has long identified the failures of psychoanalysis in regard to gender but has not yet fully grasped how psychoanalytic concepts have influenced our understanding of aging and generation. Cultural critic Kathleen Woodward recounts an anecdote in which Freud discusses how, in his old age, he continued to suffer from his desire to compete with and please his long-dead father. The anecdote is telling. It shows how the Oedipal family is structured around the dyadic unit of father and son. Moreover, that relationship is inevitably adversarial, binding generations in conflict rather than continuity. And it eliminates the postmaternal woman altogether. Woodward asks "how theoretically we might find our way out of this Freudian world . . . from which older women are missing." Even more suggestively, she seeks models of cross-generational identification that anticipate the future "not as a punishment, as did Freud, but as possibility" (1999, 150). The very existence of generation "gaps" raises the question of who benefits from them.

Antonia's Line provides one answer to these questions by modeling new forms of community around a concept of continuity that is based not on Oedipal conflict but on female, generational lineage extending expansively through time. Interestingly, the film was originally titled simply *Antonia*. The English version adds the concept of "line," as well as the grammatical possessive that gives the line to Antonia, one of cinema's most unrepentant postmaternal mothers. In realizing her vision, Gorris dispenses with the cinematic rhythms and patterns of the Oedipal plot, with its linear, individually focused, conflict-ridden sense of time and its lone hero's drive to discover who he is through conquest, romantic or otherwise. Instead, she evokes another kind of time experienced in community rather than in the isolation of the individual body. And while Antonia provides the story's through-line, the film develops a collective hero of sorts, in five generations of women and the community they draw to them. Weaving together the voices of generations, *Antonia's Line* brilliantly links feminism's unresolved concerns about motherhood with its less acknowledged anxieties around aging. It models a humane understanding of identity that shows the self expanding, not shrinking, with age. And it uses the grotesque to push beyond the two familiar genres of a woman's life— romantic comedy and melodrama—that maneuver mothers into positions of erasure or loss.

The film begins on the day of Antonia's death, and then flashes decades back to when Antonia, with her adult daughter Danielle, returns to her home in a small Dutch village after World War II. Her own mother is close to death, and Antonia has come to bury her and take residence on the family farm. As the years go by, the village's outcasts and misfits find their way to her big pink farmhouse, building a small community that expands over the years with new babies and more additions from outside. Danielle, a painter, decides she wants a child but not a husband, so Antonia helps her find a father, and Danielle gives birth to Thérèse. Farmer Bas, a widower with five sons, courts Antonia, who, like her daughter, doesn't want a husband, but she accepts him as a friend and eventually a lover. Thérèse grows up to become a brilliant musician and mathematician, and gives birth to Sarah. "The seasons pass," as the narrator says, over frequent shots of convivial alfresco dinners shared by the small community. The story is not without tragedy, but the rhythms of daily life continue until one day Antonia says, "enough is enough." She summons her family to her bedside and dies.

Gorris structures the story to foreground its critical themes, beginning with the circularity of time as a force of nature indifferent to the desires of humans. Beginning on the morning of Antonia's death, the film ends by returning to that day, and with few exceptions, its events unfold in an episodic and de-dramatized fashion. Interspersed shots evoke the cycles of nature—Antonia walking through fields sowing seeds, or Mad Madonna, a lonely prisoner of her religious beliefs, howling at the moon. Measured and restrained, the narrator recounts Loony Lips's death from a tractor accident, Letta's death in childbirth, Mad Madonna's death from a broken heart, and finally the devastating rape of the child Thérèse. The film does not provide sensationalized images of the rape, or create voyeuristic suspense around it. The narrator merely records the fact that it happened, and then the film dramatizes its aftermath. By resisting the dramatic pacing of the conventional narrative film, *Antonia's Line* suggests that life deals out tragedies in random but democratic ways; one responds to them and moves on.

Antonia's Line does not fit easily into any genre. Despite its even tone, the film uses melodrama to express its interest in the vulnerability of innocence, reminding us of the genre's long history of telling the tragic stories of mothers and daughters, and of all women who step too far beyond the bounds of convention. The film takes on melodrama's nostalgia with its pastoral setting, and it is suffused with pathos caused by patriarchal institutions, such as the church, that sustain power over women through violence that is usually sexual.

However, the film's melodramatic elements are colored by the grotesque, which tempers the romanticism of its fable-like evocation of a feminist utopia. The grotesque begins with a comic faith in renewal through its identification with youth—new crops, new babies—but it sees youth as inseparable from the old. The grotesque embraces life in its totality and accepts time as a friend. Cradle and grave, sex and death, womb and tomb, new life can happen only with death. Life finally triumphs over death, not through abstractions, such as religion, but through the body, whenever it breaks beyond the boundaries of the individual to become part of a community that spans time and space. As Mikhail Bakhtin's infamous pregnant hag suggests, the female body exists in a privileged relation to the grotesque.

Gorris demonstrated her feel for the feminist potential of the grotesque in *A Question of Silence*, and she continues to mine its potential in *Antonia's Line*. The latter constructs most of its characters as carnivalesque types, many named for their grotesque physical traits: Loony Lips and Deedee, both "simple"; Russian Olga, whose makeup looks like a mask; Crooked Finger, the sad and solitary philosopher; Mad Madonna, mad from loneliness and desire for the man she loves. Antonia's mother is perhaps the film's most grotesque character. On the threshold of death, she is nearly bald, and in contrast to Antonia's composure, she is filled with rage at her no-good, long-dead husband. When it seems she has died at last, she bolts upright like an uncanny puppet to curse him one more time before finally dropping dead.

Antonia (Willeke van Ammelrooy) in *Antonia's Line* is a Demeter figure close to the cycles of nature. The film models new forms of community based on the motherline and expanding through time.

The film poetically ties its women to archaic forces of female energy and power. Touches of magic realism shown from artist Danielle's point of view give glimpses of a universe animated in unpredictable ways. Dissolving the boundaries between life and death, Danielle sees her grandmother rise again from the dead, sitting up in her coffin during her funeral service, to join a come-to-life statue of Jesus in singing "My Blue Heaven." Through the power of her thought, Danielle wills the statue of an angel in the cemetery to knock a hypocritical priest to the ground, showing the animistic power of the female artist—like Gorris herself—to make visible normally hidden layers of grotesque reality.

Feminist Space

Ultimately, *Antonia's Line* works less through dramatic tension than through the rhetorical clarity with which it examines its themes of feminist space and time. Because bodies are always understood within temporal and spatial contexts, how we understand our place in the world is conditioned by how we understand time and space. According to feminist critiques, Western philosophy is built on a mind/body split that associates the feminine with the body and the masculine with the mind. As a result, it denies the first space we all have known, the maternal body, while also creating time as a projection of male subjectivity.[10] Transforming that universe into one in which women occupy their rightful space and live in time of their own making will require not only rebuilding the relations between the sexes, but also reimagining time and space.

If, according to Elizabeth Grosz, feminist philosophers have lagged in this project, this is less true of feminist artists. Consider, for example, the radical and inspiring work of art historian and performance artist Joanna Frueh, whose *Monster/Beauty: Building the Body of Love* is a hymn to the pleasures of living in a body that is reintegrated with mind and soul.[11] Frueh's essays, poems, and performances explore the female body in time and space—that is, the female body as it ages, and the female body that literally shapes and aestheticizes itself through bodybuilding and other means of adornment. This body commands space, draws the gaze, and violates the taboos that keep women in their place.

The female body, especially the maternal body, is "sensuous and relational," Frueh writes (2001, 133), but it is abjected by a culture that repudiates the force of eros: "Eros repressed creates a repellent mother, and the repressed returns in the damaged daughter who identifies with the grotesque mother and must reject that body in order to succeed as a woman" (136). That identification has led to "intergenerational corporeal warfare" and a history of "misery, rejection, isolation, and repulsion" (133). Ultimately, a woman who distances herself from the maternal alienates herself from "mother-eros"—both in the person of her mother, and within herself. Amber Kinser extends this argument in her poetic and astute analysis of the sensuality of mothering (2008, 121–122). She explains that, lacking a language to discuss the erotic without placing men at the center, our culture has conceptually "excised" the erotic from the maternal and thus impelled feminists to expand our understanding of the erotic.

Antonia's Line gives shape to what a feminist utopia built around "mother-eros" might look like by contrasting one spatial location—a familiar "outside" world—with the "inside" world of Antonia's farm. These worlds are not distinct in space. Characters move freely between them. Indeed, an iron gate in front of the pink farmhouse symbolizes the boundary between them, and it is often open. But the two locations represent contrasting visions of community. In the most schematic terms, the outside is patriarchal and the inside matriarchal.

Antonia's pink farmhouse is the center of a feminist utopia built around "mother-eros." Its gate is always open to the misfits and rejects of the outside world.

Patriarchal space is governed by institutions, from the military and church to the family, that rule through physical and emotional force. The strong bully the weak and learn to do so from childhood. Early in the film, a group of small boys hits Loony Lips with a clod of dirt, while an adult man looks on and laughs. The film introduces the theme of male abuse of women in one of its earliest scenes, and its most brutal examples of violence are sexual. Women are condemned to silence and passivity, and Deedee's mother quietly watches her daughter suffering at the hands of her husband and sons. At the village café, Farmer Dan, Deedee's father, hauls his daughter before the assembled villagers to try to pawn her off to a husband. After her brother Pitte grabs her breasts and shakes them to amuse the men, Farmer Bas quietly escorts her outside. This incident foreshadows Bas's role as a worthy partner for Antonia. It also establishes the film's single most important moral imperative: to defend the weak. Living by this principle, Danielle sowed the seeds of her daughter's rape, the film's most tragic event, when she interrupted Pitte's rape of Deedee by throwing a pitchfork at his crotch.

The film condemns the military and the church as corrupt institutions aligned with death, and it similarly exposes the academy for its authoritarian-ism. When Pitte returns to the village for his inheritance and his revenge on Danielle, he is dressed as a soldier. Later, Thérèse incites a small insurrection in her classroom when she refuses to be intimidated by a mediocre teacher. The stern elder priest condemns Antonia and the pregnant Danielle from the pulpit, but secretly forces himself on a vulnerable parishioner. Religious beliefs keep Mad Madonna and the Protestant apart. In contrast, the happier priest discovers he can no longer suppress the force of eros within him, throws off his clerical garb and rings the church bells for joy. Crying "I'm free! I'm free!" he ecstatically joins Antonia's compound and makes up for lost time with Letta, "lovingly knocking her up," in the narrator's words, every year for the next decade.

The film emphasizes male violence against women, but its events unfold against the backdrop of World War II and its atrocities, deepening and expanding the film's critique of patriarchy. On their first day in the village, Antonia takes Danielle to the grave of Bertie, who had shared a close friendship with her and Crooked Finger years ago. Bertie had hidden a Jewish family during the war. When the Nazis caught him, they shot him and the family. "And the priest was too cowardly to bury him," she says, in earshot of the priest. This history defined Crooked Finger, who, after Antonia, holds the most moral weight in the film. Unable to reconcile the evil he witnessed with a desire to live, he retreated from life after the war. With his long stringy hair and gentle smile, he becomes a liminal figure who lives on the border between patriarchal and matriarchal space. He never leaves his house, only peers out from its clouded windows, and so Antonia comes to him, first with Danielle, then Thérèse and Sarah, and he introduces each one to the life of the mind. He does not try to evade the problem of evil with the false consolations of religion or politics. Instead, he turns to philosophy, from Plato to Nietzsche, for secular answers to life's mysteries.

Early in the film, Crooked Finger's gloomy pronouncements sound like the remarks of a quirky intellectual, affectionately indulged by Antonia and her daughters. "The world is a hell, inhabited by tormented souls and devils," he says to a teary Thérèse when he tries to comfort her after the rape. Her reply—"Schopenhauer?"—ends the tragic episode with lightness, demonstrating the film's equanimous vision of life's ups and downs. Yet, as the film's tone darkens, Crooked Finger's despair no longer seems eccentric. Little Sarah tells him he stinks, and he laughs, explaining that he smells of "time past." However, he really smells of a death born, like Mad Madonna's and the Protestant's, from a fatal alienation from the body. Crooked Finger recalls the Nordic angst of Bergman's films, and the film respects his moral sensitivity. But the philosophy he turns to bears the limitations of male knowledge. Because he is alienated from the grotesque ambivalence of the body, his knowledge leads only to despair, and he finally hangs himself.

It is easier to depict dystopias than utopias, to show the horror that exists than to imagine something better. Yet *Antonia's Line* imagines feminist principles in practice, with a character, Antonia, who represents a response to the evils of the world different from Crooked Finger's. Like Crooked Finger, she does not close her eyes to the moral corruption around her. But through her, the film turns away from the abstractions of philosophy to a knowledge grounded in the grotesque materiality of the body enmeshed in the larger forces of natural renewal. The community that results from Antonia's commitment to live a responsible life resonates with principles M. Jacqui Alexander and Chandra Talpade Mohanty identify in their description of a feminist democracy (1995, xxviii–xxix).

Drawing on socialist principles to craft an alternative vision for change, such a democracy would create a different order of relationships among people by making sexual politics central to governance and giving attention to how hierarchies of governance affect the disenfranchised. This order would be based on a new sense of agency in which "[w]omen do not imagine themselves as *victims* or *dependents* of governing structures but as agents of their own lives," lived within "feminist collectivities and organizations." It would also likely foster the practice of "othermothering," which Heather Hewett describes as common in African American communities, where "aunties, grandmothers, friends, fictive kin" share responsibilities for childcare (2009, 27). Rooted in West Africa, othermothering encourages a communal ethic of care and often social activism as well.

In the matriarchal space that takes shape around Antonia, characters exist as "agents of their own lives," actively creating an alternative way of being that doesn't retreat from the larger community but coexists with it, resisting it when necessary.[12] The film renders this utopia in terms that are less literal than poetic, concerned less with the details of how such a community might be ordered than with the feelings it would evoke, to recall Richard Dyer's "Entertainment and Utopia," an influential 1977 essay on the political work of popular culture.

Three sequences stand out for their dramatic and thematic power in evoking those feelings. The first concerns sex, the second justice, and the third the co-presence of generations in a non-linear flow of time. Halfway through the film, Lara, a teacher, comes to the farmhouse to tutor Thérèse. Danielle sees her as Botticelli's Venus and is stricken with love for her. Over a long shot of the two strolling through the meadows, the narrator says, "And then love burst out everywhere." Next, a montage links four couples engaged in sex, beginning with Danielle and Lara. As their excitement intensifies, the camera moves closer, and a brass fanfare begins on the soundtrack. Then the film cuts to Antonia and Farmer Bas, back to Danielle and Lara, then Loony Lips and Deedee, and the priest and Letta. The editing quickens, in contrast to the languid pace of the rest of the movie, and the music becomes more bombastic. Loony Lips is a foot taller than Deedee, and a witty shot shows his rocking feet extended through the bars of their bed frame well over hers. To the sounds of escalating fanfares, exuberant carnal pleasure and a communal climax, we then see Thérèse, who is perhaps five, walking down a hallway between the bedrooms, rubbing her eyes. "I can't sleep," she complains, provoking more laughter from behind the closed doors.

This sequence most fully realizes the film's utopian principles in its depiction of the earthy inclusiveness of life on Antonia's farm. A sentiment echoed in the title of bell hooks's *Feminism Is for Everybody: Passionate Politics* (2000), sex is fundamental to the vitality of the body and the community. It is for everyone.[13] In addition to the conventionally matched couple of Letta and the expriest, the montage includes the elderly, the mentally disabled, and a lesbian couple. However, life on Antonia's farm does not revolve only around the simple pleasures of the table and bed but encompasses art and ideas, not to mention the repetitious tasks of everyday life. Danielle's paintings are ever-present in the *mise en scène*, and Crooked Finger and Thérèse provide a steady stream of philosophical conversation. By joining body, mind, and soul, to recall Joanna Frueh's "monster beauty," the sex montage evokes a visceral sense of the transformed social order feminist politics aspires to.

The film radically decenters the heterosexual romance plot but not heterosexual men who can free themselves from patriarchal notions of gender. The compound's women embrace men who reject the values of the outside world—the priest, Loony Lips, Farmer Bas and his sons—but on feminist terms. When Farmer Bas asks Antonia for her hand because he needs a mother for his sons, she simply replies that she doesn't need his sons. In time, he learns to love her on her own terms, and eventually, she returns his love, telling him, "You still can't have my hand, but you can have the rest." With dignity and romance, the film shows Antonia sitting tall on Bas's tractor as he drives her across a field for their first night together and carries her over the threshold into the little shed he built for them, apart from the youthful hubbub of the main house.

Like the grotesque body with its permeable boundaries, the farmhouse opens its gate to anyone seeking refuge from the brutalities of the patriarchal world, and so the compound grows, suggesting that goodness reproduces itself. However, a feminist utopia cannot be built only by accepting nature's imperative to renew itself. It also demands the courage exemplified by Bertie of the Resistance, martyred for his principles. The film defines its vision of morality with the clarity of melodrama: evil preys on vulnerability; good stands up to protect it. And the film defines its characters by how they respond to the demand to take a stand when called for, from Antonia's punishment of the boy bullying Loony Lips to Danielle's rescue of Deedee. Both acted without hesitation or fear of reprisal, although Danielle and her daughter would pay dearly for that early act of courage.

The film's most melodramatic moment occurs in its second key sequence, when Antonia curses the evil Pitte. It begins with the narrator announcing that Pitte has raped Thérèse. A swaggering Pitte enters the bar and orders beer for everyone. When he is asked if he has something to celebrate, the film answers with a cut to Thérèse lying in bed, as Danielle kisses her teary face. Antonia and Danielle then look at each other intently, and Danielle silently hands her mother a rifle. Antonia marches out, opens the gate, and strides into the fading light. The sequence is shot and edited to align Antonia with nature and to reinforce her association with Demeter, the earth goddess who experienced unbounded rage and grief over her lost daughter. Building suspense by prolonging her hunt for Pitte, the film shows Antonia as a powerful figure rising against the night sky. Her march toward the camera past a stone cross silently juxtaposes her virtue with the hypocrisy of the church.

When she finally enters the bar, the sequence moves swiftly to show her as a commanding agent of justice. She raises her rifle and takes aim at Pitte, who is sitting with casual arrogance at a table. When she tells him to rise and he refuses, she shoots, shattering the glasses at his table. She pushes him out to the courtyard with the barrel of her gun and tells him that she would kill him if she could. "Instead," she says with measured intensity, "I will curse you, and my curse will haunt you. If you ever return, my hate will destroy you. Your bones will break, your tongue will erupt with pus . . . The water you drink will poison you, the air you breath will rot your lungs . . . for raping a child."

Other moments in the film have highlighted unrepentant motherhood—pregnant Danielle sitting confidently in church and prompting the minister's diatribe against her and her mother, and Thérèse, without guilt, relinquishing the care of her infant daughter Sarah to the child's father. But here we see

Antonia shows the full force of her power when she draws on the moral authority of the postmaternal woman to curse the man who raped her granddaughter.

Antonia in the full force of her power. Hers is not the power of Girl Culture's Final Girl, on the cusp of womanhood, but power based on the moral authority of the postmaternal mother, whose long life has endowed her with the right to name what she sees. Like a witch, she summons the forces of nature to destroy her enemy with a grotesque vengeance that would turn his body on itself.

And her curse proves potent. The young men who have witnessed the episode begin to advance on Pitte when they hear of his transgression, which has violated even the modest norms of their community, and when Antonia walks away, they surround him and beat him fiercely. His long-resentful brother finishes the job by drowning him in a cistern. The sequence ends with Antonia sitting with Bas on their bed. She finally weeps, and it is the only moment in the film when she displays such vulnerability. The shot holds for a full twenty seconds, slowing the pace of cinematic time to allow viewers to reflect on what they have just witnessed.

Feminist Time

It is important that Antonia—not the men of the compound, not Danielle—administer justice to Pitte because of her identity as a postmaternal mother, a figure central to Gullette's critique of Western culture's ideologies of age and aging.[14] This critique provides a helpful perspective on matrophobia because it demonstrates the ways age compounds it. While Gullette's critique begins with the postmaternal mother, its scope is wider, and finally calls for a radical rethinking of our culture's notions of aging and time.[15]

Like gender and race, age is a culturally created identity category that defines us, as well as a concept that applies to the entire lifespan. Yet, just as ideology applies the concept of race only to the nonwhite, age belongs mainly to the old. Age also "comes" earlier, and differently, to women than to men. As Susan Sontag wrote, women's marginality doubles as they age. Once they pass the years of reproduction, whether they are mothers are not, the sexism they suffer is compounded by ageism (1972). Moreover, as Mary Russo adds, not "acting one's age" leaves women vulnerable to ridicule, contempt, pity, and scorn, and finally, "the scandal of anachronism" (1999, 21).

American culture has been historically and notoriously fixated on youth. From its foundations in progressivism, U.S. ideology identifies all that is good ("hope, desire, understanding, and optimism") with youth, and all that it rejects ("the past, the backward, the unenlightened") with the old (Russo 1999, 21). Indeed, old and young are shorthand for bad and good. Because of this ideology, the dominant culture tends to impose a "narrative of decline" on the passage of time. The decline narrative has its appeal, and I have long been drawn to it. It underlies romantic comedy, which always privileges youth, as well as melodrama, which emphasizes the losses inflicted by time or barely avoided ("just in time"). No one who has spent time around elderly people, or has grappled herself with the physical and mental decline of old age, would be tempted to sentimentalize the costs of aging. However, by assuming that age brings *only* loss, the decline narrative marginalizes the old and narrows the possibility of connections across generations.

In contrast, when aging is viewed primarily as the passage of time, it can be recognized as bringing not only decline and loss but also growth and change. Gullette terms this vision a "progress" narrative that finds "variousness and possibilities" across the life span and values the accumulation of experience and history on the body. As Patricia Mellencamp writes, "the most interesting and powerful woman is the old woman. She is the summation of all the life that comes with old age" (1999, 325). Antonia is such a woman, and her authority—the power she exerts over the film's narrative as well as her community—comes from her age. The progress narrative shares with liberation movements such as Marxism and feminism a faith in—or at least an acceptance of—history, or the passage of time itself.

Part of the power of the progress narrative lies in its belief that life's tragedies can be surmounted. That belief is dramatized in what Gullette refers to as the "recovery" narrative, which shows protagonists suffering great losses but eventually overcoming them. *Antonia's Line* is such a narrative, conveying through its narrator an explicitly unsentimental message about suffering: "The proverb is wrong. Time does not heal all wounds. It merely softens the pain and blurs the memories." The second part of the film is colored with sadness. Death is in the air. Thérèse appears to overcome the trauma of her rape, but we sense she will struggle all her life with Crooked Finger's suicide.

However, unlike Crooked Finger, who never recovered from the wounds of World War II, Antonia steadfastly tends to the day-to-day chores that sustain her both materially and emotionally. "Life is to be lived," she sighs before rising heavily from the table after absorbing the news of yet another tragedy. Following her model of determination, Deedee echoes her words and action. This attitude does not insist on premature healing from grief, but it does trust time and resilience and in that way privileges age. The film's long view inspires courage by showing Antonia's stalwart determination to put one foot ahead of the other even when life tries to beat her down. Time passes, and the film returns repeatedly to images of her astride her Belgian horse, which shares her physical monumentality and implacable movement across not only the landscape but also time.

Closely related to age is generation, which carries similar ideological charges, as the recent history of feminism has made all too clear. Like age, generation benefits from a critical and historical approach that recognizes that age cohorts and the so-called gaps between them are neither universal nor inevitable. The nineteenth century invented childhood and the twentieth adolescence. The twenty-first will bring the old into discursive existence because of the size of the aging population. According to historian Al Richmond, during long stretches of history, generations related to each other in terms of continuity rather than combativeness.[16] As Gullette argues, when periods of generational conflict occur, they are rooted in social forces that benefit from fostering historical amnesia and minimizing the possibility of transgenerational coalitions around common interests. The highly publicized conflict between Generation X and the baby boomers, for example, covers up the real source of a widespread malaise affecting both generations as a result of the downsizing of the American dream during the New Economy in the 1990s. This downsizing, followed by the worldwide economic crisis beginning in 2008, shrank economic opportunities and security for both generations, yet as Gullette explains, "Age war obscures the cult of youth, class war from above, and globalization, world-historical facts that would otherwise seem both more dire and more resistible" (2004, 58).

Despite its adoption of the wave metaphor, feminism has yet to develop a concept of history not colored by the Freudian model of struggle between two close but emotionally and intellectually distant generations (Woodward 1999). Nor has feminism mounted a serious analysis of age, even though age is involved in all formulations of life, we belong to an aging population, and the majority of elderly people are women. The Second Wave focused largely on issues important to younger women (reproductive rights, child care, work), as has the Third Wave. Even Nancy Chodorow, in the second edition of her groundbreaking book *The Reproduction of Mothering*, admits to writing the book from "the daughter's point of view" (Gullette 2005, 153–154).

Postmaternal mothers are at a stage in their lives when the intensive responsibilities of motherhood should rightfully be diminishing. Recognition of this category would open up the possibility of what Gullette calls "joint adulthood"—mothers and children "becoming equally adults together" (2005, 128), a relation *Antonia's Line* dramatizes. When young adults displace their problems, whether personal or social, onto their midlife mothers, they are displacing anger more rightly directed at other targets, such as patriarchy or cutthroat capitalism. Blaming midlife mothers misconstrued as "wicked powerful" and as still locked in overly intense, dyadic relations with their adult children serves the interests of the status quo. The result—in both feminism and the culture at large—infantilizes and depoliticizes younger adults as well as "othering" the postmaternal woman into a narrowly construed category of mother (2005, 149). From this perspective, Rebecca Walker cannot be singled out for her failure to see her mother as a postmaternal subject, or to examine her own ambivalences from a political perspective.

The ending of *Antonia's Line* returns to where the film began, the day of Antonia's death, and in its last segments, Sarah, a small child of perhaps six or seven, has begun to appear more repeatedly on screen. Like her grandmother Danielle, she has an artistic and visionary nature. With her journal always in hand, Sarah is a writer, and the film's final words reveal to us that she, now an adult, has been its narrator. We often see her in close-ups intently observing the events unfolding on screen, and in reaction shots and point-of-view shots that emphasize her inquisitive gaze and move us closer to her subjectivity. She is frequently on screen with Antonia, sharing intimate moments and casual conversations about topics such as death and the absence of an afterlife. ("Where is everyone? Where is Crooked Finger? Is there a heaven?") Indeed, Sarah has a precocious awareness of death, and writes a premature elegy for Deedee to let her know before she dies how much she is loved.

As the film draws to its end, it becomes increasingly clear that Sarah has made time for the real protagonist of her story. Throughout, she describes time anthropomorphically as a force that cannot be resisted and should not be ignored. As the compound grows, she recounts, "Time gave birth, again and again and, with complete contentment, produced nothing but itself." Later, as she prepares us for Antonia's death, her commentary becomes more somber: "Time flowed, season followed season, tumbling over each other as if in their dance they wanted to end the exhausting round of birth and death." Over a shot of old Antonia and Farmer Bas walking together, she says, "Sometimes, time crept slowly onwards like an exhausted tortoise." And over a shot of a funeral procession marking a death perhaps before its time, she says, "Sometimes it tore though life like a vulture in search of prey. Time took no notice of death or life, decay or growth, love, hate, or jealousy. It ignored all those things that are so important to us that we forget time." These words introduce the film's third key sequence, which begins with Antonia and Sarah watching a giant tree being felled. The tree's fall anticipates Antonia's death.

This poignant sequence, which begins on the eve of Antonia's death, unfolds without words, beginning with a high-angle long shot of yet another of the community's dinners. A reverse shot shows Sarah from a low angle, framed by the window of the nearby barn, observing the festivities below and writing in her journal. She smiles, then looks at Antonia and Farmer Bas, who appear in a close two-shot looking knowingly and tenderly at each other. Then, one by one, characters, now dead, who have touched the lives of Antonia and her daughters begin to appear, filmed in the style of magic realism to indicate that the events that follow are indeed real, to Sarah at least.

First, Crooked Finger walks through the iron gate and smiles. Sarah, who remembers him well, is puzzled to see him alive. He beckons to her, and she laughs. Next, her great-great-grandmother appears in her coffin and makes a grotesquely funny face. Mad Madonna and the Protestant enter the compound, arm in arm at last. A cut returns us to Antonia and Bas at the long table with their loved ones, but they are now decades younger. Bas offers Antonia his arm, and they walk around the table and begin a little waltz, while the sound track shifts from its melancholy motif to a more lilting one. From a distance, Farmer Dan and his unhappy sons, including Pitte, look on.

Antonia and Bas's dance continues, intercut with shots of dead Letta, pregnant again and radiantly backlit by the sun, and dead Loony Lips, lounging, full of life, in the grass. Sarah continues to watch, stroking her face with curiosity, and Antonia and Bas return to their current ages. He bows to her, and as the family claps he escorts her back toward the farmhouse. The camera moves closer to Antonia, framing her alone in the screen, and she lifts her eyes to Sarah. The old woman and small child hold each other's gaze, conveying the intimate connection between them, and as the camera moves closer to both, Antonia smiles at Sarah and beckons her to follow. In the next shot, Sarah enters Antonia's room to find her in bed, and Antonia tells her she is going to die.

In this sequence, space and time have merged. As with the festive endings of Shakespeare's comedies, the film depicts an imaginary community flexible enough to include all of its characters, even its villains. In tone, however, it recalls later romances, such as *The Tempest* and *The Winter's Tale*, in which time works to reconcile conflicts. While the narration has increasingly emphasized the relentless, forward movement of time, here time becomes fluid and nonlinear, loosening the sequential ordering of generations. Antonia shares the screen with her long-dead mother. She also shares it with her daughter Danielle, but as women of the same age. By showing the co-presence of ages within an individual's life, we see time reversing itself to display the commonalities across generations. Antonia is at once old and young, ready to die but also filled with the life she has lived. From this perspective, an old woman such as Antonia is a monumental testimony to a rich life, well lived.

Similarly, the film rids death of the fear commonly attached to it. In the film's opening sequence, Sarah announces that, unlike most people, Antonia was ready to die because she knew when "enough is enough." Speaking of herself in the third person, Sarah describes the presence of Antonia's great-granddaughter who would not leave her deathbed "until she knew exactly how the miracle of death would embrace her beloved grandmother," using the language of the grotesque to join death with its regenerative aspect (an "embrace"). When the film returns to Antonia's death at the end, the camera recalls Antonia and Bas's last waltz, and the movement of the plot itself, by circling her bed. Antonia, surrounded by her family, begins her farewells, and

ABOVE: Sarah (Thyrza Ravesteijn), the film's narrator, watches a miraculous scene unfold as dead friends (and enemies) return for Antonia's last meal and dance. BELOW: Time collapses as Antonia and Bas (Jan Decleir), momentarily restored to their younger years, share a last dance. As in Shakespeare's festive comedies, the film's imaginary community makes room for everyone.

all grapple with her imminent death in their own ways. In voice-over, Sarah recounts her desire as a child to be with Antonia "when death parted Antonia's soul from her formidable body." Again recalling the grotesque, Sarah's words echo Antonia's earlier assurance that "nothing dies forever. Something always remains, from which something new grows."

Through its perfectly balanced interplay of image and sound, the film's formal properties model the possibility of a new relation between mothers and daughters, and women across time. Yi-Lin Yu, in her thoughtful essay on Amy Tan's *The Joy Luck Club*, describes the integration of mothers' and daughters' voices into a "double voice" of interdependence or a "multiple female consciousness." This double voice allows for the co-presence of two subjects who interact with both resonance and difference. This intersubjectivity, she writes, is threatening in a culture that values individuality.[17] But invoking it, especially through storytelling, is essential to maintaining connections among generations, especially in immigrant communities. In telling Antonia's story, and with it, Danielle's and Thérèse's, Sarah does not appropriate their voices. Nor does her commentary dominate their images, which command the screen. Glossing these images, which include some of herself as a child, Sarah as an adult tells the story of generations joined in continuity rather than rupture, and in so doing shows how the stories of her maternal ancestors are hers as well.

No longer compelled to fight over psychoanalysis's value to feminism, feminists can continue to glean helpful insights from Freud's influential work. His essay titled "Femininity," for example, gestures toward the possibility of the kind of intergenerational continuity among women at the core of *Antonia's Line*. It argues that when a little girl plays with dolls she inhabits two generations simultaneously, maintaining her sense of herself as a child but imagining herself as a mother. This play sets the stage for a model of generational continuity based on a legacy of mutual caregiving, with each generation modeling for the next what it learned from the previous one. This model is not based on a struggle for domination, but on "pleasurable interaction (play) and care" (Woodward 1999, 151), much as the girl plays with her doll.[18] Citing Ernst Abelin, Kathleen Woodward explains that in the patriarchal family, boys form their identity within the triad of self, father, and mother, along the lines of sexual difference and competition with each other (152). In contrast, girls form their identity through another triad: mother, self, and baby, basing the connections among them on a heritage of care for the next generation.

Antonia's Line lyrically evokes a world governed by such an ethos of care, which flows not simply toward the next generation, but more universally toward the weak and vulnerable. Feminism could do worse than remembering this simple value. In the hands of feminist philosophers such as Sara Ruddick, such maternal thinking could become the foundation for feminist action in the service of a politics of resistance and peace. This politics would not be based on a sentimentalized notion of caregiving as an inclination inborn in women, or a task belonging primarily to the weak and disenfranchised. But it would make use of capacities honed in people who do maternal work: "attentiveness, realism, and a welcoming attitude toward change, . . . resilient cheerfulness, a grasping of truth that is caring, and a tolerance for ambiguity and ambivalence" (Ruddick 1989, 220).[19]

A "Wicked Powerful" Feminism

This book began with a discussion of *Titanic*, a postfeminist text that celebrated the power of a girl's desire for romantic love at the expense of understanding her mother, shown to be self-pitying and calculating. *Antonia's Line*, on the other hand, imagines the possibility of unruly girls and unrepentant mothers in relationships defined by mutual support and a shared commitment to social justice and the common good. American academic feminism has long been insulated by its class and racial privilege, and *Antonia's Line*, the work of a white woman from northern Europe, once again asserts the vision of an artist culturally privileged in the global hierarchy of geographic regions. But the film engages with specific types of difference—age and generation—particularly pertinent to my argument, and in ways that are generalizable to other categories of difference. Because its setting in a rural Dutch community distances it from contemporary life, the film's utopian vision does not include the more complicated pleasures of consumer culture embraced by Girl World. Instead, it celebrates the social and physical pleasures of everyday life, pursued with a sense of entitlement to "the best in everything," as the narrator explains when Thérèse, as a university student, sends an inadequate lover packing. In removing itself from the frenzied social environment of *Thirteen*, the film considers questions rarely asked in current political discourse, such as the extent to which the pathologies of contemporary life are fueled by simple but unsatisfied hungers for communities built on social justice and mutual care.

In 1981, Merle Woo called for a new feminist paradigm "created in a community bonded not by color, sex, or class, but by love and the common goal for the liberation of mind, heart, and spirit" (quoted in Sandoval 1990, 60). This vision of oppositional consciousness, associated with U.S. Third World feminism, enabled feminists of color to sustain their solidarity from the 1960s through the 1980s, despite the differences among them. It also conveyed a rare and forthright sense of a movement driven not only by ethics but also love. A few years later, Adrienne Rich revised the introduction to her feminist classic *Of Woman Born* for its tenth-anniversary edition to reflect her new realization that the inequities of gender do not trump those of class in the struggle for a more just social order. Instead, she writes, all social change must happen "hand in hand" with a dedication to "the claim to personhood" denied for centuries to women and many men—a claim that underlies the humanism of *Antonia's Line*. As an influential voice of the Second Wave, Rich shows a feminism willing to examine itself and change.

Academic feminism has devoted much of its intellectual energy in recent decades to a critique of identity, and not always toward productive ends. Mridula Nath Chakraborty notes that just as the Western literary establishment announced the death of the author when women began to claim a place in the canon, "hegemonic feminism deployed what Naomi Schor calls 'the shock troops of anti-essentialism'" when feminists of color began organizing around common racial and cultural grounds (2004, 206).[20] In contrast, Ella Shohat, echoing Woo, has called for a "multicultural feminist politics of identification, affiliation, and social transformation" based on a sense of identity as something one "does" rather than something one "has"—an understanding that resonates with the views of other theorists such as Ruddick and Marianne Hirsch who call for considering mothering as a practice (Shohat 1998, 9).

Such a movement, based on the principles of dialogism and relationality Shohat articulated with Robert Stam in *Unthinking Eurocentrism*, would transcend narrow identity politics in a common commitment to eradicating the boundaries between privilege and disenfranchisement across the globe.[21] It would join a worldwide struggle against the intensifying forces of global capitalism, imperialism, and militarism, making visible the connections among these forces as well as the ways they are supported by ideologies of heteronormativity, race, and nation. "We must be present *as feminists*," Chandra Talpade Mohanty argues, "in the full range of movements resisting empire."[22] This feminism would challenge capitalism by unmasking the role of consumerism in our lives, and join in the process of decolonization by recognizing that psychological and social domination occurs across multiple axes. Teen girls who embrace Girl Culture tap into the expressive possibilities of consumer culture, but they are also implicated in its materialism and the ways class controls their access to it. Conservative blockbusters such as *Titanic* are worldwide phenomena, while the visionary *Antonia's Line* is not.

Throughout this book, I have referred to the most recent expressions of Western feminism as the Third Wave. While I use this term with some hesitation because of the unfinished business it sidesteps concerning mothers, I've recognized the reasons for its appeal to young feminists and its acceptance in the academy. However, the name raises other concerns as well. In trying to avoid the minefield of generations, it has perpetuated a Eurocentric narrative of feminist history, based on key events and personalities of the West (Narain 2004, 240).[23] As Shohat argues, the struggles of American women of color and Third World women over the past decades cannot be made to conform to this orthodox sequence of waves. Nor can multicultural feminism be seen as a "recent bandwagon phenomenon" when in fact it is a response to a "five-hundred-year history of gendered colonialist dispossession in the past and of massive postcolonialist displacements in the present" (Shohat 1998, 19). Even more forcefully, Chakraborty argues that "there can be no Third Wave or transnational feminist unity or utopic global" until hegemonic feminism confronts the ways its use of the rhetoric of global sisterhood perpetuates a dynamic of center/periphery and first/third world.

There is no simple response to these challenges, or any easy way for feminism to renew itself on a platform of transnational solidarity built on difference. Yet one untapped source of strength lies in the potential for solidarity across the boundaries of *time* as well as those of class, race, and nation. To tap into this strength, feminism must first root out its ambivalences about motherhood and aging. In an eloquent and impassioned argument for the value of age, Gullette writes, "The life course should make its claim to a kind of sacredness. This is different from the sanctity of 'life' . . . but [demands] that we acknowledge the increasing value of a life lived in time" (2004, 96). Elsewhere she suggests the political potential of the old: "Age is a cause—like race and gender—that rightfully allies itself with principles of narrative freedom, economic justice, and human rights. There are many ways to contribute to a revolution" (2004, 196). To create new futures for ourselves, not to mention for the generations that will follow us, women need to create new narratives and images of aging women filled with possibility, rather than with the pessimism of the narrative of decline.

Gullette uses the playful phrase "wicked powerful" to capture the cultural ambivalence aroused by the postmaternal woman, seen to possess both more and less power than she actually has. I like the idea of a feminism made "wicked powerful" through the embrace of a motherline or connection among women of all ages, across history. A wicked powerful feminism would rescue the figure of the mother, and grandmother, from the culture's matrophobia and harness her unruliness and unrepentance.⁴ The mother inevitably carries prodigious ideological baggage. A wicked powerful feminism would sort through that baggage for what is of value in it. It would reconstruct mothering along the lines of what Shohat describes as necessary for any identity: it is something one chooses through action. From this perspective, to mother, to "be" a mother, means to take up the work of nurturing and defending the weak, standing up for justice, advocating for peace.

Finally, redeeming the mother from the burden of matrophobia doesn't mean that the conventional family must be the basis for generational relations among women. I have suggested that mothering is available to all who identify themselves with feminism. The postmaternal is a crucial corrective to concepts of mothering that cripple both women and their adult children, as well as discourage men from taking up new identities as parents. As an example, Kathleen Woodward cites Nancy Chodorow's discovery that a group of women trained as psychoanalysts in the 1930s had attitudes toward gender that were perplexingly different from hers. She soon realized that to expect these women to mirror back her own views, or to debate with her as if they were all adolescents, would be "vain and immature." By recognizing them as postmaternal women with no obligations to mother her as a needy child, she succeeded in *knowing* them not as mothers or grandmothers but as professional women of another generation. Chodorow was able to find generational continuity with them based on a friendship rooted in everyday life (Woodward 1999, 154).

Antonia's Line ends with the following postscript on the screen: "And as this long chronicle reaches its conclusion, nothing has come to an end . . ." Filled with the spirit of grotesque ambivalence, these words acknowledge the film's chronicle as finite, much like this book's account of one group of films and television programs in the postfeminist United States. But these words also embed that partial story in a history that is unbounded, a generational line that extends both backward and forward in time beyond the parade of figures Sarah can call up in her imagination. I would like to think of the waves of time in *Antonia's Line* as evoking the ebb and flow of the feminist struggle, which like any other liberation movement, experiences retreats as well as advances in its march toward justice. I would also like to see the spirit of the film's unruly, unrepentant women and girls nudging us toward a feminism that is ever more wicked powerful.

Afterword

And as this long chronicle reaches its conclusion, nothing has come to an end.
—SARAH, *ANTONIA'S LINE*

A S I BRING *this* chronicle to its end, I realize there is some
unfinished business that still lingers. But first, a few words
on how unfinished business haunts most academic work.
Feminism has taken us a long way toward recognizing the
standpoints from which we make our scholarly claims, and
how those standpoints limit the scope and authority of those claims. But we
still remain uneasy about revealing the *personal* stakes behind our work—why
we're drawn to one project rather than another, what unfinished emotional
business we circle around from the safe distance of our intellects. Whatever
gives purpose to our work does not spring from a place of cool disinterest.
One guilty pleasure I have long enjoyed is reading the scholarship of my colleagues and friends not only for what I can learn about their subjects, but also
for what I might learn—or even only speculate—about them. The people
closest to me probably suspect where my interest in female unruliness comes
from, although that interest might be hard to fathom for anyone who simply
observed the surface of my life.

The question that remains for me now is why I have more easily written in the voice of the mother than that of the daughter. Of course, there are abundant impersonal reasons to recuperate the voice of the silenced mother, as I hope this book has demonstrated. But my identity as mother has also marked every aspect of my being and necessarily shaped this book. When my daughters were teens and one started wearing baggy flannels and boots, I realized she was channeling Angela Chase of *My So-Called Life*. When another started wearing her underwear as outerwear, I knew she was channeling Madonna. I tried to look at the popular culture that influenced my girls from their eyes. Doing so didn't necessarily ease the stormy years of their adolescence but I learned as I went, personally and professionally.

Clueless, Mean Girls, Buffy the Vampire Slayer, even *Ugly Betty*—these Girl Culture texts often intermingle in unsettling ways the values of the Third Wave with those of postfeminism. These works are founded on a set of assumptions that compromise and often undermine their messages of female empowerment: "true beauty" means conforming to fashion industry or Hollywood standards; people of color are less important than white people and/or are morally inferior to them; consumerism and fashion are enjoyable and satisfying for all "normal" girls and women; a young woman who has sex outside romantic relationships is either evil or emotionally troubled; and alliances based on such commonalities as race or class are suspect because individualism is the key to a good life.[1] It is crucial never to lose sight of these assumptions, which are present in virtually all mainstream culture. But it is also crucial to have confidence in the young women who are drawn to the popular culture of their times. Without demonstrating trust in their ability to make sound decisions for themselves, we will not get far in building the intergenerational alliances that will benefit us all.

My more difficult unfinished business concerns my identity as a daughter. While I have looked ahead to my daughters in writing this book, a part of me has also looked back to my mother, whom I lost almost a decade ago and I will always wish to have known better. My awareness of the painfully heavy burden of judgment that mothers bear has made it hard for me to acknowledge my ambivalence toward my own mother. As a mother, she was imperfect, like all mothers. As a person, or "something else beside a mother," she was extraordinary: a teacher, an intellectual, a beauty, a person of formidable strength and courage.

At this stage in my life, I am still sorting out my mother's legacy to me and to my daughters. I also know that thinking about the relationships among us has sensitized me to feminism's generational struggles. Perhaps my mother's greatest gift to me was her insistence that I trust my daughters to get the important things right. And as time goes by, her identity as a mother matters less to me than the fullness and complexity of who she was as a person. She never felt the need to justify or explain herself, as far as I can tell, and I finally recognize that she is the figure of maternal self-possession and unrepentance that inspired this book.

My recognition of my mother's unrepentance also helps me see myself in a framework of mothering that moves beyond my dyadic relationship with her. I never knew my grandmothers well. They were from the "old country," and my parents, as first-generation Americans, had little nostalgia for their roots. It also remains to be seen whether grandchildren, let alone granddaughters, will enter my life. But in addition to my own daughters, I am connected to girls and women of all ages, both giving and receiving care and love from them. The sum of these relationships has not been a linear motherline, but something similar—uneven, raggedy, stronger in some places than in others—that has given meaning to my life and demonstrated the profound rewards of mothering as a practice.

As time passes, my daughters and I have "become adults together," and the flow of caretaking changes direction as circumstances require, in a dance that recalls the scene of miraculous time-shifting toward the end of *Antonia's Line*. And so an answer to that nagging question about competing voices emerges. The rupture between mothers and daughters that Adrienne Rich wrote about is, I suspect, more illusory than our culture would have us believe. In *White Oleander*, the daughter, freed at last, walks out of her mother's life—only to become an artist, just like her mother. We carve out identities that are separate from our mothers, as our daughters do with us, but we are always still a part of each other. When we speak as one, the other is still there.

Notes

1. The quote is from Camille Paglia, a controversial figure among feminist scholars.
2. *Titanic* is renowned for its production costs, awards, and global popularity. It won eleven Academy Awards, including best picture, and with its $200 million budget and global grosses of $1.8 billion, it is one of the most expensive and lucrative films ever made.
3. Feminism's Second Wave is associated with the women's liberation movement of the early 1960s through the 1970s. The First Wave began with the women's suffrage movement of the late nineteenth and early twentieth centuries.
4. Warner's best seller *Perfect Madness* and Ayelet Waldman's *Bad Mother* address this pressure on modern mothers. See also D. Lynn O'Brien Hallstein. Susan J. Douglas and Meredith W. Michaels's *The Mommy Myth* provides an excellent analysis of the historical roots of momism, a term that originated with Philip Wylie's influential *A Generation of Vipers* (1942).
5. Astrid Henry uses the term, coined by Rebecca Dakin Quinn, throughout *Not My Mother's Sister*.
6. One of the most important early debates in feminist film theory occurred between E. Ann Kaplan (1983) and Linda Williams (1984) over the maternal melodrama *Stella Dallas* (1937).

7. See Sarah Projansky's "Gender, Race, Feminism, and the International Girl Hero" for a concise overview of the rise of Girl Culture in the early to mid-1990s, including pertinent television shows, magazines and films.

8. Timothy Shary has extensively documented the rise and spread of youth culture in the United States and internationally.

9. The book takes its title from *Hamlet's* Ophelia, who lost her mind, then her life, after losing Hamlet's love. Pipher argues that today's girls lose their authentic selves in adolescence, when they replace the confidence of their girlhoods with an excessive desire to please others.

10. Buffy Shutt, quoted in Bernard Weinraub (1998). Jamie Kellner, one-time CEO at the WB network, adds: "What the female teens want is empowered female teen characters, which is something that has been missing for a long time on television."

11. In the late 1990s, two major feminist journals took important steps to rectify this situation by publishing relevant special issues: *Hypatia* on Third Wave feminism (1997) and *Signs* on feminism and youth cultures (1998). Both journals leaned more heavily toward alternative subcultures such as riot grrrls than toward mainstream popular culture. Similarly, Mary Celeste Kearney, a leading scholar in the new area of Girls Studies, has emphasized alternative more than mainstream forms of media production and reception.

12. Anxiety about the influence of popular culture on teens increased dramatically after the high school shootings in the late 1990s. This anxiety focused on media violence and its appeal to boys, although popular accounts of the shootings have rarely noted that they were performed *by* boys. Discussions of media influence on girls have generally focused on sex.

13. With a few exceptions, cinema has yet to exploit the dramatic possibility of female sports teams. Those exceptions include *Bring It On* (2000), in which cheerleading stands in for sports competition, and *Love and Basketball* (2000), which I discuss in chapter seven. The film depicts a girl's passion for basketball, but her relationship with her teammates is overshadowed by her romance with a male player.

14. Again, exceptions exist, such as *Mermaids* (1990), *Anywhere But Here* (1999), and *Mamma Mia* (2008), but these stand out from the norm.

15. Joanne Hollows and Rachel Moseley make this case throughout *Feminism in Popular Culture*.

16. Catherine M. Orr takes a similar position in the conclusion of her thoughtful essay on Third Wave feminism.

17. See Beretta Smith-Shomade on Oprah Winfrey, and Linda Mizejewski on Josephine Baker and Queen Latifah.

18. With thanks to Julia Lesage for proposing "unrepentant" to describe these mothers. The term's lingering tone of religiousness captures some of the sanctimoniousness often attached to motherhood, even in secular contexts.

19. Cobb quotes *New York Times* writer Kara Jesella here on how the new momism is a central feature of postfeminism.

20. See *The Unruly Woman*, especially its brief reading of *Stella Dallas* (110–115) and its more fully developed analysis of *Moonstruck* (191–212).

21. Patriarchy has generally viewed mother-daughter intimacy, like all forms of closeness between women, as more threatening than father-daughter intimacy, despite the incest taboo.

22. I used this quotation in *The Unruly Woman* (112) in a more general discussion of gender and genre.

23. In *Cinematernity*, Lucy Fischer identifies these polarities in Eadweard Muybridge's motion studies, which contrast images of a "Good Mother" with others of a "Bad Mother." For more work on motherhood in film studies, see E. Ann Kaplan. For more in the context of melodrama and the woman's film, see Linda Williams, Mary Ann Doane, Jackie Byars, Barbara Klinger, and others who work on melodrama in television and film.

24. Both draw on French feminists Luce Irigaray, Julia Kristeva, and Hélène Cixous, who brought continental philosophy to Anglo American feminism.

25. Bergman's revered *Persona* (1966) is a case in point. Drawing on the Elektra myth, it ties an actress's unrepentant refusal to speak with her lack of maternal feelings toward her son. Director Jane Campion recodes the gesture of silence in the strongwilled protagonist of *The Piano* (1993), who is also an artist and mother, but of a daughter.

26. Two of the most famous are by George Cukor (1933) and Gillian Armstrong (1994).

27. Roth's survey of genres includes the historical romance, independent film, romantic comedy, action film, thriller, and European art film. See also Susan Owen, et al., on the missing or incompetent mother in films and TV shows about young female computer wizards (2007, 63–89).

28. See Richard Dyer's *White*.

29. The significance of the Oedipus plot has been extensively analyzed in feminist theory and criticism influenced by psychoanalysis, including scholarship associated with *Camera Obscura*.

30. See also Cathy N. Davidson and E. M. Broner (1980).

31. One interesting exception is Voltaire's version of *Oedipus Rex*, which retells the tale as Jocasta's tragedy. Joanna Frueh in *Monster/Beauty* also speculates about Jocasta as an emblem of the taboo against sexual desire between an older woman and younger man.

32. Greek dramatist Euripides drew on the same mythologies as Aeschylus and Sophocles, but his plays (including *Electra*, *The Bacchae*, *Medea*, and *The Trojan Women*), which were noted for their realism, emphasized female perspectives, and orchestrations of drama and emotion that today are considered melodramatic. During his lifetime he was considered a lesser playwright than Aeschylus and Sophocles, but his works eventually surpassed theirs in popularity, if not influence.

33. These include the tragedies *Othello*, *The Tempest*, and *King Lear*, the problem plays *The Merchant of Venice* and *Measure for Measure*, as well as many of the comedies, including *Love's Labour's Lost*, *The Taming of the Shrew*, *As You Like It*, *Much Ado About Nothing*, and *Twelfth Night*.

34. Even in *The Winter's Tale*, whose character Hermione is Shakespeare's most sympathetic mother, the daughter is reborn into a comic/pastoral world without mothers.

35. I used this quotation in *The Unruly Woman* (112). Rich wrote *Of Woman Born* in 1976 and updated it in 1986, and references to it occur throughout Amber Kinser's anthology *Mothering in the Third Wave*, suggesting its continued influence. In the second edition, Rich added a thoughtful new introduction, extending her analysis beyond her original insistence on gender as the preeminent identity category for women.

36. See Ty Burr for a review of Generation X's taste for "makeovers" of canonical works of literature.

37. Michelle Citron's experimental film *Daughter Rite* (1979) stands as one of the most influential explorations of daughters struggling to understand their mothers' implication in patriarchy. Her *Mother Rite*, which tells the mother's side of the story, is less widely known.

38. Lorde wrote to Daly in 1979. Four months after receiving no reply, she shared her letter with a community of women, then published it in 1984.

39. Hirsch quoted the passage, which was originally published in *Signs*, in her 1989 book (19).

40. Tania Modleski made a similar claim, noting that women of color have led the way toward reconceptualizing identity in ways that are flexible enough to incorporate multiple allegiances (20). Feminist philosopher Sara Ruddick (1989, 1995) recalls the struggle early in the Second Wave to legitimize the use of "woman" as a means of demonstrating that the supposed gender-neutrality of the dominant discourse did not in fact exist.

41. Still, this definition is not tidy, bounded as it is by the limits of language (what, then, does "paternal" mean?). And it cannot entirely escape biology because maternal work begins, as Ruddick notes, with the labor of "some particular woman" in delivering her child.

42. With thanks to Carter Soles for fruitful conversations about slackers, geeks, and fanboys. For more on fanboys, see Rebecca Keegan Winters.

CHAPTER ONE

1. For more perspectives on the backlash against feminism, see Debra Baker Beck, Alyson Cole, and Ann Oakley and Juliet Mitchell. See also the introductions to books by Leslie Heywood and Jennifer Drake, and Nan Bauer Maglin and Donna Perry.

2. Sample titles include Elizabeth Fox-Genovese's *Feminism Is Not the Story of My Life* and Christina Hoff Sommers's *Who Stole Feminism? How Women Have Betrayed Women* and *The War Against Boys: How Misguided Feminism is Harming Our Young Men.*

3. Among the most critical voices on postfeminism have been those of women of color, such as bell hooks and Angela Davis. Kimberly Springer argues that postfeminism perpetuates liberal feminism's key weakness: calling for equality without including an analysis of race.

4. The conference "Interrogating Postfeminism: Gender and the Politics of Popular Culture," held in East Anglia (UK) in 2004, generated substantial transatlantic discussion and an anthology (Tasker and Negra 2007). See also Rosalind Gill and Elena Herdieckerhoff, and Joanne Hollows and Rachel Moseley. Of particular interest are Hollow and Moseley's global perspective and their discussion of the pressure to keep feminism "outside" the popular. See Diane Negra's excellent survey of contemporary popular culture in the context of postfeminism (2009); Sarah Projansky (2001, 2005, 2007); and Emma Bell on the politics of Girl Power in the UK. Sarah Gamble's *The Routledge Critical Dictionary of Feminism and Postfeminism* places postfeminism in a historical framework beginning in the eighteenth century.

5. For Third Wave accounts of generational tension in feminism, see Baumgartner and Richards, Astrid Henry, and Deborah Siegel.

6. See Henry's discussion of individualism in the Third Wave in *Not My Mother's Sister* (41, 106, 125). See also Susan Owen, who writes that girls, now free to imagine themselves as international spies and demon killers, have been "liberated from the burdens of the past, from their mother memory—they are free to disconnect" (2007, 231).

7. Gilligan's earlier work (1982) argued that girls develop a "different voice" from boys because of the disconnection they experience in early adolescence between reality as they experience it and reality as it is interpreted to them by those on whom they depend. See also Ann Oakley and Juliet Mitchell (1997), and Cressida J. Heyes (2000, especially 103–137). Gilligan's influence can be found in Mary Pipher's *Reviving Ophelia.*

8. See Michelle Sidler in Heywood and Drake.

9. Arguing that orthodox Second Wave feminism offered no place for "non-complicitous heterosexuality," Carol Siegel demonstrates how feminism became complicit in capitalism's repression of eros.

10. See Henry Jenkins. The inflammatory issue of child pornography, for example, is often used in campaigns to control the Internet by groups also targeting gay and lesbian rights.

11. See Chela Sandoval's influential report on the conference (Anzaldúa 1990). Since then, U.S. Third World feminism has evolved into an inclusive movement embracing scholarship on race, decolonization, cyberfeminism, and queer studies by such scholars as Chandra Talpade Mohanty, Cherríe Moraga, Trihn Min Ha, bell hooks,

and Lisa Lowe. Still, it has remained peripheral to what Sandoval calls "hegemonic feminism" (see Sandoval 2000, especially 186n9).

12. See Ednie Kaeh Garrison's excellent overview of the relation between Third Wave feminism and subcultural movements. Collections based partially or entirely on personal testimonies include Carlip; Taormino; and Rebecca Walker (1995). More theoretically oriented anthologies include Heywood and Drake, and Maglin and Perry.

13. In addition to Henry's scholarly history, see Deborah Siegel for an account of the Second and Third Wave organized in terms of mothers and daughters and designed for classroom use.

14. MTV, despite its history of excluding black artists and promoting misogynistic videos, provided young people with enlightened depictions of homosexuality and interracial relations long before adult-oriented network and cable programming did.

15. Other makers of "smart films" include Kevin Smith and Quentin Tarantino, who may affect "dumbness" but with canny self-awareness; and Ang Lee, Atom Egoyan, and Todd Haynes, whose "cold melodramas" feature stylized *mises en scène* and characters paralyzed with passivity. In *The Cinema of Sincerity*, her work in progress, Sarah Kozloff argues that the cynicism recently in fashion often covers up not only political apathy but racism and misogyny.

16. These films (*The Fellowship of the Ring* [2001], *The Two Towers* [2002], and *The Return of the King* [2003]), offer disturbing insights into contemporary fantasies about patriarchal authority, militarism, and race. Their nostalgia for strong fathers neatly parallels the anxieties around strong mothers I examine in this book.

17. The global popularity of *Titanic* suggests that its appeal extends far beyond those aspects of melodrama at the root of U.S. national identity.

18. The phrase is from Peter Brooks's influential *The Melodramatic Imagination* (1976). See John Mercer and Martin Shingler's review of the literature on melodrama.

19. DiCaprio himself distanced himself from pinup status in favor of cultivating his image as a serious actor, and saw his proximity to feminized iconography and female fans as "degrading" (Lahti and Nashi 1999, 71).

20. Curtis and Weaver's star texts carried "final girl" associations before their work with Cameron—Curtis in the *Halloween* films and Weaver in *Alien*.

21. Wood eventually became an artist. The description of her as a "titanic figure of the avant-garde" (in her *New York Times* obituary, January 3, 1999) has taken on some anachronistic irony after Cameron's film. She was also known as the "Mama of Dada," and her romantic involvements with Marcel Duchamp and Henri-Pierre Roche may have inspired Truffaut's famous New Wave film *Jules et Jim* (1962). She lived to 105 and attributed her longevity to "chocolate and young men."

22. Christine Geraghty finds feminist content in Rose's physicality as played by Winslet, with her "full bosom, strong body," and white skin that showed her strong emotions by flushing easily. She argues that Winslet's star text in this film uniquely

combines the formal British "lady" with the more vulgar American "dame."

23. See Lubin for echoes of other films in *Titanic*.

24. As Peter Lehman notes, Jack's character recalls a long tradition that romanticizes working-class men who rescue well-bred women from the sexual repression of their class.

25. The historical Brown, the daughter of Irish immigrants, was a well-known activist on behalf of women's and labor rights. After surviving the sinking of the Titanic, she became known as the Unsinkable Molly Brown, and her life inspired a stage musical (1960) and film (1964). Bates's star text brings its own unruliness to the character from her long career of playing strong women (*Misery* [1990], *Dolores Claiborne* [1995], *Fried Green Tomatoes* [1991], and the TV series *Six Feet Under* [2001–2005]).

CHAPTER TWO

1. *Armageddon* grossed $201 million in box office receipts, compared to *American Beauty*'s $130 million.

2. Incest, or at least sexual abuse, is an unspoken presence in the tragic and still-unsolved case of JonBenét Ramsey, the five-year-old beauty queen murdered in her home in 1996.

3. See the work of cognitive psychologist Jennifer Freyd on this subject (1996, and with Cindy B. Veldhuis, 1999). Freyd's work has made her the target of a well-orchestrated backlash against scholars and therapists investigating the incidence of childhood sexual abuse.

4. Other action films that build the father's heroism around the daughter's vulnerability include *Commando* (1985), *Predator* (1987), and *The Last Boy Scout* (1991).

5. One could argue, like Frank Tomasulo does, that masculinity has always been in crisis. What I refer to here is the period of crisis that followed the social liberation movements of the 1960s, especially the women's movement. See Linda Kintz, Mark Gallagher, and Andrew Hacker, the latter of whom provides statistical evidence for the trend of "men's liberation." The term refers "not to a sensitivity on the part of men to women's rights, but rather the freedom that enables husbands to leave their wives and children, with little or no social censure and seldom at drastic financial cost" (2003, 43).

6. My analysis here depends on a psychoanalytic reading of the white middle-class family, and one could argue the continued appeal of psychoanalysis in cultural analysis is tied to the academy's Eurocentrism. My argument's relevance for other racial and ethnic communities is necessarily more limited.

7. Teresa de Lauretis's "Desire in Narrative," a chapter from her book *Alice Doesn't*, is a feminist classic on woman's place in this narrative (1984).

8. In her analysis of D. W. Griffith's 1919 film *Broken Blossoms*, Julia Lesage demonstrates how incest connects the nymphet and the romantic hero. See also Joan Driscoll Lynch for an argument similar to my own (1987).

9. Marianne Sinclair's *Hollywood Lolitas* gives an interesting and well-illustrated account of the nymphet. In addition to the more familiar examples noted above, Sinclair includes the following who played nymphets for at least part of their careers: Mabel Norman, Mary Miles Minter, Judy Garland, Deanna Durbin, Elizabeth Taylor, Carroll Baker, Audrey Hepburn, Tuesday Weld, Hayley Mills, Carol Lynley, Linda Blair, Tatum O'Neal, Nastassja Kinski, Jodie Foster, and Brooke Shields. Benjamin Langton has wittily described precociously sexual girls as "prosti-tots."

10. Valerie Walkerdine, *Daddy's Girl: Young Girls and Popular Culture*, 140–141. Throughout the 1930s, Graham reviewed a number of Temple's films in the magazine *Night and Day*, which he edited. In his review of *Captain January* (1936), he attributed Temple's popularity to a "coquetry as mature as Claudette Colbert's and an oddly precocious body as voluptuous in gray flannels as Miss Dietrich's." In his review of *Wee Willie Winkie* (1937), he wrote of her "neat and well-developed rump" and her "dimpled depravity."

11. With thanks to Chuck Kleinhans for this information. According to Kleinhans, the "barely legal" theme was used in commercial pornography in the 1970s, banned in the 1980s and much of the 1990s, but reemerged in the late 1990s. These shifts have occurred because of changing definitions of what is legal and how those legal standards can be enforced. Current concerns center on virtual child pornography, or computer-generated images of children, which according to some reports, is one of the most popular types of site on the Internet.

12. Recent research consistently confirms Kinsey's 1953 figures suggesting that one in four women has experienced childhood sexual abuse. Conservative estimates today report that ten percent of women and five percent of men have experienced serious childhood sexual abuse. See Freyd (1996, 36–38), Judith Herman with Lisa Hirschman (1981), and Rivera (1999).

13. Foucault's *The History of Sexuality*, a historical analysis of the multiple ways sexual desire is incited and regulated in the social world, avoids the universalizing that often occurs around highly charged subjects such as incest.

14. See Vikki Bell's *Interrogating Incest: Feminism, Foucault, and the Law*.

15. See Judith Herman with Lisa Hirschman (1981) for a lucid summary of this history.

16. The 1983 McMartin case in California is perhaps the most notorious example. Initial charges of ritualized sexual abuse at the McMartin Preschool escalated in an atmosphere of hysteria and paranoia that eventually involved hundreds of children. None of the charges was ever substantiated despite a $15 million criminal trial. See Douglas J. Besharvo (1990).

17. Janet Walker and Diane Waldman (1990) give a detailed analysis of Freud's relevant writings on the subject, including *The Interpretation of Dreams*.

18. See also Lynn Sacco's 2001 dissertation, *Not Talking About "It": A History of Incest in the U.S., 1890–1940*, especially 300–341.

19. Psychiatric literature has long charged the mother in an incestuous family with forcing her daughter to take her place because of her own shortcomings as a wife. This literature has described mothers as "frigid, hostile, unloving women" and even "very unattractive" (Herman with Hirschman 1981, 43). According to Herman, the theme of maternal absence is emphasized almost to the exclusion of everything else (45). At the same time, much feminist work, both creative and critical, has struggled to come to terms with mothers who have been unable to protect, or acknowledge, victims of incest within their families. In addition to her influential film *Daughter Rite*, Michelle Citron has written about similar experiences in *Home Movies and Other Necessary Fictions*.

20. In African American families, the father's absence is a more acute problem for daughters, according to Jonetta Rose Barras (2000). See also Hortense Spillers's analysis of the African American family (1989).

21. The well-funded Repressed Memory Syndrome Foundation, founded in the early 1990s, uses social class to defend fathers against charges of incest. It poses a rhetorical question, "How do we know we are not representing pedophiles?" Then an answer: "We are a good-looking bunch of people: graying hair, well-dressed, healthy, smiling . . . someone you would likely find interesting and want to count as a friend" (quoted in Freyd 1996, 36–37). However, as Herman notes, "The concept of repression might more aptly be invoked to describe the social response to the reality of incest" (1981, 21).

22. Some of the most influential works by these writers include Laura Mulvey's "Visual Pleasure and Narrative Cinema"; works by Juliet Mitchell, Jacqueline Rose, Jane Gallop, and Kaja Silverman; and Constance Penley's anthology *Feminism and Film Theory*.

23. See Janet Walker and Diane Waldman (1990) and Walker (1999). Integrating testimony by incest survivors with recent work on trauma and memory, Walker argues that feminism must avoid simplistic "either/or" thinking about the relation between fantasy and real events and must continue to study the way the two are interrelated.

24. See Elizabeth A. Waites, Janice Haaken, Lenore Terr, and Susan L. Reviere.

25. Jennifer Freyd and Cindy Veldhuis in "Groomed for Silence, Groomed for Betrayal" argue that abusers prepare their victims for abuse by singling them out for their vulnerability and then cultivating intimacy with them. This process takes advantage of a child's dependency on parents and ignorance of sexual behavior. Their research also documents the social pressure for silence that occurs when speaking the truth would threaten the stability of the family. For this reason, the more extreme the abuse, the less likely an account of it will be believed.

26. This process, identified by Freyd, also describes the history of the False Memory Syndrome Foundation, which has mounted its counterattacks against charges of abuse by using stereotypes of women as gullible, unreliable, and easily manipulated.

27. Films such as *American Beauty*, while ultimately affirming patriarchal privilege, may still draw criticism from conservative religious groups because that affirmation is veiled by a more overt and sensationalized critique of the middle-class family.

28. Ellen Seiter also has discussed the ideology of childhood innocence in *Sold Separately: Children and Parents in Consumer Culture*.

29. See Walkerdine's analysis of the appeal of the "Little Orphan Annie" cartoon strip during the Depression and the incestuous aspects of the character's relation with Daddy Warbucks.

30. During the White House years, Chelsea Clinton was shielded from much public scrutiny and maintained an image that was chaste and innocent of sexuality. Unlike her mother, she appeared to embody a quiet femininity that did not threaten middle-class patriarchal values.

31. Reviews of the film tended to describe it as a "biting suburban satire" in the tradition of such "bourgeoisie-barbecuing movies" as *The Graduate* and *Election*. See Janet Maslin's "*American Beauty*: Dad's Dead and He's Still a Funny Guy." Few noted, as Andrew O'Hehir did, that the wife/mother character bore the brunt of the film's satire: she was an "embodiment of American materialism," and a misogynistic caricature that served "no good purpose."

32. Jane's voice is easily "read" at first as a voice-over because the relation between the image track and sound is not immediately clear. A female voice-over privileges female subjectivity, and it is rare in mainstream cinema.

33. Consider Roger Ebert's widely syndicated review, which explains that the film is "not about a Lolita relationship, anyway. It's about yearning after youth, respect, power, and, of course, beauty."

34. In addition to Christina Hoff Sommers's *The War Against Boys*, see *Real Boys: Rescuing Our Sons from the Myths of Boyhood* by William S. Pollack. The subtitle of Pollack's book echoes Mary Pipher's influential *Reviving Ophelia: Saving the Selves of Adolescent Girls*.

35. Richard Corliss provides interesting production information about the film, including the matter of censorship. By creating an older Lolita than Nabokov did in his novel, Kubrick evaded the issues of pedophilia the novel explores more directly.

36. Robin Morgan, a founding figure of the Second Wave, wrote "In Support of Hillary Rodham Clinton: Good-bye to All That, Part II," a richly detailed account of the sexism Clinton suffered during her campaign. The article, which circulated widely on the Internet, picks up themes from her famous 1970 essay.

37. *American Beauty*'s treatment of homosexuality is particularly interesting given screenwriter Alan Ball's role in creating HBO's *Six Feet Under*, which features compelling gay characters in major storylines, including a reprisal of the duo of the repressed homosexual male and his neurotic mother.

38. Steven Spielberg's *E.T. The Extra-Terrestrial* is one of the few mainstream films that explores the effects of a father's absence from the middle-class white family.

39. Mother-blaming in the United States reached its greatest intensity in the 1940s, with Philip Wylie's *Generation of Vipers* (1942), but remains alive today. See Molly Ladd-Taylor and Lauri Umansky, eds., *"Bad" Mothers: The Politics of Blame in Twentieth-Century America*, and Janet Liebman Jacobs, "Reassessing Mother Blame in Incest."

40. The autobiographical experimental film *Art for Teachers of Children* by Jennifer Montgomery (1995) takes a hard look at the painful aftermath of a teen girl's affair with an exploitative male teacher.

41. Angela anticipates Evie, the charismatic "bad girl" of *Thirteen* (chapter six), who is also sexually precocious and invades the good girl's family. Evie claims a history of abuse, although her credibility is suspect. See Joan Jacobs Brumberg's *The Body Project: An Intimate History of American Girls*.

42. *Our Monica, Ourselves*, a collection of academic writing on Monica Lewinsky, attempts to come to grips with her place in the culture, with a title that pays homage to the Second Wave feminist health classic *Our Bodies, Ourselves* (1976).

43. Of course, S&M sexual practices emphasize role-playing and choice. Carol Siegel's *New Millennial Sexstyles* describes the appeal of S&M among youth subcultures that view gender in more fluid terms than mainstream culture does.

44. See film and video works by Lydia Lunch, Michelle Citron, and Lynn Hirschman.

CHAPTER THREE

1. Other interesting films about the culture of teen girls (as opposed to "Girl Culture") include *Girls Town* (1996), *Foxfire* (1996), and *Girl, Interrupted* (1999).

2. Numerous film adaptations of Jane Austen's novels have been made since 1995: *Sense and Sensibility* (1995); *Emma* (1996); *Pride and Prejudice* (2005); and *Bride and Prejudice* (2004), a Bollywood version by Gurinder Chadha, who also directed the Girl Power film *Bend It Like Beckham* (2002). Television adaptations include the BBC 1995 miniseries *Pride and Prejudice* and A&E's *Emma* (1996).

3. Kim Akass and Janet McCabe's introduction to *Reading Sex and the City* (2004) describes the condescension of male critics, and some female ones as well, toward the series. See also Kathleen Sweeney's discussion of the impact of the series on teenage girls (2008, 31).

4. I discuss the professor hero and dumb blonde in *The Unruly Woman* (chapter five, "Professor Heroes and Brides on Top," and chapter six, "Dumb Blondes").

5. *Coming Soon* (Colette Burson, 1999) is unusual in its treatment of adolescent female sexuality because of its interest in girls' naïveté about their own sexual pleasure.

6. The witty animated TV series *Daria*, created by Glenn Eichler and Susie Lewis Lynn, features another smart girl and her best friend, an artist, who are outcasts at their high school. The series, a spin-off from *Beavis and Butthead*, ran on MTV from 1997 to 2002, and two movies were made based on the franchise: *Is It Fall Yet?* (2000) and *Is It College Yet?* (2002).

7. See Huttner, "Jan Chats with Aline Brosh McKenna" (2006).

8. See Akass and McCabe for excellent analyses of *Sex and the City*. See also Joanna Frueh, whose radical work connects female power with aestheticizing the body.

9. Much feminist work has been done on the ubiquity of eating disorders, especially among white girls. See Susie Orbach's classic *Fat Is a Feminist Issue*, as well as Jean Kilbourne's *Killing Us Softly* videos, which are popular in university classrooms for exploring the relation between advertising and body image problems among girls and women.

CHAPTER FOUR

1. Other examples include Jennifer Garner of TV's *Alias* (2001–2006) series, and Uma Thurman and Lucy Liu of *Kill Bill: Vol.* 1 (2003) and *Vol.* 2 (2004). See Marc O'Day, in Tasker (2004). See also L. S. Kim, on Asian cinema's stars such as Anita Miu, Maggie Cheung, Michelle Yeoh, and Zhang Ziyi, who combine action and femininity.

2. See Linda Mizejewski (2004) on the female detective.

3. See note seven in chapter one.

4. The genre of horror took on new life with a series of teen-oriented films that began with *Halloween* (1978), *Friday the 13th* (1980), and *Nightmare on Elm Street* (1984). Linda Williams (1991), Carol Clover (1992), and Barbara Creed (1993) established the genre's importance for feminist criticism, along with Rhona J. Berenstein and others. While much of this work has considered horror a primarily masculine discourse, Isabel Cristina Pinedo (1997) has studied its appeal to women.

5. Robin Wood (1979) is an important exception.

6. Drew Barrymore brings to this role her history of childhood exploitation and victimization.

7. The avenging mother as killer appears in other slasher films, including the original *Friday the 13th*. Tania Modleski's work on Hitchcock sheds light on the mother-as-murderer (2005, 108–109), and homages to Hitchcock are common in the slasher genre. For example, the early death of Drew Barrymore's character in *Scream* recalls the similar fate of the *Psycho* character played by Janet Leigh, another well-known blonde star, and Loomis, the boyfriend's name in *Psycho*, is also the name of the avenging psychiatrist in *Halloween*.

8. Metcalf gained national visibility in the 1980s and 1990s playing comedian Roseanne's sister on the sitcom *Roseanne*. Her role as Mrs. Loomis is an apt rejoinder to Roseanne's joke that anyone can tell women are second-class citizens because there are no legendary female serial killers.

9. "Roman" evokes director Roman Polanski, associated with horror in his work (*Rosemary's Baby* [1968]) and his private life (the violent murder of his wife Sharon Tate by the Charles Manson clan). Polanski fled the United States in 1977 after pleading guilty to charges of raping a thirteen-year-old girl. His case resurfaced in the fall of 2009 when police in Switzerland, where he resides, arrested him at the

request of U.S. authorities. He was placed in house arrest while awaiting the outcome of his appeal to resist extradition.

10. Almost since the invention of cinema, film theorists have speculated on how its moving images evoke life where there is none. In 1945, André Bazin linked film's power to the "mummy complex," or its seeming ability to defeat death by stopping time (Braudy and Cohen 1999).

11. John Milton was the author of the epic seventeenth-century poems *Paradise Lost* and *Paradise Regained*, an allusion that suggests Hollywood's place in today's culture as a purveyor of paradises and dreams. Milton was also a legendary antifeminist and oppressor of his own daughters, casting an even more ironic light on the Edenic ending of this film. (Thanks to James Earl for these observations.)

12. This theme pervades the *Friday the 13th* movies.

13. From a conversation with Kate Sullivan, whose work on horror includes her dissertation on suffering masculinity and an article on serial killer Ed Gein.

14. Basic information from Wikipedia.

15. Mythology-based shows such as *Xena: Warrior Princess, Twin Peaks, The X-Files*, and *Star Trek* have often attracted avid fans that participate in ancillary media, conventions, and Internet forums.

16. Most early scholarship on *Buffy*, including Rhonda Wilcox and David Lavery's (2002, 2005), did not originate in television studies and focused on asserting the validity of the series as art. By 2007, more scholarship (Elana Levine and Lisa Parks) engaged with the series *as* television.

17. As Carol Siegel argues (2007), *Buffy* carefully regulates its vision of acceptable sexuality and punishes relations, such as Buffy's with Spike, that venture outside its norms.

18. Michael Gershman shot all but two of the episodes between 1997–2001 and is credited with establishing the series's look.

19. See Elana Levine's "Buffy and the 'New Girl Order.'" In *X-Men: The Last Stand* (2006), Kitty Pryde was played by Ellen Page, whose career took a leap forward when she played the lead in *Juno* (2007).

20. Examples include Cynthia Fuchs (2007), who contrasts *Buffy* with *Dark Angel*, another TV series about a girl with superhuman powers; Vivian Chin, who questions the claim that "everyone can identify with Buffy" (2003, 96); and Jes Battis, who argues that the series's treatment of race and class reflects the desire of the show's writers (all white) to reach large audiences (2005, 73). See also Jason Middleton (2007, 162) on Buffy as Final Girl. Elyce Rae Helford (2002) argues that *Buffy* projects difference on monsters and other characters associated with excess and racial and class difference.

21. When Buffy has to support herself and her sister after her mother's death, the series avoids looking at the difficulties of single motherhood or of finding jobs that pay a living wage (Battis 2005). This failure was exacerbated when, as the series

wound down, its producers created a high-priced eBay auction "for the fans" to buy mementos (Stenger 2006). In doing so, they contradicted the show's espoused egalitarianism and exposed the consumerism implicit in Sarah Michelle Gellar's trendy wardrobe.

22. My comments here are restricted to the film. In the novels later in the series, Bella and Edward can finally have sex. Bella must become a vampire but her alternative is premature death, and she had already decided that she wanted to become a vampire anyway.

23. The title of the band's demo tape (1991). Teen video artist Sadie Benning ended her short Pixelvision film "It Wasn't Love" (1992) calling for "girl power everywhere."

CHAPTER FIVE

1. Julia Roberts had reigned as America's Sweetheart since her 1990 hit *Pretty Woman*. The designation of top-earning star changes from year to year and depends on what is included in the calculation. Other recent top-earners include Nicole Kidman, Cameron Diaz, Kiera Knightly, Angelina Jolie, and Jennifer Aniston.

2. Slackers have been an important demographic group since the 1990s. See Ron Rentel's *Karma Queens, Geek Gods, and Innerpreneurs*.

3. The list included Meryl Streep and Jodie Foster.

4. Romantic comedy has always worked from the premise that its apparently mismatched lovers are in fact perfect for each other because of their equality of spirit and wit. See Leger Grindon (2007) on the tension between ambivalence and grotesquerie in recent examples of the genre.

5. See Alex Williams (2007) on the situation she calls "dating down," wherein young professional women date men who make less money than they do.

6. In addition to Denby, see Sandra Kobrin (2007) for a discussion of *Knocked Up's* anti-choice rhetoric.

7. Space does not permit me to discuss all of Witherspoon's works, and I've omitted *Vanity Fair*, *Pleasantville*, and others that give additional layers of complexity to her star text.

8. Paul Scott, *Daily Mail* (2006). Much other factual information about Witherspoon's life is taken from Wikipedia. Other quotes are from a survey I conducted online in November 2007 of nearly one thousand English-language news articles.

9. "The Dork who Grew Into a Hollywood Princess," the London *Sunday Times*.

10. Witherspoon's decision to be known as Reese (her full name is Laura Jeanne Reese Witherspoon) showed "a certain mix of nerve," according to David Thompson (1999).

11. One exception: in 2006 she was included in a list of the "100 Sexiest Women in the World," by FHM (*For Him Magazine*).

12. These couples include Hilary Swank and Chad Lowe, Halle Berry and Eric Benet,

Helen Hunt and Hank Azaria, Emma Thompson and Kenneth Branagh, Nicole Kidman and Tom Cruise.

13. Jim Slotek in the *Toronto Sun* (1999) quotes Witherspoon's description of *American Psycho* as a "dark satire of a male response to the sexual liberation of women in the early 1980s." The film also shows that the racism, anti-Semitism, and misogyny exposed in the acclaimed TV series *Mad Men* persisted among the generation of privileged white men at the top of the New Economy of the 1990s.

14. See Kimberley Roberts (2002) for an excellent reading of the film in the context of Girl Culture.

15. The incident alludes to John Waters's *Female Trouble* (1974), in which the unruly transvestite Divine plays a character who remains unrepentant toward the legal system when she is imprisoned for an incident that involved acid-throwing.

16. Alexander Payne also directed *Citizen Ruth* (1996), as well as two later films about male midlife crises: *About Schmidt* (2002) and *Sideways* (2004).

17. With thanks to Carol Siegel for these references.

18. This film exemplifies the trope of "retreatism" that Diane Negra finds in numerous examples of popular culture (2004).

CHAPTER SIX

1. I wrote about this film in Celestino Deleyto and Peter Williams Evans's *Terms of Endearment: Hollywood Romantic Comedy of the 1980s and 1990s* (1998).

2. First aired on ABC in 1994–1995, then rebroadcast on MTV, *My So-Called Life* attracted renewed attention in 2007 with the release of a DVD set, produced in part because of fan pressure (Bellafante 2007). At the same time, the show's producers Marshall Herskovitz and Ed Zwick, also known for ABC's yuppie melodrama *thirtysomething* (1987–1991), introduced *Quarterlife*, an innovative webcast program that NBC picked up but canceled after one episode (2008).

3. Danes was also reluctant to continue for a second season because she wanted to shift her focus to film, a fact that the series's fans disputed at the time. In 1996, after making *Romeo + Juliet* with Leonardo DiCaprio, she was offered the chance to play opposite DiCaprio again, as Rose in *Titanic*, but turned it down.

4. From DVD commentary by Herskovitz, Zwick, and Winnie Holzman.

5. According to the show's producers, Angela is the descendent of Buddy, a character played by Kristy McNichol in the drama *Family* (1976–1980), which they also produced.

6. Alicia Silverstone auditioned for the part but was rejected because of her polish and self-possession (DVD commentary). Typically, teen characters are played by actors at least eighteen years old and often in their twenties because labor laws restrict working hours for child actors.

7. With the arrival of the money soaps (*Beverly Hills, 90210* and later *Freaks and Geeks*), these boundaries begin to disappear. Finally, in *Gilmore Girls* (2000–2007), mother

and daughter share the same taste in music, books, and films. *Gilmore Girls* has attracted critical acclaim for its fast-paced and witty dialogue. Originally broadcast on the WB, it runs in syndication on ABC's Family Channel.

8. *Thirteen* won or was nominated for awards for its screenplay and performances by Evan Rachel Wood and Nikki Reed. Stephanie Zacharek (2003) criticized the film as a "cinematic *Reviving Ophelia*." Feminist film scholars have diverged widely on the film (see Carol Siegel [2006] and Angela McRobbie [2003]).

9. Some examples of the ways ideology influences the flow of and access to legal drugs include international responses to the AIDS catastrophe in Africa, the fight over the "morning after" birth-control pill in the United States, deals engineered by pharmaceutical giants to keep generic drugs off the market, and the American health-care crisis, especially for uninsured working and poor people.

10. Cazdyn cites such Japanese films such as *Kyua* (Kioshi Kurosawa, 1997), but others come to mind as well, including the Korean *Oldboy* (Chan-wook Park, 2003), and in the United States, *Fight Club* (David Fincher, 1999), *Memento* (Chris Nolan, 2000), and *Eternal Sunshine of the Spotless Mind* (Michel Gondry, 2004), all of which have enjoyed considerable popularity among young people.

11. Latin American scholar Walter Mignolo presented his research on decolonization in a faculty seminar at the University of Oregon in 2006.

12. Through a provocative contrast with Catherine Breillat's *A ma soeur!* (2001), Siegel argues that *Thirteen* exemplifies a conservative feminism based on the mother-daughter bond. Her reading places these films in the different traditions of American and French feminism. Whereas she sees the film as naturalizing consumerism, domesticity, and body issues that continue to afflict girls and women, I see it as criticizing them.

CHAPTER SEVEN

1. Like gender, race has become "posted," and so, along with postfeminism, cultural critics have identified and debated the concept of a postracial society. See Anoop Nayak, as well as Herman Gray and Bambi Haggins.

2. *Different Wavelengths* (Jo Reger, ed.) and *Colonize This! Young Women of Color on Today's Feminism* (Daisy Hernandez and Bushra Rehman, eds.) include wide-ranging essays on racial and class difference in the contemporary women's movement.

3. Many young women of color have experienced a feminism that clashes with their cultural values. Cecilia Balli struggled to reconcile the orthodox feminist position on abortion with her own culturally instilled belief that "no baby should be killed" (2002, 196).

4. As Cecilia Balli argues, American feminism teaches women that they should not sacrifice themselves for others. "Yet many women of color have reminded us that sacrifice and motherhood go hand in hand . . . Does it follow that mothers cannot be feminists? . . . From the moment a woman conceives her child, she offers up part of her body for something bigger" (2002, 196).

5. *Save the Last Dance* (2001) is an important exception. Interracial romances featuring unruly women of color such as Whoopi Goldberg or Queen Latifah are often played for farce. See Linda Mizejewski (2007), and Priscilla Ovalle (2011) on Latina stars in interracial romances.

6. In a short feature accompanying the DVD, Maxine Waters, Geraldine Ferraro, and Donna Lopiano discuss the importance of Title IX, passed in 1972.

7. See Joanne Hollows, "Can I Go Home Yet? Feminism, Post-Feminism, and Domesticity," in *Feminism in Popular Culture* (2006).

8. The DVD commentary by Prince-Bythewood and Sanaa Lathan concludes with both reflecting on their desires to be mothers. Prince-Bythewood, who had earlier wanted sons, now wanted a daughter.

9. It is possible, according to the DVD commentary by Cardoso and Lopez, that the character really was ignorant about menopause.

10. Cardoso and Lopez describe Carmen's withholding of praise for Ana throughout the film as consistent with their culture: "All of us want our parents to say 'We're so proud of you,' but for a lot of us, they're unable to say that. Humility is something very important to us."

11. *Real Women Have Curves* had a $3 million budget, and earned just under $6 million in U.S. box office. *The Sisterhood of the Traveling Pants* had a $25 million budget and $40 million U.S. box office. In 2008, a sequel, *The Sisterhood of the Traveling Pants 2*, was released.

12. From the Wikipedia entry on *Ugly Betty*.

13. In *West Side Story* (1961), the song is sung in counterpoint to "Tonight" over intercut scenes of the film's characters preparing for the evening.

14. The episode even borrows a song, KT Tunstall's "Suddenly I See," from the opening sequence of *The Devil Wears Prada*.

15. Susan Sontag's classic essay emphasizes camp's links with male homosexual subcultures. More recently, queer theorists such as Alexander Doty have added yet another dimension of analysis to camp.

16. Actor and cartoonist Lela Lee created the character "Angry Little Asian Girl" for her comics, animated films, and website, "Angry Little Girls." She intended the website for girls who are "disenchanted, crazy, fresh, gloomy, and all-around angry."

17. The game is based on *Charlie's Angels*, the popular 1976–1981 TV show that featured three beautiful female investigators who regularly found themselves in dangerous predicaments. It has been made into two films (2000, 2003).

18. The series makes frequent references to popular culture—here, to *Educating Rita* (1983).

19. Throughout his career, Wang has produced work about women and their relationships across the boundaries of generation, class, and ethnicity. *Dim Sum: A Little Bit of Heart* (1985) is a poignant exploration of the ties between a sixty-two-year-old Chinese widow, her thirty-something daughter, and her brother-in-law. *The Joy Luck Club*, based on four pairs of daughters and mothers, uses the familiar formula

for a commercially successful film about women: multiple plot lines and roles for strong female actors. Wang's later work (including *Anywhere But Here* [1999] and *Maid in Manhattan* [2002]) explores similar material.

20. See Richard Von Busack's interview with Wu. Martin Tsai criticizes Wu for falling into the same trap as Ang Lee by pandering to heterosexual and non-Asian audiences and using ethnic stereotypes.

21. See, for example, Huttner, "Jan Chats with Alice Wu and Joan Chen about Their New Film *Saving Face*" (2005).

22. As these unruly women come out with their own desire, their allegiance to Chinese tradition gives way to more Western ideologies of sexuality. Thanks to my student Yin-Chin Chen for her insights into this film.

CHAPTER EIGHT

1. In Kathleen Woodward's *Figuring Age*, Mary Russo, E. Ann Kaplan, and Patricia Mellencamp make extended references to *Antonia's Line*.

2. Other films outside the U.S. mainstream also offer compelling depictions of matriarchal communities. For example, Julie Dash's *Daughters of the Dust* (1991) is a sweeping exploration of change within an African American family living in isolation off the coast of South Carolina. Spanish director Pedro Almodóvar's long-standing interest in strong and interesting women reached new heights with *All About My Mother* (1999) and especially *Volver* (2006), which, like *Antonia's Line*, made inspired use of magical realism and the grotesque.

3. My source is Gullette's "Wicked Powerful," from which I borrow the title of this chapter.

4. As Woodward notes, "Ageism is entrenched in feminism itself" (1999, xi).

5. *Juno*'s authorship has been attributed as much to screenwriter Diablo Cody and actor Ellen Page as to its director Jason Reitman.

6. For a sample of reviews, see Susanna Tully.

7. In contrast, *Baby Mama* (2008) directly confronts these anxieties by having a single career woman (Tina Fey) hire another (Amy Poehler) as a surrogate mother. The film also highlights the class issues surrounding access to reproductive technology.

8. Not surprisingly, these films have attracted harsh criticism for evading realities about not only motherhood but also the fragility of reproductive rights during the Bush years. See Ellen Goodman, who notes that teen pregnancies have risen for the first time since 1991 after one billion dollars of federal money was spent on abstinence-only sex education.

9. The term "motherline" is not common in feminist scholarship, although Andrea O'Reilly and Sharon Abbey use it in their anthology on mothers and daughters, and it is central to O'Reilly's 2004 study of Toni Morrison. It is also common in New Age writings about the Goddess and female empowerment.

10. For critiques of western philosophy, see Jane Gallop (1988), Jane Flax (1990), and Elizabeth Grosz, especially chapter five, "Space, Time, and Bodies," in her 2005 book *Space, Time, and Perversion*. From associating the feminine with the body, it is a small step to upholding the mind and creation by abjecting the less esteemed categories of motherhood and procreation.

11. Frueh's work ranges widely and provocatively on subjects from erotic attachments between female professors and students to vampires. See in particular her chapter "The Passionate Wife, the Passionate Daughter."

12. In using "matriarchy" to describe *Antonia's Line*, I am not concerned with a romanticized matriarchy of the past or future, but about the suggestive aspects of the concept. Indeed, elements of matriarchy do exist in the United States today as residual traces of cultures brutalized by our history. Slavery weakened the connections between African American fathers and their children, resulting in a form of matriarchy named and stigmatized in Patrick Moynihan's influential 1960s analysis of the black American family. See Hortense Spillers and Jonetta Rose Barras on the impact of this history on the African American family. Traditions of matriarchy also existed among some Native American tribes.

13. So is love, as hooks argues in *Communion: The Female Search for Love* (2002) where she challenges feminism to address the ways patriarchy has warped women's needs to give and receive love. *Communion* is the third book in hooks's *Love Trilogy*, which also includes *All About Love: New Visions* (1999) and *Salvation: Black People and Love* (2001).

14. In a conversation on July 20, 2008, Bill Cadbury argued that the film would be more successful if it allowed Antonia to kill Pitte herself. By calling in the men to finish the task, it sentimentalizes women as somehow above such dirty work and diminishes some of Antonia's power.

15. See Sadie Wearing's excellent analysis of age and gender in postfeminist culture, including efforts to "girl" the aging woman (2007).

16. Quoted in Gullette (2004, 57).

17. Carol Gilligan has written extensively on this topic, as I note in chapter three.

18. This structure resonates with the "emotional attunement and mutual recognition" many of the contributors to Woodward's collection remember about their relations with their mothers and grandmothers (149). Their experiences contrast with the "envy, fear, hostility, guilt, and jealousy" in psychoanalytic accounts of father-son relations.

19. Ruddick cites the mothers and grandmothers of Argentina who drew on their claims as mothers to become human rights activists during the "Dirty War" (82).

20. Chakraborty, quoting Naomi Schor's introduction to *The Essential Difference* (1994, vii).

21. Chela Sandoval's concept of differential feminism (2000) and Yi-Lin Yu's intersubjective feminism similarly theorize difference as a source of power.

22. These comments are taken from Mohanty's talk at the University of Oregon on April 4, 2005.

23. Denise deCaires Narain (2004, 240) quotes Alka Kurian (from Gamble 1999, 66–79) in describing how the now-accepted division of feminism's history into waves marginalizes the struggles of nonwestern feminists.

24. Gullette argues that learning to see the mother-as-person is "generalizable" to other human relations (2005, 130).

AFTERWORD

1. With thanks to Carol Siegel for affirming the liberating aspects of youth cultures without compromising her critical perspective.

Works Cited

Aikau, Hokulani K., Karla A. Erickson, and Jennifer L. Pierce. 2007. *Feminist Waves, Feminist Generations: Life Stories from the Academy*. Minneapolis: University of Minnesota Press.

Akass, Kim, and Janet McCabe, eds. 2004. *Reading Sex and the City*. London: I.B. Tauris.

Alexander, M. Jacqui, and Chandra Talpade Mohanty, eds. 1995. *Feminist Genealogies, Colonial Legacies, Democratic Futures*. New York: Routledge.

Anders, Allison. 2003. "A Film Maven at the Margins." *Variety* 2: 100.

Anzaldúa, Gloria, ed. 1990. *Making Face, Making Soul: Creative and Critical Perspectives by Feminists of Color*. San Francisco: Aunt Lute Foundation Books.

Austin, Paula. 2002. "Femme-Inism: Lessons of My Mother." In *Colonize This! Young Women of Color on Today's Feminism*. Eds. Daisy Hernandez and Bushra Rehman. New York: Seal Press.

Balli, Cecilia. 2002. "Thirty-Eight." In *Colonize This! Young Women of Color on Today's Feminism*. Eds. Daisy Hernandez and Bushra Rehman. New York: Seal Press.

Banet-Weiser, Sarah. 2007. "What's Your Flava? Race and Postfeminism in Media Culture." In *Interrogating Postfeminism: Gender and the Politics of Popular Culture*, eds. Yvonne Tasker and Diane Negra, 201–26. Durham: Duke University Press.

Barras, Jonetta Rose. 2000. *Whatever Happened to Daddy's Little Girl? The Impact of Fatherlessness on Black Women*. New York: Ballantine Pub. Group.

Battis, Jes. 2005. *Blood Relations: Chosen Families in "Buffy the Vampire Slayer" and "Angel."* Jefferson: McFarland.

Baumgardner, Amy, and Jennifer Richards, eds. 2000. *Manifesta: Young Women, Feminism, and the Future.* New York: Farrar, Straus, and Giroux.

Bazin, André. 1999. "What is Cinema?" In *Film Theory and Criticism*, eds. Leo Braudy and Marshall Cohen, 195–199. New York: Oxford University Press. (Orig. pub. 1945)

Beck, Debra Baker. 1998. "The 'F' Word: How the Media Stole Feminism." *National Women's Studies Association Journal* 10, no. 1: 139–149.

Bell, Emma. 2008. "From Bad Girl to Mad Girl." *Genders OnLine Journal* 48.

Bell, Vikki. 1993. *Interrogating Incest: Feminism, Foucault, and the Law.* New York: Routledge.

Bellafante, Ginia. 2007. "A Teenager in Love (So-Called)." *New York Times*, Oct. 28, 2007.

Berenstein, Rhona. 1995. *Attack of the Leading Ladies.* New York: Columbia University Press.

Bergstrom, Janet. 1999. *Endless Night: Cinema and Psychoanalysis, Parallel Histories.* Berkeley: University of California Press.

Berlant, Lauren Gail, and Lisa Duggan, eds. 2001. *Our Monica, Ourselves: The Clinton Affair and the National Interest.* New York: New York University Press.

Besharvo, Douglas J. 1990. "Lessons from the McMartin Case." *Christian Science Monitor*, February 9, 1990.

Bhavani, Kum-Kum, Kathryn R. Kent, and France Winddance Twine, eds. 1998. "Special Issue on Feminisms and Youth Cultures." *Signs* 23, no. 3.

Boose, Lynda E., and Betty S. Flowers. 1989. *Daughters and Fathers.* Baltimore: Johns Hopkins University Press.

Boston Women's Health Collective. 1976. *Our Bodies, Ourselves: A Book by and for Women.* 2nd ed. New York: Simon & Schuster.

Bovkis, Elen A. 1997. "The Magical World of the Ultimate Matriarch." *CineAction* 43: 50–57.

Bowers, Andy. "Hillary's Inner Tracy Flick." *Slate V*, 2008.

Braun, Beth. 2000. "*The X-Files* and *Buffy the Vampire Slayer*: The Ambiguity of Evil in Supernatural Representations." *Journal of Popular Film and Television* 28, no. 2: 88–94.

Brooks, Peter. 1976. *The Melodramatic Imagination: Balzac, Henry James, Melodrama, and the Mode of Excess.* New Haven: Yale University Press.

Brooks, Siobhan. 2002. "Black Feminism in Everyday Life: Race, Mental Illness, Poverty, and Motherhood." In *Colonize This! Young Women of Color on Today's Feminism*, eds. Daisy Hernandez and Bushra Rehman, 99–118. New York: Seal Press.

Browne, Nick, ed. 1998. *Refiguring American Film Genres: History and Theory.* Berkeley and Los Angeles: University of California Press.

Brumberg, Joan Jacobs. 1997. *The Body Project: An Intimate History of American Girls.* New York: Random House.

Burr, Ty. 1998. "Let There Be Lite." *Entertainment Weekly*. July 24. http://www.mentaurs.com/cachestream?url=http://www.cnn.com/ew/article/0,284094,00.html&word=.

Busack, Richard Von. 2005. "Face Time." *Metroactive*. May 25–31.

Butler, Judith. 2000. *Antigone's Claim: Kinship Between Life and Death*. New York: Columbia University Press.

Byars, Jackie. 1991. *All That Hollywood Allows: Re-Reading Gender in 1950s Melodrama*. Chapel Hill: University of North Carolina Press.

Byers, Michele. 1998. "Gender/Sexuality/Desire: Subversion of Difference and Construction of Loss in the Adolescent Drama of *My So-Called Life*." *Signs* 23, no. 3: 711–734.

Carlip, Hillary. 1995. *Girl Power*. New York: Warner Books.

Cazdyn, Eric. 2006. "Candor the World Over: Bioeconomics and Culture Today." Lecture presented at the University of Oregon, May 25.

Chakraborty, Mridula Nath. 2004. "Wa(i)ving It All Away: Producing Subject and Knowledge in Feminisms of Colour." In *Third Wave Feminism: A Critical Exploration*, eds. Stacy Gillis, Gillian Munford, and Rebecca Howie, 205–215. New York: Palgrave Macmillan.

Chin, Vivian. 2003. "Buffy? She's Like Me, She's Not Like Me—She's Rad." *Athena's Daughters: Television's New Women Warriors*, ed. Frances H. Early and Kathleen Kennedy, 92–104. Syracuse: Syracuse University Press.

Chodorow, Nancy. 1978. *The Reproduction of Mothering: Psychoanalysis and the Sociology of Gender*. 2nd ed. Berkeley: University of California Press.

Citron, Michelle. 1999. *Home Movies and Other Necessary Fictions*. Minneapolis: University of Minnesota Press.

Cixous, Hélène. 1976. "The Laugh of the Medusa." *Signs* 1, no. 4: 875–893.

Clover, Carol J. 1992. *Men, Women, and Chainsaws: Gender in the Modern Horror Film*. Princeton: Princeton University Press.

Cobb, Shelley. 2008. "Mother of the Year: Kathy Hilton, Lynne Spears, Dina Lohan, and Bad Celebrity Motherhood." *Genders OnLine Journal* 48.

Cole, Alyson. 1998. "There Are No Victims in This Class." *National Women's Studies Association Journal* 10, no. 1: 72–85.

Connolly, Ceci. 2006. "More Teenage Girls Smoking, Drinking, Abusing Drugs." *Washington Post*, February 9.

Corliss, Richard. 1994. *Lolita*. London: British Film Institute.

Creed, Barbara. 1993. *The Monstrous-Feminine: Film, Feminism, Psychoanalysis*. New York: Routledge.

Creekmur, Corey K., and Alexander Doty, eds. 1995. *Out in Culture: Gay, Lesbian, and Queer Essays on Popular Culture*. Durham: Duke University Press.

Dassanowsky, Robert von. 2001. "A Mountain of a Ship: Locating the Bergfilm in James Cameron's *Titanic*." *Cinema Journal* 40, no. 4: 18–35.

Dave, Paul. 2006. *Visions of England: Class and Culture in Contemporary Cinema*. London: Berg.

Davidson, Cathy N., and E. M. Broner, eds. 1980. *The Lost Tradition: Mothers and Daughters in Literature*. New York: F. Ungar Pub. Co.

De Lauretis, Teresa. 1984. *Alice Doesn't: Feminism, Semiotics, Cinema.* Bloomington: Indiana University Press.

——, ed. *Feminist Studies, Critical Studies.* 1986. Bloomington: Indiana University Press.

Denby, David. 2007. "A Fine Romance: A New Comedy of the Sexes." *The New Yorker,* July 23.

Dicker, Rory Cooke, and Alison Piepmeier, eds. 2003. *Catching a Wave: Reclaiming Feminism for the 21st Century.* Boston: Northeastern University Press.

Di Mattia, Joanna. 2004. "'What's the Harm in Believing?' Mr. Big, Mr. Perfect, and the Romantic Quest for *Sex and the City*'s Mr. Right." In *Reading Sex and the City*, eds. Kim Akass and Janet McCabe, 17–32. New York: I.B. Tauris.

Doane, Mary Ann. 1987. *The Desire to Desire: The Woman's Film of the 1940s.* Bloomington: Indiana University Press.

Doherty, Thomas. 1995. "Clueless Kids." *Cineaste* 4: 14–16.

Doty, Alexander. 1993. *Making Things Perfectly Queer: Interpreting Mass Culture.* Minneapolis: University of Minnesota Press.

Douglas, Susan J., and Meredith W. Michaels. 2004. *The Mommy Myth: The Idealization of Motherhood and How It Has Undermined Women.* New York: Free Press.

Driver, Susan. 2007. "Girls Looking at Girls Looking for Girls: The Visual Pleasures and Social Empowerment of Queer Teen Romance Flicks." In *Youth Culture in Global Cinema*, eds. Timothy Shary and Alexandra Seibel, 241–255. Austin: University of Texas Press.

Dyer, Richard. 1997. *White: Essays on Race and Culture.* London: Routledge.

——. 1999. "Entertainment and Utopia." In *The Cultural Studies Reader*, ed. Simon During, 371–381. 2nd ed. London: Routledge. Originally published in *Movie* 24 (Spring 1977).

Ebert, Roger. 1999. "Review of *American Beauty*." *Chicago Sun-Times*, September 9.

Faludi, Susan. 1991. *Backlash: The Undeclared War Against American Women.* New York: Crown.

Findlen, Barbara, ed. 1995. *Listen Up: Voices from the Next Feminist Generation.* Seattle: Seal Press.

Fischer, Lucy. 1996. *Cinematernity: Film, Motherhood, Genre.* Princeton: Princeton University Press.

Flax, Jane. 1990. *Thinking Fragments: Psychoanalysis, Feminism, and Postmodernism in the Contemporary West.* Berkeley: University of California Press.

Foucault, Michel. 1978. *The History of Sexuality.* Trans. Robert Hurley. New York: Pantheon Books.

Fox-Genovese, Elizabeth. 1996. *Feminism Is Not the Story of My Life: How Today's Feminist Elite Has Lost Touch with the Real Concerns of Women.* New York: Nan A. Talese.

Freud, Sigmund. 1999. *The Interpretation of Dreams.* New York: Oxford University Press. (Orig. pub. 1913.)

Freud, Sigmund, and Wilhelm Fliess. 1954. *The Origins of Psycho-Analysis: Letters to Wilhelm Fliess, Drafts, and Notes, 1887–1902.* New York: Basic Books.

Freyd, Jennifer J. 1996. *Betrayal Trauma: The Logic of Forgetting Childhood Abuse.* Cambridge: Harvard University Press.

Freyd, Jennifer J., and Cindy B. Veldhuis. 1999. "Groomed for Silence, Groomed for Betrayal." In *Fragment by Fragment: Feminist Perspectives on Memory and Child Sexual Abuse,* ed. Margo Rivera, 253–282. Charlottetown, P.E.I.: Gynergy Books.

Frueh, Joanna. 2001. *Monster/Beauty: Building the Body of Love.* Berkeley: University of California Press.

Frye, Northrop. 1949. "The Argument of Comedy." In *English Institute Essays, 1948,* 58–74. New York: Columbia University Press.

———. 1957. *Anatomy of Criticism: Four Essays.* Princeton: Princeton University Press.

Fuchs, Cynthia. 2007. "'Did Anyone Ever Explain to You What "Secret Identity" Means?': Race and Displacement in *Buffy* and *Dark Angel.*" In *Undead TV: Essays on "Buffy the Vampire Slayer,"* eds. Elana Levine and Lisa Parks, 96–116. Durham: Duke University Press.

Gallagher, Mark. 2006. *Action Figures: Men, Action Films, and Contemporary Adventure Narratives.* New York: Palgrave Macmillan.

Gallop, Jane. 1982. *The Daughter's Seduction: Feminism and Psychoanalysis.* Ithaca: Cornell University Press.

———. 1988. *Thinking Through the Body.* New York: Columbia University Press.

———. 1989. "The Father's Seduction." In *Daughters and Fathers,* eds. Lynda E. Boose and Betty S. Flowers, 97–110. Baltimore: Johns Hopkins University Press.

Gamble, Sarah. 1999. *The Icon Critical Dictionary of Feminism and Postfeminism.* Cambridge: Icon.

———. 2000. *The Routledge Critical Dictionary of Feminism and Postfeminism.* New York: Routledge.

———. 2001. *The Routledge Companion to Feminism and Postfeminism.* New York: Routledge.

Garrison, Ednie Kaeh. 2000. "U.S. Feminism-Grrrl Style! Youth (Sub)Cultures and the Technologies of the Third Wave." *Feminist Studies* 26, no. 1: 141–170.

Gateward, Frances K., and Murray Pomerance, eds. 2002. *Sugar, Spice, and Everything Nice: Cinemas of Girlhood.* Detroit: Wayne State University Press.

Geraghty, Christine. 2002. "Crossing Over: Performing as a Lady and a Dame." *Screen* 43, no. 1: 41–56.

Geraghty, Lincoln. 2006. "Love's Fantastic Voyage: Crossing between Science Fiction and Romantic Comedy in Innerspace." *Extrapolation: A Journal of Science Fiction and Fantasy* 47, no. 1: 123–133.

Gibson, Pamela Church. 2004. *More Dirty Looks: Gender, Pornography, and Power.* 2nd ed. London: British Film Institute.

Gill, Rosalind, and Elena Herdieckerhoff. 2006. "Rewriting the Romance: New Femininities in Chick Lit?" *Feminist Media Studies* 6, no. 4: 487–504.

Gilligan, Carol. 1982. *In a Different Voice: Psychological Theory and Women's Development.* Cambridge: Harvard University Press.

———. 1997. "Getting Civilized." In *Who's Afraid of Feminism? Seeing through the Backlash*, eds. Ann Mitchell and Juliet Oakley, 13–28. New York: New Press.

Gillis, Stacy, Gillian Howie, and Rebecca Munford, eds. 2004. *Third Wave Feminism: A Critical Exploration*. New York: Palgrave Macmillan.

Gilroy, Paul. 2000. *Against Race: Imagining Political Culture Beyond the Color Line*. Cambridge: Belknap Press of Harvard University Press.

———. 2005. *Postcolonial Melancholia*. New York: Columbia University Press.

Gledhill, Christine, ed. 1987. *Home Is Where the Heart Is: Studies in Melodrama and the Woman's Film*. London: British Film Institute.

Goodman, Ellen. 2008. "Movies Put Spin on Abortion Debate." *Register Guard*, January 4.

Gray, Herman. 2004. *Watching Race: Television and the Struggle for Blackness*. Minneapolis: University of Minnesota Press.

Greene, Adam Isaiah. 2002. "Gay but Not Queer: Toward a Post-Queer Study of Sexuality." *Theory and Society* 31, no. 4: 521–545.

Grindon, Leger. 2007. "From the Grotesque to the Ambivalent: Recent Developments in the Hollywood Romantic Comedy, 1997–2007." Paper presented at the annual meeting of the Society for Cinema Studies, Vancouver, BC.

Grosz, Elizabeth. 1995. *Space, Time, and Perversion*. New York: Routledge.

Gullette, Margaret Morganroth. 2004. *Aged by Culture*. Chicago: University of Chicago Press.

———. 2005. "Wicked Powerful: The Postmaternal in Contemporary Film and Psychoanalytic Theory." *Gender and Psychoanalysis* 5: 107–139.

Haaken, Janice. 1998. *Pillar of Salt: Gender, Memory, and the Perils of Looking Back*. New Brunswick: Rutgers University Press.

Hacker, Andrew. 2003. *Mismatch: The Growing Gulf between Women and Men*. New York: Scribner.

Haggins, Bambi. 2007. *Laughing Mad: The Black Comic Persona in Post-Soul America*. New Brunswick: Rutgers University Press.

Hallstein, D. Lynn O'Brien. 2008. "Second Wave Silences and Third Wave Intensive Mothering." In *Mothering in the Third Wave*, ed. Amber E. Kinser, 107–118. Toronto: Demeter Press.

Hanigsberg, Julia E., and Sara Ruddick, eds. 1999. *Mother Troubles: Rethinking Contemporary Maternal Dilemmas*. Boston: Beacon Press.

Hartsoe, Steve. 2006. "Americans' Circle of Friends Narrows to Two." *Register-Guard*. June 24.

Hatch, Kristen. 2002. "Fille Fatale: Regulating Images of Adolescent Girls, 1962–1996." In *Sugar, Spice and Everything Nice: Cinemas of Girlhood*, eds. Frances K. Gateward and Murray Pomerance, 163–181. Detroit: Wayne State University Press.

Helford, Elyce Rae. 2002. "My Emotions Give Me Power: The Containment of Girls' Anger in *Buffy*." In *Fighting the Forces: What's at Stake in "Buffy the Vampire Slayer*," eds. Rhonda Wilcox and David Lavery, 18–34. Lanham, MD: Rowman & Littlefield.

Hendershot, Heather. 2006. "The Good, the Bad, and the Ugly: From *Buffy the Vampire Slayer* to *Dr. 90210*." *Camera Obscura* 21, no. 61: 47–51.

Henry, Astrid. 2004. *Not My Mother's Sister: Generational Conflict and Third-Wave Feminism.* Bloomington: Indiana University Press.

Herman, Judith Lewis, and Lisa Hirschman. 1981. *Father-Daughter Incest.* Cambridge: Harvard University Press.

Herman, Nini. 1999. *Too Long a Child: The Mother-Daughter Dyad.* London: Whurr Publishers.

Hernandez, Daisy, and Bushra Rehman, eds. 2002. *Colonize This! Young Women of Color on Today's Feminism.* New York: Seal Press.

Hewett, Heather. 2009. "Of Motherhood Born." In *Mothering in the Third Wave,* ed. Amber E. Kinser. Toronto: Demeter Press.

Heyes, Cressida J. 2000. *Line Drawings: Defining Women through Feminist Practice.* Ithaca: Cornell University Press.

Heywood, Leslie, and Jennifer Drake, eds. 1997. *Third Wave Agenda: Being Feminist, Doing Feminism.* Minneapolis: University of Minnesota Press.

Hirsch, Marianne. 1981. "Mothers and Daughters: A Review Essay." *Signs* 7, no. 1: 200–222.

———. 1989. *The Mother/Daughter Plot: Narrative, Psychoanalysis, Feminism.* Bloomington: Indiana University Press.

Hirsch, Marianne, and Evelyn Fox Keller. 1990. *Conflicts in Feminism.* New York: Routledge.

Hollows, Joanne. 2006. "Can I Go Home Yet? Feminism, Post-Feminism, and Domesticity." In *Feminism in Popular Culture,* eds. Joanne Hollows and Moseley Rachel, 97–118. New York: Berg.

Hollows, Joanne, and Rachel Moseley, eds. 2006. *Feminism in Popular Culture.* New York: Berg.

hooks, bell. 1999. *All About Love: New Visions.* New York: William Morrow.

———. 2000. *Feminism Is for Everybody: Passionate Politics.* Cambridge, MA: South End Press.

———. 2001. *Salvation: Black People and Love.* New York, William Morrow.

———. 2002. *Communion: The Female Search for Love.* New York: William Morrow.

Howie, Gillian, Stacy Gillis, and Rebecca Munford, eds. 2004. *Third Wave Feminism: A Critical Exploration.* Basingstoke, UK: Palgrave Macmillan.

Hunt, Susan, and Peter Lehman. 1999. "Something and Someone Else: The Mind, the Body and Sexuality in *Titanic*." In *Titanic: Anatomy of a Blockbuster,* eds. Kevin S. Sandler and Gaylyn Studlar, 89–107. New Brunswick: Rutgers University Press.

Hurdis, Rebecca. 2002. "Heartbroken: Women of Color Feminism and the Third Wave." In *Colonize This! Young Women of Color on Today's Feminism,* eds. Daisy Hernandez and Bushra Rehman, 279–294. New York: Seal Press.

Huttner, Jan Lisa. 2005. "Jan Chats with Alice Wu and Joan Chen About Their New Film *Saving Face*." http://www.films42.com/chats/alice_wu.asp.

―――. 2006. "Jan Chats with Aline Brosh McKenna." http://www.films42.com/chats/aline-mckenna.asp.

Jacobs, Janet Liebman. 1990. "Reassessing Mother Blame in Incest." *Signs* 15, no. 3: 500–514.

Jaehne, Karen. 1996. "*Antonia's Line.*" *Film Quarterly* 50, no. 1: 27–30.

Jenkins, Henry. 1997. "Empowering Children in the Digital Age." *Radical Teacher* 50: 30–35.

Johnson, Merri Lisa, ed. 2007. *Third Wave Feminism and Television: Jane Puts It in a Box.* New York: I.B. Tauris.

Jones, Darice. 2002. "Falling off the Tightrope onto a Bed of Feathers." In *Colonize This! Young Women of Color on Today's Feminism*, eds. Daisy Hernandez and Bushra Rehman, 312–325. New York: Seal Press.

Jones, Lisa. 1995. "She Came with the Rodeo (an Excerpt)." In *To Be Real: Telling the Truth and Changing the Face of Feminism*, ed. Rebecca Walker, 253–266. New York: Random House.

Kamen, Paula. 2000. *Her Way: Young Women Remake the Sexual Revolution.* New York: New York University.

Kaplan, E. Ann. 1983. "The Case of the Missing Mother: Maternal Issues in Vidor's *Stella Dallas.*" *Heresies* 16: 81–85.

―――. 1992. *Motherhood and Representation: The Mother in Popular Culture and Melodrama.* London: Routledge.

―――. 1999. "Trauma and Aging: Marlene Dietrich, Melanie Klein, and Marguerite Duras." In *Figuring Age: Women, Bodies, Generations*, ed. Kathleen Woodward, 171–194. Bloomington: Indiana University Press.

Karlyn, Kathleen Rowe. 1990. "Roseanne: Unruly Woman as Domestic Goddess." *Screen* 4: 408–419.

―――. 1998. "Allison Anders's *Gas Food Lodging*: Independent Cinema and the New Romance." In *Terms of Endearment: Hollywood Romantic Comedy of the 1980s and 1990s*, eds. Peter William Evans and Celestino Deleyto, 168–187. Edinburgh, Scotland: Edinburgh University Press.

Karras, Irene. 2002. "The Third Wave's Final Girl: Buffy the Vampire Slayer." *thirdspace*, no. 1. http://www.thirdspace.ca/journal.htm.

Kearney, Mary Celeste. 2006. *Girls Make Media.* New York: Routledge.

Kim, L. S. 2006. "Making Women Warriors—A Transnational Reading of Asian Action Heroes." *Jump Cut* 48.

King, Geoff. 2000. *Spectacular Narratives: Hollywood in the Age of the Blockbuster.* London: I.B. Tauris.

Kinser, Amber E. 2008. *Mothering in the Third Wave.* Toronto: Demeter Press.

Kintz, Linda. 1997. *Between Jesus and the Market: The Emotions That Matter in Right-Wing America.* Durham: Duke University Press.

Kleinhans, Chuck. 2004. "Virtual Child Porn: The Law and Semiotics of the Image." In

More Dirty Looks: Gender, Pornography and Power, ed. Pamela Church Gibson, 71–84. 2nd ed. London: British Film Institute.

Klinger, Barbara. 1994. *Melodrama and Meaning: History, Culture, and the Films of Douglas Sirk*. Bloomington: Indiana University Press.

Kobrin, Sandra. 2007. "*Knocked Up* Bans Abortion from Script." *Women's e-News*. http://www.womensenews.org/story/uncovering-gender/070620/knocked-bans-abortion-script.

Krämer, Peter. 1999. "Women First." In *Titanic: Anatomy of a Blockbuster*, eds. Kevin S. Sandler and Gaylyn Studlar, 108–131. New Brunswick: Rutgers University Press.

———. 2006. "Big Pictures: Studying Contemporary Hollywood Cinema through Its Greatest Hits." In *Screen Methods: Comparative Readings in Film Studies*, eds. Jacqueline Furby and Karen Randell, 124–132. London: Wallflower.

Kristeva, Julia. 1979. "Women's Time." In *The Kristeva Reader*, Toril Moi, 187–213. New York: Columbia University Press.

Kuenzli, Rudolf E. 1987. *Dada and Surrealist Film*. New York: Willis, Locker, & Owens.

Labre, Magdala Peixoto, and Lisa Duke. 2004. "Nothing Like a Brisk Walk and a Spot of Demon Slaughter to Make a Girl's Night: The Construction of the Female Hero in the *Buffy* Video Game." *Journal of Communication Inquiry* 28, no. 2: 138–156.

Ladd-Taylor, Molly, and Lauri Umansky. 1998. "*Bad*" *Mothers: The Politics of Blame in Twentieth-Century America*. New York: New York University Press.

Lee, Lela. "Angry Little Girls." Comic from August 15, 2009. http://www.angrylittlea siangirl.com.

Lehman, Peter, ed. 1990. *Close Viewings: An Anthology of New Film Criticism*. Tallahassee: Florida State University Press.

Lesage, Julia. 1987. "Artful Racism, Artful Rape in *Broken Blossoms*." In *Home Is Where the Heart Is: Studies in Melodrama and the Woman's Film*, ed. Christine Gledhill, 235–254. London: British Film Institute.

Levine, Elena. 2007. "Buffy and the 'New Girl Order': Defining Feminism and Femininity." In *Undead TV: Essays on "Buffy the Vampire Slayer*," eds. Elena Levine and Lisa Parks, 168–189. Durham: Duke University Press.

Levine, Elena, and Lisa Parks, eds. 2007. *Undead TV: Essays on "Buffy the Vampire Slayer."* Durham: Duke University Press.

Lévi-Strauss, Claude. 1963. *Structural Anthropology*. Trans. Claire Jacobson and Brooke Grundfest Schoepf. New York: Basic Books.

Levy, Ariel. 2005. *Female Chauvinist Pigs: Women and the Rise of Raunch Culture*. New York: Free Press.

Li, David Leiwei. 2001. "Introduction to Special Issue: Globalization and the Humanities." *Comparative Literature* 53, no. 4: 275–282.

Liggett, Lori. 2002. "Maiden Voyage: From Edwardian Girl to Millennial Women in *Titanic*." In *Sugar, Spice, and Everything Nice: Cinemas of Girlhood*, eds. Frances K. Gateward and Murray Pomerance, 183–200. Detroit: Wayne State University Press.

Looser, Devoney, and E. Ann Kaplan, eds. 1997. *Generations: Academic Feminists in Dialogue*. Minneapolis: University of Minnesota Press.

Lorde, Audre. 1984. *Sister Outsider: Essays and Speeches*. Trumansburg, NY: Crossing Press.

Lubin, David M. 1999. *Titanic*. London: British Film Institute.

Lumby, Catherine. 1997. *Bad Girls: The Media, Sex, and Feminism in the 90s*. Sydney: Allen & Unwin.

Luscombe, Belinda. 2007. "Who Killed the Love Story?" *Time*, August 9.

Lynch, Joan Driscoll. 2002. "Incest Discourse and Cinematic Representation." *Journal of Film and Video* 54, nos. 2–3: 43–55.

Maatita, Florence. 2005. "*Que Viva la Mujer!* Negotiating Chicana Feminist Identities." In *Different Wavelengths: Studies of the Contemporary Women's Movement*, ed. Jo Reger. New York: Routledge.

Maglin, Nan Bauer, and Donna Marie Perry, eds. 1996. *"Bad Girls"/"Good Girls": Women, Sex, and Power in the Nineties*. New Brunswick: Rutgers University Press.

Mann, Bonnie. 2009. "Vampire Love: The Second Sex Negotiates the 21st Century." Lecture in Eugene, Oregon, at the University of Oregon.

Martin, Biddy, and Chandra Talpade Mohanty. 1986. "Feminist Politics: What's Home Got to Do with It?" In *Feminist Studies, Critical Studies*, ed. Teresa de Lauretis, 191–212. Bloomington: Indiana University Press.

Maslin, Janet. 1999. "*American Beauty*: Dad's Dead, and He's Still a Funny Guy." *New York Times*, September 15.

McGill, Hannah. 2004. "Not Sharp Enough to Cut It: *Vanity Fair* Is Lush, but Reese Witherspoon Just Can't Get to Grips with Its Smart English Heroine." *The Herald*, December 11.

McRobbie, Angela. 2003. "Sugar and Spice: Why Growing Up Is So Hard." *Sight & Sound* 13, no. 12: 55–56.

———. 2004. "Postfeminism and Popular Culture." *Feminist Media Studies* 4, no. 3: 255–264.

Medved, Michael. 2005. "Leading Ladies: More Glamour, Less Grit." *USA Today*, September 20.

Mellencamp, Patricia. 1992. *High Anxiety Catastrophe, Scandal, Age, and Comedy*. Bloomington: Indiana University Press.

———. 1999. "From Anxiety to Equanimity: Crisis and Generational Continuity on TV, at the Movies, in Life, in Death." In *Figuring Age: Women, Bodies, Generations*, ed. Kathleen M. Woodward, 310–328. Bloomington: Indiana University Press.

Mercer, John, and Martin Shingler. 2004. *Melodrama: Genre, Style, Sensibility*. London: Wallflower Press.

Middleton, Jason. 2007. "Buffy as Femme Fatale: The Cult Heroine and the Male Spectator." In *Undead TV: Essays on "Buffy the Vampire Slayer,"* eds. Elena Levine and Lisa Parks, 145–167. Durham: Duke University Press.

Mignolo, Walter. 2006. "Decolonial Thinking and the Decolonization of Knowledge." Lecture in Eugene, Oregon, at the University of Oregon.

Mitchell, Juliet. 1974. *Psychoanalysis and Feminism*. New York: Pantheon Books.

Mizejewski, Linda. 2004. *Hardboiled & High Heeled: The Woman Detective in Popular Culture*. New York: Routledge.

———. 2005. "In Focus: Postfeminism and Contemporary Media Studies." *Cinema Journal* 44, no. 2: 121–127.

———. 2007. "Queen Latifah, Unruly Women, and the Bodies of Romantic Comedy." *Genders* 46.

Modleski, Tania, ed. 1986. *Studies in Entertainment: Critical Approaches to Mass Culture*. Bloomington: Indiana University Press.

———. 1991. *Feminism without Women: Culture and Criticism in a Postfeminist Age*. New York: Routledge. (Orig. pub. 1988)

———. 2005. *The Women Who Knew Too Much: Hitchcock and Feminist Theory*. 2nd ed. New York: Routledge.

Mohanty, Chandra Talpade. 2003. *Feminism without Borders: Decolonizing Theory, Practicing Solidarity*. Durham: Duke University Press.

———. 2005. "Global Feminism." Lecture in Eugene, Oregon, at the University of Oregon.

Moraga, Cherríe, and Gloria Anzaldúa. 1983. *This Bridge Called My Back: Writings by Radical Women of Color*. 2nd ed. New York: Kitchen Table, Women of Color Press.

Morgan, Joan. 1999. *When Chickenheads Come Home to Roost: My Life as a Hip-Hop Feminist*. New York: Simon & Schuster.

Morgan, Robin. 2008. "In Support of Hillary Rodham Clinton: Good-bye to All That, Part II," *Women's Media Center*, http://www.womensmediacenter.com.

Morrison, Susan, ed. 2008. *Thirty Ways of Looking at Hillary: Reflections by Women Writers*. New York: Harper Collins.

Morrow, Fiona. 1996. "Line Drawing." *Time Out*, no. 1361.

Mulvey, Laura. 1975. "Visual Pleasure and Narrative Cinema." *Screen* 16, no. 3: 6–15.

———. 1989. *Visual and Other Pleasures*. Theories of Representation and Difference. Bloomington: Indiana University Press.

Munford, Rebecca. 2004. "'Wake up and Smell the Lipgloss': Gender, Generations, and the (A)politics of Girl Power." In *Third Wave Feminism: A Critical Exploration*, eds. Stacy Gillis, Gillian Howie, and Rebecca Munford, 142–153. New York: Palgrave Macmillan.

Murray, Susan. 1999. "Saving Our So-Called Lives: Girl Fandom, Adolescent Subjectivity, and *My So-Called Life*." *Kids' Media Culture*: 221–235.

Narain, Denise deCaires. 2004. "What Happened to Global Sisterhood? Writing and Reading 'the' Postcolonial Woman." In *Third Wave Feminism: A Critical Exploration*, eds. Stacy Gillis, Gillian Howie, and Rebecca Munford, 240–251. New York: Palgrave Macmillan.

Nash, Melanie, and Marti Lahti. 1999. "'Almost Ashamed to Say I Am One of Those Girls': Titanic, Leonardo DiCaprio, and the Paradoxes of Girls' Fandom." In Titanic: Anatomy of a Blockbuster, eds. Kevin S. Sandler and Gaylyn Studlar, 64–87. New Brunswick: Rutgers University Press.

Nayak, Anoop. 2006. "After Race: Ethnography, Race, and Post-Race Theory." Ethnic & Racial Studies 29, no. 3: 411–430.

Neal, Mark Anthony. 2002. Soul Babies: Black Popular Culture and the Post-Soul Aesthetic. New York: Routledge.

Negra, Diane. 2004. "'Quality Postfeminism?' Sex and the Single Girl on HBO." Genders 39.

———. 2009. What a Girl Wants? Fantasizing the Reclamation of Self in Postfeminism. London: Routledge.

Niesel, Jeff. 2007. "Hip-Hop Matters: Rewriting the Sexual Politics of Rap Music." In Third Wave Agenda: Being Feminist, Doing Feminism, eds. Leslie Heywood and Jennifer Drake, 239–254. Minneapolis: University of Minnesota Press.

Oakley, Ann, and Juliet Mitchell, eds. 1997. Who's Afraid of Feminism? Seeing through the Backlash. New York: New Press.

O'Day, Mark. 2004. "Beauty in Motion: Gender, Spectacle and the Action Babe." In Action and Adventure Cinema, ed. Yvonne Tasker, 201–218. London: Routledge.

O'Hehir, Andrew. 1999. "Kevin Spacey Keeps a Biting Urban Satire from Eating Itself Alive." Salon, September 15. http://www.salon.com/ent/movies/review/1999/09/15/beauty/index.html?CP=SAL&DN=110.

Ojumu, Akin. 2003. "Golden Girl: Reese Witherspoon." The Observer, July 20.

Orbach, Susie. 1978. Fat Is a Feminist Issue: The Anti-Diet Guide to Permanent Weight Loss. New York: Paddington Press.

O'Reilly, Andrea, and Sharon Abbey, eds. 2000. Mothers and Daughters: Connection, Empowerment, and Transformation. Lanham, MD: Rowman & Littlefield.

O'Reilly, Julie D. 2005. "The Wonder Woman Precedent: Female (Super)Heroism on Trial." The Journal of American Culture 28, no. 3: 273–283.

Orenstein, Peggy. 2007. "Your Gamete, Myself." New York Times Magazine, July 15.

Orr, Catherine M. 1997. "Charting the Currents of the Third Wave." Hypatia: A Journal of Feminist Philosophy 12, no. 3: 29–45.

Ovalle, Priscilla Peña. 2007. "Framing Jennifer Lopez: Mobilizing Race from the Wide Shot to the Close-Up." In The Persistence of Whiteness, ed. Daniel Bernardi. New York: Routledge.

———. 2010. Dance and the Hollywood Latina: Race, Sex, and Stardom. New Brunswick: Rutgers University Press.

Owen, A. Susan, Leah R. Vande Berg, and Sarah R. Stein. 2007. Bad Girls: Cultural Politics and Media Representations of Transgressive Women. New York: P. Lang.

Penley, Constance. 1988. Feminism and Film Theory. New York: Routledge.

Phillips, Shelley. 1996. Beyond the Myths: Mother-Daughter Relationships in Psychology, History, Literature, and Everyday Life. New York: Penguin. (Published in the UK in 1991.)

Pinedo, Isabel Cristina. 1997. *Recreational Terror: Women and the Pleasures of Horror Film Viewing.* Albany: State University of New York.

Pipher, Mary Bray. 1994. *Reviving Ophelia: Saving the Selves of Adolescent Girls.* New York: Putnam.

Plagens, Peter. 2008. "The Lady and the Ramp." *Newsweek,* June 16.

Pollack, William S. 1998. *Real Boys: Rescuing Our Sons from the Myths of Boyhood.* New York: Random House.

Pomerance, Murray, and Frances K. Gateward, eds. 2005. *Where the Boys Are: Cinemas of Masculinity and Youth.* Detroit: Wayne State University Press.

Powers, Ann. 1997. "Everything and the Girl." *Spin,* November.

Projanksky, Sarah. 2001. *Watching Rape: Film and Television in Postfeminist Culture.* New York: New York University Press.

———. 2007. "Gender, Race, Feminism, and the International Girl Hero: The Unremarkable U.S. Popular Press Reception of *Bend It Like Beckham* and *Whale Rider.*" In *Youth Culture in Global Cinema,* eds. Timothy Shary and Alexandra Seibel, 189–206. Austin: University of Texas Press.

Purdum, Todd S. 2009. "It Came from Wasilla." *Vanity Fair,* August. http://www.vanityfair.com/politics/features/2009/08/sarah-palin200908.

Quinn, Rebecca Dakin. 1997. "An Open Letter to Institutional Mothers." In *Generations: Academic Feminists in Dialogue,* eds. Devoney Looser and E. Ann Kaplan, 174–182. Minneapolis: University of Minnesota Press.

Reger, Jo, ed. 2005. *Different Wavelengths: Studies of the Contemporary Women's Movement.* New York: Routledge.

Rentel, Ron. 2007. *Karma Queens, Geek Gods, and Innerpreneurs: Meet the Nine Consumer Types Shaping Today's Marketplace.* New York: McGraw-Hill.

Reviere, Susan L. 1996. *Memory of Childhood Trauma: A Clinician's Guide to the Literature.* New York: Guilford Press.

Rich, Adrienne Cecile. 1986. *Of Woman Born: Motherhood as Experience and Institution.* 10th anniversary ed. New York: Norton.

Rivera, Margo. 1999. *Fragment by Fragment: Feminist Perspectives on Memory and Child Sexual Abuse.* Charlottetown, P.E.I.: Gynergy Books.

Roberts, Kimberley. 2002. "Pleasures and Problems of the 'Angry Girl.'" In *Sugar, Spice, and Everything Nice: Cinemas of Girlhood,* eds. Frances K. Gateward and Murray Pomerance, 216–234. Detroit: Wayne State University Press.

Rose, Jacqueline. 1986. *Sexuality in the Field of Vision.* London: Verso.

Rose, Mary Beth. 1991. "Where Are the Mothers in Shakespeare? Options for Gender Representation in the English Renaissance." *Shakespeare Quarterly* 42, no. 3: 291–314.

Roth, Elaine. 2005. "Momophobia: Incapacitated Mothers and Their Adult Children in 1990s Films." *Quarterly Review of Film and Video* 22, no. 2: 189–202.

Rowe (Karlyn), Kathleen. 1995. *The Unruly Woman: Gender and the Genres of Laughter.* Austin: University of Texas Press.

Ruddick, Sara. 1989. *Maternal Thinking: Toward a Politics of Peace.* Boston: Beacon Press.

Russo, Mary J. 1986. "Female Grotesques: Carnival and Theory." In *Feminist Studies, Critical Studies*, ed. Teresa de Lauretis, 318–334. Bloomington: Indiana University Press.

———. 1999. "Aging and the Scandal of Anachronism." In *Figuring Age: Women, Bodies, Generations*, ed. Kathleen M. Woodward. Bloomington: Indiana University Press.

Sacco, Lynn. 2001. "Not Talking About 'It': A History of Incest in the United States, 1890–1940." Dissertation, University of Southern California.

Sandler, Kevin S., and Gaylyn Studlar. 1999. *Titanic: Anatomy of a Blockbuster*. New Brunswick: Rutgers University Press.

Sandoval, Chela. 1990. "The Struggle Within: A Report on the 1981 N.W.S.A. Conference." In *Making Face, Making Soul: Creative and Critical Perspectives by Feminists of Color*, ed. Gloria Anzaldúa, 53–74. San Francisco: Aunt Lute Foundation Books.

———. 2000. *Methodology of the Oppressed*. Minneapolis, MN: University of Minnesota Press.

Scheman, Naomi. 1988. "Missing Mothers/Desiring Daughters: Framing the Sight of Women." *Critical Inquiry* 15, no. 1: 62–89.

Schor, Naomi. 1994. "Introduction." In *The Essential Difference*, eds. Naomi Schor and Elizabeth Weed, vii–xvii. Bloomington: Indiana University Press.

Sconce, Jeffrey. 2002. "Irony, Nihilism, and the New American 'Smart' Film." *Screen* 43, no. 4: 329–369.

Scott, A. O. 2007. "Bye-Bye, Bong. Hello, Baby." *New York Times*, June 1.

Scott, Paul. 2006. "Now Reese Has an Oscar, but Can She Keep Her Husband?" *Daily Mail*, March 7.

Seiter, Ellen. 1989. *Remote Control: Television, Audiences, and Cultural Power*. London: Routledge.

———. 1993. *Sold Separately: Children and Parents in Consumer Culture*. New Brunswick: Rutgers University Press.

———. 1999. *Television and New Media Audiences*. Oxford: Clarendon Press.

Shary, Timothy. 2002. *Generation Multiplex: The Image of Youth in Contemporary American Cinema*. Austin: University of Texas Press.

———. 2005. *Teen Movies: American Youth on Screen*. London: Wallflower.

Shary, Timothy, and Alexandra Seibel, eds. 2007. *Youth Culture in Global Cinema*. Austin: University of Texas Press.

Shohat, Ella, ed. 1998. *Talking Visions: Multicultural Feminism in a Transnational Age*. Cambridge, MA: New Museum of Contemporary Art.

Shohat, Ella, and Robert Stam. 1994. *Unthinking Eurocentrism: Multiculturalism and the Media*. New York: Routledge.

Sidler, Michelle. 1997. "Living in McJobdom: Third Wave Feminism and Class Inequity." In *Third Wave Agenda: Being Feminist, Doing Feminism*, eds. Leslie Heywood and Jennifer Drake, 25–39. Minneapolis: University of Minnesota Press.

Siegel, Carol. 2000. *New Millennial Sexstyles*. Bloomington: Indiana University Press.

———. 2006. "Irreconcilable Feminisms and the Cultural Construction of Virginity's

Loss: *A ma soeur!* and *Thirteen*." Paper presented at the annual meeting of the Society for Cinema Studies, Vancouver B.C.

———. 2007. "Female Heterosexual Sadism: The Final Feminist Taboo in *Buffy the Vampire Slayer* and the Anita Blake Vampire Hunter Series." In *Third Wave Feminism and Television: Jane Puts It in a Box*, ed. Merri Lisa Johnson, 56–90. London: New York.

Siegel, Deborah. 2007. *Sisterhood, Interrupted: From Radical Women to Grrls Gone Wild*. New York: Palgrave Macmillan.

Silverman, Kaja. 1988. *The Acoustic Mirror: The Female Voice in Psychoanalysis and Cinema*. Bloomington: Indiana University Press.

Sinclair, Marianne. 1988. *Hollywood Lolitas: The Nymphet Syndrome in the Movies*. New York: Henry Holt.

Sklar, Robert. 1996. "The Lighter Side of Feminism: An Interview with Marleen Gorris." *Cineaste* 1.

Slotek, Jim. 1999. "Reese Argues for *American Psycho* Film, Goes Ahead in Toronto Despite Vociferous Objections." *The Toronto Sun*, February 24.

Smith, Kevin. 2005. *Silent Bob Speaks: The Collected Writings of Kevin Smith*. New York: Miramax Books.

Smith, Sean. 2007. "The Fifty Smartest People in Hollywood." *EW.com*, November 28.

Smith-Shomade, Beretta E. 2002. *Shaded Lives: African American Women and Television*. New Brunswick: Rutgers University Press.

Soles, Carter. 2008. "Kevin Smith, Queerness, and Independent Film." Dissertation, University of Oregon.

Sommers, Christina Hoff. 1994. *Who Stole Feminism?: How Women Have Betrayed Women*. New York: Simon & Schuster.

———. 2000. *The War Against Boys: How Misguided Feminism Is Harming Our Young Men*. New York: Simon & Schuster.

Sontag, Susan. 1964. "Notes on Camp." *Partisan Review* 31, no. 4: 515–530.

———. 1972. "The Double Standard of Aging." *Saturday Review* (September): 29–38.

Spencer, Liese. 1996. "*Antonia's Line/Antonia*." *Sight & Sound* 9, no. 6 (September): 34–35.

Spiegelman, Art. 2006. "Comix 101." Lecture presented as part of the Comparative Literature Lecture Series in Eugene, Oregon, at the University of Oregon.

Spillers, Hortense J. 1987. "Mama's Baby, Papa's Maybe: An American Grammar Book." *Diacritics: A Review of Contemporary Criticism* 17, no. 2: 65–81.

Springer, Kimberley. 2007. "Divas, Evil Black Bitches, and Bitter Black Women." In *Interrogating Postfeminism: Gender and the Politics of Popular Culture*, eds. Yvonne Tasker and Diane Negra, 247–276. Durham: Duke University Press.

Stabile, Carol. 2007. "Fighting the Terror Warriors." Paper presented at the annual meeting of the Cultural Studies Association in Portland, Oregon.

Stenger, Josh. 2006. "The Clothes Make the Fan: Fashion and Online Fandom When Buffy the Vampire Slayer Goes to Ebay." *Cinema Journal* 45, no. 4: 26–44.

Stoller, Eleanor, Palo Gibson, and Rose Campbell, eds. 2000. *Worlds of Difference: Inequality in the Aging Experience*. 3rd ed. Thousand Oaks, CA: Pine Forge Press.

Stringer, Julian, ed. 2003. *Movie Blockbusters*. New York: Routledge.

Sullivan, Kathleen Erin. 2000. "Suffering Men/Male Suffering: The Construction of Masculinity in the Works of Stephen King and Peter Straub." Dissertation, University of Oregon.

———. 2000. "Ed Gein and the Figure of the Trangendered Serial Killer." *Jump Cut* 43: 38–47.

Sunday Times (London). 2006. "The Dork Who Grew into a Hollywood Princess." March 5.

Sweeney, Kathleen. 2008. *Maiden USA: Girl Icons Come of Age*. New York: Peter Lang.

Taormino, Tristan, and Karen Green. 1997. *A Girl's Guide to Taking Over the World: Writings from the Girl Zine Revolution*. New York: St. Martin's Griffin.

Tasker, Yvonne, ed. 2004. *Action and Adventure Cinema*. New York: Routledge.

Tasker, Yvonne, and Diane Negra. 2005. "In Focus: Postfeminism and Contemporary Media Studies." *Cinema Journal* 44, no. 2: 107–133.

———, eds. 2007. *Interrogating Postfeminism: Gender and the Politics of Popular Culture*. Durham: Duke University Press.

Taylor, Charles. 1996. "Little Red Riding Hood's Revenge." *Salon*, November 11. http://www.salon.com/nov96/freeway961111.html.

Terr, Lenore. 1990. *Too Scared to Cry: Psychic Trauma in Childhood*. New York: Harper & Row.

———. 1994. *Unchained Memories: True Stories of Traumatic Memories, Lost and Found*. New York: Basic Books.

Thompson, David. 1999. "She's Classy. She's Presidential. She's Reese." *The Independent*, September 5.

———. 2007. "Reese Witherspoon Can Play Nasty Girls. But You Don't Get $15m a Time for Those Outsiders." *Guardian*, October 12.

Thompson, Mary. 2006. "Third Wave Feminism and the Politics of Motherhood." *Genders* 43.

Thompson, Ruthe. 1997. "Working Mother." In *Generations: Academic Feminists in Dialogue*, eds. Devoney Looser and E. Ann Kaplan, 197–218. Minneapolis: University of Minnesota Press.

Tomasula, Frank P. 1996. "Masculine/Feminine: The 'New Masculinity' in *Tootsie* (1982)." *Velvet Light Trap* 38, no. 4: 4–14.

Troyer, John, and Chani Marchiselli. 2005. "Slack, Slacker, Slackest: Homosocial Bonding Practices in Contemporary Dude Cinema." In *Where the Boys Are: Cinemas of Masculinity and Youth*, eds. Murray Pomerance and Frances K. Gateward, 264–276. Detroit: Wayne State University Press.

Tsai, Martin. 2005. "Saving Face." *The Bitter Critic*, http://www.martintsai.com/2005/07/saving-face.html.

Tully, Susanna. 2008. "The Year of Unplanned Pregnancies." *The Chronicle of Higher Education*, February 8.

Waites, Elizabeth A. 1993. *Trauma and Survival: Post-Traumatic and Dissociative Disorders in Women*. New York: Norton.

Wald, Gayle. 1999. "Clueless in the Neocolonial World Order." *Camera Obscura* 42: 51–69.

Waldman, Ayelet. 2009. *Bad Mother: A Chronicle of Maternal Crimes, Minor Calamities, and Occasional Moments of Grace*. New York: Doubleday.

Walker, Janet. 1999. "Textual Trauma: *King's Row* and Freud." In *Endless Night: Cinema and Psychoanalysis, Parallel Histories*, ed. Janet Bergstrom, 171–187. Berkeley: University of California Press.

Walker, Janet, and Diane Waldman. 1990. "John Huston's *Freud* and Textual Repression." In *Close Viewings: An Anthology of New Film Criticism*, ed. Peter Lehman, 282–299. Tallahassee: Florida State University Press.

Walker, Rebecca. 1992. "Becoming the Third Wave." *Ms.*, Jan./Feb.: 39–41.

———, ed. 1995. *To Be Real: Telling the Truth and Changing the Face of Feminism*. New York: Anchor Books.

———. 2007. *Baby Love: Choosing Motherhood after a Lifetime of Ambivalence*. New York: Riverhead Books.

Walkerdine, Valerie. 1997. *Daddy's Girl: Young Girls and Popular Culture*. Cambridge, MA: Harvard University Press.

Warner, Judith. 2005. *Perfect Madness: Motherhood in the Age of Anxiety*. New York: Riverhead Books.

Wearing, Sadie. 2007. "Subjects of Rejuvenation: Aging in Postfeminist Culture." In *Interrogating Postfeminism*, eds. Yvonne Tasker and Diane Negra, 277–310. Durham: Duke University Press.

Weinraub, Bernard. 1995. "A Surprise Film Hit About Rich Teen-Age Girls." *New York Times*, July 24.

———. 1998. "Who's Lining up at Box Office? Lots and Lots of Girls; Studios Aim at Teen-Agers, a Vast, Growing Audience." *New York Times*, February 23.

Weiss, Rick. 2005. "Study: U.S. Leads in Mental Illness, Lags in Treatment." *Washington Post*, June 7.

Wikipedia. "Beatrice Wood." http://en.wikipedia.org/wiki/Beatrice_Wood.

———. "Claire Danes." http://en.wikipedia.org/wiki/Claire_Danes.

———. "*My So-Called Life*." http://en.wikipedia.org/wiki/My_So-Called_Life.

———. "*Titanic*." http://en.wikipedia.org/wiki/Titanic_(1997_film).

———. "Ugly Betty." http://en.wikipedia.org/wiki/Ugly_Betty.

Wilcox, Rhonda. 2005. *Why Buffy Matters: The Art of "Buffy the Vampire Slayer."* New York: I.B. Tauris.

Wilcox, Rhonda, and David Lavery, eds. 2002. *Fighting the Forces: What's at Stake in "Buffy the Vampire Slayer."* Lanham, MD: Rowman & Littlefield.

Williams, Alex. 2007. "Putting Money on the Table." *New York Times*, September 23.

Williams, J. P. 2002. "'Choosing Your Own Mother': Mother-Daughter Conflicts in *Buffy*." In *Fighting the Forces: What's at Stake in Buffy the Vampire Slayer*, eds. Rhonda Wilcox and David Lavery, 61–72. Lanham, MD: Rowman & Littlefield.

Williams, Linda. 1984. "'Something Else Besides a Mother': *Stella Dallas* and the Women's Film." *Cinema Journal* 24: 2–27.

———. 1991. "Film Bodies: Gender, Genre and Excess." *Film Quarterly* 44, no. 4: 2–13.

———. 1998. "Melodrama Revised." In *Refiguring American Film Genres: History and Theory*, ed. Nick Browne, 42–88. Berkeley: University of California Press.

———. 2001. *Playing the Race Card: Melodramas of Black and White from Uncle Tom to O. J. Simpson*. Princeton: Princeton University Press.

Winters, Rebecca Keegan. 2007. "Boys Who Like Toys." *Time*, April 30.

Wiseman, Rosalind. 2002. *Queen Bees and Wannabes: Helping Your Daughter Survive Cliques, Gossip, Boyfriends, and Other Realities of Adolescence*. New York: Crown Publishers.

Wood, Robin. 1985. "An Introduction to the American Horror Film." In Vol. 2 of *Movies and Methods*, ed. Bill Nichols, 195–220. Berkeley: University of California Press.

———. 2004. "Neglected Nightmares." In *The Horror Film Reader*, eds. Alain Silver and James Ursini, 111–128. Compton Plains, NJ: Limelight Editions.

Woodward, Kathleen M. 1999. *Figuring Age: Women, Bodies, Generations*. Bloomington: Indiana University Press.

Wurtzel, Elizabeth. 1998. *Bitch: In Praise of Difficult Women*. New York: Doubleday.

Wylie, Philip. 1955. *Generation of Vipers*. New annotated ed. New York: Holt, Rinehart, and Winston.

Yu, Yi-Lin. 2002. "Relocating Maternal Subjectivity: Storytelling and Mother-Daughter Voices in Amy Tan's *The Joy Luck Club*." *thirdspace* 1, no. 2 (March), http://www.third space.ca/journal/article/view/yu/49.

Zacharek, Stephanie. 2003. Review of *Thirteen*. Salon.com, Aug. 20. http://dir.salon.com/story/ent/movies/review/2003/08/20/thirteen/index.html.

Zita, Jacquelyn N., ed. 1997. "Third Wave Feminism." Special issue, *Hypatia: A Journal of Feminist Philosophy* 12, no. 3.

Index

slogan, 7, 79; popular texts of, 134; in the *Scream* trilogy, 101, 112; sexuality and pop culture as weapons of, 52, 53, 215. *See also* Girl Culture

girls, teenage. *See* teen girls

girls/women of color, 29, 31, 47, 67, 172, 178, 191–226, 251, 252, 256, 274nn3,4. *See also* African Americans; Asians; Latinas; race

Girl World, 82, 125, 130, 159, 250; definition of, 78–79, 97–98; as depicted in action, horror, and fantasy films and TV shows, 99; as depicted in comedies, 80, 88, 92, 141, 146, 149; as depicted in melodramas, 172; as depicted in shows featuring women of color, 191, 192, 193, 201, 202

Gish, Lillian and Dorothy, 54

Gledhill, Christine, 10

Glee, 11

globalization, 8, 29, 177, 178, 179, 245

Goodman, Ellen, 230, 276n8

Gorris, Marleen, 10, 23, 228, 232–233, 234, 235

Greene, Graham, 55, 266n10

Grey's Anatomy, 13

Griffith, D. W., 54, 265n8

Grosz, Elizabeth, 236

grotesque, the, 10–11, 12, 18, 23, 210, 234, 235, 236, 239, 241, 247, 249, 276n2

Gullette, Margaret Morganroth, 229, 243, 244–245, 252, 278n24

Halloween, 103, 270n4

Hamilton, Linda, 38, 99

Hardwicke, Catherine, 124, 162, 171, 173

Harris, Charlaine, 124

Hathaway, Anne, 92, 95

Hayek, Salma, 206, 214

Hayworth, Rita, 185

Heathers, 78

Heckerling, Amy, 6, 77, 78, 85, 87

Hedaya, Dan, 81, 83

Henry, Astrid, 4, 19

Hepburn, Katherine, 84

Herman, Judith, 57, 64, 75, 267n19

Hernandez, Daisy, 194, 195, 196

Herskovitz, Marshall, 162, 163, 273n2

heterosexuality, 36, 170, 199, 219; as decentered in *Antonia's Line*, 240; as decentered in *Thirteen*, 180, 186; father/daughter relationship as the basis of, 59; and happy Hollywood endings, 106; as privileged in society, 32, 193, 276n20; and the rescue fantasy, 40; Second Wave's view of, 30; seen as dangerous, 102, 173–174; Third Wave's view of, 33

Hill, Amy, 216

Hill, Anita, 31–32

Hills Have Eyes, The, 105

Hilton, Paris, 11

hip-hop, 34, 186

Hirsch, Marianne, 15, 16, 18, 251

Hoff-Sommers, Christina, 27

homophobia, 31, 170, 207, 215

homosexuality. *See* gays; lesbians

hooks, bell, 240, 277n13

horror films, 22, 37, 100, 103, 105, 111, 112, 116, 119, 227, 270n4. *See also* slasher films

Howie, Gillian, 30

Hudgens, Vanessa, 184

Hughes, John, 71, 77, 81, 163

Hunter, Holly, 173, 174, 181, 188, 189

Hurdis, Rebecca, 194

immigrants/immigration, 8, 175, 208, 249

incest, 22, 50–75, 83, 107, 135, 138–139, 175, 261n21, 265n2, 265n8, 266n13, 267nn21,25. *See also* sexual abuse

Indiana Jones films, 215

Indigo Girls, 105

interracial relationships, 185–186, 197–198, 264n14, 275n5

It's Just Lunch, 178

Jervis, Lisa, 34

Jolie, Angelina, 99, 272n1

CPSIA information can be obtained at www.ICGtesting.com
Printed in the USA
245558LV00002B/13/P